THE INVENTION OF JEWISH THEOCRACY

THE INVENTION OF JEWISH THEOCRACY

The Struggle for Legal Authority in Modern Israel

Alexander Kaye

OXFORD
UNIVERSITY PRESS

Oxford University Press is a department of the University of Oxford. It furthers
the University's objective of excellence in research, scholarship, and education
by publishing worldwide. Oxford is a registered trade mark of Oxford University
Press in the UK and certain other countries.

Published in the United States of America by Oxford University Press
198 Madison Avenue, New York, NY 10016, United States of America.

Library of Congress Cataloging-in-Publication Data
Names: Kaye, Alexander, author.
Title: The invention of Jewish theocracy : the struggle for legal authority
in modern Israel / Alexander Kaye.
Description: New York : Oxford University Press, 2020. |
Includes bibliographical references and index. |
Identifiers: LCCN 2019035294 (print) | LCCN 2019035295 (ebook) |
ISBN 9780190922740 (hardback) | ISBN 9780190922764 (epub) | ISBN 9780190922757 (updf)
Subjects: LCSH: Religious Zionism—Israel—History. | Religious Zionism—Philosophy. |
Religious Zionists—Israel—Attitudes. | Judaism and state—Israel.
Classification: LCC DS150.R39 I7545 2020 (print) | LCC DS150.R39 (ebook) |
DDC 322/.1095694—dc23
LC record available at https://lccn.loc.gov/2019035294
LC ebook record available at https://lccn.loc.gov/201903529

9 8 7 6 5 4 3 2 1

Printed by Sheridan Books, Inc., United States of America

For my parents

CONTENTS

ACKNOWLEDGMENTS

This work owes a great debt to the generosity of family, friends, colleagues, and teachers. These brief words cannot do justice to the thanks that they are due.

Rabbi Dr. Yehuda Abel, Rabbi Mordechai Friedman, and Rabbi Dov Linzer taught me how to read and appreciate Jewish texts. My historical training began in earnest at the University of Cambridge, and I still try to follow the example of Annabel Brett, Chris Clark, William Golding, and, especially, Quentin Skinner, who set me on the path of the history of political thought. David Abulafia, the supervisor of my undergraduate thesis and M.Phil. dissertation, encouraged me to write Jewish intellectual history for the first time. My advisor at Columbia University, Michael Stanislawski, shaped me as a scholar and continues to be a valued mentor. Samuel Moyn and Suzanne Last Stone have been generous guides and inspirational teachers.

I am deeply grateful for the privilege of studying under Professor Yosef H. Yerushalmi and of serving as his last graduate teaching assistant. In the time following his retirement, which turned out to be the last years of his life, he continued to offer both scholarly advice and empathy. He taught me how to be a Jewish historian.

The following deserve special recognition for their contributions to this project: Leora Batnitzky, Elisheva Carlebach, Arye Edrei, David Ellenson, Moshe Halbertal, Lynn Kaye, Assaf Likhovski, Yehudah Mirsky, David Myers, Derek Penslar, Amihai Radzyner, Jonathan Sarna, Nomi Stolzenberg, Joshua Teplitsky, and Steven Wilf.

This research has been enhanced by the knowledge and insight of innumerable people, who have shared ideas, alerted me to archival material, read drafts, and supported my work in other ways. They include Hanina Ben-Menahem, Hillel Ben Sasson, Volker R. Berghahn, Michael Brenner, Naomi Brenner, Rabbi She'ar Yashuv Cohen, Levi Cooper, Jeremy Dauber, Yaacob Dweck, Matt Goldish, Jonathan Gribetz, Aviad Hacohen, Yitzchak Herzog, David Horowitz, Motti Inbari, Ronit Irshai, Amos Israel, Bernard Jackson, Robin Judd, David Kaye, Shira

Kohn, Eugene Korn, Yehuda Kurtzer, Shahar Lifshitz, Menachem Lorberbaum, Yair Lorberbaum, Shaul Magid, Tamara Mann, Jessica Marglin, Menachem Mautner, Ari Mermelstein, Naphtali Meshel, Douglas Morris, Kenneth Moss, David Novak, Daniel Price, Lawrence Rosen, Tamar Ross, Yaakov Ross, Pinchas Roth, Alan Rubinstein, Avi Sagi, Arieh Saposnik, David Schorr, Dov Schwartz, Alan Segal, Joshua Shanes, Anita Shapira, Eugene Sheppard, Elana Stein-Hain, Michael Walzer, Itamar Warhaftig, Yaakov Warhaftig, David Weinfeld, Julie Yanofsky-Goldstein, Jennifer Young, and Ron Zweig.

My research was facilitated by the staff at a number of archives, particularly those at the Central Zionist Archive, the Israel State Archive, the archives of the Religious Kibbutz Movement at Kvutsat Yavneh, the personal papers of Rabbi Isaac Herzog, which were housed in Hekhal Shlomo in Jerusalem when my work on them began, the Religious Zionist Archives at Mosad Ha-rav Kook in Jerusalem, and the Religious Zionist Archives at Bar-Ilan University Library. I am grateful to the foundations and institutions that have supported my work. They include the ACLS/Mellon Foundation, the Foundation for Jewish Culture, and the Memorial Foundation for Jewish Culture. My research has benefited from fellowships and visiting scholarships at Cardozo Law School's Center for Jewish Law and Contemporary Civilization, the Herbert D. Katz Center for Advanced Judaic Studies, the Yad Hanadiv/Beracha Foundation, the David Berg Foundation Institute for Law and History at the Buchmann Faculty of Law at Tel Aviv University, and the Kogod Research Center for Contemporary Jewish Thought at the Shalom Hartman Institute in Jerusalem. The publication of the book was supported by the Institute for Israel and Jewish Studies at Columbia University and the Schusterman Center for Israel Studies at Brandeis University. I offer my thanks for all the support of colleagues and friends at my home institutions these past years: Princeton University, The Ohio State University, and Brandeis University. I am grateful to the people of Oxford University Press, who have been steady companions in bringing this book to fruition. I have special gratitude for my editor, Nancy Toff, whose advice careful comments helped to shape the voice of the final draft.

Finally, I want to express my gratitude to my family. I owe everything to my parents, David and Lindsey Kaye. I could do no better than to emulate the love, grace, and strength of my grandparents, Louis and Rhoda Kaye of blessed memory, and Harry, of blessed memory, and Rita Kushner. I want to thank my sister, Tamara, and my in-laws, Sally Zanger and Daniel Nadis, Joe and Becky, and Maya. To Lynn, nothing I could say here could possibly suffice.

INTRODUCTION

THE HALAKHIC STATE

"Step by step, we will bestow the laws of the Torah upon the citizens of Israel and we will turn halakha into the binding law of the nation." This promise was made by Israel's minister of justice, Yaakov Ne'eman, an Orthodox Jew, to a gathering of rabbis in 2009.[1] Ne'eman's call for the laws of the Torah—by which he meant Orthodox Jewish law—to be imposed on the citizens of a modern democracy provoked a fierce backlash. One politician described the comments as a move toward the "Talibanization of Israel."[2] The Ministry of Justice later "clarified" Ne'eman's comments, but did not retract them; his spokesperson insisted that Ne'eman merely "spoke in broad and general terms about restoring the stature of Jewish law and about the importance of Jewish law to the life of the country."[3]

This furor was a typical moment in a decades-long culture war in Israeli society, revolving around the idea of the halakhic state. Halakha, in the understanding of Orthodox Judaism, is the law revealed by God, which is binding on every Jew. Those calling for Israel to be a halakhic state want it to be governed by that law. Debates over whether Israel should be a halakhic state have generated existential controversies about the role of religion, and religious figures, in public life, the legitimacy of Israel's courts and legislature, and even Israel's claims to the West Bank.

Both supporters and opponents of the halakhic state have referred to such a regime as a "theocracy." Fundamentally, this contentious term refers to a political body whose laws are the laws of God, not of human beings. For opponents of the halakhic state, "theocracy" conjures up the image of an archaic and coercive regime unfit for a modern state. For its supporters, it means the establishment of a perfect law and the fulfillment of divine command. Both those who idealize theocracy and those who demonize it typically imagine the idea of a Jewish theocracy, the halakhic state, to be a very old idea, an ancient archetype of Jewish politics. In fact, though, the idea of the halakhic state was invented no earlier than the 1940s. This book investigates its genealogy. It traces the intellectual history of the idea of the halakhic state among religious Zionist thinkers, recovers the position of Orthodox thinkers before its emergence, analyzes the reasons for its widespread adoption by

The Invention of Jewish Theocracy. Alexander Kaye, Oxford University Press (2020). © Oxford University Press.
DOI: 10.1093/oso/9780190922740.001.0001

Jewish thinkers in the State of Israel, and traces its transformation in Israel's first decades.

In addition to being indispensable for a full understanding of contemporary Israel, this genealogy also opens avenues of comparison with other states around the world in which powerful religious groups both resist and adapt to democratic constitutions. It offers insight into some of the most urgent questions of political life in the twenty-first century: Must fundamentalist religion and democracy inevitably conflict with each other, or can they cooperate? How do religious communities relate to legislation that they believe contradicts divine law? Can religious traditions offer a productive critique of the modern state without entirely undermining its existence?

An unlikely starting point for the idea of the halakhic state is Dublin, in December 1921. Great Britain had just signed a treaty with Irish republican forces that created the Irish Free State. The treaty, however, fell short of granting full independence to Ireland, which remained legally subordinate to Britain. In the summer of 1922, violence broke out between two heavily armed factions within the Irish Republican movement, one supporting the compromise and the other opposing it. Thousands were wounded and hundreds killed. During the conflict, Éamon de Valera, the head of the so-called anti-treatyites, who was unwilling to compromise for anything less than a fully independent Irish constitution, took refuge for his life. The place de Valera chose to hide was the house of Isaac Herzog, the chief rabbi of Dublin.[4] The two men were personal friends and also political allies. Herzog was a supporter of Irish independence from the British, and de Valera was a supporter of Zionism, a cause close to the heart of Herzog, who would go on to become the State of Israel's first Ashkenazic Chief Rabbi.[5] Indeed, the two men, like many Irish Catholics and Jews, came to see a similarity between Zionism and Irish Republicanism, which were both nationalist movements fighting British Imperial control for what they considered the right to establish independent states in their own homelands.[6]

De Valera and Herzog each lived to see the fulfillment of his nationalist dream. Within forty years of de Valera's taking refuge in the Herzog home, the British Empire had withdrawn from almost all of its colonies. In the aftermath of World War II, a bankrupt Britain withdrew from the Indian subcontinent (1947) and Palestine (1948). By the end of the 1960s it had relinquished most of its Asian and African colonies. As the empires of Britain and other European powers declined, independent nation-states were established in their wake. These included the Republic of Ireland in 1937 and the State of Israel in 1948.

By some accounts, religious leaders like Herzog have little to do with this grand narrative of imperial decline and nationalist ascendancy. Most post-imperial nationalist movements were dominated by secular leaders, and Zionism was no exception. Zionism was a "secular revolution," designed not only to achieve an independent Jewish state but also as an effort to liberate Jews from their religious past.[7] Myths and motifs of traditional Judaism were routinely exploited by Zionist leaders, but only in support of their broadly secular project.[8] In this sense, Zionism was akin to many other nationalist movements, from Algeria and Egypt to Turkey, Iraq, and Syria, all of which attempted to "free" nations from their religious past.[9]

Religious Zionism, the common name for the Orthodox Jewish religious nationalism that Herzog represented, did not fit into this picture. At a time when Jewish nationalism was associated with secularism, religious Zionists were committed nationalists who nonetheless persisted in their adherence to traditional religion. Although, since the 1970s, religious Zionism has come to play an increasingly powerful role in Israeli politics, its influence was marginal at best in the first decades of the state.[10] By the late 1940s, the Holocaust had destroyed Orthodox Jewish life in Eastern Europe and most Jews in America and Palestine were abandoning the religious beliefs and lifestyle of their parents. In this light, Orthodox Jews adhering to a religious version of nationalism could easily be dismissed as outliers, a historical anomaly in the context of modern nationalism and a fading remnant of an abandoned world.

This book comes to a different conclusion. It argues that the religious Zionism of Herzog and his followers was not an anomaly of modern times but was, in fact, a product of modernity. It was shaped by the logic of the modern liberal state and was therefore firmly part of the story of Zionism and modern European nationalism more broadly. Religious Zionists produced few political manifestos or works of legal philosophy. They tended to write halakhic tracts and commentaries on religious texts in a rabbinic idiom, replete with references and allusions to the traditional canon, that are difficult to decipher, even for most Hebrew speakers. And yet, this book argues that the writings of Herzog and others like him bear the mark of an unmistakably modern legal and political theory. Although it was articulated through sources of the Talmud and medieval rabbinical literature, Herzog's imagined halakhic state was a new phenomenon in Jewish history.

Before religious Zionism, halakha had never been associated with a modern state. Unlike the centralized legal systems of modern states, halakha was a decentralized system of law. Indeed, it is debatable whether halakha should be considered a "system" at all.[11] Rabbinical courts were not part of a single, hierarchical institution; every rabbinical judge was independent, and there was no formal relationship between one court and the next. Jews all over the world followed different laws, depending on local custom and judicial rulings. Furthermore, whereas modern states tend to claim that their laws have exclusive legal authority within their territory, halakha worked alongside other kinds of law, like the laws of non-Jewish rulers and non-halakhic legislation of Jewish lay leaders, which were also considered authoritative by Jews. Finally, whereas the rule of law in the modern state requires the law to apply equally to all citizens within its borders, halakha claimed authority only over Jews and never over members of other religious communities. Personal identity and not geographical boundaries determined the limits of its jurisdiction.

Herzog's idea of a halakhic state, however, re-imagined the history of halakha according to the model of the modern state. He and his allies envisaged a halakhic system centralized into a single body, recorded in law books explicitly modeled on the legal codes of modern European states. They created a hierarchical system of halakhic courts that, contrary to ancient precedent, included a court of appeals.[12] They also proposed that, just like the law of the modern state, the law of the halakhic state would apply to all citizens, of whatever religion. This recasting of halakha, and the practical program for implementing it, represented a radical departure from the historical precedent to which religious Zionists appealed for legitimacy.

These innovations reflect the fact that many religious Zionist rabbinical leaders were immersed in the intellectual currents of modern European law and politics. Their writings should therefore be read in the context of the rise of modern nationalism, the struggle of independence movements against the control of European empires, and the centrality of legal philosophy in that struggle. The image of de Valera taking refuge in Herzog's house reminds us how deeply embedded Herzog and other religious Zionists were in the historical adventures of the time. Like Herzog, de Valera considered law and constitutionalism to be a primary tool in the battle for full independence from Britain. De Valera finally achieved that goal with the constitution of an independent Ireland, which was ratified in 1937. Herzog was familiar with the Irish constitution; he consulted with de Valera over the clauses regarding the place of religious communities in the new Ireland. Herzog could not fail to have been impressed by the way in which the democratic Irish constitution upheld a central place for religion and religious law in the state. In the very same year that the Irish constitution was ratified, Herzog was appointed as Ashkenazic Chief Rabbi of Palestine and took up the cudgel in his own battles over law in the Zionist context. He fought against the secular Zionists who wanted a constitution that drew from the "foreign wells" of British and Ottoman law rather than the sacred canon of halakha.[13] Like de Valera, Herzog pushed for the creation of an independent state, while maintaining the central role of religious law in that state. Far from being an anomaly in an age of modern nationalism, Herzog's religious Jewish nationalism was produced by it.[14]

Varieties of Religious Zionism

The term "religious Zionist" requires clarification. Commonly used to refer to Orthodox Jewish Zionists, the term covers tremendously diverse ideologies and ways of life. Indeed, the flagship political party of religious Zionism, the National Religious Party (*Mafdal*), which functioned from 1956 to 2008, has been described as a party of "institutionalized factionalism."[15] Religious Zionism has included socialists and bourgeois capitalists, those devoted to rabbinic authority and those skeptical of it, and people with disparate views on politics, theology, and many other key issues. It has also has undergone many changes in its history of more than a century.[16]

As early as the 1860s, Orthodox Jews began writing about the religious value of Jewish settlement in the Land of Israel. Yehudah Alkalai (1798–1878) and Zvi Hirsch Kalischer (1795–1874), rabbis in Sarajevo and Prussia respectively, each advocated for Jewish settlement in the Land of Israel, both out of concern for the fate of indigent European Jews and out of a certain kind of messianic ideology. Their writing had limited impact, however, and it was not until the 1880s, following a series of repressive antisemitic measures in the Russian Empire, that emigration to Ottoman Palestine became a serious option for many European Jews. In those years, the Hibat Zion movement promoted Jewish immigration to Palestine and attracted many Orthodox Jews, particularly from Eastern Europe.[17] Because of internal divisions and the difficult conditions in Palestine, most of the Hibat Zion settlements had failed by the time Theodor Herzl formally established political Zionism as a world movement in 1897. That failure is why the historian Dov Schwartz dates the real genesis of religious Zionism to 1902, when the Mizrahi party was founded.[18] Mizrahi was an Orthodox Zionist party, whose name was a contraction of *merkaz ruhani*, meaning "spiritual center." Its slogan was "the Land of Israel for the People of Israel according to the Torah of Israel." The founding of Mizrahi marked the moment at which Orthodox Jews began to conceive of themselves as a part of the wider current of Jewish nationalism represented by the Zionist movement.

Religious Zionism was paradoxical. Defined on the one hand by its conservative adherence to the Jewish tradition, it also aimed to bring about revolutionary change. Thus, religious Zionism was deemed by some of its adherents to be a "sacred rebellion"; elements of both sanctity and rebellion were central to its identity.[19] The rebellious element of religious Zionism was expressed primarily in its embrace of Zionism against the objections of most other Orthodox Jews. (Only after the Holocaust did the majority of Orthodox Jews begin to affiliate with Zionism.) Zionism was often opposed by Orthodox Jews for two reasons. First, they balked at the fact that most Zionists defined their movement as a way to escape the religious world of their parents and to replace the enervated, degenerate "exilic" Jew of the religious past with a muscular liberated "New Jew" in a national homeland. Rabbinic teachings had little place in this vision. Second, in the eyes of most Orthodox leaders, Zionism represented an attempt to "force the end," taking the salvation of the Jewish people into their own hands, and thereby arrogantly replacing God as redeemer.[20] Through a mixture of innovative interpretations of canonical texts and pragmatic alliances with secular Jewish Zionists, religious Zionists allowed themselves to join the Zionist movement against the protests of the majority of Orthodox rabbis of the time.

At the same time, religious Zionists understood their project to be deeply sacred. In his prayer for the State of Israel, composed by Herzog in 1948 and immediately adopted by religious Zionists into synagogue services, the state was described as "the beginning of the flowering of the redemption."[21] Religious Zionist leaders believed from the start that their mission would have apocalyptic consequences and that Zionism, rather than usurping the role of redeemer from God, would actually enjoin God to bring about the messianic age. This outcome would lead to the redemption not only of the Jewish people but also of the entire world. Some religious Zionists concealed their eschatological beliefs in an attempt to appease non-Orthodox Zionists. Yitzhak Yaakov Reines, for example, the founder of Mizrahi, claimed that his support of Zionism was purely a matter of political exigency in order to protect the oppressed Jews of Eastern Europe.[22] Others, however, such as Isaiah Bernstein, a central figure in Ha-Po'el Ha-Mizrahi, the socialist wing of the Mizrahi movement, were more explicit about the religious value of Zionism. "The battle we are now waging for the freedom and redemption of Israel and for the establishment of a Jewish state is not confined to us," wrote Bernstein. "The return of Israel to their land and the renewal of their spirit are a significant contribution to peace in the world."[23]

Because they believed that Zionism was an instrument of divine redemption, religious Zionists tended to think that secular Zionists, even those who explicitly opposed religion, were unconsciously motivated by a latent religious impulse. According to Yitzhak Nissenbaum, a Mizrahi leader, Zionist activity of any kind was always impelled by "faith in the power of Judaism."[24] Similarly, Abraham Isaac Kook, a rabbi who was never technically a registered Zionist but who was revered as a figurehead of the religious Zionist movement, claimed that "while [secular Zionists] may believe that the good they accomplish is contrary to the Torah, it is in fact of its very essence."[25] For Kook, secular Zionists were tools of God whether they knew it or not.[26]

As part of their messianic vision, religious Zionists saw the Zionist movement as a way to open up new spiritual avenues for the Jewish people. They believed that the return of Jews to the Land of Israel would allow Jews to follow biblical and rabbinic law in areas of life that were not available to them in their exile, such as laws pertaining to agricultural life and, eventually, the rebuilding of the Temple in Jerusalem. They also believed that Jews in their newly redeemed state would follow Jewish law. Shlomo Zalman Shragai, another Mizrahi leader, wrote that, because "observing the Torah and fulfilling its commandments in their entirety is possible only in the land of Israel," the ultimate purpose of Zionism is "a means to realize the goal of fulfilling and observing the Torah."[27]

Within the basic parameters of this worldview, streams of religious Zionism proliferated, adopting different perspectives on a host of issues. Members of the Mizrahi party by and large continued to adhere to a conservative religious outlook coupled with a moderate political platform. By contrast, Ha-Po'el Ha-Mizrahi, an organization established in 1922 by Orthodox Zionist youth who disapproved of what they saw as the bourgeois values of many religious leaders, attempted to con-nect religious Zionism to the secular Zionist workers' movement. The religious kibbutz movement, a network of religious socialist communes that were affiliated with Ha-Po'el Ha-Mizrahi, were generally skeptical of rabbinic authority and had a freer interpretation of Orthodox Jewish law. They worked toward the creation of a redeemed Jewish society in which physical labor and communion with the land were cardinal virtues.[28] Meanwhile, religious Zionists emanating from the circle of Abraham Isaac Kook were drawn to his unusual mix of traditionalism, romantic nationalism, and mysticism.[29]

After the 1967 war, religious Zionism produced still more variants. *Gush Emunim*, the "Bloc of the Faithful," was a religious Zionist movement that emphasized the Jewish settlement of the territories occupied by Israel during the war as a primary religious value. The eschatological impulse that had been pres-ent in religious Zionism from the start became more explicit and imminent in religious Zionist thought from the 1970s. It also became more violent. Religious Zionists mounted fierce resistance against the state's policy of exchanging "land for peace" with its neighbors. This opposition expressed itself in rhetoric, politi-cal action and, occasionally, physical conflict. In 1995, Prime Minister Yitzhak Rabin, the Israeli champion of the peace process, was assassinated by a religious Zionist student. The trauma caused by the event is still palpable in Israeli society.

Since the 1980s, religious Zionism has diversified still further under the influ-ence of global trends toward multiculturalism and, later, the potential of the inter-net to strengthen and give voice to otherwise marginal groups. In recent decades, religious Zionism has developed in various, often opposing, directions. Some religious Zionists have incorporated feminist insights and the higher criticism of Scripture into religious life. Others have embraced extreme right-wing activism, or Hasidically inflected new-age artistic expressionism.[30] Still, however, wider Israeli society seems to associate religious Zionism primarily with the campaign for continued Israeli control over the Occupied Territories. A study from 2014 found that 22% of Israeli Jews identified themselves as "religious nationalist" even though only 10% of Israeli Jews identified themselves as "religious."[31] This data seems to indicate that, for some, "religious Zionist" has become a proxy for Israeli territorial maximalism represented by political parties like The Jewish Home.[32]

Obstacles to the Halakhic State

The mission of religious Zionists to create a halakhic state had to contend with severe obstacles, some arising from the political circumstances of their time and others inherent in the Jewish tradition itself. Among the political obstacles was the commitment of the overwhelming majority of Zionists to a liberal democratic legal constitution for the Jewish state and a deep opposition to the idea of religious rule. Immediately after the establishment of Israel, the provisional government set up a committee to prepare a constitution for the new state. The government committee considered several constitutional drafts. Their proposals regarding the place of religion in the state were comparable to other democratic constitutions of the period. At the time, a complete separation between religion and state was rare, even in liberal democracies. Even in the United States, the erection of a "wall of separation" between religion and state did not become a mainstay of Supreme Court decisions until the second half of the twentieth century.[33] Despite the lack of a sharp distinction between church and state, however, democratic constitutions tended to protect the freedom of, and from, religion.

Typical of this approach was the draft written by Leo Kohn, a jurist and professor of international relations who also worked for Israel's Foreign Ministry. Kohn drew inspiration mainly from the constitutions of France, Ireland, and the Weimar Republic, as well as those of the United States and China, rather than from the Jewish tradition, and certainly not from Jewish law. His proposal was accepted as the formal basis for the deliberations of Israel's government in August 1948.[34] It opened with an affirmation of the place of God in Jewish history: "We, the children of Israel, giving thanks and praise to God, the Creator of the world, who brought us out from slavery to freedom and returned us to the land that He promised to our forefathers."[35] But it defined Israel as "a sovereign, independent, democratic republic," maintained that the state would not discriminate among its citizens on the basis of "race, religion, language or sex," and had little religious content beyond its opening words.[36] Under pressure from religious Zionist critics, Kohn added more references to the Jewish tradition to the second and third drafts of his constitution. Those references, however, remained largely symbolic and incidental to the main substance of his proposal. In this respect, Kohn's draft constitution was similar to many European constitutions of the time that included a reference to God in their preambles but not substantive religious norms.

Religious Zionists were not satisfied with Kohn's cursory gesture to religion. Zerah Warhaftig, a religious Zionist representative of the United Religious Front party who was the chair of the constitutional committee lamented that, other than the preamble, Kohn's constitution contained "nothing concerning religion." He complained that its "formulation is liberal and avoids giving a clear answer to issues of religion." Warhaftig believed, by contrast, that "the religion of Israel should be given a status in the State of Israel."[37]

The disappointment of Warhaftig and other religious Zionists was predictable, and points to a fundamental opposition between the idea of a halakhic state and the secular democracy embraced by secular Zionists. As early as 1922, Meir Berlin (later Bar-Ilan), a religious Zionist activist who later became the president of the World Mizrahi organization, had marked out the Jewish approach to religion as distinct from that of Christian European countries:

> Our case is different. Our Torah and traditions are not man-made constitutions, but God's own law. . . . We have no "church" that is not also concerned with matters of state, just as we have no state which is not also concerned with "church" matters. In Jewish life these are not two separate spheres.[38]

John Locke, the Enlightenment thinker, whose writings on the role of religion in the state laid the groundwork for many modern constitutions, attempted "to distinguish exactly the Business of Civil Government from that of Religion, and to settle the just Bounds that lie between the one and the other."[39] Meir Berlin rejected the application of Locke's distinction to the Jewish case. He argued that Judaism, in contrast to the liberal tradition that had emerged from a Christian heritage, does not recognize a sphere of religion distinct from the civil politics that is the business of the state. Rather, Berlin, like all religious Zionists, believed that Jewish national and religious identities were deeply integrated. More specifically, he argued that Judaism had an inherently legal character. It followed that the constitution of a Jewish state could not simply be another one of those "man-made constitutions." In the constitution of a Jewish state, the Torah, "God's own law," had to play a central role.

The political obstacles to the realization of a halakhic state were even deeper than the fundamental divide between religious Zionists and the rest of the Zionist movement over the place of religion in the constitution. Many Zionists displayed not only an antipathy to the idea of the halakhic state but to traditional Judaism more broadly. Max Nordau, for example, a close collaborator of Theodor

Herzl in the foundation of political Zionism, wrote of the Hebrew Bible that its "conception of the universe is childish and its morality revolting." He considered it to be full of superstition and faulty history, along with poems and stories that "are rarely distinguished by beauties of the highest order but frequently by superfluity of expression, coarseness, bad taste, and genuine Oriental sensuality."[40]

David Ben-Gurion, the architect of the Jewish state and Israel's first Prime Minister, relied heavily on the Bible as a source for a Jewish nationalist mythos, but he too had no interest in Orthodox Judaism or in halakha as a normative practice.[41] For Ben-Gurion, Zionism was heir to the Jewish sovereignty and political heroism described in the Bible, but he dismissed the "exilic" period between biblical times and the rise of Zionism—which included the entire rabbinic period and the formation of halakha—as "apolitical, particularistic, prone to an exaggerated spiritualism and withdrawal."[42]

For all these reasons, religious Zionists faced an uphill battle in their attempt to convince the Zionist movement to adopt a constitution on the basis of the Torah. Although many of them believed that, as part of the unfolding of a messianic vision, the Jewish masses would eventually repent and return to the Torah, they did not know exactly when this event would happen.[43] As a result, the establishment of a halakhic state required them to win over a population that ranged from the skeptical to the openly antagonistic.

Aside from the political obstacles arising from the negative attitude of many Zionists toward religion, religious Zionists also faced a set of intellectual obstacles that flowed from the numerous tensions between halakha and democracy. Democracy posed four key challenges to the idea of the halakhic state. The first was the challenge of anachronism. Most of the corpus of halakha was formulated before the period of the modern state. As such, its political categories are ostensibly unsuited for dealing with modern politics. Halakhic sources speak of kings, priests, and prophets, and have very little to say about parliamentary democracy, bureaucracy, and the modern judiciary. The second challenge was that of scale. Halakha developed among Jews who lived under Gentile rule. Their communities were sometimes very large, and certainly had a rich political life. They did not, however, require either the legal structure or the administrative capacity of the modern state. Halakha therefore says almost nothing about questions that are fundamental to the politics of the state, such as foreign policy, the role of the army, the structure of government, or the procedures of mass representation. The third challenge was one of social and political discrimination. Orthodox interpretations of halakha distinguish in numerous areas of law between men and women, between Jews and Gentiles, and between Jews who observe halakha and those who do not. Many rabbis believed that halakha would not permit either non-Jews or Jewish women to hold positions of political or judicial authority. Already in the years following World War I, several religious Zionist rabbis had attempted, and failed, to deny the franchise to Jewish women in Palestine.[44] This kind of discrimination was in direct tension with modern democratic values. Finally, there was the challenge of authority. The cornerstone of democratic politics is that the people govern themselves. The people are the source of all legal and political authority; laws have authority only if they are endorsed by their will. In halakha, however, the source of legal authority is not the people but God. Halakha is considered to be the will of God as revealed in the Bible and interpreted by rabbis, its authorized interpreters. God's laws are binding whether or not the people accept them, and new rules cannot simply be invented by a parliament; they must be consistent with generations of halakhic precedent.

These challenges could not simply be ignored by religious Zionists. By the 1920s, it had already become clear that a Jewish state, should it be established, would be democratic. The *Va'ad Le'umi*, the Jewish National Council that organized Jewish life in Palestine and became the structural foundation for the Israeli government, was democratic. Indeed, it was not only the majority of the Zionist movement but also the international community that demanded that the Jewish state should be an egalitarian democracy. When the United Nations voted in 1947 to partition Palestine into a Jewish and an Arab state, it specified that both states should have a democratic constitution and a legislative body elected by universal suffrage and should not allow discrimination based on "race, religion, language or sex."[45] To convince others to govern the Jewish state by halakha, religious Zionists would have to present a picture of a halakhic state in which women, non-Jews, and non-Orthodox Jews could hold positions of power. They would have to propose a constitutional arrangement that was compatible with their understanding of the Jewish tradition but would also allow a woman to be the Prime Minister and a Muslim to be a judge.

Legal Pluralism and Legal Centralism

Broadly speaking, there were two ways in which religious Zionists attempted to grapple with the obstacles that stood in the way of applying halakha to a modern Jewish state. In the language of legal theory, one approach would be called legal pluralism and the other would be called legal centralism. It is a central claim of this book that, around the end of the 1940s, religious Zionist elites abandoned legal pluralism, which had until then been the framework for their constitutional thinking, and embraced religious centralism. A clear definition of these terms and their place in Jewish history and legal scholarship is therefore crucial.

According to the ideology of legal centralism, a political territory may have only one system of law, derived from a single source of authority and arranged in a single legal hierarchy. In modern legal theory, this single legal system is typically that of the state and its ultimate source of authority is called the sovereign.[46] In democratic states, the sovereign is usually understood to be the people. So, according to legal centralism, it is the will of the people that ultimately bestows authority upon all the law in the state. Although the people may delegate the business of making law to various institutions (parliaments, regulatory commissions, and so on) they are ultimately responsible for all laws, from the law against murder to zoning laws on the local high street. Here is how legal centralism was described by John Griffiths, a pioneering legal theorist:

> [L]aw is and should be the law of the state, uniform for all persons, exclusive of all other law, and administered by a single set of state institutions. To the extent that other, lesser normative orderings, such as the church, the family, the voluntary association and the economic organization exist, they ought to be and in fact are hierarchically subordinate to the law and institutions of the state. . . . In the legal centralist conception, law is an exclusive, systematic and unified hierarchical ordering of normative propositions.[47]

Legal centralism has advantages as a descriptive account of law. The theory tends to be intuitive for citizens of modern states who tend to think it is self-evident that the government has the exclusive authority to make laws. Legal centralism is also appealing in its simplicity. The law that convicts a murderer is the same law that prohibits parking on a busy road during rush hour.

There is also another way of imagining the law: legal pluralism. According to this alternative theory, multiple legal systems may coexist in the same social field.[48] Each system has its own source of authority, often distinct from the state. Proponents of legal pluralism claim that it is a more accurate representation of how law works in reality. A private contract between individuals, for example, may indeed be enforced by the law of the state. But in the minds of the parties to the contract, other normative systems such as moral or religious obligations may be more important than state legislation. Legal pluralists, then, recognize the existence of multiple overlapping sources of normative authority. These various sources do not necessarily coexist in a systematic way and coincide in ways that, in the words of Griffiths, "may support, complement, ignore, or frustrate one another."[49]

There are two key debates among legal philosophers around the concepts of legal centralism and legal pluralism. One debate is normative. It revolves around the question of whether legal pluralism or centralism is a better way to organize law in the modern state. Another debate is descriptive. Some jurists believe that legal centralism accurately describes the function of law in the state, whereas others believe that, despite appearances, even modern states actually include several legal regimes.[50] These debates aside, most legal historians agree that legal pluralism does accurately describe the way law worked in two specific historical contexts. The first context was the Middle Ages, in which everyone in the Christian and Muslim worlds lived under a legally pluralistic regime, which had a wide array of diverse legal institutions and authorities that related to each other in fluid and generally unsystematic ways, sometimes in conflict, sometimes in cooperation.[51] The second was the colonial context. From the nineteenth century, even as European imperial powers attempted to enforce legal centralism in their own states, they retained in their colonies a system of legal pluralism in which all kinds of local, religious, and "tribal" law were recognized alongside the law imported by the colonizers.[52]

These medieval and colonial contexts, in which legal pluralism dominated, were especially significant for the legal thinking of religious Zionists. The legal pluralism of the Middle Ages was a primary point of reference for religious Zionists. Much of the halakhic precedent that they deemed authoritative was produced in that period, when halakha was only one of a number of sources of law. Alongside halakha, the non-halakhic legislation of Jewish lay leaders and the laws of non-Jewish rulers were both considered binding by Jews. Legal pluralism was therefore taken for granted by many of the medieval Jewish jurists whose works were accepted as precedent by religious Zionists. Similarly, the colonial context of the British Mandate for Palestine, which formed the de facto starting point for Zionist discussions of law, was also legally pluralistic. Under Ottoman rule, religious communities in Palestine had exclusive authority over the personal law pertaining to their members. (Personal law included, among other things, laws of marriage, divorce, and inheritance.)[53] After the British conquered Palestine in 1917, they continued to recognize the independence of Palestine's religious courts.[54] Even the most liberal drafts of a constitution for Israel did not consider altering this state of affairs;[55] thus, the law of Mandate Palestine was not unified into a single hierarchy but was distributed among different communities and legal institutions. As a result, legal pluralism characterized not only the medieval precedent for religious Zionist legal thinkers but also their lived reality.

It is therefore to be expected that, before 1948, most proposals of religious Zionists regarding the role of halakha in the state were legally pluralistic. They suggested that halakha should play a role in the state, but not that it should have exclusive legal authority. They typically imagined a Jewish state in which halakha would exist in parallel with the legislation of a democratically elected parliament.

They acknowledged that many aspects of the state would be governed by laws created by human legislators, many of whom would not have any affiliation with religious Orthodoxy, and who might not be Jewish at all. This legally pluralistic approach provided a way for religious Zionists to address the practical and theoretical challenges of applying halakha in a democratic state. It also allowed them to legitimize both democratic legislation and halakha simultaneously, granting religious legitimacy to secular legislation while bestowing the imprimatur of the state on halakha.

At the end of the 1940s, however, a sea change occurred. For the first time, religious Zionist legal thinking began to reject the model of legal pluralism and to adopt the approach of legal centralism. A key instigator of this change was Isaac Herzog, who vehemently opposed the very idea of legal pluralism. He and his followers argued that the State of Israel should be governed exclusively by a single, centralized system of halakha, proposing that Israel's constitution include a clause designating the Torah as the fundamental law of the state. Herzog himself described his envisioned constitution as a "theocracy." He converted many followers to this point of view and convened a large group of rabbis who set about composing halakhic legal codes in the form of modern law books. "We will not give up on the law of the Torah," he insisted. "I am ready to sacrifice my life for it. Only on the Torah of Israel may the state of Israel be built."[56] Ultimately, Herzog's aspirations for a modern Jewish theocracy were ignored by Israel's political leaders. By the mid-1950s, even Herzog himself had to admit that his dream of a centralized halakhic state would never be realized. Despite the failure of his ambitions, however, the legal centralism that Herzog championed continued to shape the legal thinking of religious Zionists in the ensuing decades, and its echoes can be heard in Israeli political discourse to the present day.

The shift from legal pluralism to legal centralism can be explained by the fact that religious Zionists, for all their resistance to the secularizing tendencies of the Zionist movement, were embedded in a European legal and political culture that similarly repudiated legal pluralism in favor of the undivided sovereignty of the centralized state. This tendency was not unique to Zionism but was typical of postcolonial nationalist movements. On the Indian subcontinent, all over Africa and elsewhere, nationalists, who were often educated in European imperial centers, adopted legally centralist aspirations as they fought against imperial hegemony. Having been educated in London and Paris, and having been so intimately involved in the Irish struggle for independence from Britain, Herzog was particularly entrenched in this culture. His influence in Palestine after he was appointed chief rabbi in 1937 allowed him to disseminate, promote, and fund his philosophy of halakha and his view of the relationship between religion and the state.

There is a large and contentious literature that deals with the relationship between Zionism and colonialism. Some scholars see Zionism as an example of European settler colonialism. Others maintain that the two phenomena have nothing to do with each other. The unique place of Jews in *fin de siècle* Europe makes the truth more complicated than either of these positions. Many Jews were party to European culture and politics, including its colonialist assumptions. But many Jews (indeed, many of the same Jews) were also marginalized and oppressed by European society. The analytical tools of postcolonial theory, then, need to be applied to the history of Zionism with caution.

As Derek Penslar, one of the foremost historians of Zionism, has pointed out, "Zionism was historically and conceptually situated between colonial, anti-colonial and postcolonial discourse and practice."[57] Even though the attitude of Zionists toward Palestinian Arabs shared some features with the *mission civilatrice* of European colonialism, it also differed in important respects. Zionists understood themselves not only to be colonizing Palestine, but also as a nationalist movement, resisting the colonial rule of the British Empire and, ultimately, establishing their own postcolonial state in their ancient homeland. These nationalist and postcolonial contexts are especially relevant for the analysis of religious Zionist legal philosophy, which grappled with the legacy of European imperialism and used it in the struggle to establish a state in the wake of its retreat.

Implications

The core arguments of this book, therefore, yield two main insights. The first is that, about halfway through the twentieth century, religious Zionists invented the idea of a halakhic state, a legally centralist modern state run exclusively by halakha, which was called a "theocracy" by its leading proponent. The second is that this ideological development can best be understood by placing religious Zionist legal theory against the backdrop of modern European jurisprudence, and in the context of global postcolonial nationalist movements.

To be sure, religious Zionist rabbinical elites always believed that halakha should play some sort of role in a modern Jewish state. They understood, however, that the realization of this goal required them to contend with the political and intellectual obstacles that resulted from the tensions between halakha and modern democratic principles. Earlier religious Zionists responded to these challenges with legally pluralistic solutions, proposing that halakha and democratic legislation should exist in parallel in the Jewish state. From the end of the 1940s, however, most religious Zionists began to adopt responses that were legally centralist, insisting that the state could have only a single, halakhic, legal system. A primary reason for this shift was the deep influence of modern European legal philosophy, which informed the most fundamental assumptions of religious Zionist legal thinking. While remaining committed to their idiosyncratic and traditionalist vision of Jewish law, religious Zionists also followed trends toward legal centralism that they held in common with many postcolonial modern nationalist movements. Religious Zionist aspirations to a centralist halakhic state predictably failed to materialize. This setback required religious Zionists thinkers to create new strategies to deal with what they considered to be Israel's flawed legal order. Despite their failures, however, they never abandoned the principle that a legally centralist halakhic state was the ideal. The persistence of that idea continues to color Israeli political discourse.

These arguments have particular implications for two areas of contemporary interest: the study of the modern state of Israel and the study of the relationship between religion and the modern state more generally.

The analysis of religious Zionist legal philosophy is critical for an understanding of contemporary tensions in Israeli society. Since the mid-1970s, relations between religious and secular groups in Israel have become increasingly tense, often erupting into violence. The root of these tensions, and in particular the role of the 1967 war in Israel's evolution, is the subject of a historiographical debate. Many scholars understand 1967 to be a crucial turning point. They claim that before 1967, most religious Zionists were pragmatists who did what they could to support the secular Zionist establishment. They were conscious of their relatively weak position in Israeli society and did not generally try to enforce their religious way of life onto others.[58] After 1967, however, younger members of the religious Zionist community became a major component of the settler movement, which was also supported in many ways by the Israeli government itself.[59] Religious rhetoric, sidelined in the days of the hegemony of socialist political leadership, returned to the Israeli mainstream in the "euphoria" that followed the war.[60] The religious Zionist community in Israeli society was gradually emboldened, with its members attaining senior positions in the military and the government. By the end of the 1970s, secular elites had begun to warn that Israel was "sliding into clerical dictatorship" and that Israeli democracy was being replaced by a halakhic state.[61] Tensions between newly invigorated and politicized religious Zionists and the state quickly escalated over the policy of "land for peace." Mass protests among religious Zionists against the evacuations of settlements such as Yamit in the Sinai (1982), Gush Qatif in the Gaza strip (2005), and Amona in the West Bank (2006 and 2017), not to mention the assassination of Prime Minister Rabin, placed an intense strain on relations between religious Zionists and the state.[62]

This book offers a different perspective. Without minimizing the consequences of the 1967 war, it argues that religious-secular tension was already built into the legal philosophy of religious Zionism by the late 1940s. The adoption by religious Zionists, around the years of the establishment of the state, of a legally centralist vision, which lay claim to the entire hierarchy of the state's legal authority, established the potential for conflict. While religious Zionists remained politically weak, there was no opportunity for this vision to be applied to reality. It became a subterranean desire that emerged forcefully after decades of suppression. The principle of legal centralism, however, was present from the state's founding.

The forgotten beginnings of religious Zionist theocratic thinking recovered in this book are not only a matter of academic interest. The idea of the halakhic state continues to play an important role in religious Zionist thought and in the public discourse of the State of Israel. Struggles over the control of Israel's key institutions frequently erupt. Rabbinical courts in Israel are constantly vying with the civil courts over the extent of their authority. Religious Zionist leaders push for the application of halakha over the public sphere and rabbis urge resistance against certain policies of Israel's armed forces.[63] The idea of the halakhic state has even reached the highest political office. Even Prime Minister Netanyahu reportedly recently called for the Talmud, the foundational text of halakha, to be the "basis for the Israeli legal system."[64] All of these developments are outgrowths of the discourse of religious Zionism in the first years of the state. An intellectual history of the religious Zionism of those years is therefore crucial to an understanding of these recent developments.

The history of the idea of the halakhic state in the Israeli context also illuminates urgent contemporary global questions about the relationship between religion, law, and politics in the context of the modern state. It has been widely observed that the predictions by early-twentieth-century scholars that religion would disappear in a "disenchanted" modernity were severely misguided. The revival of a politically engaged Christian right in the United States, the emergence of political Islam in the Middle East, the ascendance of Hindu nationalism in India, and the surge of radical Jewish politics in Israel all challenge the notion that modernity, liberal democracy, and secularism inevitably go hand in hand. Indeed, the impact on global politics of newly politicized religious groups has generated a far-reaching reassessment of theories of secularization.[65] Studies of these phenomena, however, are overwhelmingly focused on Christianity or Islam and tend to overlook Judaism. Bringing the history of religious Zionism into conversation with the scholarly literature on secularization provides a new comparative perspective on a global phenomenon.

Until recently, a largely unexamined myth in Western political thought was that of the "Great Separation."[66] According to this myth, the formation of the modern state from the sixteenth century onward was a response to the European wars of religion. It was an attempt to escape religious violence by divorcing religion from political life. According to this narrative, modernity was necessarily accompanied by secularization, which was a trend comprising several components: differentiation—the separation of the sphere of politics from the sphere of religion; privatization—the retreat of religious life away from public state institutions into the personal lives of individuals and voluntary organizations; and decline—the inexorable weakening of religious belief and practice in the face of a powerful demystifying scientific worldview.[67]

The "Great Separation" thesis is more than a historical claim. It also implicitly entails the normative claim that religion is prone to violence because religious passions claim total and exclusive authority over all spheres of life. It contrasts this view to secular politics, which it holds up as rational, allowing for toleration between diverse groups. According to this understanding, secularization was a rational response that saved modern Europe from the intolerance and violence of religious conflict. This myth implies that there is something special (and better) about Western Christian society, which, alone among the world's "civilizations," developed a rational secular politics.[68] This position tends to support the notion that, even today, secular politics remains an essential bulwark against the danger of politicized religious radicalism.

In this reading, a clear distinction can be made between "political theology" and "modern political philosophy."[69] Political theology is a kind of politics in which the ultimate authority is God and in which human action is oriented toward spiritual salvation in an eschatological future. By contrast, modern political philosophy is an approach to politics in which the ultimate authority is not God but the will of the people and in which human action is oriented toward the good of people in the "immanent frame" rather than to some kind of transcendent salvation.[70]

Scholars have taken issue with both the descriptive and the prescriptive aspects of the "Great Separation" thesis. Descriptively, the thesis fails to explain why religion has demonstrably not, in fact, been relegated to the private sphere. Even in modernity, religion continues to play a major role in political life, as the daily headlines repeatedly confirm. Scholars have also pointed out that even the aspects of modern politics that appear to be secular are in fact intrinsically theological. Locke, Hobbes, and other founders of modern political theory based their works on readings of the Bible and other religious texts.[71] In his critique of liberalism, Carl Schmitt pointed out as early as the 1920s that modern notions of the state and sovereignty are nothing but medieval theological ideas dressed in a new garb and that "the central concepts of modern state theory are all secularized theological concepts."[72] Specifically, he argued, the sovereignty of God, and the loyalty that flowed from it, has been inherited by the sovereignty of the state that replaces God as the source of political authority.

Prescriptive aspects of the theory of secularization, which make claims about what should be, rather than what actually is, have also been criticized. Scholars have objected to the contrast between irrational, violent religious politics and rational, tolerant secular politics. They point out that modern forms of violent conflict are not a function of religion, but rather the outcome of structural changes brought about by modern state formation. In other words, the modern state was not formed in order to escape religious violence; religious violence is an outcome of the modern state.[73] According to this position, conflict and violence today are not caused by an anachronistic eruption of religious fanaticism; they are a function of the internal logic of the modern state itself. It is the modern secular state, not religion, that demands the monopoly on the legitimate use of force and the power to legislate almost every aspect of life. It is the state that expresses its instinct toward violence (against its own citizens and against people beyond its borders) and total authority over law within its borders. These impulses then spread around the globe, migrating along the routes of European colonialism.[74] Taken together, these criticisms blur the distinction between "secular" and "religious" and challenge the notion that a clear distinction can be made between "political theology" and "modern political philosophy."

Contemporary scholarship, then, is currently in the midst of a wide-ranging series of debates over whether a "Great Separation" ever occurred, over the nature of "religion" and "secularism" and over the relationship between them. The intellectual history of religious Zionism contributes to this debate.

Ostensibly, the example of religious Zionism lends credence to the position that there is a sharp distinction between secular and religious politics. Secular Zionism, it could be argued, is a classic example of "modern political philosophy," a movement that attempted to strip Judaism of its theological content and to set up a Jewish state on the model of other modern states. By contrast, religious Zionism championed political theology against modern political thought, explicitly appealing to God, not the people's will, as the ultimate authority, and orienting Zionist politics toward a messianic future.

At the same time, the phenomenon of religious Zionism can also be shown to undermine the distinction between secular and religious politics. Although the ultimate goal of religious Zionism was explicitly eschatological, the entire structure of religious Zionist legal and political thinking was based on archetypally modern categories such as democracy, territorial sovereignty and, most of all, the state. For the first time in Jewish history, under religious Zionism the state became a primary vehicle of religious meaning and a key category of halakhic discourse. Schmitt thought that modern politics was based on "secularized theological concepts." Religious Zionist theories of politics, the mirror image of Schmitt's conception, might be termed sanctified secular concepts.

The religious Zionist philosophy of law is a particularly strong example of modern ideas being absorbed into a religious framework and imbued with sacred significance. Religious Zionists incorporated into their legal thinking a series of deeply held assumptions that underpinned the legal philosophy of twentieth-century Europe. They accepted from modern European jurisprudence the principles that everyone within the territory of the state, whatever his or her religious affiliation, was subject to the same system of laws and that all legal authority in the state was centralized, hierarchically organized, and flowed from a single source. To many modern readers, these principles might seem unremarkable because they form the basis of modern Western jurisprudence. In the history of Jewish law, however, they are quite unusual; before the twentieth century, no Jewish thinker had thought about halakha in quite this way. The religious Zionist embrace of the principles of state sovereignty and democratic constitutionalism is therefore striking.

This analysis does not somehow mean that religious Zionism was "secular" as opposed to "religious." Although the structure of religious Zionist legal theory was derived from the jurisprudence of modern Europe, its content was quite distinct. The fact that modern concepts such as democracy and the state were raised to new prominence in religious dialogue must not obscure the fact that the foundation of its normative system remained the will of God, not the people, or that the goal of its political agenda was eschatological as well as temporal. Indeed, religious Zionists fiercely resisted many elements of secularization, including differentiation, privatization, and the decline of religious commitment.

The case of religious Zionism does not, then, unambiguously support or contradict the notion of a "Great Separation" between secular politics and political theology. Rather, it demonstrates that intellectual exchange on a deep level may take place between groups that define themselves as "secular" and "religious" even while fundamental tensions between the groups persist. In fact, in the Israeli case, it is the very similarity between the ways that religious and secular political structures are imagined that exacerbate the tensions between them. The prominence of legal centralism in religious Zionist thought, which it inherited from modern European jurisprudence, brought it into direct conflict with the state itself. Because both religious and secular communities considered the state to be the exclusive locus of political and legal authority, they found themselves fighting over exclusive control of its legal apparatus. This conflict has contributed to a cultural war that lasts to this day.

Methodology

In recovering the genealogy of the idea of the halakhic state, this book draws on two overlapping historical methodologies. It is, first of all, a work of intellectual history. It undertakes a close reading of religious Zionist texts, attempting to piece together the internal logic of their patterns of thought and to reconstruct the discourses of which they were a part. This approach involves identifying their "commonplaces," the general assumptions that are taken for granted in the construction of their arguments.[75] Often, what is left unsaid in a historical source reveals more than what was explicitly expressed. Statements made as an aside, without any need for justification or explanation, may warrant more attention from the historian than statements that are emphasized by the author. This is because the peripheral or incidental elements of a text are often the key to recovering the scaffolding that undergirds the rhetorical web in which it is embedded. The historical meaning of a text can be ascertained only after identifying the matrix of other texts to which it is implicitly or explicitly responding.[76]

This book is also informed by the methodology of the field of cultural legal history and its fundamental insight that law and culture construct each other.[77] By providing the categories through which we think about ourselves as individuals, social groups, and national units, law creates the structures through which we make meaning.[78] By appreciating the role of law in constituting meaning, rather than merely as a tool to bring about practical ends, we can read law as a discourse through which identity, power, and social roles are negotiated.

This approach to law can be particularly effective in the study of people or groups who feel marginalized or threatened by a state's hegemonic authority. For them, the law can become a battlefield on which struggles for identity are asserted and power imbalances addressed. Often the significance of legal argument is in its rhetoric as much as its ability to bring about a practical outcome; the use of law to mount social resistance or to shore up identity can be no less important than its political outcome. This insight refines our understanding of why cultural debates over law were so important to religious Zionists. Their fixation on law was not only because they wanted to achieve real social change (though, certainly, it was about that as well). Even when such change was out of reach, their continued principled arguments about law in public forums acted as a marker of their own social identity and resisted the secular hegemony of a state that, they believed, had abandoned God.

As the first intellectual history of the halakhic state, this book adds a Jewish case study to the growing field that is dedicated to an exploration of the meaning of the "religious" and the "secular" in the modern state and the relationship between them. Like works that focus on other religious traditions, this book analyzes the complex and counterintuitive interaction between "modern" and "traditional," "religious" and "secular." The Jewish case, however, is different in an important way. Whereas, historically, several states have officially established religions such as Christianity or Islam, the halakhic state has only ever existed in imagination, an ideal to be achieved or a nightmare to be avoided. Although traces of Jewish law are encoded in Israeli legislation and although Jewish religious courts, like the courts of other religious communities, have some jurisdiction in Israel, nothing like the theocracy proposed by Isaac Herzog ever came to fruition. It is impossible to know how a halakhic Jewish state would have unfolded over the decades had Herzog's proposals been accepted. The array of anthropological and ethnographic data available in the study of other states, where religions have officially been established, simply does not exist, with an important methodological consequence. The sources for the study of the halakhic state are limited to the intellectual output of the religious Zionist elites who invented, debated, and attempted to implement the idea during the middle decades of the twentieth century. These historical subjects are almost exclusively Orthodox rabbis. They are all male. They are also mostly (though not exclusively) Ashkenazim, of European origin.[79] They are not the rank and file religious Zionists whose outlook often differed from those of the rabbinical elites. They are certainly not women, Palestinians, migrant laborers, or other members of early Israeli society who would have been largely oblivious to the esoteric rabbinical writing on the halakhic state. Although the voices of these groups are not represented in the relevant sources, the history of the halakhic state nevertheless has significant implications for their place in Israeli society. Questions of inclusion, equality, and representation deeply preoccupied theorists of the halakhic state. Among other things, this book explicates religious Zionist thinking about groups that have historically been disadvantaged from the perspective of Orthodox Jewish law. These attitudes continue to have a significant effect on Israeli society today, even though the halakhic state never became Israel's official constitutional model.

Although the main texts analyzed in this book were written before the end of the 1960s, it is difficult to overestimate the consequences of the history of the idea of the halakhic state on contemporary Israel. The role of religious Zionism in Israel's politics today can be seen in a new light once the historical foundations of the theocratic idea have been taken into account. While the importance of 1967 can scarcely be overstated, it is impossible to understand religious Zionism in the twenty-first century, or Israeli society more broadly, without coming to grips with the genealogy of the idea of the halakhic state that began decades earlier. Although early religious Zionist leaders, including Isaac Herzog himself, were in many respects far more accommodating and liberal than their spiritual heirs, they unwittingly laid the intellectual foundations for the religious Zionist fundamentalism that intensified from the 1970s onward. Therefore, the act of historical recovery attempted in this book might have practical implications for Israeli society today. Appreciation for the long history of Jewish legal pluralism provides tools that could allow parties to religious-secular conflict to understand their differences in less acrimonious ways. The recovery of forgotten byways in legal and political religious thought offers strategies to ameliorate the tensions between secular and religious communities in Israel today and, by extension, in other parts of the world.

1 THE PLURALISTIC ROOTS OF RELIGIOUS ZIONISM

A popular Israeli bumper sticker from the 1980s read, "*medinat halakhah halkhah ha-medinah*." It may be roughly translated as "a halakhic state— the state is lost," although this translation does not convey the crisp wordplay of the original.[1] It expressed resistance to what many Israelis perceived as an attempt by religious leaders and politicians to convert Israel's secular democracy into a state run by religious law. It echoed sentiments that self-defined secular Israelis had been articulating for years. The influential left-wing politician Shulamit Aloni had warned in 1970 that "it seems that the principle of 'a state of law' is being gradually eroded and the principle of 'a state of halakha' established."[2] These fears rested on an implicit assumption that there is a zero-sum conflict between halakha and modern democracy: the more of one, the less of the other.

These fears also found expression in intellectual circles. In 1976, the Israeli philosopher Gershon Weiler published a book called *Jewish Theocracy* in which he asserted that "the Jewish religion . . . is inevitably bound to be destructive of a real state in the real world."[3] Weiler thought that halakha claimed supremacy over all other kinds of law. Because its authority derives ultimately from divine revelation, he wrote that followers of halakha must necessarily believe that it should take precedence over any other kind of law, including democratic legislation. Two years after the Iranian revolution, Weiler intensified his claim that religious law and democracy are mutually exclusive by comparing the legal philosophy of Israel's rabbis with that of Iran's Supreme Leader. "We are sliding into clerical dictatorship," he wrote. "If you read Khomeini's lectures on jurisprudence, in principle it is the same as what the rabbis are saying. . . . The American notion of a constitution expressing the will of the people is anathema to religious Moslems and Jews."[4]

The belief that halakha aspires to legal supremacy, rising above democratic law, was not limited to secular thinkers and politicians.

The Invention of Jewish Theocracy. Alexander Kaye, Oxford University Press (2020). © Oxford University Press.
DOI: 10.1093/oso/9780190922740.001.0001

From the middle of the twentieth century, many religious Zionist rabbis, politicians, and leaders promoted the same idea. For example, one of Israel's chief rabbis, Isaac Herzog, pondered the ideal form of government for a Jewish state by asking, "Should it be a theocracy?" His answer was "Absolutely yes."[5] Similarly, Meir Berlin, a senior religious Zionist leader, wrote that his goal was to create "a state law that is based on the laws of our holy Torah. . . . This law and no other, none besides it."[6] Both Herzog and Berlin wanted the laws of the state to be halakha. This position was shared by Ze'ev Falk, a religious Zionist professor of law, who drafted a proposal for Israel's constitution that began with the following clause: "The State of Israel declares the laws of the Torah as they have been transmitted from generation to generation as the laws of the state."[7] It bears emphasizing that these religious Zionist thinkers and many others like them thought that halakha should not only have a place in Israel's public discourse in a vague sense. Rather, they promoted the specific position that the law of the state should be halakha.

So both religious and secular Israelis have, for decades, shared the belief that halakha and the laws of the state are in tension. They have agreed that the laws of the state can either derive from God or from the people but not both, and they have differed only about which kind of law should have supremacy. Secular Israelis tend to want halakha to be expunged from the state's laws and religious Zionists tend to advocate for halakha to be incorporated into, or even to replace, them. In Israel, this fundamental difference is expressed daily in bitter arguments over whether public transport should run on the Sabbath, who has the power to decide who is a Jew, the role of religious doctrine in peace negotiations, and countless other political and social questions.

The historical record, however, paints a very different picture. Jewish religious thinkers over many centuries believed that there is nothing at all inevitable about a conflict between halakha and other kinds of law. The idea of a halakhic state is in fact relatively new. Among religious Zionists, it was not until the end of the 1940s that the idea of a state run exclusively by halakha was suggested for the first time. Most writing on this topic by religious Zionists before the establishment of the State of Israel imagined a state in which halakha had a role but did not eclipse the will of the people and did not override democratic legislation.

Given the widespread consensus today that halakha and democracy are necessarily in tension, it is all the more important to engage in a conscious excavation of earlier positions of religious Zionists who thought differently. Their forgotten voices may offer an important corrective to religious Zionist dialogue today and play a part in ameliorating religious-secular tensions in Israel.

Haim Ozer Grodzinski

Until the late 1970s, religious Zionists had very little influence in the wider Zionist movement. They constituted a small group whose opinions were generally ignored by Zionist leaders, many of whom were opposed to traditional religion, some militantly so. This opposition did not stop them, however, from talking among themselves about their wishes for the future Jewish state. As people who were existentially committed both to the Jewish tradition and to contemporary Jewish nationalism, they considered the synthesis of these two commitments to be an urgent necessity.

Before the late 1940s, most significant attempts by religious Zionists to formulate a constitutional approach to the Jewish state were based on a legally pluralistic framework. They contended that religious and democratic norms could exist side by side without any necessary conflict between them. They imagined a single Jewish state that recognized two legal systems, each with its own source of authority and its own system of courts. One of these legal systems would be halakha, traditional Jewish law as interpreted by the rabbis, and the other would be a modern legal system legislated by an elected parliament. In the case of legal conflict, the former would be judged in rabbinical courts and the latter in civil courts. Religious Zionists disagreed over the ways in which this theory would play out in practice and about the precise parameters of the role of halakha in the state, but they broadly agreed about this pluralistic approach to legal philosophy.

A short epistolary exchange from 1937 provides a perfect example of this kind of legal pluralism, offering an outline in miniature of the position that was embraced by so many religious Zionists of that period. In July of that year, the Palestine Royal Commission (commonly known as the Peel Commission after the name of its chairman, Earl Peel), tasked with investigating the "disturbances" in Palestine, issued a report advocating the partition of Palestine into a Jewish and an Arab state.[8] Zionists rejoiced that the establishment of a Jewish state seemed within reach. Isaac Herzog, who had assumed the post of Ashkenazic Chief Rabbi of Palestine six months earlier, began to address the question of how to synthesize the legal and political requirements of a modern Jewish state with those of halakha. He was acutely aware of the challenges that such a project entailed. Seeking advice on how to proceed, Herzog wrote to one of the preeminent rabbinic personalities of the period, Haim Ozer Grodzinski.

Grodzinski was one of the most influential Orthodox leaders of his time. He was not a religious Zionist but rather a distinguished Ultra-Orthodox rabbi, the primary representative of Lithuanian Orthodoxy, who held the prestigious position of a rabbinical judge in Vilna. Like many Orthodox leaders of the time, he was opposed to Zionism in principle. At the same time, Grodzinski was a pragmatist, and he supported Jewish life and politics in Palestine. He had good relations with Abraham Isaac Kook, a supporter of Zionism, and he championed the cause of Orthodox immigrants to Palestine. In the late 1920s, he supported the abortive plan for the unification of the two Orthodox groups, the anti-Zionist Agudat Yisrael (which he had helped to found) and the Zionist Mizrahi.[9]

Herzog wrote to Grodzinski, asking his opinion about one of the main tensions between halakha and democracy: "the difficulty confronting us in the matter of public appointments of Gentiles."[10] Herzog wanted Grodzinski's advice on how to devise a solution to the halakhic prohibition on non-Jews holding positions of authority in a Jewish polity. Grodzinski's response went beyond the parameters of Herzog's question. In just a few lines, he sketched an entire constitutional proposal:

> In regard to furnishing a constitution for the rule of Torah in the Hebrew state: Regarding [civil] law, this is truly a difficult matter in need of much reflection. My initial thought is perhaps to arrange matters so that the judges in civil cases between two Jews would be rabbis whose power of subpoena and whose judgment would be recognized by law. Cases between a Jew and a non-Jew would be adjudicated according to the general law. Concerning theft and robbery and criminal law in general, it appears to follow from the responsum of the Ran that there was a separate royal law alongside the rabbinical court administering Torah law. For it would truly impair the order of the polity if the full punishment for theft would be to pay double [the cost of the stolen item]. You must necessarily concede that the polity should legislate for such cases.[11]

Grodzinski's plan bore the unmistakable hallmarks of legal pluralism. He imagined a Jewish state in which there were two kinds of law: halakha, and "general law," by which he meant the laws of a democratically elected legislature. He proposed that these two kinds of law should have parallel judicial systems. Halakhic cases would be judged by rabbis and "general law" cases, he implied, by judges appointed by the state. The two legal systems would also apply to different groups in different circumstances. He imagined that civil cases involving only Jews would be judged by rabbis according to halakha but that cases with a non-Jewish party and criminal cases of all kinds should appear before the state's own civil courts. Halakhic criminal law, he claimed, was simply incapable of governing society properly.

Grodzinski supported his position by appealing to the precedent of "the Ran," the fourteenth-century rabbi, Nisim of Gerona. Grodzinski maintained that halakha should have a role in a Jewish state but should not be—and is incapable of being—the state's only law. He adopted this view not only because it would have been difficult to convince secular Jews to accept halakha as Israel's exclusive law. Rather, Grodzinski believed that halakha had inherent limitations that prevented it from being an effective way of governing society, especially in the area of criminal law. He illustrated this point by referring to the halakhic punishment for theft, which is simply to return the stolen item and to pay a fine equal to its value. Grodzinski, like the Ran centuries earlier, doubted that this punishment would effectively deter theft if it were the only penalty for the crime. He therefore advocated a legally pluralistic system in which halakha had a limited role, existing alongside a "general law" that would be legislated by "the polity" and not by rabbis or religious figures.

Despite the fact that Herzog had approached Grodzinski, the revered leader of European Orthodox Jewry, for advice, Herzog refused to accept his suggestion. Herzog responded that Grodzinski's was "not an acceptable solution" and rejected it out of hand.[12] Some scholars have explained this disagreement by pointing out that Grodzinski was an anti-Zionist who wanted to protect halakha against the threats that might be posed to it by modern political attitudes, whereas Herzog was a religious Zionist who had an interest in applying halakha to the Jewish state.[13] This is a case, however, of hindsight becoming a handicap. In fact, the debate between the two men did not grow out of their different approaches to Zionism. Indeed, Grodzinski's argument was not unique to non-Zionists. Several religious Zionist thinkers approached the problem of halakha in the Jewish state from the same legally pluralistic perspective. Herzog's rejection of Grodzinski is not a self-explanatory consequence of Herzog's Zionism but a radical departure from halakhic precedent, a historical puzzle that requires explanation.

The Medieval Legacy

For Grodzinski, as for religious Zionists, the problems of the present could not be solved without an appeal to the past. Halakhic precedent inspired religious Zionist thinkers and bolstered their authority. It also limited them in that their arguments would be diminished if they contradicted earlier authorities. As a result, a crucial context of religious Zionist discourse is the theory and practice of premodern Jewish law and politics.

Legal pluralism defined the legal institutions of the premodern Jewish community. In fact, before the rise of the modern state, not just Jews but also Muslims, Christians, and others were governed by a network of overlapping legal orders and institutions. In Christian Europe, these included local customs, feudal law, mercantile law, canon law and Roman law, and the judicial institutions of guilds, universities, manorial estates, cities, and the royal court.[14] Under Islam, they include sharia, different *madhhab*s (schools of sharia jurisprudence, often operating in parallel in the same court system), *mazalim* (courts of complaint, distinct from sharia courts), *hajib* courts (which applied Mongol law in the Mamluk empire), civil courts (which operated alongside sharia courts, especially in the late Ottoman empire), and various functionaries with judicial authority, such as the inspector of markets and censor of public morals (*muhtasib*), the chief of police (*rats al-shurta*), and the investigator of complaints (*sahib al-mazalim*).[15]

These systems of law often overlapped and occasionally conflicted with one another, but most of the time multiple systems of law happily coexisted. A medieval peasant in Christian Europe, for example, would acknowledge that the local baron permitted him to hunt in some areas and not others; that the church imposed tithes and told him whom he could or could not marry; that the town council set the price at which he could sell grain; and that the king sent traveling judges to hear grievances. This system was not considered to be odd or confusing. It was how things were.

This picture of legal pluralism equally characterizes premodern Jewish communities. Just like the societies in which they were embedded, Jews understood themselves to be governed by many overlapping systems of law. They considered themselves to be bound to halakha, which, in their understanding, derived its authority from God's revelation on Sinai, accompanied by the interpretations and injunctions of the rabbis. However, they also recognized the binding authority of both Jewish and non-Jewish political institutions.[16] Jews submitted themselves to the authority of Gentile legal regimes not only out of the fear of coercive force or the need for protection, but also out of a principled obedience to governmental legal authority.[17] There was an understanding that without extra-halakhic laws and government there would be no social order.

This basic orientation in Jewish legal history has very old roots. As an early rabbinic source taught, "Pray for the welfare of the monarchy, for without fear of it people would swallow each other alive."[18] Over time, there developed a principle of "the law of the land is the law" (*dina de-malkhuta dina*), which articulated the acceptance by Jewish communities of the authority of the laws of Gentile governments.[19] Indeed, Jewish courts throughout history made heavy use of the laws and legal procedures of the Gentile communities around them. They often used, for example, Latin and Arabic contracts for wills and business transactions. Sometimes these contracts were drafted alongside equivalent halakhic documents and sometimes they served instead of them.[20] There is even a recorded case of a Jewish court ceding a criminal to the courts of Gentile authorities to be sentenced to death.[21] The source of the authority of "the law of the land" was not the Sinaitic revelation but the Gentile government. It was adjudicated by governmental institutions, not rabbinical courts. It was an independent legal regime, parallel to halakha, which was recognized as authoritative by the Jewish tradition.[22]

Another source of legal norms for premodern Jews was their own political institutions, which were often quite distinct from rabbinic institutions. According to the biblical narrative, the coronation of the first Israelite king, Saul, was accompanied by a divine warning that according to the "king's law" (*mishpat ha-melekh*), Saul would force the people to work and fight for him and would take their land and property.[23] Jewish interpreters over the years debated whether this behavior was endorsed by God or not. According to many, the king legitimately wielded this authority.[24] In other words, although under halakha it would be considered theft for the king to take someone's property for his own use, under the "king's law" it would be legitimate. This belief laid the groundwork for the Jewish recognition of binding law, emerging from political institutions, which operated alongside, and sometimes in conflict with, halakha.

On that model, around the tenth century there emerged the *kehilla* or *kahal* as "an autonomous body that fulfilled internal political functions in all areas of communal life."[25] The leaders of the kehilla, often called the *tuvei ha-ir*, the "good men of the city," were communal lay leaders who served alongside the rabbinical authorities. The Talmud itself recognizes the authority of non-rabbinic leadership, asserting that "the townspeople are authorized to set measures, prices, and wages, and to punish those who violate them."[26] Rabbis recognized the authority of the leaders of the kehilla to enact binding legislation and to tax its members, coercing those who refused to pay. Extensive communal legislation known as *taqanot ha-qahal* comprised the public and administrative law that effectively governed Jewish communities.[27] In addition to their legislative function, lay leaders in many Jewish communities acted as judges on permanent courts, which were set up to adjudicate matters connected to lay legislation.[28] This all meant that the lay leadership of the kehilla was nothing less than a "civil sovereign."[29] Communal legislation existed alongside halakhic rules and "in the sphere of social and particularly economic activity could circumvent halakhic norms or even deviate from them."[30]

Rabbinical courts not only recognized this non-halakhic law and these non-rabbinical institutions; they also often appealed to them when dealing with legal procedures that went beyond their own halakhic authority. Solomon ibn Adret, known as Rashba, for example, was a leading rabbinic and communal leader of thirteenth-century Spanish Jewry. He was fiercely protective of the importance of halakha in Jewish communal life. Even he, however, had frequent recourse to extra-halakhic procedures, such as the use of the testimony of women or of a single witness. His reason for this approach was clear: halakhic rules were not capable of governing any society, even the Jewish community, without being supplemented by other norms.

> For if you were to restrict everything to the laws stipulated in the Torah and punish only in accordance with the Torah's penal [code] in cases of assault and the like, the world would be destroyed, because we would require two witnesses and [prior] warning. The Rabbis have already said that "Jerusalem was destroyed only because they restricted their judgments to Torah law."[31]

Despite his deep commitment to halakha as a communal law, Rashba acknowledged the necessity for other legal systems to operate alongside it.

In short, the notion that halakha was the only law that ever governed Jews is a myth. The existence of many parallel, sometimes conflicting, normative systems was a basic feature of Jewish communal organization from before the time of the Talmud through to the modern period. As a result, the greatest Jewish legal thinkers created conceptual frameworks through which to understand the legal pluralism that they encountered every day. One of the most systematic of such frameworks was proposed by "the Ran," Nisim of Gerona, the important medieval talmudic commentator and legal scholar, to whom Grodzinski had referred. His writing on the subject was an important touchstone for religious Zionist thinking in the twentieth century.

In his "Eleventh Sermon," one of a collection of long discourses, the Ran laid out a comprehensive constitutional theory. His guiding principle was that Jewish polities have always been governed by a dualistic legal regime, consisting of both halakha and the "law of the King" operating side by side.[32] For the Ran, this dualism was not a concession to an unredeemed world or a consequence of the powerlessness of Jews in exile. Rather, it was the ideal model for Jewish society. The archetype for this model was the biblical narrative, according to which the Jews were subordinate to both the Law of the Torah and the "king's law." The reason, the Ran posited, that the king was needed alongside halakha is that halakha alone was incapable of governing society. He noted that the halakhic punishment for theft, (the return of the stolen object along with a fine of the same value), was scarcely a sufficient deterrent, especially for people of means. Indeed, it would be close to impossible to convict anyone of any crime in a halakhic court. A halakhic conviction could be carried out only if two unimpeachable eyewitnesses observed the crime and if the accused was warned of the punishment for the crime immediately before carrying it out. According to the Ran, therefore, halakha is simply not capable of keeping social order. Indeed, he wrote, "some of the laws and procedures of the [Gentile] nations may be more effective in enhancing political order than some of the Torah's laws."[33]

If society is governed by the King's law, what then, for the Ran, was the point of halakhic civil and criminal law? The Ran's answer to this question is extremely provocative:

> [Unlike] the laws of the nations of the world, the laws and command-ments of our Torah . . . include commandments that are ultimately not concerned with political order. Rather, their effect is to bring about the appearance of the divine flow within our nation and [to make it] cleave unto us.[34]

The Ran held that halakha, while imperfect as a practical system of good governance, is perfect in its justice. Following its dictates in all areas of life—both ritual and political—invites a flow of divine energy. He therefore believed that an ideal Jewish polity should indeed have courts run by religious judges according to the laws and procedures of halakha. These courts, however, would not be intended for the practical running of a state. Their value would be metaphysical, not political. The task of real governance is left to a parallel legal regime. In biblical times, the Ran maintained, this parallel regime was the law of the Jewish king. Since the end of the Jewish monarchy, its authority was inherited by other kinds of Jewish political leaders, such as the leaders of the *kahal*, who, he understood, were representatives of the king's law in the absence of a monarchy.

In sum, the Ran believed that the Jewish constitution called for two distinct court systems operating in parallel. Lay courts, under the control of the king or subsequent political leaders, would be responsible for establishing law and order. Alongside them, rabbinical courts would be responsible for bringing the metaphysical benefits of halakha to the community. Halakha would not be charged with governance in any practical sense. It certainly had no claim to being the exclusive legal system for the Jewish state.[35] Although the full details of the Ran's position were not accepted by every Jewish thinker, its basic outline was widely held.[36] Premodern Jewish religious leaders typically believed that a non-halakhic political law had to govern the Jewish community alongside halakha, that the Jewish king performed that function in biblical society, and that the king's authority was inherited by Jewish lay leaders after the decline of the monarchy.

Religious Zionist Applications

The religious Zionists who grappled with the constitutional questions of a modern Jewish state had a deep history on which to draw. They were heirs to generations of discussion and practice of Jewish political life. The legal pluralism described previously, a hallmark of the premodern Jewish community, was the basis of religious Zionist constitutional writing before the establishment of the State of Israel.

Haim Ozer Grodzinski's advice to Isaac Herzog about the place of halakha in a modern Jewish state relied heavily on the legal pluralism of previous generations. He thought that halakha could not be the exclusive law of a modern state, because it lacked the capacity to govern effectively. Explicitly referring to the Ran's legal pluralism, Grodzinski recommended that the new Jewish state have two sets of laws: rabbinic law and civil general law running side by side. Before the late 1940s, the general consensus among religious Zionists followed the same pattern. Religious Zionist rabbis and thinkers generally agreed that halakha is not the only law binding upon Jews and that precedent from the Bible and the rabbinical canon supported the application of non-halakhic legal systems alongside halakha to create effective governance.

Religious Zionists did not write a great deal about constitutional questions before the establishment of Israel. Like all leaders of the Zionist movement, they were preoccupied with the practical considerations of state building and other urgent concerns relating to the safety of Jews in Palestine and beyond. These were the years of increasing antisemitism in Europe, the Holocaust, Jewish-Arab conflict, and British restrictions that made legal Jewish immigration to Palestine almost impossible. As a result, before the 1940s little was written by any Zionist thinker about what the laws of a Jewish state might be.[37] There were exceptions, however, and those religious Zionist thinkers who did write on this subject drew on the precedent of Jewish legal pluralism, arguing for a role of halakha in the Jewish state but rejecting the notion that halakha should be its exclusive law.

Rabbi Abraham Isaac Kook offered one of the earliest statements on this subject. Kook was born in the Russian Empire and educated at the Volozhin yeshiva in Lithuania. He moved to Ottoman Palestine in 1904 and later became the first Ashkenazic Chief Rabbi of Palestine in 1921. He spent most of World War I in Europe, first in St. Galen, Switzerland and then in London. During the end of his time in St. Galen, in December 1915, Kook wrote a long responsum, a written rabbinic judicial decision, in the course of which he made a single pithy comment on the question of non-halakhic Jewish authority. He wrote, "It seems to me that when there is no king, since the king's laws relate to the general state of the nation, the rights of these laws return to the hands of the nation in its entirety."[38]

In this one sentence, Kook extended medieval precedent quite radically. He accepted the venerable position that the Jewish tradition endorses systems of law besides halakha, and that these were represented by the institution of the monarchy. He also believed, like many before him, that the political authority of the king persisted even after the demise of the Israelite monarchy. Kook's innovation, however, is in saying that the monarch's authority "return[s] to the hands of the nation in its entirety." In other words, in the absence of a king, Jewish political authority resides in the entire Jewish people. Whereas many before him had talked about the leadership of the Jewish community, Kook's turn of phrase was exceptional in his location of political authority in the people as a whole. Writing at the dawn of the age of mass politics, Kook was contemplating a more democratic Jewish political thought, in which power was not held exclusively by political elites.

It is difficult to establish how much significance Kook himself placed on his precise formulation. The statement was written in passing, in the course of discussing a different topic. Indeed, it is unlikely that he was thinking in any practical way about Jewish governance of a modern state. His responsum was written over a year before the Balfour Declaration, at a time when the achievement of a Jewish home in Palestine seemed far from realization. (Kook died in 1935, over a decade before Israel was established, and even before the events—the British Partition Plan of 1937, the Shoah, the UN endorsement of partition in 1947—that accelerated its establishment.) For the future of religious Zionism, however, Kook's comment became very significant. In time, Kook became a towering figure for religious Zionists and remains their spiritual figurehead to this day. As a result, his brief statement became an important basis for future discussions among religious Zionists about political and legal authority in Israel.

Aside from Kook's general comment, several religious Zionists thinkers did write explicitly, and at greater length, about the legal system in an imagined future Jewish state. All of them adopted the principles of legal pluralism.

Reuven Margulies

Reuven Margulies was one of the earliest thinkers to offer a treatment of the constitution of a Jewish state from a religious Zionist perspective. Born in Lwow, Poland, Margulies was a rabbinical scholar who was associated with the religious Zionist party, Mizrahi, for most of his life. He moved to Palestine in 1935 and wrote prolifically on Jewish law and thought. He dealt with the question of religion and law in a Jewish state in a 1922 article called "The Courts of Law in the Land of Israel."[39] At the beginning of his work, Margulies immediately made both his religious and his Zionist commitments clear. Writing in the years after the

Balfour Declaration, Margulies believed that providence had given his generation the responsibility of "laying the foundation stone for Hebrew life in the land of Israel upon which the Israelite people will develop as it arises from the dust of exile."[40]

For Margulies, setting up a "Hebrew life" in a Jewish state meant, among other things, that its laws had to be drawn from Jewish tradition. He particularly objected to the possibility of the Jewish state adopting the laws of other nations. Just as the Jewish nation had its own history, land, and language, the Torah was its own law. "We cannot choose for ourselves a political program according to the processes of other lands and their laws," he wrote, "because all our ways of life are one unique package according to the laws of the Torah."[41] The idea that nations each have a unique and precious way of life was very common among nationalists of all stripes. Nationalists generally assumed that nations are organic entities, each with its own distinctive history, language, and law. Among religious Zionists, the position was intensified because of the belief that the legal heritage of the Jewish nation was not only an important historical legacy but also an eternal law given by God.

Given this commitment to the unique law of the Hebrew nation, one might expect Margulies to have been a legal centralist, arguing for halakha to be the exclusive law in Israel. But this was not the case. Like many before him, Margulies was dubious about the ability of halakha to govern in practice. The fact that halakha had never encountered modern Jewish sovereignty meant that "any institution founded to correlate to the spirit of the Torah and Judaism is like a new creation ex nihilo."[42] He also acknowledged, as did the Ran and many others, that halakha is not sufficiently able to deal with criminal behavior: "[The Torah is lacking] an important law book in an area which is important and urgent for maintaining society. We know today that [in the modern state] . . . in addition to the civil law there is also a law book especially for criminal law."[43]

Margulies was also conscious of the presence of non-Jews in Palestine and the necessity of creating a social order that could accommodate the members of all religions in an egalitarian way. He supported his call for egalitarianism both by appealing to a sense of justice, and also to the political situation of Jews in the interwar period. As a vulnerable, dispersed population, Jews were protective of their own rights in countries where they lived as minorities. For Margulies, it was inconceivable that Jews would not grant the same rights to others when they found themselves in the position of the majority.

We have to take account of the fact that even when the percentage of Jews in the land of Israel increases, we will not be a people dwelling there alone.[44] . . . There will be members of three religions living there. Therefore we, who request minority law in all the lands of the Diaspora, must set an example to the nations about extending rights to the other people who live in our land, and must also take their opinions into account.[45]

This view meant that the halakhic discrimination between Jews and others made it unsuitable for governing a polity with Jews and Gentiles living side by side. "Let's assume," Margulies wrote, "that the government of the land has already been transferred to us and we have to appoint judges. Shall we not appoint Gentiles because they are invalid witnesses? And what of their testimony? Will the law of the land discriminate between residents?"[46]

Margulies addressed these issues by way of his own historical reconstruction of the constitutional history of the Jewish people. He emphasized the long-held recognition among Jewish thinkers of a political authority distinct from halakha. Initially, he wrote, before the age of monarchy, the Judges ruled in Israel. In this period, there was chaos "because the laws of the sages of Torah ... could not alone govern social life. Then they asked for a king who would establish the earth in justice."[47] The kings had the power to rule differently from how halakha did: "When the Torah permitted the appointment of the king who has in his power the strength of rulers like all the nations, it thereby also gave him an unlimited power of legislation."[48] This power was not only vested in kings but passed to every future political leader as well.[49] This political authority extended to the present day: "From this historical investigation we learn that the Torah authorized the current leader of the people to make governments in the land [and] to run national courts which punish on the authority of the government."[50]

Margulies's historical reconstruction closely echoed the Ran's model of legal pluralism. Like the Ran, Margulies considered the law of the king in ancient Israel to have existed alongside halakha. And like the Ran, Margulies asserted that after the end of the Jewish monarchy, the independent legal authority of the king passed to the political leadership of each generation. Laws enacted in a modern Jewish state would address criminal law more effectively than halakha. They would also bypass the impractical evidentiary procedures of halakha and would be able to incorporate Gentiles and women fully into the legal process:

It is in the power of the head of state to enact a general law that every resident who is presumed to tell the truth is qualified to testify, and one who knows the laws is qualified to judge. And this state law is authorized by the authority that the Torah gave to the head of state to enact whatever he thinks will be for the benefit of the State.[51]

Margulies's legal pluralism is highlighted by his language, which distinguishes state legislation, to which he refers by terms like *hoq* or *mishpat*, from rabbinical law, to which he refers by terms like *din* or *halakhah*. Similarly, he calls non-halakhic courts *batei mishpat amami'im*, distinguishing them from halakhic courts, *batei din*. This designation of non-halakhic courts as *amami*—"national," or even "folk" or "people's" courts—reinforces the idea that the rules they follow are not halakhic; they derive from the people, not from Sinai.

What would be the relationship between the "national courts" and halakha? Margulies argued that the difference between halakha and legislation that derived from royal (or state) authority was that halakhic courts ruled on the basis of fixed law, whereas kings could rule on the basis of their discretion in a given situation. For Margulies, this argument explained why very few of the kings' laws survived the generations. They were not intended to comprise a permanent legal code but rather to be temporary laws that would deal justice in particular circumstances. In this understanding, there was a clear difference between the two kinds of law. Halakha was a rigid law with established procedures, which operated on principles of pure justice. The law of the king or other political leaders was intended to mitigate the rigidity of halakha by operating with discretion in a particular moment.

In the new situation of a modern state, however, Margulies believed that Jewish political legislation should no longer be quite so flexible. It would have to depart from its traditional roots and become more rigid and predictable, "a clear law in a logical order." Although these "state laws in the land of the Hebrews" would be quite independent from halakha, Margulies considered them to be the "laws of Israel" because they would be the modern equivalent of the king's law of ancient times. Furthermore, because these laws would be created by Jewish legislators, they would be imbued with "the spirit of righteousness and ethics of ancient Israel and its Torah," and they would therefore be sufficiently distinct from the laws of other nations to be considered an organic production of the Jewish people.[52] Although Margulies wanted areas of law with a ritual aspect such as marriage and divorce to remain under the purview of halakha, he argued that other areas of law should not be dependent on halakha or rabbinic authority. This opinion satisfied Margulies's Jewish nationalism as well as his commitment to the Torah. It also allowed him to imagine a legal-political regime that was consistent with the Jewish tradition without discriminating against Gentiles.

Shlomo Gorontchik (Goren)

Margulies was writing more than twenty years before the State of Israel was ultimately established, and his thoughts remained largely in the abstract. Years later, a similar approach was proposed in greater detail by another religious Zionist rabbi by the name of Shlomo Gorontchik. Gorontchik wrote his constitutional proposal in early 1948, after the UN had already voted to recognize a Jewish state, and he attempted to translate the framework of legal pluralism into a practical vision.

Gorontchik was born in the Polish town of Zambrów in 1918 and immigrated with his parents to Palestine at the age of seven. He served in the Haganah, became the chaplain of the newly constituted Israel Defense Forces, and was later appointed as its chief rabbi. In 1973, having changed his name to Goren, he became the Ashkenazic Chief Rabbi of Israel. Only months before the Declaration of Independence, Gorontchik wrote an article about Jewish law in the Jewish state in the religious newspaper *Ha-tsofeh*.[53]

Gorontchik was deeply invested in the theological and eschatological significance of the Jewish state that was about to be established. He felt that the moment called for urgent attention to the "great and holy task" to produce "a detailed Torah constitution for the State of Israel," and he believed that this act would pave the way for "the return of the crown of the Torah to its former glory, for the establishment of the Sanhedrin and for the complete redemption."[54]

However, although Gorontchik considered his work to be a "Torah constitution," he did not think that halakha should be the state's only law. Gorontchik was a legal pluralist who believed that it would be impossible to base a constitution solely on halakha. His concerns are the same as those who had come before him:

> The halakha of judges and witnesses will impinge on the rights of minorities, women and others and will arouse a strong opposition both from the secular population of the Yishuv and from the United Nations. The Torah constitution disqualifies sinners and, it goes without saying, Gentiles, from being judges or witnesses. It disqualifies women from testifying, except in certain circumstances. These difficulties almost preclude the practical possibility of a full Torah constitution for the ordering of the new courts.[55]

Rather than pushing for a change to the procedures of halakhic courts, making them more egalitarian, Gorontchik suggested that the Jewish state should have a parallel legal system, with a democratic judicial and legislative system operating alongside a halakhic one. He wanted to provide, from within the Jewish tradition, "the legal and practical possibility of establishing a new court, according to the Torah in the Jewish state, for full equal rights, so that all parts of the population may be appointed as judges and to be accepted as witnesses."[56] This new court would judge both civil and criminal matters. Citing the long tradition of extra-halakhic communal legislation, Gorontchik wrote that "the community is able to enact legislation . . . according to the discretion of the judges or legislators for the sake of public order."[57]

Gorontchik emphasized that the new court system he was proposing would not replace the halakhic system but would run in parallel to it. Each court system would operate according to its own procedures and would enforce a different set of laws. Rabbinical judges would judge according to halakha. Judges in the other courts would judge according to a new civil code distinct from halakha. Like Margulies, Gorontchik differentiated the courts by both name and function. There would be halakhic courts, called *batei din torani'im,* and "new courts," called *batei mishpat,* which will "derive their legal authority from the power of public consent." Goren made this distinction quite clear: "These courts will not have the name 'Torah court' because their Torah authority comes from the community, and not direct[ly from the Torah], and by this authority even those disqualified from judging or giving testimony [according to halakha] will be qualified [in those courts]."[58]

As precedent for his proposal, Gorontchik turned to a talmudic passage that mentions "Syrian Courts" (*arkha'ot she-be-surya*).[59] The context of the passage in the Babylonian Talmud indicates that these were Jewish courts that were distinct from regular rabbinical courts and that did not rule according to halakha.[60] After examining a parallel passage in the Palestinian Talmud and interpretations of several medieval commentaries, Gorontchik emphasized the fact that these Jewish courts did not judge according to halakha. He described the so-called "Syrian Courts," like his proposed non-halakhic courts for the modern Jewish state, as *batei mishpat* and maintained that "their authority was derived from the general consent of the community." The judges in these courts were not proficient in halakha. "They judged cases according to their 'reasoned discretion' and not according to the law of the Torah because they were not knowledgeable in Torah law."[61]

Gorontchik supported his interpretation by borrowing a phrase of Menahem Meiri, a thirteenth-century Provençal rabbi. Meiri had written that the judges in these courts "were not fluent in Torah law but judged according to their reasoned discretion and statutes and mores. . . . And if all the people of the land accepted them in this way, then I say that there is no claim [against their validity]."[62]

Gorontchik conceded that according to some interpreters, such a court is valid only in a situation in which no experts in Torah law are available, making lay courts the only option for establishing justice. Such an interpretation would have made this talmudic precedent inapplicable in the State of Israel, where rabbis were in no short supply. Other interpreters, however, including Meiri and the distinguished sixteenth-century Polish rabbinic authority Moses Isserles, held that such courts could operate even in the presence of a Torah scholar. Gorontchik followed their interpretation and concluded that the non-halakhic

"Syrian Courts," accepted as authoritative by the Talmud itself, constituted ample precedent for non-rabbinical courts, even in a place where rabbis were available:

> So we have clarified two fundamental matters. . . . 1) Courts of this type are not connected to any Torah courts but rather are permitted to establish special laws to judge "according to their reasoned discretion and statues and mores." 2) It is possible and lawful to establish [such courts] on a state-wide basis "if all the people of the land accept them."[63]

Gorontchik anticipated a possible critique of his position. If the Jewish state had a court system that is independent from rabbinical law and authority, what would become of the laws of the Torah? Would they be completely replaced? After acknowledging the seriousness of the question, Gorontchik insisted that there was simply no choice. Legal pluralism may put the primacy of halakha at risk. But halakha is incapable of ruling a polity alone. "One has to ask," he wrote, "whether a fastidious and exact dominion of all the laws of the Torah in the life of the state . . . can support private and public order in the state," unless they are supplemented "by statutes and mores and special legislation based on popular will."[64]

Gorontchik fleshed out this position by quoting from medieval thinkers like the Ran to support his position that a Jewish state requires non-halakhic law and courts to maintain proper order. He then referred to the statement of Abraham Isaac Kook discussed previously, in which Kook proposed that after the end of the Jewish monarchy, legal and political authority had reverted to the people as a whole. In short, Gorontchik insisted, non-halakhic law in a Jewish state is both endorsed by the Jewish religious tradition, and necessary in order to govern properly and without discrimination.[65] He therefore endorsed a "dual system of courts" for the Jewish state. There would be "a network of rabbinical courts based fully on the Torah [batei din torani'im mele'im], in which all the laws of the Torah will have force," alongside "civil courts [batei mishpat], in which a special civil code, in accordance with international law, will be followed, with care that it will not contravene the laws of the Torah."[66]

Gorontchik's proposal raised a logistical problem. What would happen if there was a conflict between the two systems of law? He observed that there would need to be rules about which court system should have jurisdiction in which cases. Without discussing the matter in detail, he suggested that, generally speaking, the parties in a case should have the choice of which system to use. In the case of a disagreement between them, he wrote, if all parties were Jewish then the case should be heard in the rabbinical court, but if any party was non-Jewish, the case should be heard in the civil court.

In sum, Gorontchik composed a striking constitutional proposal from the heart of the religious Zionist camp. According to his legally pluralistic plan, a Jew in a Jewish state could in theory be judged according to a secular law by a non-Jewish judge. Gorontchik's proposal was not rooted in a lack of commitment to the halakhic system. On the contrary, his ultimate intention was to devise a practical strategy "to fight to instill the spirit of the Torah and its laws into the state until it is seen as the path to complete redemption."[67] In fact, he considered one of the advantages of his parallel system that the halakhic courts would be protected from too jarring a change in order to "safeguard the purity of the Torah law."[68] Gorontchik's pluralism allowed the halakhic system to remain almost untouched because the existence of civil courts would insulate the rabbinical courts from concessions to modern rights and egalitarianism.

Shimon Federbusch

Legal pluralism also defined the approach of religious Zionists living outside Palestine and Israel. Shimon Federbusch was a religious Zionist leader born in Galicia, who, from 1940, lived in New York. In 1952 he published *Mishpat ha-melukhah be-yisra'el*, an attempt to outline a constitutional framework based on traditional sources, for a democratic Jewish state.[69] The purpose of the book was to present what Federbusch believed should be the role of religion in the laws and society of the new state. Although it was written in America and was inflected with modern American political thought, it was composed in Hebrew and published in Jerusalem. Federbusch clearly hoped that the book would influence the political and legal discourse of the religious Zionist movement of which he was a senior member.

For Federbusch, as for Margulies, state legislation would be legitimate because it derived its authority from the ancient category of the king's law. "Every law of a state institution today," he wrote, "has the same force and effect as the law of the king in his time." In the case of the State of Israel, he continued, this force meant that "the authority to legislate and adjudicate resides in the governmental legislative and adjudicatory bodies of the State of Israel.[70]

The pluralism of Federbusch's constitutional vision is unmistakable. Indeed, he explicitly described the traditional "duality" of the legal structure of Jewish communities:

> Duality in adjudication and even in legislation has endured throughout Jewish history in various forms. That is to say legislation and adjudication in accordance with religion and the Torah side by side with legislation and adjudication that did not depend on the law of the Torah. During the

time of Israel's monarchy, the non-religious law was called the law of the king, and after the destruction [of the Temple], courts of that sort were established with the consent of the Torah sages, as lay courts, arbitration tribunals, or the like.[71]

In this sweeping statement, Federbusch rooted the principle of legal pluralism in the biblical period and subsequent generations. To lend authority to this opinion, Federbusch quoted the same comment of Abraham Isaac Kook that Gorontchik had also used as a support. Federbusch interpreted Kook's comment, that after the decline of the monarchy, legal and political authority "return[ed] to the hands of the nation in its entirety," as a legitimation of the authority of the democratic government of the State of Israel. In other words, Federbusch presented Israel's democratically elected government as the heir to the political authority of the ancient kings. Federbusch went further than Kook, however. Going beyond the simple legitimation of democratic government, he held it up as the ideal Jewish constitution. He insisted that a democratic outlook, with its emphasis on equality and freedom, not only was commensurate with traditional Judaism, but also constituted its very basis. Jewish political theory, Federbusch declared, begins with the premise that all people are created equal under God. One striking passage reveals the full extent of Federbusch's self-conscious awareness of his intellectual environment. Writing in Hebrew, he quoted de Tocqueville's *On Democracy in America* in order to liken the egalitarianism of America with that of the Jewish tradition:

> The democratic order in America has its source in the lack of social divisions of the first immigrants. "The immigrants who founded America," emphasizes Tocqueville, "all belonged to one class. In this society there were no lords, no commoners, no rich and no poor." Because of this, they laid the foundation for a democracy with no class distinctions. It is the same with the Jews. The Torah emphasizes that their formation in the house of bondage was in order to stress the total social equality of all parts of the people, in order thereby to argue for the justice of the legal and financial equality of every individual, including aliens and foreigners.[72]

Federbusch's use of de Tocqueville to praise the value of equality is all the more notable, given that the passage of *On Democracy* that Federbusch quoted was actually making a slightly different point. De Tocqueville's original point was that the Puritan colonists of New England were all from England's middle class. The significance of this for de Tocqueville was that they were educated, unlike the common classes, and idealistic, unlike the wealthy who traveled in search of riches rather than "an idea." This is what de Tocqueville meant by "neither poor, nor rich."[73] In his eagerness to laud equality, Federbusch read that passage of *On Democracy* to be doing just that.

Federbusch's belief in the inherent equality of all people in society is underlined by his emphasis on another element of democratic theory: that all people are fundamentally free. This belief means that the only legitimate laws or social orders are those that have been accepted freely. For Federbusch, the requirement that laws be freely accepted applies not only to human laws but even to those of God:

> The democratic spirit in Israel is clearly apparent in the essence of the covenant between the Jews and God. . . . The idea of the covenant is that Israel did not accept the entirety of religious and political legislation out of duress or coercion but out of goodwill, by free choice, on the basis of a contract undertaken with the people on the basis of democratic agreement.[74]

If non-coerced consent is required to make God's laws legitimate, then, argued Federbusch, the authority of human legislation must also depend entirely on the consent of the governed.[75]

The imprint of democratic politics on Federbusch's thinking is perhaps most apparent in his discussion of the relationship between religion and state. Federbusch clearly asserted that there should be a separation between religion and politics. In the context of the United States, the image of a separation between religion and state was used as early as 1802 when Thomas Jefferson wrote in a letter to the Danbury Baptist Association that the First Amendment to the Constitution built "a wall of eternal separation between Church & State." The idea, however, had limited impact on American legislation or judicial decisions before the middle of the twentieth century.[76] It was in 1947, shortly before Federbusch published *Mishpat ha-melukhah*, that the Supreme Court clearly ruled for the first time that "the First Amendment has erected a wall between church and state."[77] In the postwar period, most American Jews supported this separation and Federbusch interpreted Jewish history from its perspective.[78] He wrote that "religious and political power have been separated from each other not just in theory in Jewish philosophy but also in practice in the course of Jewish history."[79] Federbusch was deeply committed to traditional Judaism and argued that halakha should have a role in Israeli society. He believed, however, that its role should be as a persuasive moral force without any coercive authority. Religious institutions, he wrote, should be strong in order to have a positive role in society and to avoid the state interfering with private religious practice. The state, however, should have no role in enforcing religious laws.[80] On the whole, halakha should be left to voluntarist religious communities, while political government should be left to the state and its machinery.[81]

In writing about the State of Israel, Federbusch cast the tradition of Jewish legal pluralism in American terms. He believed, like the Ran, Margulies, and Gorontchik, that halakha was not able to govern society in practice, nor was it intended to do so. In his mind, the law of the state should be newly legislated by a democratically elected government, whose authority, heir to the ancient kings, was legitimate only to the extent that it earned the consent of a free people. Halakha, and the spirit of the Jewish tradition, were distinct from this system of law and existed to provide a source of moral guidance rather than enforceable legislation. By situating the separation of religion and state firmly within the Jewish tradition, Federbusch created room for the state to act according to the principles of democracy without running into any resistance from halakha.

Though both Federbusch and Gorontchik were firmly committed to the normative value of halakha and the binding nature of its precedent, they also differed in some respects. Federbusch devoted himself to interpreting the Jewish tradition through the lens of American democratic thought. To do so, he presented halakha in the role of a moral guide rather than a governing norm. By contrast, Gorontchik's motivation was not to democratize halakha but rather to rescue it from the influence and authority of the modern state, so he proposed that halakha exist in parallel with the laws of the state. Despite their different outlooks, however, the religious Zionists Federbusch, Gorontchik, and Margulies, as well as the non-Zionist Grodzinski, all adopted an attitude of legal pluralism in their proposals for the role of halakha in a Jewish state. They believed that halakha was only one normative system among others. They wanted halakha to have normative authority, but to exist alongside a distinct civil law that would be legislated by a democratic body in the new state.

Herzog's Rejection of Legal Pluralism

Given the extent of the Jewish tradition of legal pluralism, it is something of a shock to find that Isaac Herzog, Israel's first Ashkenazic Chief Rabbi, entirely rejected legal pluralism and vehemently opposed those religious Zionists who endorsed it. When he received Grodzinski's proposal that Israel should be governed by democratic and halakhic legislation in parallel (a position in line with the legal pluralism of Margulies, Grodzinski, and Federbusch), Herzog responded that "this is not an acceptable solution." Even though Herzog had approached Grodzinski for advice on this matter, he rejected Grodzinski's solution. "I maintain my position,"

Herzog wrote, "that it is inconceivable that the laws of the Torah should allow for two parallel authorities."[82]

Not only did Herzog dispute Grodzinski's opinion, but he also questioned the precedent on which it relied. Grodzinski had referred to the piece in which the Ran outlined his idea of a pluralistic Jewish constitution as a "responsum," implying that it was written as a rabbinic judicial decision. Herzog pointed out, correctly, that the piece was not a responsum, but a sermon. It is possible that Grodzinski's error indicates the high normative value that he placed on the Ran's legally pluralistic position. Nonetheless, Herzog deemed that this genre of rabbinic literature carried less weight, and he proceeded to dismiss the position of the Ran altogether.

Herzog was deeply opposed to the idea of a dual judicial system. His ambition was that the state as a whole should base its law on halakha and that the state's judiciary should be amalgamated into a single structure. Herzog acknowledged the fact that halakha as it existed then did not have the capacity to govern a national polity. He knew that for halakha to have a role in the modern state—for it to be both effective and accepted by all—it would need to be modified. Laws of procedure would have to make room for female and Gentile witnesses, and laws of inheritance would have to become more egalitarian. Herzog's approach, however, was not to allow for a parallel system of non-halakhic courts, but to introduce supplementary regulations into the halakhic system itself. He utterly rejected legal pluralism as a way to structure the Jewish state and championed instead a legal centralism whereby the state would have a single halakhic legal system: "Our main ambition is that the constitution should include a clause that lays down that the law in the state is based on the Torah."[83]

For this reason, Herzog opposed the legal pluralism of Margulies and Gorontchik just as he opposed the legal pluralism of Grodzinski. Herzog was aware of Margulies's writing on the subject.[84] However, he rejected Margulies's suggestions out of hand, minimizing it as being merely "historical research" that was not pertinent to the current situation.[85] While acknowledging that Margulies had described the Jewish political tradition accurately from a historical perspective, Herzog nevertheless took a different approach with regard to the present. Herzog continued by once again making his rejection of legal pluralism entirely explicit: "From the perspective of halakha only the authorized sources of Torah law may enter the discussion and according to them there is no basis for this suggestion of a double system of justice or two parallel authorities."[86]

If governing were left to political authorities and taken out of the hands of the rabbis, Herzog claimed, then "the Sanhedrin descends into being a kind of legal researcher and this makes no sense."[87] Whereas Margulies had held up the biblical king as the prototype for state government, Herzog believed that the king in the Israelite constitution had very limited powers. For Herzog, the king's extra-halakhic prerogative was limited to the extraordinary situation of punishing a criminal who was blatantly guilty but happened to escape conviction under the halakhic system. It was not the basis of an entire legal system alongside halakha.

Herzog rejected Gorontchik's proposal even more forcefully than the positions of Grodzinski and Margulies. He was so scandalized by Gorontchik's arguments, published on the eve of the establishment of the State of Israel, that he devoted an entire article to rebutting them.[88] Of particular significance in Herzog's rebuttal is the methodology he uses to make his argument. Herzog undertook a close reading of countless canonical authorities and made reference to many more. His writing is rigorous and often persuasive. Still, he also relied on rhetorical techniques as well as analytical arguments, giving the impression that his disagreements with Gorontchik were based less on a conflict over the reading of authoritative texts and more on a matter of a priori ideology. Herzog had a fundamentally different approach to law in general, which made it simply impossible for him to accept a pluralistic jurisprudence.

At times, Herzog's rebuttal descended into an attack on Gorontchik over minor semantic points. Gorontchik had said, for example, that under his proposal the civil courts would be governed by "a special civil code, in accordance with international law."[89] Gorontchik presumably meant that his system was intended to address the UN's stipulation that all the citizens of a Jewish state be equal under the law. Herzog's response, rather than engaging with the substance of Gorontchik's argument, merely picked holes in his formulation:

> Firstly, international law is only applicable to international matters and does not involve itself with the internal law of any state. Secondly, if he is referring to paragraph 4 of the decision of the United Nations "that there be no discrimination in the state on the basis of race, religion or sex,"[90] then if this is applied to family law then we will God forbid be required to carry out civil marriages that do not distinguish at all on the basis of sex and religion so that, God forbid, mixed marriages between Jews and Gentiles will have legal force. . . .
>
> However, we have a basis to interpret this decision in a way that will not lead to such a situation. For in another paragraph it says that "religious courts should remain as they are,"[91] meaning that the authority in personal law will not be taken from [the rabbinical courts].[92]

Herzog's comments make sense in their own right but, other than the pedantic note about Gorontchik's misuse of the term "international law," they have little to do with Gorontchik's proposal. Gorontchik agreed with Herzog that rabbinical courts should have control over Jewish marriages and should continue to operate on the basis of halakha. Herzog's choice to grapple with this straw man conveys the impression that he not only disagreed with Gorontchik on this point, but he also had a deeper principled aversion to it.

This impression is reinforced by Herzog's argument that the parallel judicial system proposed by Gorontchik would cause an assault on the primacy of the halakha. Gorontchik had written that under his proposal care would have to be taken to make sure that the laws of the civil courts were "not against the laws of the Torah." Herzog pounced on this phrase. How, he asked, could the civil courts possibly avoid contravening the laws of the Torah? "Surely, there are very few laws that the Torah does not already cover. If so, is it not a fact that in any case that is not judged according to the Torah, the verdict will be against the Torah?"[93]

On the face of it, Herzog's critique is sound. Gorontchik had proposed that the civil courts judge cases according to democratically enacted legislation rather than halakha. Halakha, however, already has laws that cover civil law and so, Herzog pointed out, any legislation covering any of these areas of law would by definition contravene the preexisting halakha. Thus, according to Herzog, Gorontchik's plan to have a non-halakhic judicial system that does not contravene halakha was necessarily impossible.

In fact, however, Herzog's critique is less devastating than it first appears, because it is not a critique of Gorontchik alone but of the entire history of Jewish legal pluralism. As Herzog was no doubt aware, halakhists had for centuries grappled with the problem of what it means that Jews are required to obey the law of the land only if it does not contravene halakha. If halakha covers all areas of life, then surely almost all non-halakhic law clashes with halakha in some fashion. Historically, this question had been answered in various ways. The most common approach was to draw a distinction between ritual and civil areas of law; to hold, for example, that the law of the land must be obeyed when it comes to contract law but not if it requires Jews to work on the Sabbath.[94] Other interpreters limited the validity of non-halakhic law to those areas with which halakha does not explicitly engage.[95] Either way, however, Herzog's critique of Gorontchik was no less a critique of generations of precedent, to which many thinkers had already offered answers.

Herzog also addressed the historical precedent that Gorontchik had marshaled for his case, particularly the talmudic case of the "Syrian Courts." Herzog was very resistant to the notion that a Jewish court could judge by a law other than the halakha. He initially tried to deny Gorontchik's view, following Meiri, that the difference between rabbinical courts and "Syrian Courts" was that the former judged by halakha and the latter by the discretion of the judges. Herzog suggested that both courts judged by halakha but that the judges of the "Syrian

Courts" were not experts in halakha and had to consult with Torah scholars. Ultimately, though, Herzog conceded that one "must follow the interpretation of the commentators," and he reluctantly accepted the prevailing opinion that the "Syrian Courts" judged not by halakha but by some other law.[96] Still, Herzog posited, this was a function of particular historical circumstances: in the absence of Torah sages, setting up a Jewish court comprising judges who were not halakhic experts was the only way to avoid resorting to Gentile courts, which was entirely forbidden. This historical precedent was therefore inapplicable to the new State of Israel, where Torah scholars were abundant. Although most Israeli judges were not yet familiar with the halakhic system, Herzog believed that they could soon become familiar enough with halakha to apply it in their courtrooms. Fundamentally, it was simply unthinkable to Herzog that a sovereign Jewish state in the Land of Israel could have a legal system that was not based on halakha:

> With regard to a Jewish settlement in Syria which is not in any case part of the Biblical Land of Israel . . . it is at least possible to imagine a circumstance like this [where Jewish courts do not judge by halakha]. But in the Jewish state in the Holy Land, which is the only place where our law could be established and enforced with state power, if a [non-halakhic] justice system like this is established, it seems to me, God forbid, like writing a divorce for the Torah and raising a hand against the law of Moses.[97]

So much for historical precedent. What about the theoretical work of the Ran and his comments about the need for a "king's law" alongside halakha? Herzog had already dismissed the approach of the Ran as a mere sermon, rather than a responsum, in his rejection of Grodzinski's opinion. He expanded on that position in his rebuttal of Gorontchik. Herzog first questioned the authorship of the Ran's *Eleventh Sermon*, presumably to diminish its authority by distancing it from such an authoritative medieval jurist.[98] He conceded that it must have been written by a competent author, but pointed out that whoever wrote the piece "did not bring proofs from the Talmud."[99] Besides, he insisted that the Ran's approach was both impractical and nonsensical. If, as the Ran maintained, the halakhic system was incapable of governing and the system of the king's law was necessary for real government, what was the purpose of the rabbinical courts in the first place? Why have two legal systems with overlapping jurisdictions, one of which was effective and the other ineffective? Surely the Ran's constitutional vision would make the halakha and its courts entirely redundant. "At the end of the day," Herzog claimed, "it is very difficult to build a fixed structure on these words of the Ran."[100]

For Herzog to claim that halakha alone is sufficient to govern a state without any resort to the king's law or communal legislation, he had to account for the deficiencies in the halakhic system. Even Herzog agreed that halakha as it had developed made it too difficult to convict and punish criminals in the context of the modern state. He offered the unconvincing suggestion that in ancient times halakha was sufficient because Jews were simply more ethical, so social order could be maintained even with the restrictive nature of halakhic procedure and its relative lack of punitive measures.[101] Since ancient times, Herzog continued, the ethics of the Jews had declined and changes to halakha would be required. But, he claimed, these changes would not be made on the authority of the "king's law," as Gorontchik had proposed. Rather, they would be made by rabbinic enactments within the halakhic system, without needing the support of a non-halakhic legal authority like that of the king.[102] For Herzog the very fact that halakha has the ability to respond to changing circumstances was itself a further argument that the "king's law" must not be as expansive as the Ran and Gorontchik had claimed. If halakha itself has the internal resources to meet new circumstances, then an expansive "king's law" is unnecessary. While the traditional sources did not allow Herzog totally to disregard the category of "king's law," he vastly limited its application to the rare occasion on which a murderer escapes proper punishment in rabbinical courts. Only then is "king's law" employed to execute true justice.

For Herzog, then, the idea of a plural legal regime was simply unthinkable. His criticism of legal pluralism went beyond textual arguments and appealed to common sense. He considered it "inconceivable" that the Torah could allow for two parallel authorities. Herzog simply refused to accept that there were ever "two authorities, a Torah bet din authority and a bet din by the power of the king, two authorities ruling as one."[103]

However, legal pluralism was not "inconceivable" at all. In fact, it had been a mainstay of Jewish legal culture for centuries.[104] Moreover, legal pluralism solved many of the problems that religious Zionists faced in their drafting of their own constitutional propositions. The discriminatory nature of halakhic distinctions between men and women and between Jews and non-Jews meant that halakha would never have been accepted by most Zionists as the exclusive law of the entire state. Legal pluralism allowed religious Zionists to argue for a constitutional regime that gave ample room to halakhic authority without foisting its discriminatory norms on an unwilling public. Legal pluralism also relieved religious Zionist rabbis from the burden of radical innovation in halakha. It made it possible to give halakha a role in the state while also insulating it from the challenges of modernity. For these reasons, legal pluralism was the way that most religious Zionists until this point in history attempted to map out a vision for the state.

Herzog's rejection of legal pluralism therefore requires an explanation. Indeed, it is not just Herzog's approach that needs to be explained but also the fact that in the course of the 1950s it had such a profound impact on the legal thinking of religious Zionists. This chapter opened with claims by secular and religious Israeli thinkers that halakha lays claim to the exclusive governance of a Jewish polity. The fact that these claims were so widely accepted, despite so much historical evidence to the contrary, indicates the extent to which Herzog's rejection of legal pluralism became accepted in Israeli society. The explanation for this phenomenon lies in the genesis of Herzog's own legal thinking in the twin contexts of modern European jurisprudence and the twilight of the age of European empires.

2 ISAAC HERZOG BEFORE PALESTINE

In the early 1950s, Isaac Herzog was scheduled to give a lecture to a group of lawyers. Before he began to read his prepared words, Herzog felt the need to correct the publicized title of his talk, which was "Knowledge and Will in Contract and Property in Torah Law in comparison with English Law." Herzog told his audience that he did not intend to compare Jewish law with anything else. "The words 'in comparison with English law' were added subsequently, without my knowledge," he announced. He went on to criticize some scholars of Jewish law for their "conspicuous proclivity . . . to invariably search for comparison and analogies from external sources." Indeed, he insisted, such a comparison is "inconceivable" because "as the heavens are higher than the earth, so the divine Torah from heaven is higher than any kind of jurisprudential system produced by human intellect and spirit." And yet, Herzog immediately proceeded to talk about the value of such comparison:

> At the most, it is useful for explanatory purposes, enlisting human intellect to invoke external concepts in explaining certain concepts of Torah Law for those who are not conversant with the classical Jewish sources, but are familiar with other legal systems. Therefore, my lecture is not devoted to comparison but rather to explanation, in other words explaining with the assistance of concepts and definitions taken from English law.[1]

Herzog believed that Jewish law is qualitatively different from any other legal system. As the word of God, it cannot be compared with other kinds of law. At the same time, Herzog seemed eager to talk about Jewish law in reference to other legal systems, English law in particular, in order to "explain" its concepts.

This simultaneous embrace and rejection of legal comparison produced a paradoxical tension that is characteristic of Herzog's oeuvre.

The Invention of Jewish Theocracy. Alexander Kaye, Oxford University Press (2020). © Oxford University Press.
DOI: 10.1093/oso/9780190922740.001.0001

He was a champion of the uniqueness and superiority of Jewish law. At the same time, however, he frequently explained aspects of Jewish law according to the categories and principles of what he called "external sources," especially English and Roman law. Herzog, then, was both a triumphalist and an apologist. He argued that Jewish law was incomparably superior to any other legal or religious system, yet attempted to demonstrate that superiority by measuring it against the very systems he deemed unworthy of comparison.

This paradox in Herzog's thought can best be understood by placing him in the context of Western European thought of the first half of the twentieth century. This context is the backdrop of his frequent engagement with two particular developments in the scholarship of his time, each of them implicitly critical of Judaism and Jewish law. The first was the application of evolutionary theory to social phenomena, particularly the belief that religion and law became more refined and more moral over time. Advocates of this approach often painted Judaism as a backward vestige of a tribal culture that Christianity and the modern West had long ago superseded. The second was the shift in European jurisprudence from legal pluralism, which allowed for multiple coexisting jurisdictions, to legal centralism, which brought all law in the state into a single organized hierarchical structure. The ascendancy of legal centralism exposed Jewish law to the criticism of being inferior by virtue of its being stateless and decentralized. Herzog's response to these theories was not to challenge their premises but to show how Judaism and Jewish law were superior even by their own assumptions. To make this case, Herzog often read Jewish sources against the grain, reinterpreting traditional sources so that they would be seen in a favorable light according to the standards of the "external sources" that he decried as inferior to halakha.

Herzog's ambivalence toward European civilization—his assertion of the superiority of Judaism coupled with his tendency to measure that superiority against modern European standards—is the foundation of his later influential writings about a halakhic constitution for the State of Israel. An understanding of Herzog's earlier writing is, therefore, critical to understanding his endorsement of the idea of the halakhic state after he moved to Palestine. And it explains why, given the justified popularity of legal pluralism among religious Zionists, Herzog fought so strongly against it.

Herzog's Early Life

Although born in Poland in 1888, Isaac Herzog was a product of Western Europe.[2] When Herzog was nine years old, his father, Yoel, brought the family to the city of Leeds in the north of England, where he took up a rabbinical position.

Isaac Herzog was by all accounts a gifted student. He received an education in traditional Torah scholarship and, even as a young man in England, corresponded with seasoned rabbinical scholars in Eastern Europe, who were deeply impressed with his erudition. In 1908 he was formally ordained by three leading rabbis in Eastern Europe.[3]

Herzog also received an extensive general education. In 1909 he received a BA from the University of London, where he concentrated on mathematics and classical and Semitic languages. In 1912, he received an MA in ancient languages. In the same year the family once again moved for Yoel Herzog's rabbinical career, this time to Paris, where Isaac earned another MA from the Sorbonne. He later returned to the University of London, which granted him a doctorate in marine biology in 1914. His dissertation, *Hebrew Porphyrology*, was a scientific and historical investigation of *tekhelet*, the blue dye used by ancient Jews to dye the *tsitsit* fringes.[4]

In 1916, Isaac Herzog relocated to Ireland to become the rabbi of Belfast. Three years later, he moved to Dublin. Herzog was a committed and energetic leader of the Jewish community of Ireland and was frequently called to defend and advocate for Jews and Judaism. He repeatedly spoke out, in the press and in private communications with political and religious leaders, against antisemitism and against Nazi sympathizers within Ireland.[5] He defended kosher slaughtering methods before the Irish parliament and delivered public lectures on Judaism and Zionism. His lecture on "The Hebrew Language, Its Position and Revival," for example, aired on Irish radio in 1934.[6] Perhaps the most significant focus of his political activism was his fight to raise immigration quotas for Jews fleeing Nazi Europe. He dedicated himself to this task while still in Ireland and continued to pursue it after his move to Palestine.[7]

Ireland, which at the time was in the throes of a war with Great Britain, was an important crucible for Herzog's thought. Herzog experienced life both in Belfast, a loyalist stronghold that later became the capital of Northern Ireland as a part of Great Britain, and in Dublin, the seat of the revolt against British rule. After the Anglo-Irish Treaty of 1922, which established the Irish Free State as an independent political entity, Herzog officially became the first Chief Rabbi of Ireland. His years in that position involved him in what the Irish saw as the struggle of an oppressed nation for their own state against the injustice of British imperial rule. The similarities between Irish separatism and the Zionist struggle against British rule in Mandate Palestine was not lost on Herzog.

Herzog had been a Zionist since his youth. An early memory was of his father's devotion to Zionism in the face of severe opposition. In the Shas and Magen Avraham Synagogue, he recalled that

. . . my father, his memory be blessed, delivered his sermon on Hibat Zion[8] and the settlement of the Land of Israel. In the town a ruckus broke out because several of the zealots strongly opposed the Hovevei Zion movement and they locked the shutters around the platform of the holy ark. The community broke the lock and father, his memory be blessed, delivered his sermon, which made an immense impression on the hundreds of listeners who crowded in. From that evening the love of Zion began to burn in me—an eternal flame that will never be extinguished—and I began to plan for my immigration to the Land of Israel.[9]

Herzog was an open advocate of Zionism while he was a rabbi in Ireland, and his experiences there colored his own approaches to Zionism. In particular, Herzog had firsthand experience in Ireland of the centrality of the role of law and constitution in nationalist movements. The place of the constitution of Ireland played a major role in the fight between the Irish and the British, as well as in internal conflicts among Irish Republicans of different philosophies. In fact, Herzog, who was a personal friend of Éamon de Valera, was consulted during the drafting of a new Irish constitution that was eventually adopted in 1937, the year that Herzog moved to Palestine.

In addition to his political activity, Herzog produced a steady scholarly output. He wrote halakhic responsa, sermons, and talmudic commentaries.[10] He also wrote many articles about Jewish thought and law for nonspecialist audiences. They were published in Jewish publications such as London's *Jewish Chronicle* newspaper and *Jewish Forum*, a journal for Orthodox Jews published in New York, as well as legal journals for a general readership.[11] Many of his articles concentrated on matters of Jewish jurisprudence and legal history, on the relationship between the Jewish tradition and science, or the relationship between Judaism and other civilizations. This period of Herzog's scholarship culminated in the late 1930s with the publication of two volumes of his magnum opus, *Main Institutions of Jewish Law*.[12]

These works display Herzog's mastery of the Jewish canon as well as his deep familiarity with non-Jewish sources and scholarship, both ancient and modern. They promoted the dignity of Jewish law in terms that were intelligible to a modern audience more familiar with Western thought than with the Talmud. It is in these publications that Herzog's triumphal apologetics is most apparent. He defended Judaism and halakha from modern critics by trying to prove that they surpassed even modern standards of morality and cultural sophistication.

Law and Evolution

Herzog's writings on Judaism and Jewish law were always implicitly in conversation with prevailing European ideas of law and religion, defending against possible critiques of the Jewish tradition and halakha. In the period before he moved to Palestine, his writing was animated by the need to defend Judaism against two prevailing ideas: the idea that civilization and law evolve from lower to higher forms and the idea that the ideal law is rational and hierarchically organized under a central authority.

From the second half of the nineteenth century, the theory of evolution came to inform many areas of scholarship, including religion.[13] Many European scholars (almost all of whom were Christians) understood Judaism to occupy a more primitive evolutionary stage than Christianity, the religion of most European scholars. This position was often reinforced by academic critics of the Hebrew Bible, who articulated theories of religion according to which Judaism is an intermediary stage between "primitive religions" and Christianity.[14] This evolutionary approach to religion confirmed the old Christian theology of supersession, according to which God intended Christianity to replace Judaism.

Legal scholars also employed evolutionary ideas in their own studies. The application of evolutionary theory to law was an outgrowth of the historicist study of law that began in Germany in the late nineteenth century. Friedrich Carl von Savigny, a central figure in the German Historical School of Law, claimed that law did not conform to abstract and universal legal principles but evolved against the background of the historical peculiarities of specific peoples. In England, the most prominent heir to Savigny's legal historicism was Henry James Sumner Maine, a jurist and historian. Maine's most influential work, *Ancient Law*, was published in 1861, two years after Darwin's *Origin of the Species* and by the same publisher.[15] Evolution formed the basis of Maine's description of the development of law. He claimed that law begins with the commands of heroic kings, before ascending through the emergence of aristocracy and the formation of law into a body of knowledge, developing into customary or common law, and, finally, reaching the stage of codification, the zenith of legal evolution.[16] For Maine, the development of law mirrored the development of the political institutions in which law is embedded. They begin as collections of families, gradually forming into tribes and eventually into larger societies governed by law. Maine believed that this evolution of law marked "the upward march of society."[17] As it evolved, he believed that law became progressively more effective, more sophisticated, and more moral.

According to this approach, which was widely accepted among legal scholars, Jewish law with its ancient origins was stuck at an earlier stage of legal evolution and was therefore inferior to the more evolved modern European law. Until the last years of the twentieth century, Jewish law was all but excluded from academic legal research because it was considered too primitive to be considered proper law. Legal academics were swayed by the influence of Maine that Judaism can be classified only as a "religion," and therefore belongs to an earlier stage of cultural development that is outside the purview of legal history.[18] By the end of the twentieth century, Jewish law had become more integrated into the scholarly study of law and was even held up as a model that could provide alternatives to elements of modern legal systems.[19] In Herzog's time, however, the evolutionary theory of law created an association between Jewish law and "primitive" or "tribal" law, which was considered by many to be immoral, violent, disorganized, and intrinsically inferior to the more evolved laws of modern European states. This approach to the history of law worked hand in hand with the assumptions of many Christian scholars of religion. Both dealt with Judaism in a deeply pejorative way.

Much of Herzog's writing can be seen as a response to the critique of Judaism derived from the evolutionary approach to religion and law. Rather than disputing the basis of these critiques of Judaism, he accepted their basic premises, agreeing that certain kinds of society were more evolved than others. He claimed, however, that Judaism was an exception to this general rule because of its divine origin. Despite its antiquity, he asserted, it was more moral than any other religion or body of law. Far from being superseded, he contended, Judaism was superior to modern civilizations and served as a basis for their morality and law. The supposedly superior Christian peoples of Europe, he wrote, "did not rise to the level of cultured peoples until thousands of years after we stood at Mount Sinai."[20] He went on to emphasize the superiority of Jewish law over the other laws, particularly those in force in Mandate Palestine: "The wisdom of their [British and Ottoman] laws . . . is like a monkey before a human being when compared to the wisdom of our [Jewish] laws."[21] For Herzog, Jewish law was more evolved than modern legal systems, not the other way round.

Herzog's strategy of accepting the premises of common criticisms of Judaism and inverting them to show Judaism's superiority is readily apparent in his 1930 article, "The Outlook of Greek Culture upon Judaism."[22] The article was presumably intended primarily for a Christian audience, as it was published in *The Hibbert Journal*, a London liberal Christian quarterly. It engaged with the binary relationship between "Hellenism" and "Hebraism," which at the time was often used to support the superiority of Christian Europeans over Jews and others. For Matthew Arnold, the most prominent popularizer of the two terms, Hebraism represented rigid virtue, traditionalism, and faith, whereas Hellenism represented flexibility of thought, reason, science, and beauty.[23] Although Arnold felt that a balance was required between these two tendencies, many Christians believed that the corollary of the superiority of Hellenism was the inferiority of the Jews.[24] It was this conclusion that Herzog protested.

In the article, Herzog offered a wide-ranging survey of pagan Hellenistic attitudes to ancient Judaism, quoting extensively from ancient sources across the Greek world, as well as from contemporary scholarship in French and Hebrew.[25] By indicating that he knew as much about contemporary scholarship as non-Jewish scholars, he established his own qualifications in claiming the superiority of Judaism. (In a later speech, Herzog made this strategy explicit, declaring that "I am talking to you as someone who is well versed in the laws of Rome and England"[26]).

Herzog accepted the basic distinction between philosophy, associated with Greece, and religion, associated with Jerusalem. He attempted to show, however, that the morality of Hebraism, and therefore of Judaism, was not merely an inflexible adherence to rules, but was the basis of all higher ethics.[27] This position was natural, he wrote, considering Judaism's "sublime ethical trend, which towered so high above the religions of all the 'barbarian' nations and even above the religion of Greece herself."[28] Then, as now, it was only irrational hatred of the Jews that prevented appreciation of them, and "even now the Jewish people and Judaism, in particular, are largely misunderstood and misjudged."[29] He concluded, however, in a more optimistic tone and described how in the final analysis there is an affinity between Judaism, which appreciated Greek philosophy and science, and the "Greek mind," which eventually rejected its pagan roots and embraced the monotheism and morality of Judaism:

> The fact that the first encounter between these two principal cultural forces generated mutual sympathy cannot fail to grip our attention. The Greek mind, repelled at last by its ancestral world-outlook, or religion, and struggling from light, was thrilled by the phenomenon of an entire nation professing a religion which comprised a God-idea, a spiritual, imageless cult and a system of morality, all singularly congenial to the circle of ideas which Greek thought was now evolving. The Jewish mind, on the other hand, was powerfully attracted by the high flights of the Greek intellect in its effort to grapple with the riddle of the universe. . . .[30]

Herzog embraced the conceptual categories prevalent in the Britain of his day. He accepted the dichotomy between the ethical, the philosophical, and the sublime on the one hand and the barbarian, the pagan, and the sensualist on the other. He rejected, however, the prevailing antisemitic implications of the dichotomy, and mobilized it in the defense of Judaism. He argued that Judaic religion and Greek science are not only compatible but are in fact mutually reinforcing. The subtext was that even in Herzog's own period, with the ascendance of scientific positivism in Europe, Judaism could be held up as a beacon of religious and ethical enlightenment. Far from being superseded, Judaism was morally superior even by the standards of modern European thought.

Herzog's writing exhibited the same triumphal apologetics with regard to Jewish law as they did with regard to the Jewish religion. An example of this is Herzog's 1931 article, "John Selden and Jewish Law," an overview of the works relating to Jewish law written by the seventeenth-century English politician, scholar, and jurist.[31] Herzog first wrote this material as a paper that he delivered to the London branch of *The Society for Jewish Jurisprudence*. The society was a group, first established by Zionist jurists in Palestine, whose goal was "the revival of our national law and its scientific development." The London branch had been established in 1926.[32]

Selden wrote several works on Jewish law, on subjects such as tithes, inheritance, marriage and divorce, courts, and the calendar.[33] Herzog read these works in the original Latin and once again did not hold back from establishing his qualifications for discussing them, informing the reader that "I decided to read no reviews or criticisms of Selden until I had covered the whole of his Rabbinic writings from beginning to end and had formed an independent opinion free from all external influences."[34]

Herzog seemed to be torn between a high regard for Selden and criticism of him. He recognized that Selden was "undoubtedly one of the most erudite men that England had ever produced" and was generally impressed with his writings on Jewish law. He was, however, unforgiving of some elementary mistakes in Selden, calling one "a blunder unworthy of the merest beginner" and at one point suggesting that "the barest acquaintance with post-talmudic Jewish history would have saved him from the subsequent pitfall into which he fell."[35] He also lamented Selden's digressive style, noting sharply that "[w]e can see at a glance that Selden tries to be exhaustive. But he succeeds in doing much more than that: he exhausts the patience of the reader."[36] In general, Herzog quoted with approval Selden's praise of rabbinic literature while, through his criticisms, implying that the ultimate right to interpret Jewish law lay exclusively with Jewish rabbinic experts like himself. Thus, Herzog paid Selden a somewhat backhanded compliment in appreciating the fact that "a man who certainly was not a Talmudist should have been able to produce what Selden has produced in the domain of Rabbinica."[37]

Herzog used the study of Selden as an opportunity to paint a picture of halakha as a superior system of law that played a critical role in the development of Western civilization. He observed that Hebrew writings had a place alongside the classical world in the Renaissance revival of ancient thought. "Christian savants in many European centres of learning," he wrote, "began to apply themselves with an ever-increasing zest to the study of Hebrew, and, gradually widening the scope of their studies and researches, they also began to pay considerable attention to talmudic and rabbinic literature."[38] The sources of Jewish law, he implied, were as important to European scholarship at the dawn of modernity as the literature of Greece and Rome.

In the same vein, Herzog wrote at length about Selden's high estimation of Jewish law, even above Protestant and Catholic interpreters of the Bible:

> There can be no doubt that Selden had great faith in Jewish tradition, which represented to him the vehicle of the true meaning of the Law of Moses. He generally treats the sages of the Mishnah and the Talmud with the profoundest respect and now and again he censures even Jewish Biblical exegetes like Ibn Ezra and Ralbag for giving interpretations at variance with tradition. With Christian writers, both Catholic and Protestant, who ignore Jewish tradition in explaining Pentateuchal law he deals very summarily. This, says Selden, is like attempting to interpret Roman law independently of the standard Roman jurists, Ulpian, Palinian, etc.[39]

Herzog used Selden to show that, far from being a superseded vestige of antiquity, an artifact of an earlier stage of cultural evolution, the Jewish legal tradition is a cornerstone of modern legal culture, and worthy of study in its own right.

The celebration of Jewish law as a superior model of jurisprudence was one of Herzog's main scholarly preoccupations of the 1930s, in the years before he took up his position as Chief Rabbi of Palestine. There is no doubt that his desire to see Jewish law applied to a new Jewish state was a primary motivation for him during these years. In his own words, "the deep-rooted consciousness that we are on the threshold of a new era which, with the help of the Eternal Guardian of Israel, will bring with it the revival of Israel's nationhood in his ancient, prophetic, cradleland and the rehabilitation of Jewish law as a living and vivifying force, has acted all along as an incessant inward urge and as a powerful incentive."[40]

Between 1929 and 1931, Herzog published seven articles on Jewish law and jurisprudence in the Scottish *Juridical Review* and the American *Temple Law Quarterly*, the law review of Temple University in Philadelphia. The articles were impressively detailed surveys of the sources of Jewish law, and the topics of possession, rights and duties, norms, and morality in Jewish law.[41] This spate of legal writing reached its apex with the publication of the first two volumes of Herzog's monumental *The Main Institutions of Jewish Law* in 1936 and 1939.[42]

In Herzog's opinion, Jewish law was an "elaborate, massive towering structure . . . of such hoary antiquity, of so majestic, awe-inspiring an origin."[43] He was dismayed, therefore, that its true genius was not recognized by the world at large and lamented that it had not received the attention it properly deserved. In Herzog's mind, the cause of the undeserved lack of attention to Jewish law was twofold. It was, first, the result of an ancient and persistent anti-Judaism. This was the fault of Rome, which "destroyed the Jewish state and drove the Jewish people out of its magic land," thereby stunting "the process of natural growth and development inherent in Israel's legal system." Ironically, it is Rome that "has been admired throughout the centuries for her juristic genius."[44] By contrast, Jewish law has been deprived of its due:

> [Rome's] victim, Judaea, on the other hand, has not yet received due appreciation for her achievement in the field of law, an achievement which so strikingly attests the intellectual powers of the Jewish race as well as its noble passion for righteousness. . . . Judaea has not yet received the meed of recognition and appreciation to which she is justly entitled upon that score.[45]

The mention of Rome in this context was not accidental. It reflected the fact that even in Herzog's day, Roman law formed the basis for European and, to a lesser extent, Anglo-American jurisprudence.[46] It also hinted at his hope that in returning to the Land of Israel, thereby reversing the termination of Jewish sovereignty by Roman conquest, the Jews would revive their religious law.

Herzog did not only lament the lack of proper respect given to Jewish law by non-Jews. He also complained about the failure of Jews themselves to recognize the wisdom in their own law: "It is, I regret to have to say, the inferiority complex from which some of our people suffer that prevents them from attaching importance to the treatment of a purely Jewish subject unless it is presented from the comparative standpoint."[47]

The Jews with an "inferiority complex" to whom Herzog referred were the scholars of the *Mishpat Ivri* movement, a group of scholars who provided a foil to Herzog's work throughout his life. At the end of the nineteenth century, the academic study of Jewish law began to be developed by Zionist law students and their German professors.[48] German law professors, who were heirs to von Savigny's German Historical School, became interested in Jewish law from the perspective of legal ethnology.[49] Their Zionist students, meanwhile, embraced the academic study of Jewish law as part of a movement of Hebrew national revival. Just as Zionists, influenced by romantic nationalist movements in Eastern Europe, considered the revival of the Hebrew language to be an essential aspect of their own national revival, so they believed that the retrieval of Jewish law (which they called "Hebrew law") as an organic aspect of their national character was an important component of their Zionist aspirations. Societies arose that were dedicated to this task, the first being the Hebrew Law Society established in Moscow in 1918 under the leadership of a Swiss-educated Russian Jew, Shmuel Eisenstadt. Eisenstadt later immigrated to Palestine with colleagues such as Paltiel Dickstein and continued his attempts to revive Hebrew law. The most ambitious and expansive work on Jewish law to emerge from the movement was Asher Gulak's *Foundations of Hebrew Law*, published in Berlin in 1922, three years before Gulak took up his position as Professor of Law at the newly established Hebrew University of Jerusalem.[50] In its four volumes, Gulak's majestic work attempted systematically to cover all areas of Hebrew civil law.[51]

The Mishpat Ivri movement had a great deal in common with Herzog. Both devoted themselves to research in Jewish law with a view to reviving the culture of the Jewish people based on ancient rabbinical law. However, despite being a member of the Hebrew Law Society in London, Herzog expressed serious reservations about the entire enterprise.[52] In Israel today, the term "Mishpat Ivri" is often used interchangeably with "halakhah," and most of those who study and promote it are Orthodox Jews. This was not always the case, however. At its start, and for decades thereafter, the Mishpat Ivri movement was fundamentally a secular project. It was an attempt to construct a workable national law that was based upon religious law, but was not identical to it.[53] Mishpat Ivri scholars, much like the Zionist movement as a whole, regarded Jewish religious history as a resource for national revival but not as a binding source of law and custom.[54] This view is clear from Eisenstadt's description of the movement in a 1910 article:

> Mishpat Ivri reveals its full depth and breadth out of the confusion of the Talmud and demands its redemption from the chains of time and the rust of generations. It demands elucidation and modern illumination. It demands a new Hebrew attire, to appear in all its splendor to its people and it demands an academic scientific apparel so that it can appear in the pantheons of human knowledge.[55]

It is for this reason that the movement called itself Mishpat Ivri (Hebrew Law) rather than *Mishpat Yehudi* or *Mishpat Yisraeli* (Jewish Law). Most leaders of the Zionist movement had an ambivalent relationship to the Jewish tradition. They drew on its symbols and myths, while also rebelling against it, openly disdaining religious (as opposed to nationalist) aspects of Jewish identity. The adjective "Hebrew" connoted both a connection to the national roots of the Jewish people and a self-conscious departure from rabbinic authority and religious precedent.

The secularization of the Jewish legal tradition was anathema to Herzog.[56] He admired the scholarship of Gulak and others. He acknowledged, for example, that Gulak was the first to attempt a systematic account of Jewish law according to abstract principles.[57] Herzog could not accept, however, the repudiation of the divine origin and binding nature of halakha. For Herzog, Jewish law was the product of divine revelation and so was entirely *sui generis*. He therefore viewed the comparative methodology and the historicization of Jewish law used widely by Mishpat Ivri scholars as fundamentally flawed. He felt that such an approach would diminish the uniqueness and superiority of Jewish law and that scholars studying it in a comparative light would be more likely to judge its significance only by virtue of its relationship to other, more prominent legal systems such as Roman law. Herzog intended his *Main Institutions of Jewish Law* to be an alternative scholarly approach to Jewish law that recognized its role in Jewish national revival without rejecting its religious significance. Herzog was careful to describe the work as "neither a history nor . . . a comparative study of Jewish law."[58] It is smattered with critiques of Mishpat Ivri scholars, including Gulak and earlier scholars like Nahman Krochmal.

In *Main Institutions*, Herzog continued to affirm the superiority of halakha over modern jurisprudence, even according to modern standards. Ironically, despite Herzog's complaint that bringing a comparative methodology to the study of Jewish law was a symptom of an inferiority complex, the primary goal of *Main Institutions* was to formulate Jewish law according to the structure and conceptual categories that were familiar to scholars of modern European law. Herzog was very clear about this intent. As he put it himself, his goal was to distill "the intricate, the bewildering, semi-enigmatic nature and often semi-chaotic state of so much of the stupendous mass of material" of the totality of Jewish law into a "methodised, reasoned quintessence, presented in a Westernised and modernised form."[59]

Early in *Main Institutions*, Herzog listed the categories of Jewish law and explicitly compared them to European categories, proposing that "[t]he following classes of laws taken together would seem to constitute a body of legal matter corresponding approximately to law in the modern Western sense."[60] Herzog tried to reconcile this comparative approach with his claim that Jewish law is unique. On one occasion, he addressed this paradox by suggesting that a similarity between Jewish and Roman law may be the result of the Romans borrowing from the Jews rather than vice versa.[61] But in general, although Herzog repeatedly pointed out the ways in which "modern Western" and Jewish categories do not precisely overlap, he nonetheless persisted in drawing comparisons. "*Dinin*," for example, "would nearly but not absolutely correspond" to "civil law."[62] The halakhic category of "*dinê makkoth*" "might suggest correspondence with criminal law."[63] The entire tractate of Sanhedrin "may be taken as the Mishnaic-Talmudic approximation of what modern jurisprudence would class under administration of the law."[64] Indeed, *Main Institutions* is peppered with references and comparisons with contemporary English jurists, most often to John Salmond's *Jurisprudence* and Anson's *Law of Contract*, both of which were popular among British jurists in Herzog's time.[65]

It was not just in its details that *Main Institutions* compared Jewish and Western law, but in its very structure. Herzog clearly intended his work to mirror a book with almost the same title, *The Main Institutions of Roman Private Law*, which was published by the Cambridge University law professor W. W. Buckland in 1931, only five years before the first volume of Herzog's own *Main Institutions*. Herzog's *Main Institutions* even roughly follows the organization of Buckland's, allowing for the differences in subject matter. Both works begin with chapters on the sources of law and then consider concepts like "persons," "property," and "acquisition." Roman law in this period was extremely influential in Western Europe. As late as the nineteenth century, Roman law was the official legal system of some European states, and it was a principle influence in the codification of new civil law codes. Even in England, where the common law tradition was perhaps more influential than Roman law, the latter still played a central role in legal culture, and was part of the legal curriculum. Buckland himself had claimed that "next to Christianity, Roman law was the greatest factor in the creation of modern civilization."[66] The absence of Judaism or Jewish law from Buckland's statement might itself have been enough to arouse Herzog to offer a rebuttal in the form of his own, competing, *Main Institutions*. Surely, Herzog believed, only ignorance of Jewish law could explain how jurists routinely overlooked it. Herzog hoped to correct this neglect:

> When its literary sources have been made more accessible and its accumulated treasures of the ages have been laid bare, the world's jurists may awake one day to find to their utter amazement that Jewish law, so sadly neglected, if not contemned [*sic*], offers one of the most arresting and thought-compelling manifestations of the Jewish mind. They may yet come to realize that the utter neglect of Jewish law on the part of students of law, and of cultured persons generally, has meant a serious loss to the cultural progress of humanity.[67]

In addition to showing that Jewish law was the conceptual equal to Roman law, Herzog claimed that Jewish law was its moral superior. Roman law, he claimed "undoubtedly moves upon a lower ethical plane than Hebrew law."[68] To support this position, Herzog felt the need to address the penalties in Jewish law that made it seem like a brutal and archaic system to many modern readers. A particularly jarring example of halakhic punishment was the prescription of the death sentence for a large number of crimes, including the transgression of ritual laws. The death penalty was operative in many countries in Herzog's lifetime; in the United Kingdom, murder remained a capital crime until 1965. However, the idea of imposing capital punishment for, say, collecting sticks on the Sabbath appeared barbaric by modern standards. Herzog acknowledged as much: "I have often heard it remarked that the restoration of the Jewish State in accordance with Jewish law, would isolate the Jewish people from the modern civilized world; for the Hebrew penal code includes the death-penalty for purely ritual offences, such as the willful desecration of the Sabbath."[69]

This passage reveals that Herzog was thinking about the application of Jewish law in a Jewish state—and how to present it in a good light to critics—even before his appointment as Chief Rabbi of Palestine. In a 1931 article, he suggested that the problem was "more apparent than real" because halakhic procedure made it very difficult ever to impose capital punishment.[70] Capital, and even corporal, punishment, he explained, was highly restricted, requiring "that the culprit had been warned immediately before the commission of the offence in the presence of two adult male Israelites of unimpeachable character and conduct . . . and that he had expressly defied the warning and said that he would commit the act in the full knowledge of the penalty awaiting him."[71]

In practice, Herzog posited, even ancient Jewish courts never used the death penalty. The Jewish penal code as recorded in the Talmud, he wrote, "is more theoretical than practical" and, by the time of the Roman destruction of Jerusalem, it had almost been abolished in practice.[72] The real fault for the presence of these archaic rules in the Jewish legal system, he intimated, lay with the Romans, who interrupted the natural course of Jewish history. Had Jewish law continued along a normal line of development, capital punishment would probably have entirely dropped out of practice.[73] So Herzog portrayed the attitude to punishment in Jewish law as far from being brutal and archaic, but rather as civilized. "In this, as in many other respects," he wrote, "it is superior to the law of the majority of the most highly civilized modern states."[74]

Herzog returned to this theme five years later in *Main Institutions*. Most of his comments there were taken directly from his earlier article, but in *Main Institutions* he was even more explicit about the fact that the ancient death penalty should not prevent the implementation of Jewish law in a new Jewish state. He pointed out that even the theoretical application of the death penalty could only be carried out with the rebuilding of the Jewish Temple in Jerusalem and the resumption of its sacrificial cult. Herzog did not imagine that the Temple, which had been destroyed by the Romans in 70 CE, would be rebuilt any time soon. It "could only be restored," he wrote, "under prophetic directions" and its return entailed "insurmountable" problems. (He presumably had in mind not only halakhic complications, but also the fact that the ancient site of the Jewish

Temple had by then been the location of the Al-Aqsa Mosque, a revered place of Muslim worship, for over a millennium.) As "a matter which could only arise in the *Messianic* age," serious discussion of the death penalty could be deferred, "and need not enter into any practical calculations affecting the reconstitution of the Jewish State in Palestine." In the meantime, "no Jewish court could inflict the death-penalty even for the crime of homicide."[75]

In subverting the criticism that halakha was barbaric, by defanging halakhic writings on the death penalty, Herzog opened Jewish law up to another criticism. If a halakhic court could not convict a murderer, it might therefore appear to be incapable of enforcing law and order. In response to this apparent shortcoming, Herzog explained that the Jewish legal system had ample resources to deter crimes even without the threat of capital punishment: "It must not, however, be thought that murder could be committed with impunity in the Jewish State governed by Jewish law. We are told that when the court was convinced that wilful murder had been committed but could not, owing to the technical restrictions, pass the death-sentence, the convict was condemned to life-long imprisonment."[76]

In other areas too, the defense of halakha's morality threatened to undermine its claim for effectiveness. To avoid this dilemma, Herzog sometimes had to make some very delicate arguments. An example is his discussion of a theory of Gulak regarding the difference between Roman and Jewish approaches to legal "possession." In Roman law, Gulak noted, the physical possession of an article, even by someone other than the owner, bestows certain rights on the possessor. This is not the case in Jewish law, where physical possession is less legally significant. Gulak attributed these different attitudes to the legal significance of physical possession to the fact that in Roman law the presence of "the sovereign power" means that there is a "worship of might." Judaism, by contrast, "is the divinely ordained law in which there is no room for the worship of might, nor for its juridic protection."[77]

In engaging with Gulak's claim, Herzog trod a fine line. Although he concurred with Gulak's "sentiments in regard to the lofty ethical pedestal occupied by Hebrew law," he was reluctant to accept Gulak's contrast between Roman law, as emanating from the "sovereign power of the state," and Jewish law, as depending purely on religious morality.[78] To accept this distinction would have been to admit that Jewish law was lower down the chain of legal evolution, to portray it as religious law incapable of properly enforcing social order, and therefore inferior to the law of a modern sovereign state. Consequently, Herzog took pains to emphasize the efficiency and sovereignty of Jewish law. Like Roman law, Herzog wrote,

> Jewish law was likewise eager to maintain public peace and order, but it was not so ready as Roman law to enact sweeping measures by which

the rights of the individual would be sacrificed in the interests of the mass. . . . Jewish law was not altogether devoid of a system of discipline, but it kept that system within certain limits and bounds.[79]

In other words, Jewish law perfectly balanced a high moral standard with effectiveness in maintaining law and order. Unlike Roman law, Jewish law was capable of enforcing social order without sacrificing the "rights of the individual."

Centralizing Law

The evolutionary approach to law, with which Herzog constantly engaged, went beyond questions of morality and effectiveness. According to theories of legal evolution, the most advanced structure of a legal system was legal centralism. By contrast with the disorganized, decentralized, and arbitrary rules of primitive and tribal societies, the argument went, more evolved modern states centralized all law into a single rational, systematic, and hierarchical structure of norms. Here too, Herzog also accepted the premises of this aspect of European jurisprudence and attempted to demonstrate, against the preponderance of evidence, that Jewish law fits this model as well as any modern European legal system.

From the nineteenth century on, a series of legal reforms centralized the legal structure of many European jurisdictions. Before that point, English law, for example, had been criticized for being a disorganized muddle of overlapping legal systems. Of particular concern for critics was the parallel operation of the Courts of Common Law and the Court of Chancery. The Courts of Common Law, sometimes simply called Courts of Law, employed a corpus of judicial precedent that had grown up over many centuries. The Court of Chancery, also called the Court of Equity, was established in the Middle Ages as a mechanism for the Lord Chancellor to impose more equitable solutions in cases in which the common law solution was considered unjust. By the nineteenth century, however, chancery and common law had each developed into fully independent systems that had virtually coextensive jurisdictions and competed for business.[80] This state of affairs was widely considered to be deeply unsatisfactory. English law was convoluted, expensive, and difficult to use. Already in the previous century, the jurist William Blackstone had observed that "[i]t seems the height of judicial absurdity, that in the same cause [*sic*] between the same parties, in the examination of the same facts, a discovery by the oath of the parties should be permitted on one side of Westminster Hall, and denied on the other."[81] The Chancery courts were particularly vilified. They were the object of satire in Charles Dickens's *Bleak House* and the target of reformers such as Jeremy Bentham, who called its procedures "a volume of notorious lies" and wanted to reform all of English law to produce a centralized, rational, unified system.[82]

As a result of this kind of agitation, a series of far-reaching reforms was enacted from 1867 to 1873, with supplementary reforms continuing until the end of the century. Under the reforms, all English courts were unified into a single legal system. The reforms were popular.[83] Walter Bagehot, a contemporary writer, observed with approval that they ushered in a "new Constitution."[84] Essentially, the reforms had brought about a nationwide shift from legal pluralism to legal centralism.

The centralization of law was not unique to England; it was a hallmark of modern European law. Prior to the nineteenth century, Europe was split into innumerable localities, each governed by its own heteronomous laws. The rise of the modern nation state was accompanied by the consolidation of state power through the imposition of a single law within state boundaries. This goal was achieved by the creation of new national legal codes that were intended to bring the rigors of Enlightenment positivism to the field of law and clarity and uniformity to the legal systems of modern states.[85] The earliest example was the Napoleonic Code, a French civil code enacted in 1804. A decade later, after the beginning of German unification with the Congress of Vienna, progress began toward a German legal code.[86] Legal unification culminated with the *Bürgerliches Gesetzbuch* (BGB), Germany's civil code, which was begun in the aftermath of the final unification of Germany in 1871 and finally adopted in 1900. The BGB became the archetypal civil code and was the basis of much subsequent European legislation and codification. By Herzog's time, therefore, the move toward a rational, centralized, and ordered system of law had been adopted by virtually the entire legal establishment of Great Britain and Europe. It was taken for granted that legal centralism—the organization of all norms in the state into a single hierarchical structure—was superior to a legally pluralist regime in which different systems of law operated in parallel.

According to this new jurisprudence, Jewish law was vulnerable to significant criticism. Halakha was a totally decentralized system of law. It was not connected to any state. Its laws, far from being organized into a systematic code, were scattered over centuries of cryptic texts of different genres. No book of Jewish law was regarded as universally authoritative. Rabbinical judges were not part of a single, ordered system; every rabbinical court was independent and there was no formal relationship between one court and the next. Jews all over the world followed different laws, depending on their local customs and the judgment of their local leaders.

As part of his triumphal apologetics for Jewish law, Herzog attempted to show that halakha did in fact meet, or exceed, the standards of modern jurisprudence, even in terms of its centralized structure. Rather than challenging the prevailing belief in the superiority of legal centralism over legal pluralism, Herzog tried to demonstrate that halakha really was a legally centralist system. This impulse to show that halakha comported to what Herzog, and everyone around him, had come to regard as the most evolved and rational structure of law often required him to interpret halakhic sources in radical ways.[87]

Between 1931 and 1932, Herzog wrote a series of four articles entitled "The Administration of Justice in Ancient Israel."[88] In these articles, Herzog argued that Jewish law, even in ancient times, was not a jumbled collection of primitive rules but a system of law no less centralized, structured, efficient, and rational than a modern constitution.

Herzog's forced interpretations in support of this position are most evident in his discussion of ancient Israel's judicial institutions. According to talmudic and medieval sources, there were three kinds of courts in ancient Israel. The Great Sanhedrin of seventy-one judges sat in Jerusalem, a Small Sanhedrin of twenty-three judges sat in cities of more than 120 residents, and smaller towns could have ad hoc courts of three judges, made up of laymen (*hedyotot*), rather than ordained judges.[89] The Great and Small Sanhedrins could judge any case, including capital cases, whereas the courts of three judges could judge only civil cases. One source also mentions a "tribal court," whose purpose is debated among talmudic commentaries.[90]

Herzog set himself the task of explaining three features of this judicial structure that would have made it seem bizarre to modern European jurists. First, modern jurists would have considered it unsustainable, to require a town of only 120 residents to have twenty-three residents qualified as judges capable of sentencing people to death. Second, they would have considered it unprofessional to allow untrained laymen to administer justice in ad hoc courts. Third, they would have considered the absence of a hierarchical system of courts organized under a unified state to be primitive.

Herzog noted that Asher Gulak, the great Mishpat Ivri scholar, was also "fully congnisant of the difficulty entailed by the statement that every town of 120 citizens and upwards had to be furnished with a Sanhedrin of 23."[91] According to Herzog, Gulak's explanation for this phenomenon was that most of the judges on these Small Sanhedrins were not in fact legal experts, but community "elders" who were "ordinary laymen." [92] Gulak's description corresponded closely to Henry Sumner Maine's description of tribal law, which was, in Maine's taxonomy, close to the lowest rung of legal evolution. As a result, Herzog, at pains to show Jewish law to be highly evolved and civilized, was deeply dissatisfied with this description. Instead, Herzog entirely reinterpreted the traditional sources pertaining to the court of twenty-three judges. Contrary to the plain meaning of the rabbinical sources and their key interpreters such as Maimonides, Herzog claimed that the law did not *require* every town of 120 or more residents to have a court of twenty-three judges; rather, it *permitted* them to have one. Any other reading,

Herzog claimed, was inconceivable, considering that local elders untrained in the law would hardly have been capable of sitting on capital cases. Herzog defended his reading of the sources not by reference to halakhic texts, nor to historical evidence, but by appeal to an a priori assertion that Jewish law simply must have fit the model of centralized systematic legal systems: "It will hardly avail us to assume that during the early periods such cases were tried by the assembly of citizens in each locality and not by a distinctive body possessing specific qualifications and specially appointed for that purpose."[93]

In this passage, Herzog revealed his basic assumption that, even in antiquity, Jewish law was applied by a "distinctive body" with "specific qualifications." In his view, there were not Sanhedrins made up of legally untrained elders in every village, as the sources imply. Rather, these courts were few in number and composed of expert judges. In Herzog's interpretation, each of these courts was "district court, covering by its jurisdiction a large and distinct area."[94] He thereby made them resemble a level of the centralized hierarchy of a modern European state.

Herzog similarly reinterpreted the sources regarding the ad hoc three-person lay courts. The Talmud describes them as courts of *hedyotot*, courts of laymen with no particular legal training, a kind of arbitration panel made up of peers of the disputants. Herzog acknowledged that to the modern reader, this arrangement seemed to be "rather startling." He imagined his readers wondering "what kind of a judicial system would that be under which a plaintiff could compel the defendant to appear before any three men he may choose?"[95]

Herzog had two strategies to address this quandary. He vastly limited the application of these courts of arbitration, claiming that they were only to be used where regular courts were unavailable.[96] He also reinterpreted the meaning of *hedyot* to be a technical term meaning an expert fully trained in the law, but without formal rabbinical ordination. Thus, he argued, the courts of three were not made up of laymen at all but rather "expert-jurists, authorized by the [Jewish] Babylonian authorities."[97] Once again, Herzog cast the courts of ancient Israel in a light more palatable to modern attitudes by attributing to them standards of legal qualifications conventional in contemporary legal systems.

Herzog was also determined to demonstrate that the Jewish judicial structure was, and always had been, centralized and hierarchical. He noted that according to the Bible, the royal charter granted to Ezra in the sixth century BCE referred to judges by two different names, *shoftim* and *dayanim*. This nomenclature, Herzog claimed, showed that the charter "contemplated a grading of the judiciary into a higher and a lower order."[98] According to Herzog, the first, higher-order court was the *Knesset ha-gedolah*, the "Great Assembly," which sat at the pinnacle of the national legal and political hierarchy. Herzog dismissed the scholarly consensus that if the assembly had ever existed, it did so in a form very different from the one described in the talmudic sources. "Whatever the critics may say," he declared, "the historicity of that body cannot be questioned by sound, really scientific criticism."[99] Herzog defined the body as "a kind of academic-legal assembly charged with the reorganizing of Jewish life, private and public, in accordance with the letter and the spirit of the Torah and the Prophets."[100] Herzog refined this rather vague description in a later work. In doing so, he made it clear that he imagined the Great Assembly as something like a modern house of representatives, "a kind of legislating parliament, enacting laws in the framework of the limitations established by the written and oral Torah."[101] According to Herzog, this assembly eventually developed into the Great Sanhedrin of seventy-one judges, which he also identified in modern constitutional terms, calling it "the highest authority of the nation" and its "Supreme Court and legislative body."[102]

In these articles, then, Herzog attempted to present Jewish law according to the categories of modern European law. Even the most ancient Jewish legal institutions, in Herzog's reconstructions, were parallel to contemporary British institutions such as the Supreme Court, district courts, and parliament. Herzog's reading of the Jewish sources confronted both the neglect of Jewish law by Christian scholars and the "inferiority complex" of Jewish scholars. It presented Jewish law in "modern Western" terms to show that it was the equal, or even the superior, of contemporary European codes and constitutions.

The tension at the heart of Herzog's scholarship—by which he set out to illustrate both that the genius and moral superiority of Jewish law make it incomparable to other legal traditions, and also that Jewish law conformed to the categories and idioms of modern European legal theory—is the key to understanding his attitude toward the laws and constitution of the State of Israel. Herzog rejected outright the idea, held by many religious Zionists before him, that a Jewish state could have two sources of legal authority in parallel. This raises the question of why Herzog rejected the legal pluralism of so many of his religious Zionist precursors. The question is especially strong, given that legal pluralism was popular among religious Zionists for good reason. It was well rooted in rabbinic precedent; it solved the problem of the inadequacy of halakha to deal with the governance of a modern state; it removed the need to convince the secular majority of Zionists, and the international community, to accept a legal system that discriminated against women and non-Jews; and it protected halakha from the change that would necessarily come about if it became the formal law of an entire state.

Herzog's early writings on Jewish law help to explain his rejection of legal pluralism in a Jewish state. Before coming to Palestine, he had spent decades arguing for a vision of halakha that would satisfy the standards of modern European jurisprudence. A Jewish state on the model of legal pluralism would be vulnerable to the kinds of criticism against which he had been defending halakha for his entire adult life. It would indicate that halakha could operate only in the context of a legal structure that modern Europe had left behind. By contrast, a legally centralist Jewish state, in which halakha was the only legal system, might demonstrate how halakha lived up to the standards of modern European law.

On one occasion, Herzog explicitly connected his disapproval of legal pluralism with the history of British legal reform. In response to Haim Ozer Grodzinski's suggestion that the Jewish state should set up parallel halakhic and state courts, Herzog responded, "I maintain my position that it is inconceivable that the laws of the Torah should allow for two parallel authorities, like the Courts of Law and the Courts of Equity, the latter stemming from the authority of royal law, that operated in England in the past."[103]

Herzog's reference to nineteenth-century English law would have been quite obscure even to most of his contemporary readers. It makes total sense, however, in the context of Herzog's intellectual formation and his approach to the defense of halakha to which he had dedicated so much of his early scholarship. Herzog knew that in England there had been two distinct court systems, the "Courts of Law" and the "Courts of Equity." He also knew that the existence of two parallel courts, each with its own procedure and laws, had resulted in widely mocked chaos and that Britain, like many countries in Europe, had abolished this system in favor of one that was deemed more evolved, centralized, and rational. Herzog could not tolerate the possibility that the Torah, a perfect and divine law, could be applied in a modern Jewish state only in the context of a pluralist legal structure that was derided by European jurists as primitive and inferior. Such an outcome would have negated the claim, fundamental to Herzog's lifework, that halakha was at least as advanced than modern legal systems. The legal pluralism that many early religious Zionists considered to be the natural structure of law in a Jewish state was "inconceivable" to Herzog because his approach to the organization of law and its institutions was shaped by the domination of legal centralism in Britain and in Europe in general.

Herzog's attention to the legal theory of his day only intensified upon his move to Palestine. The principles of legal evolution and legal centralism that determined the jurisprudence of European states took on a more powerful significance in their colonies. Herzog arrived in Palestine at the moment that European colonies were beginning to win their independence from imperial powers. Legal theory had become a critical weapon in this struggle. Newly independent states established their legitimacy by holding up their own law as the equal of the law of the imperial center. After he arrived in Palestine, the tendency of Herzog's earlier scholarship to portray Jewish law as a superior version of modern European jurisprudence coincided with the colonial context of the Zionist aspiration for independence from the British Mandate. It was these circumstances that provided the background to Herzog's attempt to apply Jewish law in a Jewish state, which he and his colleagues took up in earnest at the end of the 1940s.

3

A CONSTITUTION FOR ISRAEL ACCORDING TO THE TORAH

Early 1948 was a tense time for the Zionist movement. In November 1947, the UN had voted in favor of the partition of Palestine, but it was not until May 1948 that the British were scheduled to withdraw. In the meantime, war had erupted between Jews and Arabs. During all the turmoil, Zionist leaders were setting the groundwork for the legal and political structure of the future Jewish state. Even before the name of the Jewish state was decided, constitutional drafts were produced. Almost every draft constitution seriously considered by the Zionist leadership stated that the future Jewish state would have a secular constitution. The seat of its political authority and the author of its laws would be the body of its citizens, not God or the Jewish tradition.

An exception was a constitutional draft written by Isaac Herzog. He had been working on a constitution for some years and his prescription was clear. The Jewish state had to be a theocracy, he wrote. "Is it necessary for the Jewish state which recognizes the decisive rule of the Torah to be a theocracy? The answer is clear and simple: Yes and yes!"[1]

To the twenty-first-century reader, the idea that an Orthodox rabbi like Herzog would voice a desire for the state to be ruled by religious law seems unremarkable, especially since he had spent his career in writing about what he took to be the superiority of Jewish law. Today, such a position is the clarion call of politicized religious leaders the world over. Indeed, several modern constitutions are based on religious laws.[2] In Israel today, most people take for granted that religious Zionist rabbis would want the state to be run by halakha. This was not, however, a typical position among religious Zionists at the time, and Herzog's commitment to a halakhic state would have been an outlier before the end of the 1940s. So why did Herzog think the way he did? And why has his outlook become so established that, today, few people know that there was ever an alternative approach?

The Invention of Jewish Theocracy. Alexander Kaye, Oxford University Press (2020). © Oxford University Press.
DOI: 10.1093/oso/9780190922740.001.0001

Between Theocracy and Democracy

Herzog began his work on the constitution of a Jewish state at around the time that he was appointed as Chief Rabbi of Palestine, in 1937. His work took a long hiatus of almost a decade after the outbreak of World War II, during which time Herzog's attention was focused on the plight of European Jews. During those years, Herzog devoted huge efforts to the cause of the Jews of Europe.[3] In 1938, he requested that his friend Éamon de Valera, by then the prime minister of the Irish Free State, accept Jewish doctors who had been ousted from their positions in Nazi Germany. In 1939 and 1940, Herzog again recruited de Valera, along with other acquaintances from Ireland, such as Cardinal Joseph MacRory, to help him secure an audience with the pope, with a view to enlisting the Vatican in the cause of Jewish refugees. In the early 1940s, Herzog utilized every possible diplomatic connection to find paths for Jews out of Nazi Europe, including his personal acquaintance with Ivan Maisky, the Soviet ambassador to Great Britain, who was Jewish.[4] Herzog also worked to secure the passage of students and teachers from Polish yeshivot to Palestine or other countries such as the United States, Australia, or even Rhodesia, a British colony. After the war, Herzog spent almost ten months of 1946 in traveling around Europe and endeavoring to bring Jewish refugees to a safe haven, in Palestine or anywhere else.

Herzog's approach to the crisis of European Jewry, like that of many rabbis, differed from that of the secular leaders of the Jewish Agency, the organization that oversaw Jewish immigration to Palestine. To be sure, the Jewish Agency did what it could to save vulnerable Jews. It placed this objective, however, in the context of its primary goal of achieving a Jewish state. This goal led to disagreements with Herzog, as well as other religious Zionists. After the British essentially closed Palestine to Jewish immigration at the time European Jews most needed a place to go, Herzog and his religious Zionist allies developed strategies designed to avoid the British restrictions. One was the use of fictitious marriages between Jews from Palestine and Europe, which were followed by quick divorces after visas were secured. The official position of the Jewish Agency was to oppose this practice out of a pragmatic desire to remain in good standing with the British. What visas were available the Jewish Agency preferred to allocate to Jewish immigrants who were perceived as helping the Zionist cause. This preference generally meant young secular Zionists. Non-Zionist Orthodox yeshiva students, whom the Zionist leadership saw as the archetypal "exilic" Jews, were low on the list. Herzog sharply objected to these policies, insisting that saving lives had to take precedence over political goals. Although he never openly transgressed the wishes of the Jewish Agency, he also never stopped pushing for the immigration of all Jews, irrespective of their utility to the Zionist enterprise, and he encouraged the rabbinate to officiate over fictitious marriages and divorces until new legislation made the practice ineffective.[5] He also worked extremely hard—traveling endlessly, raising money, and engaging diplomatically—on behalf of Orthodox Jews, who were deprioritized by the Jewish Agency. To do so, he took part in a network of American and British rabbis and raised funds independently. His efforts resulted in the rescue of many rabbinical leaders of European Jewry.[6] These actions were not always encouraged by the Zionist leadership, who even attempted to prevent his winter 1940 visit to London, where he hoped to acquire visas for some of Europe's Orthodox Jews. The Jewish Agency preferred to restrict such negotiations to the formal channels, and was reluctant to make an exception for Orthodox students.[7]

Herzog's work for the rescue of European Jews must have had a significant impact on his thinking about a halakhic constitution for the Jewish state. He witnessed firsthand the effect of the Holocaust on Orthodox Jews. Many of the great institutions and leaders of Torah scholarship were destroyed during those years, and the future existence of Orthodoxy was itself in question. Furthermore, it was made clear that most of the secular leaders of the Zionist movement had little interest in the survival of halakhic life. Herzog likely felt that the continuation of the world of the Torah rested on his shoulders and those of his Orthodox allies.

With these experiences fresh in Herzog's mind, he revisited the question of the constitution at the end of 1947, once the war was over and statehood imminent. In August 1947, at a meeting of the Council of the Chief Rabbinate, he urged a focus on "setting up a program for the constitution of the state in the framework of the Torah."[8] He was likely motivated by the fact that the Va'ad Le'umi, the Jewish National Council that would form the basis of the government of Israel, had formed its own committee for the writing of the constitution. Its chairman was Zerah Warhaftig, a member of the religious Zionist Mizrahi party, who was eager to incorporate his consultations with Herzog and other rabbis into the committee's deliberations.[9] Herzog decided to write a constitution himself and convened a committee of rabbis who would review it. He also conferred on the subject with experts in secular law, such as Gad Frumkin, an Orthodox Jew who would become one of the first justices of the state's Supreme Court.[10]

Herzog planned to publish a draft constitution, which was in effect a short thesis of eighteen chapters dealing with the theory of democracy and theocracy, political and judicial appointments, rabbinical enactments, elections, taxes, the presidency and ministries, the police force and army, education, the place of religion in the state, the Chief Rabbinate, and other matters.[11] Ultimately, Herzog completed only six of the eighteen chapters, of which only one was published in his lifetime.[12] The fact that the work was never completed can be attributed in part to the many pressing matters competing for Herzog's attention after the foundation of the state, in part to his eventual acceptance that his constitution would never be implemented, and in part, perhaps, to failing health in his later years. In 1989, Herzog's extant writings in connection with the constitution and related material were published by Itamar Warhaftig, Zerah Warhaftig's son, under the title *Constitution for Israel According to the Torah*.[13]

Although Herzog never finished the constitution, it is possible to piece together his constitutional and jurisprudential thinking from the chapters that do exist, in conjunction with Herzog's other writings. In Herzog's vision, the entire state would be governed by a single law: halakha. "The aspiration of all of religious Judaism in Israel and the Diaspora," he wrote, "should be that the constitution include a basic clause that the law of the land is based on the foundations of the Torah."[14]

Although Herzog explicitly described his constitution as theocratic, he knew that it also had to be democratic. On the face of it, these two constitutional approaches are mutually exclusive. Herzog, therefore, went to great pains to demonstrate that his idea of a theocracy was compatible with democracy. It is not clear if he was motivated by a genuinely egalitarian impulse or by the pragmatic concern that he had to convince secular Zionists (who made up the majority of Jews in Palestine, including virtually all of the political elite) to adopt his constitution. The bulk of Herzog's writings indicate that pragmatism was his main motivation and that his concessions to liberal considerations were intended to reassure secular Zionists that halakha would be consistent (or consistent enough) with their values. But Herzog also had to sway an entirely different constituency to his perspective. He had to convince more traditionalist Orthodox leaders, many of whom were not full supporters of the Zionist enterprise, that the goal of halakhic rule was worth the cost of being creative with the interpretation of traditional texts. Many of Herzog's writings on this topic were directed at this religiously conservative constituency. They were composed in a Hebrew saturated with references to rabbinic texts and specialized halakhic shorthand. Herzog did not take for granted his reputation among Orthodox rabbis in Palestine. Although nobody doubted Herzog's prowess as a halakhic scholar, some more conservative rabbis were suspicious about his Western education. The Ultra-Orthodox community of Palestine nominated Yaakov Moshe Harlap, a pupil of Abraham Isaac Kook, as a candidate to oppose Herzog in the election for the chief rabbi, which took place in 1936. Herzog won the election by a decisive majority but it is possible that in his rabbinic writings he still had an eye toward cultivating support among his more conservative colleagues.[15] It is therefore possible that Herzog was more progressive than his writings attest and that his dismissive remarks about liberal values were intended to appease critics for whom adherence to Torah outweighed any democratic considerations. It is more likely, though, that Herzog was

genuinely ambivalent about the values of liberal democracy and that his concessions to democracy were motivated mainly by pragmatism rather than principle.

Either way, Herzog wrote with conviction about the necessity of modifying
halakha, for it to be "in accord with the democratic nature of the state."[16] He knew
that the majority of Jews in the state, "which is far from knowledge of the Torah
and to our regret does not totally adhere to our holy tradition," would have to be
persuaded to go along with his constitutional plans.[17] He also knew that the constitution of Israel would have to be in accord with the United Nations Partition
Plan, which required the new Jewish state to have a democratic constitution, to
elect a legislative body by universal suffrage, and not to allow political, civil, or
any other discrimination against any person.[18] "The establishment of the Jewish
state," Herzog noted, "is largely dependent on the guarantee of those rights in
the spirit of that pact."[19] For it to succeed, he knew that his constitution would
therefore have to be both theocratic and democratic: "The Jewish state . . . must
of necessity be neither a total theocracy, nor a total democracy, but theocratic-
democratic. . . . But this hyphenation requires deep study and great attention and
thought on the part of Torah scholars."[20]

Much of Herzog's writing on the constitution was an attempt to describe
the nature of this hybrid relationship between theocracy and democracy. The
challenges inherent to this project were the same as those faced by all religious
Zionists. Like Margulies, Gorontchik, and others, Herzog noted that, according to halakha, neither women nor non-Jews were permitted to take up positions of political authority, to become judges, or to give testimony in a court of
law.[21] Furthermore, Herzog acknowledged, halakhic criminal and civil law was
not developed enough to govern a modern state.[22] He recognized that a failure to
address these issues would pose problems that were "impossible to surmount."[23]
Legal pluralists allowed the existence of a legal regime for the state distinct from
halakha, and thus allowed them to preserve halakha while also providing for a
parallel state law that would be acceptable to all citizens. Herzog's commitment
to legal centralism prevented him from embracing this solution. With halakha as
the only legal regime in the state, he had no option but to propose modifications
to halakha in order to make it fit with modern democracy.

There is, however, a mood of reluctance that pervades Herzog's writings on
democracy. He lamented the fact that Orthodox Jews were not in the majority
and the concessions that he was forced to make sometimes made him balk. He
was particularly reluctant to address the question of gender equality with regard
to judicial appointments. The idea of women on the bench, he wrote, was something that "surely we must oppose . . . with all force."[24] He noted that even many
democracies did not allow women to be judges and wondered "why should those
who campaign for democracy be even more democratic than many democratic

states?" It is difficult to say which states Herzog had in mind but it is certainly true that at that time, even in countries where women de jure qualified for the judiciary, they were severely underrepresented on the bench. In Britain, for example, the judiciary was officially opened to women in 1919, but the first female judge was not appointed until 1945. In the United States, as Herzog was writing, fewer than 1.5 percent of judges at the state or federal level were women.[25] Grudgingly, however, Herzog recognized that this argument was unlikely to persuade others and acknowledged that there was no way the people would accept a halakhic constitution that did not allow women to be judges. Even as he urged his followers to continue to oppose gender parity in the judiciary "to the fullest extent that we are able," he reluctantly accepted that the "evil day" would eventually arrive when women would be appointed to the bench.[26] He therefore began to look for halakhic justifications of this undesirable outcome because otherwise, he knew, his dreams of a halakhic constitution would have no hope of success.

Ultimately, Herzog's desire for a halakhic constitution that was acceptable to liberal democrats was so strong that it overrode his misgivings about egalitarianism. Herzog felt that a Jewish state that did not give full rights to non-Jews would imperil the lives of Jews around the world. This was especially the case in the context of the period. After the Holocaust, he felt, Jews "dispersed among the nations" were particularly vulnerable. He thought that establishing a halakhic state "according to how the simple meaning of halakha appears at first glance" would endanger Jews in other countries. In such a state, "non-Jewish residents would be discriminated against to a large degree," a fate that would "expose [Jews] to retaliation."[27] Having witnessed the destruction of European Jewry, Herzog was more determined than ever to preserve the rights of Jews wherever they happened to live. Without rights, he believed, Jews would suffer dishonor, which could have catastrophic consequences. "For in this era known as modernity, dishonor will eventually result in total contempt and total contempt will bring the contemptuous to thoughts—which will result in actions—that [Jews should be] denied human rights and that their blood and possessions are free for the taking."[28]

Herzog therefore felt that the danger to Jews around the world that would result from the establishment of a discriminatory legal regime in Israel was so grave that it should override any halakhic reservations:

> We have been given the opportunity to accept from the [United] Nations the power to establish a Jewish state in the land of Israel, but on condition that we tolerate those of other faiths . . . What should we do? [Should we] tell the nations: We are unable to accept this condition because our holy Torah prohibits a Jewish state from permitting Christians, and *a fortiori*

idolaters, to live in our land, and moreover it forbids us from permitting their worship in our land and forbids us from allowing them to rent land? It seems to me that there is no rabbi in Israel in his right mind who would think that we have to respond in that way, meaning that this is what the holy Torah requires of us.[29]

The basis of Herzog's argument was that in such an extreme situation it would be proper to accept any halakhic leniency that was necessary to secure international recognition of a Jewish state. This view rested on the well-established halakhic axiom that preservation of life takes precedence over almost any other religious consideration. "Even if the Jewish state would be sinning by fulfilling the condition[s of the UN]," he wrote, "I would still say that the sin is overridden by the threat to the life of the Jewish people."[30]

Despite the halakhic significance of the need to save Jewish lives, however, Herzog was unwilling to base his entire position on it. He knew that he would be more convincing to his rabbinical colleagues if he could prove that conventional halakhic reasoning supported the establishment of a halakhic-democratic state, without needing to appeal to the extenuating circumstances of Jewish vulnerability. He therefore insisted that "[w]e do not need to rely on leniencies arising from the fact that the Jewish state [is required to] save the nation" because "according to the law itself there is no sin here according to my opinion."[31] Much of Herzog's constitutional writing was dedicated to providing a persuasive halakhic rationale for an egalitarian, inclusive halakhic state.

Herzog's challenge, then, was "to solve the problem of the harmonization of a democratic government of Torah" by creating a model of a Jewish democracy that would fend off criticisms from both secular Zionists and halakhic purists.[32] The key was to find an epithet for a form of government that would be acceptable to traditionalists and liberals alike. One term that Herzog considered was "theocracy." The term did not originate with Herzog. It was the ancient Jewish historian Josephus who coined the word, in the second century CE, defining it as a system of government that "ascribes the authority and the power to God."[33] The most prominent discussion of theocracy came much later, in Spinoza's *Theological-Political Treatise*, published in 1670. Like Josephus, Spinoza also called the ancient Hebrew constitution a theocracy, defining it as a constitution in which "all their citizens had to swear allegiance to God, their supreme judge, to whom alone they had promised absolute obedience in all things."[34] Spinoza's analysis had a very particular contemporary application. He used his historical reconstruction of the Hebrew constitution to argue in favor of Erastianism, the principle (named for the sixteenth-century Swiss theologian, Thomas Erastus) that the civil sovereign should have complete control over religion.[35] According to Spinoza, Moses, and even God, after Moses's death, were civil sovereigns who had full control over religious law rather than religious leaders with civil authority. This belief supported the Erastian position of the subordination of religious law to civil government.[36]

Herzog's use of the term was different. He used "theocracy" as a blanket term for a state ruled by God's law. He had different preoccupations from those of Josephus, who had no interest in combining theocracy with democracy. He also disagreed with Spinoza's vision; contrary to Spinoza's argument against clerical authority, Herzog expected rabbis and rabbinical law to have pride of place in the Jewish state. But, even though he was aware that in the twentieth century the term would repel liberals, Herzog did not shy away from using it. He defied those who used the term pejoratively. "Say what you will! Say that [a halakhic state] is a theocracy!" he reproached his opponents. He caustically observed that the international community was happy to accept a Muslim theocracy located only a few miles away from Palestine. "Look at Saudi Arabia!" he proclaimed. "You all recognize it and you all run after it because of its oil. Yet it maintains a government, police force and legal system which is absolutely theocratic."[37]

On other occasions, though, Herzog was more circumspect. He acknowledged that "theocracy" was not a popular term and he was sensitive to the fact it conjured up images of a state ruled by religious functionaries.[38] He therefore made it clear that, by theocracy, he meant not the rule of rabbis but the rule of law, albeit religious law. In a 1953 article, Herzog alighted on a more felicitous term for the kind of state he had in mind: nomocracy. "The Jewish state," he wrote, "according to its traditional structure, is neither a complete theocracy nor a complete democracy, but a nomocracy."[39] A nomocracy, he explained, "is rule of law. But not the rule of any law; the rule of the divine law, the heavenly Torah."[40]

Herzog did not invent the term "nomocracy." It was a term apparently first used to describe the ancient Jewish constitution. The *Oxford English Dictionary* identifies the earliest use of the word in print as the 1829 *The History of the Jews* by the English priest Henry Hart Milman. The book was still in print during Herzog's lifetime and it seems reasonable that a voracious reader like Herzog might have encountered this popular English work about the Jews. Indeed, Milman's description of "nomocracy" is reminiscent of Herzog's: "If God was not the sovereign of the Jewish state, the Law was . . . If the Hebrew commonwealth was not a theocracy, it was a nomocracy."[41]

Notably, the term also occurs in a 1901 work by Oscar Straus, who became the first Jewish cabinet secretary in the United States, serving as the Secretary of Commerce and Labor under President Theodore Roosevelt. Straus sought to trace the origins of the republican form of government in the United States to "the direct and indirect influence of the Hebrew Commonwealth." He wrote,

"This [ancient Jewish] government, from the fact that God, the source of all power, the embodiment of the law, and not a king, was ruler of the nation, is termed by various writers a Theocracy, or Nomocracy (from nomos, meaning law), or a Commonwealth."[42] Like Milman and Straus, Herzog used the term "nomocracy" to emphasize the role of law in the Jewish constitution.

The term "nomocracy" performed an additional function for Herzog. It aided his attempt to convince skeptics that a halakhic constitution was essentially no different from the constitution of a modern European state. In the ancient Jewish state, which Herzog called a "theocratic monarchy," the king was "placed under the sovereignty of the Torah, just like the king of a democratic state is placed under the authority of the constitution and the law." [43] By making the analogy between the ancient Jewish king and the kings of contemporary democracies, Herzog enhanced the legitimacy of the Jewish constitution by comparing it with the constitutional model of many European states, not least the United Kingdom, which was ruling Palestine at the time these lines were written. He was implicitly indicating that the Jewish constitution, just like Britain's, defined a monarchy in which the king was subject to law. This move is familiar from his earlier writings, in which he strove to legitimize Jewish law in the eyes of non-Jewish critics by demonstrating its similarity to systems of law that were widely accepted (by Europeans, at least) as the most advanced, moral, and efficient in the world.

In a further comparison between his reconstruction of a halakhic state and modern constitutions, Herzog found a counterpart for the Great Sanhedrin, which he called the "main supreme power" in the Jewish state, in modern parliaments.[44] Although he acknowledged that the Sanhedrin was a court, on several occasions Herzog explicitly compared the Sanhedrin with a parliament, remarking that "the role of the parliament was filled by the Great Sanhedrin in no small way."[45] Elsewhere, he described the "Great Assembly," which in rabbinical literature is often considered the precursor of the Sanhedrin, as "a kind of legislative parliament, enacting laws according to the procedures set up by the written and transmitted Torah; a parliament, only not in the modern sense."[46]

Herzog self-consciously described a halakhic constitution in terms that explicitly likened it to the modern European state. For Herzog, the halakhic state is governed by the rule of law. Its power is organized in a single centralized hierarchy, according to which all legal authority derives from the sovereign. The king of Israel, like the kings of constitutional democratic monarchies, or the presidents of republican governments, was entirely subordinate to that sovereign authority. Furthermore, the halakhic constitution appoints a body whose task is to interpret old laws and create new ones. In the modern state, this role is taken by the parliament; in the ancient Jewish state it was taken by the Sanhedrin.

Herzog's subordination of the Jewish king to the law is significant beyond the fact that he used it to align his constitution with modern democracies. The "king's law" was the cornerstone of religious Zionist legal pluralism from Abraham Isaac Kook onward. According to legal pluralists, the king's law was not subordinate to halakha but rather an independent parallel legal system. The king represented the possibility of a distinct legal authority outside of halakha. Herzog sharply diverged from this approach. For him, the king's law was not parallel to halakha but subordinate to it. Herzog's Jewish constitution allowed for only one centralized system of law deriving from a single sovereign constitution: the Torah.

Strategies for Inclusion

Having laid the basis for the structure of his constitution, Herzog went on to address the potential conflicts between halakha and democracy. His primary focus was on the question of whether, and, if so how, to allow non-Orthodox Jews, women and non-Jews to be judges. Herzog made clear that he would ideally want his judiciary to be limited to Orthodox Jewish men, who were experts in Torah law. The requirements of democracy, however, demanded a compromise. Herzog was unwilling to depend on halakhic leniencies, justified by the need to preserve life. He felt that this halakhic mechanism would not have been a sustainable basis for a halakhic constitution, so he searched for other grounds for inclusion.

Herzog's initial proposal did not recommend full inclusion. He suggested that the state should have two kinds of courts, one called "rabbinical" and the other "state" (*memshalti*).[47] The rabbinical courts would have jurisdiction over personal status law and the state courts would judge civil matters.[48] Although this proposal appears to be similar to that of religious Zionist legal pluralists who advocated the establishment of parallel halakhic and civil courts, it is in fact quite different. For Herzog, both rabbinical judges and the state's civil judges would apply halakha in their courts. "Torah law," he wrote, "is also the legal code of these [civil] courts."[49] Indeed, Herzog thought that the state courts should even prosecute people for some religious transgressions, such as the public desecration of the Sabbath and sexual immorality.[50] Furthermore, for Herzog, both civil courts and rabbinical courts would have to satisfy halakhic procedural rules. Even civil courts would require at least three judges, the minimum size of a rabbinical court. He also wanted civil judges to be male Orthodox Jews. If this were impossible, he wanted them to be people with a basic respect for religious tradition, who, "at least, are not known to transgress the Sabbath or eat non-kosher food in public," and therefore would not "cause pain and strife in the heart of the believing community."[51]

So, in contrast to the pluralist model, even Herzog's "state courts" would be halakhic courts in both substance and procedure. The only distinction between "rabbinical" and "state" courts was one of jurisdiction. Herzog's proposed court system, just like that of many European states, would have different courts for family law and civil law. In Herzog's system, judges in the family courts, because of the complicated nature of family law and its critical importance for religious integrity, would have to meet higher qualifications of religious commitment and halakhic knowledge than the judges in the criminal and civil courts did. All courts, however, would be governed by, and apply, halakhic law.

Herzog realized that in practice this system could never be implemented. The exclusion of women, non-Orthodox Jewish men, and non-Jews from the judiciary would arouse "the opposition of large sectors of the public on the basis of the principle of the personal freedom of religion."[52] Herzog considered creating courts for non-Jewish citizens of Israel, "two jurisdictions and two laws, for Jews as appropriate for them, and for Arabs as appropriate for them."[53] This plan would have avoided the halakhically problematic situation of a non-Jew judging a Jew in a court run according to the Torah. But Herzog knew well that this position would also not have been accepted. The state's leaders, he believed, would claim "that this is not the way to arrive at peace and serious, free, political unity."[54]

Therefore, Herzog had to devise more far-reaching solutions. He was not willing to compromise on his position that all courts in the state must apply halakha. Within this framework, though, he attempted to devise a way to allow nonreligious, female, and non-Jewish judges to sit on those courts.

Herzog's first suggestion was to sidestep the question altogether. The halakhic prohibition of allowing non-Jews into positions of power applies only to formal political-legal authority. Halakha does not, though, prohibit business partnerships between Jews and non-Jews. Herzog observed that if the state was defined not as a political entity but as a voluntary association, "a kind of [business] partnership," then the exclusionary laws regarding non-Jews, women, and non-Orthodox Jews would not apply.[55] The modern State of Israel, he thought, is different from the ancient Jewish monarchy in that it was founded on the basis of international agreements in the United Nations. It would not exist without the involvement and agreement of other states. It could therefore be treated in a different way from that of the ancient Jewish kingdom. "In reality," he wrote, "this [state] is a partnership between the people of Israel and non-Jewish people according to conditions that guarantee the first partner [i.e., the Jews] a certain degree of control."[56] If the state is imagined as a voluntary partnership, then, just as halakha places no restrictions on the authority of partners in a business association, so will halakha permit all people, of whatever gender or religious persuasion, to have full authority in a Jewish state.

Herzog was not satisfied with this approach, however, and ultimately did not recommend it. Although he did not offer a reason for this, two possibilities suggest themselves. First, the "partnership" solution diminishes not only the political but also the theological significance of the Jewish state. The establishment of a sovereign Jewish state, to which Herzog himself ascribed the messianic description of "the first flowering of our redemption," could surely not be reduced to an innovative kind of business partnership.[57] Second, the proposal was simply not very convincing. Herzog's description of the state as civil partnership could more or less apply to any state. Taken to its logical conclusion this position could entirely eliminate the category of the political from Jewish thought. Herzog had spent his entire rabbinical career arguing that Jewish thought had as coherent and developed a legal and political theory as any modern state. Adopting this approach would have been a betrayal of that cornerstone of his life's work. Herzog dedicated only two paragraphs to this proposal before putting it to one side and exploring other avenues for justifying the appointment of all citizens to the judiciary in a Jewish state.

The first halakhic obstacle to address was the prohibition of "rulership" (serara). The prohibition is based on an extrapolation from the biblical passage about the appointment of a king who has to be "from among your brethren," implying that the king had to be an Israelite.[58] According to the influential medieval interpretation of Maimonides, the teaching regarding the appointment of the king extends to all other positions of authority: "This applies not only to the monarchy but to all positions of authority. . . . All appointments that you make must only be from among your brethren."[59]

Herzog limited the application of Maimonides's ruling by noting that it is based on a verse about the appointment of a king. Perhaps, he suggested, the ruling applies only to positions of authority that are akin to monarchy and not to appointments in a democracy. Whereas kings are appointed for life and they transmit their political authority to their heirs, appointments in a democracy generally have a fixed term and are not inherited. Furthermore, Herzog argued, a king's subjects have no say in his appointment. In a democracy, by contrast, elected officials are elected by the very people over whom they have authority. These differences between a king and democratically elected officials, he thought, may mean that Maimonides's restrictions to political appointments do not apply in the context of the democratic state.[60]

Herzog's innovative interpretation of Maimonides dealt with the general problem of the appointment of non-Jews to political authority. A further step, however, was required to justify non-Jews occupying the judicial bench and judging Jews by Jewish law. The halakhic mechanism he suggested for this purpose was that of "acceptance" (*qabalah*). Within certain parameters, if all parties to a civil case or defendants in a criminal case agree, they may accept the authority of a judge or the testimony of a witness, even if they do not meet normal halakhic requirements. This method could, Herzog suggested, allow non-Jews or women to become judges on the basis of the formal acceptance of all relevant parties. It would, however, be inefficient and potentially chaotic if cases could proceed only once every party had formally accepted the judge and witnesses. It would hardly make for a robust legal system if any party in a case could simply reject the authority of the judge before the case had even begun. Herzog therefore proposed that there could be a one-off "acceptance" of all judges, on behalf of all the residents of the state, by a binding act of the elected government. Because, he proposed, elected officials represent the entire people, they may formally accept on their behalf all judges and witnesses in the state's courts, even "witnesses and judges who are unqualified by the law of the Torah and the sages."[61] This was a radical proposal. It had no precedent in halakhic literature, and Herzog admitted that he had not "explicitly found an 'acceptance' of this kind in the commentators."[62] Without this accommodation, however, halakha would certainly not be accepted as the legal system of the state, an outcome that Herzog considered to be unthinkable. He felt that the only way for it to have a chance of acceptance was for the mechanism of "acceptance" to be employed.

The outcome of Herzog's deliberations was to propose a judicial system in which some courts, those concerned with family law most of all, would be run by Orthodox judges but the other state courts could accept judges and witnesses of any kind. Both courts, however, would be part of the same hierarchy and would have to apply halakhic law. On this he would not compromise. "Let the official law book for the entire population," he demanded, " 'for the stranger as for the sojourner in the land,' be Torah law."[63]

Clearly, this system is quite unlike the pluralist system suggested by Gorontchik in 1948. The difference is manifest even in the names that the two men used for the courts. Gorontchik called the two court systems in his constitutional proposal "rabbinical Torah courts" (*batei din rabani'im*) on the one hand and "courts of law" (*batei mishpat*) on the other. This distinction emphasized the fact that they each ruled according to a different source of law and legal authority. Herzog, by contrast, called both courts by the traditional name for Torah courts (*bet din*) and distinguished them by calling the family courts "rabbinical Torah courts" (*batei din rabani'im*) and the others "state Torah courts" (*batei din memshalti'im*). Herzog's halakhic interpretations were very creative, sometimes radical. But all this creativity was intended to produce a situation in which Israel's law would be halakha, a law that would be applied to all people in all of the state's courts.

Ireland's Religious Constitutionalism

This point raises the question: Why did Herzog take such strong exception to legal pluralism? Why did he reject a model for the Jewish state that drew firmly on halakhic precedent, provided reasonable solutions to the challenges of accommodating both halakha and democracy, and received support from within the religious Zionist community?

Part of the answer is provided by Herzog's writings from before he came to Palestine. In an intellectual environment in which religious law was considered primitive, Herzog portrayed halakha as more advanced than modern European law. Defending Judaism against scholars who held legal pluralism to be a mark of unevolved and chaotic premodern politics, Herzog argued that halakha had the same centralized structure as the modern state. The political circumstances that Herzog encountered upon his arrival in Palestine, however, intensified his commitment to a legally centralist halakhic constitution. In particular, his legal thinking was shaped by postcolonial jurisprudence, which characterized the Zionist movement and, indeed, all nationalist movements fighting for independence against European imperial powers.

The transition from British imperial control to national independence reinforced Herzog's inclination to present Jewish law in the model of modern European law and, in particular, to reimagine halakha as a centralized legal system. Even before Herzog arrived in Palestine, he became acquainted with the use of law as a tool in nationalist struggles. When he was still in Dublin, serving as Chief Rabbi of Ireland, Herzog played a significant role in the life of Éamon de Valera, the Irish nationalist leader.[64] Around 1922, at the height of the civil war between Irish unionists and nationalists, de Valera found himself in danger during violent clashes on the streets of Dublin and spent a time hiding in the Herzog home.[65] Herzog and de Valera were good friends. They shared a love of mathematics and, according to the memoirs of Herzog's son Chaim (later president of the State of Israel), de Valera would frequently visit Herzog to "unburden his heart to my father."[66]

The friendship between the two men was likely strengthened by their support for each other's nationalist causes. Herzog, according to his son, was "an open partisan of the Irish cause."[67] He even learned a little Irish in response to de Valera's friendly challenge.[68] Herzog's sympathy for Irish nationalism was presumably enhanced because he compared the Zionist movement with the struggle for Irish independence. Herzog's criticism of British policy in Palestine mirrored the Irish opposition to British policy in Ireland.[69] The comparison of Jewish and Irish independence was quite common in Ireland. Many Catholics in Ireland, for example, were strongly opposed to Britain's 1937 plan for the partition of Palestine because it reminded them of the division of Ireland that had been forced upon them by the British and their supporters.[70] Long after he had become Chief Rabbi of Palestine, Herzog continued to make this connection explicitly. An Irish newspaper reported in 1947,

[i]n a recent conversation with a "high British personality," who had demanded the Jewish community's co-operation in suppressing disorders, he [Dr. Herzog] explained that this could only be done by the Jewish people having their own Government, police and army.

Dr. Herzog said he had reminded the British official of the history of Ireland, and emphasized that the Irish people had refused to become informers when asked to do so by the British Government.

"Britain did not enlist the co-operation of Ireland in the campaign against terrorism until agreement was reached with the Irish nation, after which the Irish people liquidated the terrorists," Dr. Herzog added.[71]

De Valera, for his part, seems to have sympathized with Herzog's Zionism. In 1933 de Valera, then prime minister of Ireland, received Norman Sokolow, the president of the Jewish Agency and the World Zionist Organization, in Herzog's presence. Sokolow asked de Valera to urge the League of Nations to pressure the British into allowing more Jews into Palestine. Reportedly, de Valera promised to try.[72] De Valera's association with Zionism continued even after Herzog's departure to take up office in Palestine. In 1950, he visited Israel's first prime minister, David Ben-Gurion, in Israel and he remained close with the Herzog family for decades.[73]

De Valera's connection with both Isaac Herzog and with Zionism is reflected in the more recent account of Isaac Cohen, one of Herzog's successors as Chief Rabbi of Ireland:

During his years with the Irish Volunteers, [de Valera] developed a warm mutual friendship with a predecessor of mine, Rabbi Dr. Isaac Herzog, whom he visited in the Chief Rabbi's residence in Dublin's South Circular Road. He mentioned a number of times that he greatly admired the new-born state of Israel and welcomed its liberation from British control. He was particularly impressed by the successful revival of Hebrew as the daily spoken language in Israel. President de Valera was deeply moved when I brought him a sapling of a fir tree in 1973 from the Eamon de Valera Forest which the Irish Jewish community had planted in Cana near Nazareth in his honour. When the Israeli forestry department sent him three trees growing in the forest he was happy to plant them himself in the grounds of Aras an Uachtaráin [the residence of the Irish President] so as to have a part of the Holy Land near his home. . . . When the United Nations urged Israel to withdraw from extensive parts of the liberated areas of Palestine he said that if he had still been President of the League of Nations he would have seen to it that Israel did not give up any of the territory that it had regained after the Arab attack resulting in the Six Day War in 1967.[74]

Herzog's connection with de Valera, and the association between Zionism and Irish nationalism, must have impressed upon Herzog the importance of legal sovereignty for the cause of nationalist movements. Under the Anglo-Irish Treaty of 1922, Britain gave Ireland a measure of independent rule, but the Irish Free State, created by the treaty, remained under the ultimate sovereignty of the British crown. Many Irish accepted this compromise but others decried the submission to British control and a bloody civil war ensued. De Valera had been the first president of the Free Irish State, but he could not accept a situation in which total sovereignty did not reside in the state, and he left the Parliament in protest after the treaty was signed. After a year of civil war, he finally supported a cease-fire and dedicated himself to fighting for independence through legislative means. He succeeded fifteen years later, shepherding Ireland to full independence from Britain and becoming the first Taoiseach (prime minister) of Ireland. It was during the preparation of the new constitution for a fully sovereign Ireland that de Valera consulted with Herzog about the clause concerning minority religions.[75]

De Valera's constitution was important for Herzog as a blueprint for national independence from British rule. It was also a model of how to incorporate religious law into a modern democratic constitution. Ireland's 1937 constitution was an early example of a document that attempted to balance religious tradition and social values with modern constitutionalism.[76]

The religious framing of the constitution is impossible to overlook. It opens as follows:

> In the Name of the Most Holy Trinity, from Whom is all authority and to Whom, as our final end, all actions both of men and States must be referred,
> We, the people of Éire,

> Humbly acknowledging all our obligations to our Divine Lord, Jesus Christ, Who sustained our fathers through centuries of trial,
>
> Gratefully remembering their heroic and unremitting struggle to regain the rightful independence of our Nation,
>
> And seeking to promote the common good, with due observance of Prudence, Justice and Charity, so that the dignity and freedom of the individual may be assured, true social order attained, the unity of our country restored, and concord established with other nations,
>
> Do hereby adopt, enact, and give to ourselves this Constitution.[77]

The prominent place of Christian symbols in the Irish constitution points to its religious character. Even more significant is the inclusion of the phrase "dignity . . . of the individual," which was a concept borrowed from the Catholic Church. Although subsequently the term has largely shed its religious overtones, "human dignity" at the time was a way of expressing in ostensibly neutral language the elevation of religious natural law over democratic legislation.[78] The Irish example was the model of a constitution that was democratic and religious at the same time and promoted religious teachings in many areas of social and political life, including constitutional law.

Christian doctrine was not limited to the preamble of the Irish constitution; it also had an impact on its substantive law. While the constitution provided for freedom of conscience, outlawed discrimination on the basis of religion, and recognized minority religious communities, it also recognized "the special position of the Holy Catholic Apostolic and Roman Church as the guardian of the Faith professed by the great majority of the citizens."[79] It gave a special reverence to Catholic identity as a national heritage and as a religious value, proclaiming that "[t]he State acknowledges that the homage of public worship is due to Almighty God. It shall hold His Name in reverence, and shall respect and honour religion."[80] Indeed, under the constitution, divorce was impossible in Ireland.[81] Only under the fifteenth amendment, enacted in 1996, did divorce become lawful and, even then, constitutional restrictions remained.[82]

Herzog was keen to point out the central place of the Catholic religion in the Irish constitution. Shortly before the establishment of Israel, Herzog took issue with the draft constitution of Leo Kohn because it did not grant Judaism and halakha the prominence that Herzog desired. Herzog used Ireland as an example to support his case. In a memorandum criticizing Kohn's draft, he wrote,

> Although our country is democratic, this does not prevent the state from granting special official recognition in the constitution to the religion of the vast majority in the State of Israel.

> There is a precedent to this, which is alive and well. Ireland is also democratic, and no one has ever doubted its democracy. . . . In the Irish Constitution it says clearly that the Catholic Church is recognized as the official church of the Irish people, because it is the church of most of the citizens. However, it also says explicitly that the rights of other churches, Anglican, Presbyterian, etc. and Jewish, are firmly and energetically guaranteed. I argue that in view of the fact that there is a precedent in the constitution of a new democratic state in Western Europe, not only can the Constitution interpret that the Jewish religion has a special status as the religion of the majority of the citizens, but it must grant this respect for our holy religion.[83]

Herzog's experiences in Ireland, then, brought him into intimate contact with an independence movement that fought for years for a constitution that centralized all sovereign authority in the new state. It was also a democratic constitution that enshrined religious doctrine. The year the Irish constitution was ratified, Herzog left Dublin to become Chief Rabbi of Palestine. Herzog's experience in Ireland goes a long way to explaining his consistent commitment to the principle of legal centralism and its indispensability to Zionist national goals. It also suggests why he did not consider "theocratic-democratic" constitution to be paradoxical. If Ireland could give the Catholic religion such pride of place in its new constitution, why should Israel not do the same?[84]

Colonial Pluralism, Postcolonial Centralism

Ireland was not the only archetype for Herzog's jurisprudence; something beyond his individual experience was at play. Herzog was composing his halakhic constitution in the midst of a global trend of postcolonial nationalists creating legally centralist states.

Colonialism was bound up in legal pluralism, postcolonial independence in legal centralism. In the first years of European colonialism, imperial powers made no effort to alter the legal regimes in the places they ruled. In fact, they preserved the existence of multiple legal regimes in their colonies because this preservation made it easier to deal with the challenges of ruling unfamiliar territories with limited bureaucratic resources. They therefore did not attempt to form any kind of centralized legal order, nor did they make any claim to the monopoly on legal authority in their colonies.[85] During the nineteenth century, this policy gradually changed as European powers began to impose a more centralized and hierarchical idea of law over the areas that they controlled. Their colonies remained legally pluralistic, but the imperial state became a kind of ordering power that organized the various legal regimes within each part of the empire.[86]

With the decline of empire and the establishment of independent postcolonial states, there was a further shift, away from state-dominated pluralism and toward a full-fledged legal centralism. Law played a significant role in the achievements of independence movements, the leaders of which had often received their legal education in imperial capitals and used that training against the imperial powers in their struggle for independence.[87] This interaction between postcolonial leaders and the imperial center meant that the self-understanding of postcolonial independence movements was often based on European myths and ideas. These movements frequently absorbed the Western myth of the backwardness of colonial law and considered modern law on the European model as the pinnacle of legal evolution.[88] It was not just the hegemonic influence of imperial education that produced this effect; there was also a strategic advantage in embracing European jurisprudence.[89] Legal centralism, with its emphasis on the omnipotent sovereign power of the state and the integration of all cultural streams into a single state-based regime, was a legal philosophy that naturally supported the goals of independence movements.

The shift from the legal pluralism of imperial colonies was replicated across the globe, throughout the twentieth century, as newly independent nations repeatedly embraced legal centralism. It was the case, for example, in the 1960s and 1970s in Central Africa, where the new leaders of independent Zaire, Rwanda, and Burundi rejected the legal pluralism of the colonial period in favor of a unified legal regime in their new states.[90] Earlier, and closer to Palestine, the same dynamics were at work in Turkey. During the imperial period, in the 1870s, the Ottoman Empire had established a civil code called the Mejelle, which existed alongside religious law. The result was classic legal pluralism, in which civil and religious law, two bodies of law, which received their authority from different sources, were in force at the same time.[91] This all changed with the Turkish nationalist movement. Many of the founders of the independent state of Turkey had received their legal education in Europe. In 1926, as a founding act of the new state, the Swiss *Code civil* was received into Turkish law. This code brought an abrupt end to pluralism in Turkey. It established an all-encompassing legal centralism, which was based on European law and intended to strengthen Turkish independence.[92]

European Jurisprudence in Mandate Palestine and the State of Israel

The legal history of Palestine and Israel mirrors the pattern of the global shift from colonial pluralism to postcolonial centralism. During the period of colonial rule, the British governed Palestine as a legally pluralistic regime in much the same way that they governed India and their other colonies. The British bureaucracy imported its own regulations, particularly in the areas of commercial and criminal law, and organized and arbitrated between the legal regimes of the various religious communities.[93] The Mandate government never, however, claimed to be the source of all legal authority. It recognized, for example, that the rabbinical courts had their own systems of law, with their own sources and procedures, which preexisted the arrival of the British. Although the Mandate tried to create some kind of order among these regimes, it never claimed to be the only sovereign, the single source of all law within the state.

Yet, even as Britain governed Palestine as a pluralistic legal regime, the legal curriculum followed by law students in British Palestine presumed the superiority of legal centralism every bit as much as that in the imperial center. Henry Maine's theories of legal evolution were hugely influential in Palestine, as they were in other areas under British rule. They provided a seductive conceptual framework for an imperial society that both romanticized and scorned the cultures of "oriental" colonies.[94] Maine himself was an important figure in Britain's colonial apparatus. He served as a member of the council of the governor-general of India and was heavily involved with the codification of Indian law. His jurisprudence laid the theoretical ground for the widespread belief that the "religious" and "tribal" law of the colonies (as it was called by the British) was less evolved than the law of the civilizing imperial power.[95] Imperial rule drew its authority from, and reinforced, the myth of modern, secular, state-centered, codified law as the pinnacle of evolutionary progress.[96]

The evolutionary theory of law, for example, characterized the British approach to the law of the Ottoman Empire after its decline. In Mandate Palestine, British judges portrayed the residual Ottoman laws as "outdated and archaic, intricate and obscure, illogical and unreasonable, harsh and monstrous," not to mention inefficient and corrupt.[97] For example, one British judge in Palestine considered the Mejelle, the Ottoman legal regime, to have a "barbarous" air and believed that its backwardness indicated "how remote is the working of the Asiatic mind from that of the European."[98] Another referred to the Ottoman Penal Code as "a delightful piece of juridical nonsense," a comment that simultaneously displays both the condescending romanticism and the disdain of imperial judges toward colonial law.

These attitudes were transmitted to Zionist lawyers who, in Palestine as in other British colonies, were educated in British law. They were trained in the Law Classes, an institution established in Jerusalem in 1920 that heavily emphasized British jurisprudence. The textbook for the course on jurisprudence was *An Introduction to the Study of Law: A Handbook for the Use of Law Students in Egypt and Palestine*, by Frederic Goadby, an English jurist who had taught in England and Cairo and was brought to Palestine to direct the Law Classes there.[99] Goadby distinguished between religious and primitive legal systems and the law of the modern state. For Goadby, only state law, the will of the sovereign backed by coercive force, could be considered modern law and was the hallmark of "a high state of civilization."[100] He believed that European law had reached a higher state of evolution than the "half barbaric" legal systems outside of Europe, including those in the Ottoman Empire and the Mandate itself. This view was certainly true of religious law, which he believed to be quite backward compared to the mostly secular law of modern Europe.[101]

This pejorative approach to religious law, including Jewish law, was widespread at the time. The Law Classes for which Goadby's *Introduction* was a textbook were founded by the Attorney General of Mandate Palestine, Norman Bentwich. A British Jew, Bentwich was a Zionist who, after leaving his position with the Mandate government, remained in Palestine as a professor in the Hebrew University until 1951. In 1927, Bentwich published an article describing the role of Jewish law in the mandatory legal regime. He noted that the Jewish community, like all religious communities, had internal control over personal law like marriage and divorce. He did not oppose that arrangement in principle, but he did express a hope that Jewish religious law would in time become more modern and liberal:

> There is reason to expect that in the free atmosphere of Palestine, Jewish law will be systematically developed to accord with the liberal views of our time as to the relations of men and women. That development has been impaired by the abnormal conditions of the Jewish communities in Eastern Europe since the Middle Ages. As soon as a Jewish religious centre is established in the national home, the authority of the rabbinical body to change the law would be recognized throughout the diaspora, and Jewish law on matters of family right could be modified, as it was modified in the happier days of the great jurists of Babylon, Persia, Egypt and Spain during what are known as the Dark Ages of Europe.[102]

Bentwich, despite his general sympathy for Jews and Jewish law, was clear about the problems of its discrimination between men and women in family law, which compared unfavorably with "the liberal views of our time." Bentwich attributed this bias to the "abnormal conditions" of Ashkenazic Jewry in the previous centuries. On the face of it, this explanation is reminiscent of Herzog's laying the blame for the unnatural development of Jewish law at the feet of the Romans. There was, however, another aspect to Bentwich's analysis. Although dismissive of the dominant strain of Jewish law in recent centuries, he talked nostalgically about Jewish jurists in "Babylon, Persia, Egypt and Spain." Bentwich was presumably referring to the rabbis of Late Antiquity and the Middle Ages, particularly during the ascendancy of Spanish Jewry, when philosophers and rationalists like Sa'adia Gaon and Maimonides dominated the world of Jewish law. This romanticization of the Sephardic legacy is part of the myth of Sephardic supremacy that pervaded enlightened Jewish scholarship from the nineteenth century.[103] It is characteristic of a kind of Jewish orientalism that repudiated the apparent backwardness of Eastern European Judaism and embraced a mythical older Judaism that was more akin to the enlightened universalist monotheism of modern Europe. Therefore, even as he defended the ability of Jewish law to evolve in line with contemporary liberalism, Bentwich implicitly agreed with Goadby and others like him, that Jewish law as it was currently constituted was inferior to contemporary liberal European law.

The attraction to modern European jurisprudence even infiltrated the Mishpat Ivri movement. Although the movement had been formed to celebrate Hebrew law as a national resource, as early as the 1920s Mishpat Ivri scholars changed their approach. In an attempt to demonstrate the viability and enlightened nature of Jewish law, they began to downplay the uniqueness of Jewish law and to emphasize how similar it was to European law and how different from Muslim and Ottoman law. Imitating European jurists, they characterized Muslim law as primitive, passive, and tribal and they took pains to emphasize its difference from Jewish law, which they characterized as more refined and evolved.[104]

The influence of European jurisprudence was also apparent among Zionists in Palestine during Herzog's tenure as chief rabbi. In the late 1940s, on the verge of independence, there were renewed calls among Israeli jurists and politicians for the creation of a national law that would be based on Jewish law.[105] Even supporters of this goal, however, had no interest in a halakhic constitution. They intended to create a modern, secular law that, in the interests of national revival, could draw on Jewish precedent. In 1947, the Zionist National Council set up a Legal Council to discuss the legal system of the future state.[106] The council had a special subcommittee to deal with Jewish law, headed by Abraham Haim Freimann, a scholar of Maimonides and medieval Jewish law. The subcommittee did not complete its work, in part because Freimann was killed in the ambush of a Jewish convoy to Mount Scopus in April 1948. In any case, the interest of the Legal Council in Jewish law was primarily the function of a nationalist rather than a religious impulse and would never have advocated for the indiscriminate imposition of halakha in Israel.

Moshe Silberg, an Orthodox Jew who later became an Israeli Supreme Court Justice, was one of the most consistent supporters of Mishpat Ivri. Even he, however, believed that Israeli law could not simply adopt traditional Jewish law wholesale. Discussing the proposal to write a law for Israel based on halakha, he wrote,

> This code will not be in the nature of a "condensed *Shulhan Arukh*," and it will not claim for itself the traditional authority—religious and sacred—of the existing codes. This will be a civil-secular creation which will accept, wherever possible, the basic principles of Jewish law, with the explicit exception of the archaic conclusions which are superimposed on them. The objective will be: to winnow and sift, to bring closer and to reestablish what still cleaves to life, and to keep away and reject the dry growth which became shriveled and impoverished in the course of centuries. In other words somewhat more graphic: to pour out the wine that has become sour, and to keep the barrel so as to fill it with new wine which will become permeated with the aroma that has seeped into it, and that its aroma and its taste may be like the aroma and the taste of the old wine.[107]

In short, even the most ardent supporters of Mishpat Ivri wanted Israel to be governed by modern secular law. To the extent that Jewish law would have any place in the modern state, it would be as a nationalist institution, not a religious one, and its authority would flow from the secular state and not from divine command.

The Zionist commitment to modern European jurisprudence was also expressed in the interest in a constitution and in codification. Israel's Declaration of Independence of May 14, 1948 explicitly called for the adoption of a constitution no later than October of the same year. It was assumed by almost all major jurists and politicians in the late 1940s and early 1950s that a constitution would soon be adopted.[108] Ultimately, though, a constitution was not adopted, primarily because of Ben-Gurion's reluctance to constrain his executive powers at a time of war and political fragility. Even Ben-Gurion, however, wanted the state eventually to adopt a constitutional legal regime based on the British or European model.[109]

Israeli jurists also desired a codified legal system on the European model. Although the Mandate had imported Britain's common law tradition into Palestine, there was a strong move among Zionist jurists toward a continental-style codification.[110] Like the constitutional project, the codification project stalled in 1948, in part because of a reluctance to borrow from German culture in the aftermath of World War II and the Holocaust. It did not, however, dissipate entirely. The move to codification re-emerged in the 1960s and intensified in the 1970s under the tenure of Aharon Barak, who was then attorney general of Israel and later became a particularly influential Supreme Court Justice. (A civil code was finally adopted in Israel in 2004.)[111]

It was not just the British authorities, then, but also the Zionists themselves who regarded as ideal the European legal model, complete with a constitution and a civil code. Zionist jurists had been educated under the auspices of the British in Palestine or in European universities that espoused the same ideology of the supremacy of the law of the centralized state.[112] The legal culture among the Zionist elite was deeply rooted in continental Europe.

With the establishment of the State of Israel, Zionist leaders deepened their adherence to legal centralism. The British Mandate, even as it used law as a tool to serve its imperial ends, had remained legally pluralistic. Despite having disdained the supposedly less evolved systems of religious law, it continued to respect its jurisdiction over personal status law and to recognize that its authority originated not in the Mandate's sovereignty but in the various communities that preexisted British rule. This pluralistic attitude is articulated well in the following description of the place of religious law in the Mandate constitution, by a professor of law at the Hebrew University:

> [W]hat is the status of those norms of Jewish law which are recognized by our legislator? . . . Can we say that the Jewish law has become merged into the law of the state? If by "merged" as distinguished from "linked up" we mean . . . that their autonomy is denied, the answer is in the negative. . . . When the Palestine legislator in the Palestine Order in Council, 1922, made Jewish law and the systems of the other religious communities sources of Palestine law, with regard to a certain class of legal relations, he intended to incorporate it into his system as autonomous law.[113]

In other words, the British Mandate was a legally pluralistic regime. Religious law was deemed to be an autonomous law with its own source of authority, distinct from British law. This was typical in colonial regimes. Things changed, however, after the state was established. The jurists of the new State of Israel insisted that sovereignty belonged to the state alone and that the source of all law was the state. Even though religious courts continued to exist and to have jurisdiction over personal law, their status changed after 1948. They no longer had independent authority but were made part of the legal hierarchy of the state. As far as Israel's leading jurists were concerned, religious courts had become one branch of the judicial administration of the state.

This is an important point because to this day in the State of Israel, personal status law (the law governing marriage, divorce, etc.) is under the jurisdiction of religious courts. It is sometimes believed that the State of Israel has more than one parallel legal system. From the perspective of the state, however, this is not the case. The state has a single, centralized legal system with a single source of authority. The state chooses to grant authority to properly registered rabbis and other religious officials in certain areas of law. This choice does not, however, diminish the centralist nature of the state's legal regime. Ben-Gurion himself clearly expressed this legal philosophy. In response to rabbinical resistance to the Women's Equal Rights Law of 1951, he declared that, to give legal force to their rulings, "the rabbinical courts require . . . the sovereign authority that is given by the power of the state."[114] The previous year, during a debate with some religious politicians, he expressed the same sentiment even more forcefully. "The office of the Rabbinate," he proclaimed, "does not exist by the authority of [the religious law code] the *Shulhan Arukh* but by the law of [Norman] Bentwich [the first Attorney-General in Mandate Palestine]. And it is certainly possible to repeal Bentwich's law."[115]

This centralist approach to Israel's religious courts also formed the basis for judicial decisions. A landmark case in 1951, *Skornik v. Skornik*, dealt with the status in Israel of a civil, nonreligious marriage between two Jews that had been contracted outside Israel. The question arose of the jurisdiction of the religious courts in the matter. Justice Alfred Witkon answered in a distinctly centralist vein, "Every religious law, in its application in this country, flows from an act of the secular legislator . . . and derives its force therefrom."[116] Itzhak England, a leading Israeli legal scholar who later became an Israeli Supreme Court Justice, wrote extensively about how religious law has no authority in Israel in its own right. Only when power is granted to them by the state do religious courts have any legitimate jurisdiction.[117]

The same theme arose in many cases that were decided by the Supreme Court in the early years of the state.[118] For example, in a 1959 case dealing with a conflict between a husband and wife over spousal support, the case turned on the extent to which legislation in the Knesset could interfere with the application of rabbinical law in the rabbinical courts.[119] Fundamentally, the question at stake was the extent to which the rabbinical courts were under the centralized authority of the state. Moshe Silberg, an Orthodox Jew, offered the sole dissenting opinion, reasoning that the rabbinical courts were independent within the area of their own jurisdiction because "the secular legislature . . . is not the source of the religious legislation."[120] The majority opinion, however, ruled that the state may indeed interfere in the jurisdiction of her religious courts because ultimately their authority flows from the state. As Justice Yitzhak Olshan, author of the majority opinion, put it, "I find no basis for the claim that the secular legislator cannot annul a religious law. In the absence of a constitution, the legislator is all powerful."[121]

A similar attitude was expressed in a 1964 Supreme Court case in which the Chief Rabbinate was challenging the right of the civil court to hear an appeal to a rabbinical court decision. The rabbinate maintained that religious courts operated independently of the civil judiciary so the Supreme Court had no authority to hear an appeal to a rabbinical decision. Justice Yitzhak Kister of the Supreme Court disagreed. "When they are acting as rabbis with the authority bestowed upon them by the legislator," he ruled, "rabbinical judges are an arm of the government and are subject to supervision like other authorities of the state."[122]

There was, then, a distinct difference between the way that the Mandate authorities and the Israeli government understood the basis for the legal authority of the state's religious courts. As with so many other newly independent postcolonial nations in which national unity was a priority, the legal pluralism of Mandate Palestine gave way to the strict centralism of the State of Israel. Although in Israel the religious courts continued to have jurisdiction over personal status law as they had under Mandate rule, the jurisprudential basis for that arrangement was quite different. Whereas the Mandate considered the various courts within the state to be operating autonomously and to have their own sources of validity, the State of Israel considered all law to flow directly from its centralized sovereignty. That has remained the case to the present day. Aharon Barak described Israel's law thus:

> Even the application of *Torah* law in the areas of marriage and divorce among Jews derives from a secular law. . . . From the standpoint of the State, the secular legislature is empowered to adopt a given set of religious law norms and to reject others. The application of religious law derives, then, from its absorption by the secular law. By the process of this absorption, the religious law becomes a law with a secular source.[123]

The history of the association between legal pluralism and colonial rule and the corresponding association between nationalism and legal centralism adds to the explanation of Herzog's rejection of legal centralism as he formulated a halakhic constitution. Herzog's intellectual life had begun among British scholars who disdained pluralist religious law as primitive and who had championed modern European centralist law as the telos of legal evolution. In Palestine, these ideas had been confirmed as secular Zionists created a national jurisprudence on a centralist model. Religious Zionists who proposed constitutional arrangements for the Jewish state before 1948 suggested models that were, at their core, legally pluralistic. They conceived of the Jewish polity as incorporating a number of parallel systems of law that, although they all were under the authority of God, each had its own source of authority and had distinct rules and procedures. Herzog repudiated this line of thinking and sharply opposed the notion that a Jewish constitution might accommodate multiple legal systems. The Jewish state, he argued, had to be a centralized, all-encompassing regime with a single legal hierarchy. Postcolonial nationalists from the Middle East to Central Africa adopted European-style centralized legal regimes in order to show themselves to be the equal of the European states from which they claimed independence and in order to support national unity. Herzog too believed that only a legally centralist constitution would be a viable model for a new state shrugging off the control of imperial domination. He also thought that halakha would have a chance of being made into the law of a new Jewish state only if it was considered to be the equal of modern European law. He therefore took great pains to describe Jewish law in centralist terms, taking every opportunity to demonstrate parallels between the ancient Jewish constitution, as he portrayed it, and the constitutions of modern Europe. He did this even though it required him to make substantial accommodations in his halakhic reasoning.

Ostensibly, there is an irresolvable tension between Herzog's theocratic constitution and the democratic constitutional drafts of secular Zionists. After all, in Herzog's halakhic state, the Torah would be the ultimate authority, whereas in a democracy the people are sovereign. But this tension masks a deeper identity between Herzog and secular jurists. Both had a constitutional vision in which the state was the exclusive source of legal authority and in which only one legal regime could rule within its borders. Ironically, the fact that the same centralist outlook was shared by Herzog and secular Zionists made the conflict between them more intractable. Because they both rejected legal pluralism, and both wanted exclusive authority for the legal regimes they championed, there was little room for compromise between them. The religious-secular tensions in Israel today may, in large part, be traced back to this basic disagreement.

The speed with which Herzog's constitutional thinking rose to dominate the legal thought of the religious Zionist camp might indicate how clearly it resonated with general Zionist jurisprudence. Within a few years after the establishment of the State of Israel, legal centralism became a defining feature of the legislative goals of the religious Zionist leadership, and was the incentive for the institutionalization and bureaucratization of the Chief Rabbinate and the rabbinical courts.

The Chief Rabbinate, and the rabbinical court system that it over-sees, is among the most contentious institutions in the State of Israel. For many secular Israelis, it is a reviled blemish on Israeli democracy. Meanwhile, most religious Israelis, even those who acknowledge some of its flaws, condone the Rabbinate's control over all Jewish marriages and divorces in the state. Few of its supporters or detractors know just how new the institution is. What is more, its ideological origins are counterintuitive. The rabbinate is often taken to be a bulwark against secularizing forces in Israeli society (for better or for worse). Many of its defining features, however, were modeled on modern European law. Far from being a holdover in a modern state, the Israeli rabbinate is, in many important details, quite unlike any previous Jewish institu-tion. In designing the rabbinate as they did, its architects explicitly departed from halakhic precedent in numerous ways.

The formation of the Israeli rabbinate is an outgrowth of the legal philosophy of religious Zionism. Just as Isaac Herzog's creation of a legally centralist constitution for a halakhic state was a departure from the legally pluralist approach to law of religious Zionists who preceded him, so the creation of a centralized rabbinic authority was a departure from the pluralistic structure of rabbinic institutions before the 1940s. The new rabbinate was created in conscious imitation of modern legal institutions, in the hope of convincing Israelis that halakhic authority was capable of having a central role in the modern state. It deliberately adopted practices that were unprecedented in the history of halakhic institutions but were vital aspects of modern legal systems. These prac-tices included the centralization of regional rabbinical courts into a single court system, the creation of a halakhic court of appeals, the promulgation of rules of procedure for rabbinical courts, the official publication of rabbinical rulings, and the homogenization of halakhic practice among Israel's diverse Jewish communities.

The Invention of Jewish Theocracy. Alexander Kaye, Oxford University Press (2020). © Oxford University Press.
DOI: 10.1093/oso/9780190922740.001.0001

The Sanhedrin

The Great Sanhedrin, which rabbinic literature presents as the most important Jewish court of antiquity, was long considered an idealized model for the rabbinate in a Jewish state. After World War I, as the prospects for the establishment of a Jewish state appeared increasingly plausible, religious Zionist leaders dreamed of the reconstitution of this ancient body. The ways in which religious Zionist rabbis imagined their new Sanhedrin changed over time. Early attempts to establish a new Sanhedrin anticipated that it would be a kind of annual rabbinic conference, a religious body for the global Jewish community. Later attempts, however, which coincided with the shift to legal centralism spearheaded by Herzog and his followers, imagined it as a national Israeli institution, part of the legislative branch of a modern government. This change reflects wider developments in religious Zionist thought and points the way to the ideology of the halakhic state.

The nature of the Great Sanhedrin is disputed by historians.[1] Religious Zionists generally accepted the rabbinic tradition according to which it was an ancient Judean supreme religious body, which functioned as a high court and also advised on difficult questions of rabbinic law. Throughout Jewish history, the memory of the Sanhedrin functioned as a symbol of supreme rabbinic authority. It was also loaded with eschatological significance. In religious thought, the reinstitution of the Sanhedrin accompanied the return of Jewish sovereignty in the Land of Israel and the central role of rabbinic authority in Jewish governance. The idea of a restoration commonly accompanied messianic yearnings through centuries of Jewish history.[2] Indeed, many believed that its re-establishment was a necessary condition for the advent of the Messiah.[3] It is therefore no surprise that some religious Zionists, who saw messianic significance in the rise of the Zionist movement and Jewish migration to Palestine, should have attempted to bring about the establishment of the Sanhedrin in their own time.

One initiative to reconstitute the Sanhedrin came from Tsvi Makovsky. Originally the rabbi of Melitopol, in Soviet Ukraine, Makovsky migrated to Palestine and became a rabbi in the Tel Aviv–Jaffa district. He believed that the immigration of Jews to the Land of Israel in his generation was a sign that "there has been awakened in the heart of the people of Israel [a desire] to redeem its soul."[4] For Makovsky, Zionism had brought about a redemption not just in theory but also in practice. "Zion has already ceased to be merely [a] romantic [fantasy]," he wrote. "It is an established fact and has become a desired refuge for all the groups among our people."[5] The time was right, he believed, for the re-establishment of the Sanhedrin. He composed a long pamphlet, which was published in 1928, in which he laid out his halakhic arguments in favor of the endeavor, along with responses that he elicited from many of Europe's senior rabbinical figures. Most of the responses approved of the plan in theory but rejected it in practice as impractical and potentially divisive. Few rabbis thought it would be possible to achieve the level of consensus required to make the project a success.

The comments of Abraham Isaac Kook are particularly instructive as a window into attitudes among religious Zionists during this period. In the last year of his life, Kook wrote to Makovsky, expressing a general enthusiasm for his plan but advising against its immediate implementation. Kook warned that he saw "no possibility of creating a consensus among the Torah scholars of our generation" and that therefore proceeding "without prior heartfelt and practical preparation will lead only to polemic and no practical benefit will come out of it."[6] However, Kook wrote, he had long been in favor of some kind of global rabbinical assembly based in Jerusalem. He remarked that early in his time as Ashkenazic Chief Rabbi, at the beginning of the British Mandate, he had proposed the following enterprise:

> If we are able to organize the rabbinate properly in the Land of Israel in its branches and centers, then we will be able to turn to the whole people of Israel, especially the most influential rabbis and scholars in the exile, ... so that they will be our partners in a single association, and send representatives from all over the exile. . . . Every year, one month will be designated for the representatives to appear. . . . The joint meeting, which will include the greatest of the rabbis of the Holy Land and of the exile, this great conference, will be called "the general rabbinate," meaning the rabbinate of the entire Jewish people. And if God desires, we will be successful and this conference and its association will achieve right and good things, whether to strengthen the state of the Torah in all areas of religion, or to solve the greatest most general questions connected with the life of the people in the Land of Israel and in the exile, or to improve the situation of the people with regard to its external relations to the nations.[7]

So although he opposed Makovsky's call for a formal reinstitution of the ancient Sanhedrin, Kook let him know that he had previously recommended the establishment of a global rabbinic network that would send delegates annually to a meeting in Jerusalem. Kook's plans for a global rabbinical assembly never materialized, presumably because it required the collaboration of too many rabbis with different outlooks and allegiances. Kook himself, though beloved by many, was excoriated by others who were disgusted by his willingness to collaborate with secular Jews.[8]

Kook's unrealized plan is significant as much for what it was not as for what it was. His proposed rabbinical assembly would have been a glorified religious convention. He never imagined that it would play a central role in the apparatus of a Jewish state. Moreover, the proposed rabbinical body would have been global, rather than national. It did not resemble a national legislature but rather an international scholarly conference. To be sure, Kook entirely supported the idea of Jerusalem being a Jewish religious center. The thought of a rabbinic body based there inevitably resonated with his strong messianic orientation. There is not, though, any hint that he imagined that it would be a supreme rabbinic body responsible for all the laws of a Jewish state in Palestine. A few years later, another attempt to revive the Sanhedrin had a very different outlook. A comparison of the two attempts indicates a shift in the understanding of religious Zionists of the role of halakha in the legal institutions of the Jewish State.

The second attempt of the twentieth century to reinstitute the Sanhedrin took place in the late 1940s. In contrast with the dreams of Makovsky and Kook earlier in the century, the Sanhedrin was imagined for the first time as a central legislative institution in the framework of a modern state. This attempt was championed by Yehudah-Leib Fishman-Maimon. Born in Russia, Maimon migrated to Palestine from Russia in 1913 and became an early leader of the Mizrahi movement.[9] He was a rabbi and educator who was close to Rabbi Kook, founding a publishing house in his name. After the establishment of the state, he became Israel's first Minister of Religious Affairs. A signatory of the Declaration of Independence, he was also one of the few religious Zionist leaders who had a friendly relationship with Ben-Gurion. Ben-Gurion appreciated Maimon's boldness and flexibility and called him "one of the finest men in Orthodox Judaism in our times, if not the finest."[10]

In language reminiscent of Herzog's, Maimon made clear his desire to see halakha become the basis of Israeli law. In a 1949 article published in the religious newspaper *Ha-tsofeh*, he wrote, "I hope that just as I have had the privilege of seeing the rebirth of the State of Israel, I will be privileged to witness the revival and flowering of Israeli jurisprudence, a system of law that is built upon the foundations of the Torah and the tradition, based on equity and justice the likes of which are not to be found in the jurisprudence of any other nation, ancient or modern."[11]

Like all religious Zionists who aspired to apply halakha to the modern Jewish state, Maimon recognized the challenges involved in this project, challenges that arose from the incommensurability of halakha and democratic politics. Maimon's solution was the reinstitution of the Sanhedrin. He expressed this vision to the Mizrahi convention in 1949. "The challenge of linking the Torah and the State is new and difficult," he acknowledged. "It is not the task of individuals, even especially great scholars, but of a large team of men of distinguished eminence, a select rabbinic body that possesses supreme Torah authority and governmental power, namely: a paramount legislative institution in the image of a Sanhedrin."[12]

Maimon claimed that his proposal was based upon that of Abraham Isaac Kook, noting that Kook had hoped that the Chief Rabbinate would serve as a foundation for a future Sanhedrin. He failed to note, however, the significant ways in which his vision of the Sanhedrin differed from Kook's earlier description. Whereas Kook had imagined an institution that would serve as a global rabbinical assembly, Maimon dreamed of a Sanhedrin that would be a "legislative institution." This term implied that Maimon's Sanhedrin would not merely "solve . . . questions," as Kook had proposed, but it would also create new halakhic legislation, fit to be applied in a modern Jewish state.

Maimon worked for years to garner support for this project. He wrote about it incessantly, in particular in a series of articles in *Ha-tsofeh*.[13] He was also joined by partners such as Shlomo Zalman Shragai, a leader in Ha-Po'el Ha-Mizrahi. Because of his authority in the religious Zionist community and his position as chief rabbi, Herzog's approval was also crucial to the success of Maimon's Sanhedrin. Although Herzog agreed with Maimon's vision of a halakhic law for the State of Israel, he did not throw his weight behind the institution of the Sanhedrin. He expressed abstract approval of the project but repeatedly postponed dealing with it in practice. When he did address it directly, it was to counsel patience and pragmatism. Even though Maimon insisted that the Sanhedrin would "adopt regulations, not reforms," Herzog was afraid that Maimon's idea would be criticized by more conservative rabbis as an attempt to evade the strictures of halakha by using the Sanhedrin to change rabbinic law.[14] For many Orthodox rabbis, this approach smacked of the methods of Reform rabbis, who openly revised or rejected halakha. Even Herzog himself was concerned that there was public interest in the Sanhedrin among "people who don't have full faith in the Torah" and who wrongly thought that the Sanhedrin would have "the power to change the laws" so as to release them from their halakhic obligations. This interest, which was "not totally pure," Herzog wrote, moved him to oppose the establishment of a Sanhedrin, "despite my strong desire for a kingdom of Torah in Israel."[15]

Herzog was also skeptical of the project because he was sure the Sanhedrin would not be accepted by the Zionist leadership. Herzog, like Maimon, understood the proposed Sanhedrin to be a state institution with political power and he was certain that "the government of Israel will in no way allow a committee of rabbis . . . to deal with political matters and the like."[16] Furthermore, Herzog was concerned that establishing a formal Sanhedrin as a branch of government could also become a threat to halakha. Because, he wrote, "we live in a democratic era," the members of the Sanhedrin would be democratically elected. That process would remove control over the institution from the rabbinate, and make it impossible to determine its members. As a result, "it is clear that against our will we will be tripped up and that inappropriate people, from the perspective of their [observance of the] Torah and their fear [of God], will be brought in."[17]

The nature of Herzog's hesitation makes it clear that he envisaged a modern Sanhedrin that would not simply be a religious organization but would also be an official institution of the government of Israel. He assumed that it would therefore have to be constituted democratically, like other state institutions. A democratically elected Sanhedrin, he feared, would be vulnerable to control by the secular majority, opening up the possibility of the state's most powerful halakhic body including members who knew nothing about halakha and who were not committed to its practice. Herzog's objections eventually led to the demise of Maimon's idea; the reinstitution of the Sanhedrin became a footnote in the history of religious Zionism.[18]

Herzog's objections to the reinstitution of the Sanhedrin were based, to a degree, on a pragmatic fear of failure that had also characterized Kook's lukewarm reception of Makovsky's proposal fifteen years earlier. However, there are some important differences between the two episodes. Whereas for Makovsky and Kook the idea of a Sanhedrin was primarily a matter of religious revival and a way to deal with the halakhic problems of world Jewry, Maimon and Herzog both imagined it as an institution that would be responsible primarily for the Jews of Israel. Furthermore, both Maimon and Herzog imagined that the Sanhedrin would be an official state institution. These differences offer insight into changes in the outlook of religious Zionism that were taking place in the late 1940s. During that time, religious Zionist leaders began to think of rabbinic leadership as intrinsically bound up with the state, as associated not only with religious law but also with civil legislation. This change in outlook was also reflected in institutional changes in one of the most important religious institutions in the State of Israel: the rabbinical court system itself.

Centralization of the Rabbinical Courts

Ironically, considering its subsequent embrace by religious Zionists, the Chief Rabbinate was in fact the invention of the British Empire. It was an office that initially had to be forced onto rabbinical leaders, who were reluctant to accept its authority. In its early days, the bureaucracy of the Chief Rabbinate was resisted by many rabbis, including Kook himself, who objected to the role of secular authorities in its establishment.[19] By the 1940s, however, the Chief Rabbinate was embraced by Isaac Herzog and his followers. This shift in attitude is yet another illustration of the tendency, from the 1940s, to interpret halakha according to the model of modern European law and to embrace the political and legal centralization that were hallmarks of the modern state.

Since the nineteenth century, the Ottoman Empire had recognized the Jewish community as a formal political body whose official representative was the *Hakham Bashi*, or Head Rabbi. After their conquest of Palestine in 1917, the British, as elsewhere in their empire, had an interest in recognizing the religious courts that existed before they took control. They had neither the desire nor the capacity to rule their colonial subjects by English law, and so continued to allow religious communities to control their own affairs in matters of personal law. They did, however, require communal religious courts to conform to what the British considered to be proper legal procedure. They demanded that all courts in Palestine must have an appeals process, formally register their judges, and enact official rules of procedure.

The office of the Hakham Bashi did not fulfill these requirements. On British initiative, therefore, the Chief Rabbinate was created in 1921 as an institution that would satisfy their administrative and procedural demands. It was, in fact, the first institution of the Jewish community of Palestine to be formally recognized by the Mandate authorities. Abraham Isaac Kook became the first Ashkenazic Chief Rabbi and Yitzhak Nisim the first Sephardic Chief Rabbi.[20] With the establishment of the Chief Rabbinate, a new series of rules was promulgated for all the rabbinic courts in the country. These rules covered everything from the location of trials, to the composition of the courts to the procedures for appeal.[21] In addition, a rabbinical court of appeals was introduced. Before the establishment of the Chief Rabbinate, the rabbinical court of Jerusalem had no special status. It was simply one of a number of regional rabbinical courts. From 1921, however, it was given an additional function and a new name. It became the *bet din ha-gadol*, the Great Rabbinical Court, and was given the power to act as a court of appeals for cases heard in any of the other rabbinical courts. This change effectively demoted the other rabbinical courts, making them first-tier courts in a new juridical framework in which the Jerusalem court held, for the first time, higher authority.

These changes were resisted by rabbinical authorities, including Kook himself, because they were not a Jewish initiative but a British one and they were not drafted by rabbis, but by lawyers.[22] Furthermore, the creation of a rabbinical court of appeals was a radical innovation in halakhic terms. Halakha provides no right to appeal as a privilege of the due process of law and there was almost no precedent in Jewish history of a judicial institution that existed to scrutinize the decisions of other rabbinical courts.[23] Some of the new procedural rules were also departures from halakha. They stated, for example, that the rabbinical judge must formally record the reasons for his ruling. This rule was required for the proper administration of a court of appeals because an appeal cannot take place unless the court of first instance has duly recorded its decision. The classic Jewish codes, however, explicitly state that the rabbinical judge need not record his reasoning.[24]

It was not just Kook who objected to these innovations. The four regional rabbinical courts (Haifa, Tel Aviv–Jaffa, Petah Tikvah, and Jerusalem) typically ignored the new regulations and each continued to follow its own procedures, which were generally ad hoc and often even internally inconsistent. Indeed, there were frequent complaints from lawyers about the unpredictability of the rabbinical court system, attesting to the fact that the rabbinical courts were not systematically following the new procedural rules.[25] Although the court in Jerusalem did hear many appeals, the regional rabbinical courts frequently objected to its jurisdiction. The new requirement for rabbinical judges to record their reasoning was also widely disregarded. Until the 1940s, rabbinical court records often consisted of a terse summary of the court's ruling, with no accompanying explanation. In short, the procedural regulations of 1921 made little impact on the rabbinical courts.[26]

With Isaac Herzog's installation as Chief Rabbi in 1937, following Kook's death, the attitude of his office to the rabbinical court of appeals and to the new procedural regulations quickly changed. This change once again reflects the shifting attitude of religious Zionists who were beginning to reimagine halakha as a centralized legal system on the model of modern European jurisprudence. The initial impetus for the change was a landmark case in 1939, in which, for the very first time, the High Court of the British Mandate reversed a ruling of the rabbinical court in Jerusalem. The grounds for the reversal were the failure of the rabbinical court to adhere to the regulations that had been promulgated in 1921. The British ruling was fiercely contested by both chief rabbis, who considered the ruling to be an unjustified interference in their jurisdiction. The jurisdiction of rabbinical courts over personal law, they claimed, extended not only to the law itself but also to legal procedure. They believed that they should have autonomy to rule "not only according to the material law of the Jewish community but also according to laws and principles of judgment that are customary in the Jewish religious courts and which constitute an inseparable part of the general Jewish law."[27]

This moment marked a turning point in the administration of the rabbinical courts. To avoid future appeals to the Mandate courts, the Zionist government of the Jewish community of Palestine, the Va'ad Le'umi, proposed, yet again, new procedural regulations for the rabbinical courts. Within a year, lawyers for the Va'ad Le'umi had composed the regulations. They were presented to the chief rabbis, who made few changes, and they were published in November 1942.

Although the 1942 regulations were very similar to those of 1921, their reception was entirely different. The 1921 regulations had made such little impact that even experts, oblivious to the similar regulations promulgated less than twenty years earlier, thought that the new regulations of 1942 were the first of their kind.[28] By contrast, the 1942 regulations were publicly defended and enforced by the chief rabbis. The different attitudes to the regulations of 1921 and 1942 are, in large part, a result of the shift in approach to Jewish law that had come about in the leadership of religious Zionism in the intervening two decades.[29] Gradually, the Chief Rabbinate had thrown its authority behind a regulatory apparatus that transformed a disparate body of loosely connected rabbinical courts with inconsistent procedures into a single hierarchical structure with uniform procedural regulations.

Even before the new regulations were written, the chief rabbis had begun to insist on the authority of the Great Rabbinical Court in Jerusalem to request case materials from lower courts in order to properly conduct appeals. In 1937, the Chief Rabbinate wrote to the notoriously independent rabbinate of Tel Aviv–Jaffa with regard to a family law case: "We have not been honored with a response to our correspondence of 28 Iyyar 5697 [May 9, 1937] and we still have not received the legal material in your possession regarding Shlomo and Sophia Skorokhod. As this is impeding the appeal hearing, we would be grateful if you would request your agents promptly to send to us the full material of this case."[30]

This letter was sent on 28 Sivan (June 7) a full month after the earlier request for the material. Behind the stylized honorifics, the reader senses the impatience of the Chief Rabbinate with the Tel Aviv–Jaffa court, which had not only failed to fulfill proper procedure, but had ignored their request altogether. This response was not unusual. The Tel Aviv–Jaffa rabbinate in particular objected strenuously to the centralizing thrust of the new regulations. In a private meeting with the Chief Rabbinate, the regional rabbis asserted that the Great Rabbinical Court was authorized to write regulations only for itself, and not for the regional courts. If regulations were required, they insisted that they be allowed to write their own. Besides, they claimed, the regulations contained rules that were contrary to halakha, such as the establishment of a rabbinical appeals court. The members of the Tel Aviv–Jaffa rabbinical court were unanimous in their opposition. One member said that the imposition of a rabbinical court of appeals would result in their total opposition to the regulations; another said he would organize all the rabbis in the country against them; a third labeled the regulations "Reform," a forceful criticism in the eyes of the avowedly Orthodox rabbinate.[31] Even after the 1942 regulations had been published, a commission of the Va'ad Le'umi found that the Tel Aviv–Jaffa rabbinate was still ignoring them. In blatant and explicit contravention of the regulations, they attempted to dissuade parties from challenging their rulings in the Great Rabbinical Court in Jerusalem by levying a tax on parties who sought an appeal.[32]

Despite all of this opposition, however, the chief rabbis began to enforce the regulations assiduously. To be sure, there was no overnight change. Over time, however, the chief rabbis, and Herzog in particular, fought to change this state of affairs and to strengthen Jerusalem's position at the apex of the new hierarchy of rabbinical courts. In support of the status of the Great Rabbinical Court in Jerusalem as a court of appeals, Herzog attempted to enforce the rule that lower rabbinical courts had to keep a written record of their judicial reasoning. Without a record of judicial reasoning the system of appeals would be undermined because the appeals court would not be able to consider the legal basis on which earlier decisions had been made. In the face of explicit statements in halakhic codes that rabbinical judges do not need to record their reasoning, Herzog made the argument that under the new circumstances, halakha did mandate the cooperation of the lower courts. In a responsum of 1948, he accepted that "according to the strict halakha there is no right to request written arguments" and he recognized that the opposing rabbis relied on this long-established precedent. He even conceded that the regulations were "a great innovation." Nevertheless, he wrote, these rabbinical courts "are not acting properly," because "they are contravening our enactment which was made with their agreement."[33]

Notably, Herzog made no mention of the fact that the regulations had originated with the insistence of the British authorities. He took full ownership of them and threw the weight of his authority behind them. Even though the regulations were written by lawyers and not by rabbis, Herzog attributed halakhic authority to the regulations on the basis that this was "our enactment." In other words, he argued that the new regulations had the status of a rabbinical enactment with the binding force of halakha, and not merely of the Mandate authorities. He even stated that the enactment had received the approval of the regional courts, although it was not in fact the case.

Similarly, the Jerusalem court insisted on its right to hear appeals from the regional rabbinical courts. In 1950, a case was heard in the Tel Aviv–Jaffa rabbinical court in a civil matter. This was a legal field over which the rabbinical courts had no state-enforced jurisdiction. From the perspective of the state, therefore, the court was functioning merely in the capacity of an arbitration board and not as a formal court.[34] Herzog claimed that even in this instance, the parties had the right to appeal, "for our authority as a rabbinical court of appeals flows from a communal enactment."[35] In other words, he argued, the centralization of the rabbinical court system was not a result of enforcement by the secular state alone; it had real halakhic validity. This approach was repeatedly affirmed in discussions in Great Rabbinical Court cases about the jurisdiction of the rabbinical court of appeals. In one example of many, the court ruled in a 1945 case, "The Great Rabbinical Court finds that it indeed does have the authority to judge this appeal, since the matter of appeals was accepted by rabbinical enactment, which is [as authoritative] as a law of our holy Torah. Therefore, anyone who comes to court comes with this in mind."[36]

Here again, the rabbinical court in Jerusalem insisted upon its authority to overturn the decision of a lower court. They defended this authority on the basis that the new regulations of 1942 were "accepted by rabbinical enactment." The rabbinical court thereby incorporated the desire of the British Mandate to impose its legal infrastructure, with its tendency to centralization and hierarchy, onto Jewish law. Far from resisting this as the imposition of a foreign legal system, they accepted it as their own innovation and took pains to enforce it. Against halakhic precedent, and against the protests of local rabbinic authorities, the rabbinical court system was gradually remade in the image of a European court system. Today, few people are aware of the British origins of the Israeli rabbinical courts, and it is very rare for a local rabbinical court to resist the right of appeal to the Great Rabbinical court in Jerusalem.

Another sign of the transformation of Israel's rabbinical courts system into a modern court structure on the European model was the decision of the Chief Rabbinate to begin to publish official collections of rabbinical court rulings.[37] The first volume was published in 1950 and edited by Zerah Warhaftig, a religious Zionist politician and lawyer with close ties to Herzog. The book was the first of its kind. For centuries, rabbis had published collections of responsa, which sometimes included the rulings of their rabbinical courts. The formal records of Jewish communities also frequently included the final rulings of rabbinical cases. Warhaftig's collection, however, was quite different. Its format was far from that of traditional responsa and evinced the newly institutionalized and centralized bureaucracy of the rabbinical system. Its arrangement and design were almost identical to that of the records of the Supreme Court of Israel, which were first published at around the same time. Like the publications of the secular court reports, each case in the rabbinical collection bears a reference number and the name of the court. It then lists the names of all of the judges, the president of the court for the hearing, the plaintiff, the respondent, and their legal counsel.[38] There follows a short summary of the subject of the case, a statement of the facts, the terms of the decision, the reasoning of the judges, and a numbered list of the "conclusions," meaning points of law decided in the case that could be applied as binding precedent in future cases.

The new rabbinical court reports were a striking departure from earlier practices of the rabbinical courts in Palestine and Israel. Before 1950, there were no formal collections of rabbinical court rulings. When those rulings were issued in writing, they took the form of simple typed letters, signed by the rabbinical judges who heard the case. Unlike the later published reports, earlier decisions make no mention of the points of law considered in the case, or the findings of fact. And unlike the later reports, which tended to cover several pages, the earlier decisions were typically very short. One decision from 1938, for example, which has been preserved in the archives, consists of a single sheet of paper bearing the letterhead of The Chief Rabbinate of Palestine. It begins with the names of the plaintiff and defendant and the subject of the case and concludes with the signatures of three rabbinical judges. The rest of it, in its entirety, reads as follows:

> There have appeared before us in law Mr. Pinhas Ehrlichman, plaintiff, and his representative, Mr. Goldberg Esq., and Mrs. Rivkah Shapira-Ehrlichman, respondent, and her representative Rabbi Yitzhak Levi. After hearing the claims and responses of the two sides, we have decided: According to the inquiry she is held to be a married women. The plaintiff may not force her to accept a divorce until he pays her damages in the sum of 15 Palestinian pounds. Then he will be exempt from marital support.[39]

No law or political pressure pushed the rabbinical court to change this state of affairs. The innovative decision to print its court reports in a new format, identical to the printed reports of the secular courts of Israel, was born of a desire to present the rabbinical courts as professional, regulated, and uniform; to encourage the Jewish population of Israel to patronize the rabbinical courts rather than the secular courts; and to centralize the authority of the rabbinical courts into a hierarchy with the Jerusalem court at its peak.

The initiative to publish the decisions of the rabbinical court came from Warhaftig himself. He was assisted by a number of lawyers, including Mordekhai Levanon, who was one of the authors of the procedural regulations of both 1921 and 1944. The reports were not verbatim copies of the rabbinical rulings, but were "abstracted by the editors" from court materials.[40] As a result, some rabbis were initially resistant to the project and had to be reassured by the editors.[41] According to Warhaftig, the goal of publishing the decisions was to modernize the workings of the rabbinical court and to showcase the world of halakha to those unfamiliar with it, to provide "jurists and scholars with access to the world of the rabbinical courts and the methods by which they reach their decisions."[42] Warhaftig recognized the challenge of presenting the rulings of rabbinical courts in a language that could be understood by nonspecialists and acknowledged "the doubters," who questioned whether he would "succeed in getting the rabbinical judges to speak in a general legal fashion." [43] Ultimately, he found that these doubters were "pleasantly surprised" with the outcome.[44] As he published their rulings, Warhaftig found that rabbis used to writing in the traditional mold began to express themselves in a more accessible way, "to communicate their opinions in a clear and orderly manner comprehensible to those unschooled in Jewish law, whether jurists or members of the public."[45] Warhaftig's hope was that if the halakhic process could be widely understood, then people would not question the competence of rabbinical courts to operate under modern conditions. He anticipated that they would thereby be endorsed by the Israeli public as a key element of Israel's legal establishment.

The commitment of the Chief Rabbinate to legal centralism and bureaucratization is also evident in a flurry of rabbinic legislation from the middle of the 1940s. Before that time, rabbinical courts tended to apply customary Jewish law, inscribed in halakhic texts and communal practice, rather than regulations that they had drafted themselves. Abraham Isaac Kook had considered the possibility of rabbinic legislation but, even in the abstract, he thought that this should only be a rare event, reserved for times of pressing need, and he never created any legislation in practice.[46] The only regulations that the Chief Rabbinate did endorse were the procedural regulations discussed previously. While significant in their own way, these regulations were entirely procedural and did not address any substantive legal issues. This all changed in 1944, when the Chief Rabbinate enacted a series of substantive statutory regulations for the first time. More regulations followed in 1950. This fact in itself is an indication of a centralizing approach. These statutes diminished the interpretive authority of individual judges, further serving the centralization of legal authority and the imposition of uniform practice.

The statutes of the Chief Rabbinate were concerned primarily with Jewish marriage law.[47] They set a formal structure for the Jewish marriage ceremony and set a minimum age for marriage of sixteen years for women. They also outlawed polygamy and the practice of levirate marriage. (In the case that a married man with a brother dies childless, halakha requires either that his brother marry his widow—levirate marriage—or that the *halitsah* ceremony, by which the brother is released from that obligation, be performed.) The statutes were designed to bring the workings of the rabbinical courts in line with the norms of modern European society. They also had another consequence, however, which was to efface the communal practice of many of Israel's Sephardic communities.

Hundreds of thousands of Sephardic Jews from North Africa and the Middle East arrived in Israel in its first few years, and many of them had practices that differed from Ashkenazic custom. The rabbinate favored Ashkenazic practice, in part because Ashkenazic rabbis were more numerous at the time, but in part because their custom in marriage law was closer to the accepted norms of

modern Europe. Sephardic and Ashkenazic practices surrounding marriage differed in a number of important ways. Whereas Ashkenazic custom had banned
the practice of polygamy early in the Middle Ages, polygamy continued in some
Sephardic communities.[48] The Yemenite Jewish community maintained the custom of men betrothing young girls, sometimes girls even younger than twelve,
who were therefore minors from a halakhic perspective. (This practice was criticized by other Sephardic communities as well as by Ashkenazim.)[49] More general
Sephardic practice was also to estimate a lower value for the silver shekels mentioned in a traditional *ketubah* marriage document (which specifies the obligations of the husband toward the wife), meaning that Ashkenazic rabbis granted
women higher marriage settlements in real terms. Furthermore, Sephardim
tended to perform levirate marriages, whereas Ashkenazim tended to prefer
the *halitsah* ceremony. The new statutes forbade all of these Sephardic customs
in Israel's rabbinical courts. They outlawed polygamy, specified that no woman
younger than the age of sixteen years and one day could be betrothed, aligned the
real value of the ketubah with the Ashkenazic custom, and mandated *halitsah*,
thereby attempting to eradicate levirate marriage.

Ironically, in 1938, only six years before the promulgation of the first round
of the new statutes, Herzog had defended Jewish polygamy, one of the very practices that the new regulations prohibited. Soon after Herzog became chief rabbi,
he had been asked to provide his expert opinion in a case in the British Mandate
courts in which an Ashkenazic Jewish man was being prosecuted for polygamy.
Herzog's defense was that the man's own religious law, halakha, allowed polygamy.
Given that personal status came under the exclusive jurisdiction of the religious
courts, he argued, the man should not be convicted. Herzog maintained that
polygamy was not a criminal act even for Ashkenazim and that therefore both
the man's first and second marriages were legal and valid.[50] It seems clear, however, that Herzog's vociferous defense of this polygamous act came from his desire
to preserve rabbinic autonomy in marriage law before the British courts.[51] When
it came to his own rabbinical court, he was loathe to accept the practice. Indeed,
not only did he uphold the traditional eschewal of polygamy for Ashkenazim,
but he also pushed for its abolition among Sephardim. Historically, it was unremarkable for different Jewish communities to follow their own customs and laws,
even if they lived side by side with one another. The various Jewish communities
of Palestine had followed diverse customs for centuries. This legal diversity, however, could not be countenanced by a centralized rabbinical authority.

It did not escape the attention of Sephardic rabbis that the statutes imposed
uniformity according to the Ashkenazic rite. The reasons for this choice are not
difficult to discern. At the time, the majority of the rabbinical authorities in
Israel were Ashkenazic. More importantly, people like Herzog, whose entire legal

philosophy was motivated by the desire to create a halakha that would be seen to compete with any modern state's legal system, wanted to eradicate practices such as child marriage and polygamy that would have made halakha seem backward, even barbaric, to modern observers. In a sense, the statutes not only represented the imposition of a centralized rabbinical authority; they also supported a kind of civilizing mission with regard to the newer immigrants from Middle Eastern countries that characterized the policies of the State of Israel in those years.[52] This rabbinical orientalism was resisted by rabbis such as Ovadiah Yosef, who became a champion of Sephardic independence. In 1951, just one year after the statute mandating *halitsah*, a case came before Yosef in the rabbinical court of Petah Tikvah. He ruled that, irrespective of the new statute, Sephardim should continue to perform levirate marriages rather than *halitsah*. The legislation of the Chief Rabbinate, he concluded, should be ignored because "they have no authority in this matter."[53]

Yosef correctly perceived this legislation as an attempt both to centralize authority in the Chief Rabbinate and to impose a uniform law on all Jews in the state at the expense of Sephardic custom. He resisted both tendencies.[54] His criticisms, however, were not sufficient to stand in the way of the centralization of the rabbinate. The new rabbinical statutes, like the establishment of a rabbinical court of appeals and the new publication of rabbinical court records, were part of the inexorable trend toward modernization, centralization, and bureaucratization that recreated Israel's Chief Rabbinate in the image of a modern legal system.

Halakhic Legislation for a Modern State

This modernizing dynamic also characterized the remarkable attempt by religious Zionists to draft a comprehensive halakhic law for the State of Israel. Like other reforms, this massive effort to codify new halakhic legislation exemplifies the tension between resistance to "foreign" law and adoption of its basic structures and methods. In pursuing their goal to present halakha as the equal of modern Western jurisprudence, vying to replace it as the law governing the state, religious Zionist rabbinical leaders embraced the nature of the very jurisprudence that they wanted to reject.

The codifying project went even further than Herzog's earlier attempt to sketch out the basic structure of a halakhic state. It was an attempt to write a complete series of halakhic legal codes for all areas of law. The objective was to produce halakhic law books that could be understood even by those without rabbinical training and would be adopted as the legal code of the entire state. Yet, although the idea of the project was to promote halakha in place of the British law that Israel had inherited or the European-style civil codes that were being considered by the Knesset, the newly written halakhic codes were themselves based on a modern European legal model.

The project was initiated in 1948 by one of the most senior religious Zionist leaders of the time. Rabbi Meir Bar-Ilan was born Meir Berlin in Volozhin, then part of the Russian Empire, to a preeminent rabbinical family. His father was the revered Rabbi Naftali Tsvi Yehudah Berlin (widely known by the acronym Netziv), head of the Volozhin Yeshiva. After receiving an extensive religious education, Berlin attended the University of Berlin. It was in Germany that he became a member of the Mizrahi party and later the secretary of the world Mizrahi movement. After his move to Jerusalem in 1926, he became the president of the Center of World Mizrahi, holding that office until his death in 1949. In 1948, Bar-Ilan was one of the senior representatives of the Yishuv, the grandfather of religious Zionism, and a deeply authoritative voice who was connected to the religious establishment of prewar Europe.

Given his deep investment in religious Zionism, Bar-Ilan had naturally given thought to the relationship between politics and Judaism. As early as 1922, he made the claim that the Jewish tradition knows of no separation between church and state.[55] His thoughts remained in the realm of theory for decades. It was not until 1948 that he outlined a detailed position on what a modern Jewish state might look like in practice. In the immediate aftermath of the Declaration of Independence, only months before his death, he published an article called "Law and Justice in our State."[56] Originally a memorandum circulated among like-minded rabbinical scholars, the article was later reprinted in *Yavneh*, a newly founded journal of religious Zionism. At the time, Herzog's work had not yet been published or widely shared, so this was one of the first and most detailed treatments of the role of halakha in the laws of the state.

The article began with Bar-Ilan stating outright that he believed that all areas of law in the Jewish state, including civil law, should be governed by halakha. "Foreign" law, he believed, had no place in the Jewish state: "We are obliged to . . . arrange statutes and laws, not just in matters of religious ritual [*isur ve-heter*] but also in matters of civil law [*hiyuv u-petur*], by which we will live and by which we will judge in our independent and sovereign state."[57]

Bar-Ilan conceded that there were serious obstacles to this goal of imposing a halakhic civil law on the citizens of a modern state. Like Herzog, he recognized that modifications would have to be made, in order to allow the full participation of women and Gentiles in public life. Without this, he knew, halakha would certainly not be adopted by the majority of citizens, in which case "the whole shape of social life in our state will be neither by our spirit, nor according to our outlook."[58] He also acknowledged that Jewish law, particularly criminal law, fell short of what the modern state required. He readily admitted that in their exile, Jewish communities had not generally been responsible for administering their own criminal or civil law without the oversight of non-Jewish authorities.[59] This was no small admission. The two millennia of Jewish exile, which Bar-Ilan portrayed as merely an unfortunate historical hiccup, actually incorporated the entire history of halakhic development. Nevertheless, Bar-Ilan maintained that the Torah in principle contained all the necessary resources for governing a modern state. All that was needed was reorganization. "We have the entire Torah," he wrote, and "we have only to put these laws in *order* and to make their realization in day to day life to a real possibility."[60]

Bar-Ilan excoriated the popular view that the state would have to adopt the laws of other nations, "to go and graze in other fields and to draw the basis of the laws of our state from the strange wells of the other nations."[61] This assumption, he believed, was nothing but "the evil inclination [produced by] the long exile."[62] The halakhic corpus, he insisted, had all the resources necessary to create a modern civil code. He observed that even within the Orthodox community itself there were those who were prepared to accept a pluralistic legal model in which halakha could operate in parallel with a secular legislation. "Within our religious circles," he wrote, "there is a kind of secret agreement that if the State of Israel has a double system of law, with religious or rabbinical courts, on the one hand and secular ones on the other . . . that will be enough for them and they will not ask for more."[63]

For Bar-Ilan, however, as for Herzog, this legally pluralist solution was entirely unacceptable. He expressed this view in a bold, even aggressive, way.

> The only path for every believing Jew is to request with all force and to strive with all might and every effort for us to have *one law in all realms* of our state. Not just for us but for all those who live in the state, even those who are not of the covenant, just as in every land and country the political territory determines [the law] and not personal [religious] affiliation . . . and this one law should be based on the Torah of Israel and what derives from it, and not on another law and another Torah.
>
> . . . Therefore it is our obligation . . . to prepare immediately for war, with the right and with the left, for a state law that is based on the laws of our holy Torah in all the streets of our state and in all the fields of its life. This law and no other, none besides it.[64] [Emphases in the original.]

In this striking passage, Bar-Ilan explicitly articulated his belief that halakha must be the only legal system endorsed by the state. He stopped short of calling for the imposition of all ritual aspects of halakha, such as dietary law, on every citizen. He did, however, issue a call to arms in the struggle to establish a halakhic civil and criminal law as the only law for every resident in the state, whether they were Jewish or not. The originality of this statement cannot be overstated. It was a radical innovation to seek to impose the civil and criminal aspects of Jewish law not just on Jews but on all those within the territory of the state, irrespective of their religious identity. His picture of the law represented the epitome of legal centralism and he was willing to tolerate serious divergences from tradition in order to establish and defend it.

The strength of Bar-Ilan's rhetoric belied its paradoxical nature. He maintained that Jewish law is capable of governing a modern state and that the adoption of a pluralistic legal system, incorporating the laws of other nations, would be folly. Despite this belief, however, he fought for a centralist model of halakha precisely on the grounds that this was the legal model of other modern states. He argued that the halakha should apply to everyone, "just as in every land and country [where] the political territory determines [the law] and not personal [religious] affiliation." So even as he called for a pure Jewish law unsullied by foreign influence, he promoted innovations that would make Jewish law more like the law of other nations, especially the European countries where legal centralism reigned supreme.

Bar-Ilan laid out the method by which the halakhic code would be compiled. He called for the formation of committees of Torah scholars, which would each focus on a specific area of law. They would "conduct a great search in the responsa from the early to the late" in order to find applicable halakhic material. The fruit of these committees would be reviewed by a further set of committees, after which a final product would be composed. Even this, however, would first need to be edited into "a concise and pithy literary form." In addition to halakhic experts, Bar-Ilan assumed that the work would have to recruit "[secular] lawyers familiar with the Torah and perhaps other proof readers." Once complete, the code, he imagined, would then be placed "in the hands of every judge" so that even judges without a prior knowledge of halakha would be able to apply it.[65] The modern bureaucratic nature of this endeavor is remarkable. Never before had a halakhic code been compiled by committee.

Bar-Ilan also wanted the form of his halakhic code to resemble the form of the law codes of other modern states. He took pains to explain to his potential collaborators that the finished product should not contain the extended legal analysis customarily found in halakhic texts. Rather, it was to be concise and consistent. It was to contain the law and nothing more. In this respect, Bar-Ilan acknowledged the innovative nature of the project he was proposing and explicitly acknowledged its distinctiveness from earlier modes of halakhic literature:

Every generation has its own literary form. . . . In this generation and for the needs of our time a book of laws has to be edited in the accepted form of [modern secular] law books, with sources at the bottom [of the page] and, in exceptional cases, comments as either footnotes or endnotes. But the people working on this should not include in the law books the many new theories and lengthy explanations that will certainly occur to them [because the law books] will be in the hands of every judge, including those who are not real Torah scholars.[66]

It is difficult to overlook Bar-Ilan's apologetic tone and the fact that he felt the need to defend the literary form of his proposed code. He was quite aware that the form he was describing had little in common with traditional halakhic compilations, which were typically incomprehensible to nonexperts and were published together with commentaries whose sheer volume dwarfed the main text. In place of this traditional model, Bar-Ilan wanted the new halakhic code to mirror European codes like the German BGB or the French *Code civil*. It would be composed of precise and well-organized legal statements. References to the original halakhic sources would be kept out of the main text. Commentary would be rare and unobtrusive.

The language with which Bar-Ilan described his vision of the new halakhic code gives a sense of the extent to which modern European law was the touchstone for his entire project. Many of the terms that Bar-Ilan used were direct Hebrew translations of terms from German jurisprudence. Thus, he called his legal code a "law book" (*sefer huqim*), a direct translation of the German *Gesetzbuch*. He referred to "civil law" (*hoq ezrahi*), a translation of *bürgerliches Recht*; "penal (i.e., criminal) law" (*hoq pelili*), a translation of *Strafrecht*; and "public law" (*hoq tsiburi*), a translation of *öffentliches Recht*. This terminology was common in legal circles in the Berlin of Bar-Ilan's youth and also among the secular jurists of the State of Israel, who were mostly educated in the German legal system. It is, however, entirely foreign to the Jewish legal tradition. There is not a single instance of any of these terms in halakhic literature before the rise of religious Zionist jurisprudence. Indeed, these are not just foreign terms, but foreign categories as well. Halakha knows no distinction between, for example, civil and criminal damages; they are both categorized under "damages" (*neziqin*). Nor does halakha know of a "law book" in the sense of a modern civil code. No halakhic code, however influential, is ultimately authoritative in every situation. Case law and "compromise" (*pesharah*) are as important to halakhic adjudication as halakhic codes. Yet despite the categorical differences between halakha as traditionally applied and modern European law, Bar-Ilan chose to adopt this terminology for his legal code.

Bar-Ilan insisted on using an unadulterated Jewish law for the Jewish state. But his entire vision of that law, its application to the citizens of a state rather than to a religious community, its all-encompassing scope, its codification, its terminology, and its central categories were drawn entirely from modern European jurisprudence. The adaptation of halakha to this foreign model required innovations that Bar-Ilan, for the sake of his vision, was ready to accept. He understood that legal centralism was the only kind of legal model that was valued by modern jurists. For halakha to be taken seriously and to make its mark in a newly independent state, it had to be refashioned according to that structure.

Bar-Ilan set about implementing his vision of a halakhic civil code together with Herzog. The two of them had the seniority, funding, and institutional respectability to take practical steps to bring their ideas to fruition. In the summer of 1948, only weeks after the proclamation of independence, Bar-Ilan and Herzog convened a "legislative committee" of the World Mizrahi movement.[67] The committee, as its secretary Zvi Kaplan later described, was to pursue the following goal:

> The preparation of a book of laws for the State of Israel according to our Torah . . . It is forbidden for two kinds of law to rule in our state, a "civil" law and a Torah law. *All* the state and *all* the courts[68] within it must be run according to the law of the Torah. . . . To that end . . . there is the need first of all for internal work in order to create a book of laws in the modern form so that it will be comprehensible to every judge and lawyer, even those who are not religious.[69] [Emphasis in the original.]

Kaplan's description precisely echoed Bar-Ilan's call for a single halakhic law for the state and for a new halakhic code that would be comprehensible to all the state's lawyers and judges, including those with no experience of halakha.

On August 17 of that same year, Bar-Ilan personally wrote to a number of rabbis to enlist their participation in the project.[70] He explained the urgency "to go as fast as possible to prepare samples of a book of laws in topical matters in both civil and criminal matters." He presumably knew that the sooner the halakhic code would be ready, the higher the chance of its success. He outlined a tremendous array of specific areas of law that required their attention. These included contract, extortion, insurance, tort, treason, espionage, draft evasion, forging currency, theft, robbery, and murder. Although religious Zionist jurists sometimes said that they would limit the application of halakha to civil matters, and not to criminal law, Bar-Ilan and Herzog at this point clearly intended to compose halakhic codes dealing with criminal law too. Bar-Ilan also mentioned some of the procedural problems that needed to be overcome in the application of halakha to the state such as the appointment of judges and the inclusion of testimony from women or Gentiles. The work, he said, would require them to find appropriate precedent and work it into the form of the finished code. He encouraged the rabbis to tell him which areas of law they most wanted to research and how much they would like to be paid. Ultimately, a fixed committee was established, comprising nine rabbis, whose work was supplemented by other members.[71]

The work of this committee, and the intellectual problems that it encountered, reflected the paradoxical nature of the project, which was caught between the repudiation of foreign sources of law and the reliance on European legal models. First, there were questions about the literary form of the work. Bar-Ilan had already stipulated that the halakhic code would have to be written in the genre of a European civil code, quite different from the discursive nature of most rabbinical legal texts. He reiterated this requirement in a meeting of the legislative committee on April 11, 1949:

> Whatever is published must be acceptable to the public and must be intended for this particular purpose. There is no place for length but for summary. The give and take of halakha must be curtailed. The work must be edited by one, directed hand. . . . Attention must be paid to the form, which must be comprehensible not just to Torah scholars, for our work is not just intended for them.[72]

Despite his clear instructions, though, not all members of the committee understood what was required. Kaplan had to write to one of the rabbis on the committee, who had apparently failed to follow the required format: "You must understand that this work with which we are occupied is not intended for the sake of study alone;[73] it has a practical goal: the ordering of a law book for the State of Israel. And in the context of this work, we must attend only to matters pertaining *directly* to the laws of the contemporary state and not to other matters."[74] [Emphasis in the original.] The rabbi's confusion over what was expected of him underlines the differences between the proposed modern halakhic code and the conventional forms and methods of halakhic scholarship.

The paradoxical nature of the project also surfaced in the search for legal materials on which to base the code. Members of the committee were conscious of the paucity of relevant materials in the halakhic corpus, especially pertaining to criminal matters. One of them called their work "a creation ex nihilo," clearly identifying the innovative nature of the project.[75] Avraham Shapira, who later served on the rabbinical court in Jerusalem and, from 1983 through 1993, as the Ashkenazic Chief Rabbi of Israel, was also a member of the committee. His letter to Bar-Ilan perfectly manifested the tension implicit in undertaking such a radically new project while claiming that it arose naturally from traditional sources. He began by expressing his confidence that "any legal problem in any area can find a fitting solution according to the foundations and roots of traditional halakha."[76] However, he went on to undermine this certainty, particularly with regard to criminal law. "Apart from the paucity of material in our possession," he wrote, "there is the additional factor that criminal law, apart from establishing guilt or innocence, needs to effect punishments that fit the crime. This is an indispensable part of the law and in this area there are no sources at all in the halakha."[77] Whereas in theory Shapira shared Bar-Ilan's belief that halakha could be implemented as the law of a modern state, he had substantial reservations in practice. He was bothered by the lack of relevant precedent in halakhic criminal law. Most of all, he realized that the punishments for criminal acts recognized by halakha were scarcely fitting for modern circumstances.

Despite these problems, and hesitations, the project to create a halakhic law for the State of Israel forged ahead. By April 1949, less than a year after it had begun, the committee had produced pamphlets on murder, theft, robbery, extortion, incarceration, contract, business law, laws of partnerships, tort, labor law, inheritance law, laws pertaining to the national mint, and the jurisdiction of rabbinical courts. Not all of it had been edited, but some had been approved by Bar-Ilan and Herzog.[78]

In this same month, though, Bar-Ilan died. The project found itself without a leader and consequently without a budget. It appears that the entire undertaking was shut down, at least temporarily. The Mizrahi archive contains letters from participants in the project who had been informed that it would have to be closed because of lack of funds. All was not lost, however. Yehudah Leib Fishman-Maimon, the champion of the failed attempt to re-establish the Great Sanhedrin, had become Israel's first Minister of Religious Affairs and apportioned funds to the project. Funding was also provided by the Harry Fischel Institute. The institute was named for its patron, a Russian-born Orthodox Jew who had become a successful real estate developer and philanthropist in New York. The institute had been funding Torah scholarship in Jerusalem for some years and eventually absorbed the efforts toward a halakhic codification under its auspices.

After Bar-Ilan's death, the project remained under the ultimate supervision of Herzog, but its management passed to Binyamin Rabinowitz-Te'omim. Rabinowitz-Te'omim, a nephew of Abraham Isaac Kook's second wife, had been educated in the Slobodka Yeshiva in Kovno, Lithuania, and immigrated to Palestine in 1930. He had been a member of the original committee on halakhic codification and published a programmatic pamphlet about its future in March 1950.[79] As the pamphlet made clear, the intellectual problems and the inherent paradox of the project persisted, despite its change of management. Like his predecessors, Rabinowitz-Te'omim stressed the importance of a uniquely Jewish approach to law but at the same time conceded the need to consult with experts in other legal systems. He especially recommended the consultation of "Swiss law which is accepted in many countries."[80] Indeed, one adviser to the project was Zvi Arman, a law graduate of the University of Bern and an expert on Swiss law. Rabinowitz-Te'omim explicitly stated that there was a need to use new terminology of the kind Bar-Ilan had already introduced. He also repeated the requests, already made by Bar-Ilan and other leaders of the project, that the law be understood by anyone, even those who were not scholars of the Torah.

Ultimately, Bar-Ilan's dream was realized only in part. The Harry Fischel Institute published two books of Jewish law, one dealing with commercial law, the other with the authority of the courts and government, and the laws of murder.[81] These books were the first legal codes ever produced in the rabbinical tradition that were intended to apply to all the citizens of a modern state. They roughly fit the literary form that Bar-Ilan had envisioned, although they contain more commentary and digression than he would probably have approved; the traditional rabbinic idiom was apparently too difficult to break away from entirely. Each book presents the law in clear, numbered paragraphs. Beneath the main text there are footnotes that direct the reader to the sources of the law and a commentary that delves into the law in greater detail, occasionally making comparisons with other legal systems. The section on criminal liability, for example, surveyed German, Ottoman, and British Mandate law before discussing halakha.[82] These law books were the only ones published before it became clear that they would never be accepted as law by the secular Israeli establishment. The Harry Fischel Institute continues to produce works of Jewish law to this day and also trains halakhic judges for Israel's rabbinical courts. Bar-Ilan's great initiative, however, never achieved its goal of establishing a halakhic law for all residents of the State of Israel.

The efforts of religious Zionist leaders in these early years of the state was, by their own standards, a failure. They had undertaken a reform of the Israeli rabbinate and a reimagining of halakha in a modern idiom in the hope that secular leaders would be convinced that halakha could meet the modern state on its own terms and would grant it pride of place in the state's legal apparatus. This endeavor produced the paradoxical effect that religious Zionist leaders consistently lobbied for the rejection of "foreign" influence on Jewish law while simultaneously remaking halakha, sometimes in radically new ways, on the very model of the law they were trying to reject. By the early 1950s, however, it had become clear that the state would not adopt halakha as its national code. Despite this failure, however, the bold new thinking of their leaders in these years established among religious Zionists the principle that the state can and should be run according to halakha. The principle was pursued with such force in that critical period that it has persevered over the decades and continues to motivate many religious Zionists even today.

5 FAILURE AND RESISTANCE

By the early 1950s, it became clear that the halakhic state would not be realized, at least in the short term. Resigning themselves to the fact that Israel would not be governed entirely by halakha, religious Zionists redirected their efforts toward more modest goals. Although it fell very short of the dream of a fully halakhic state, they pushed for what became known as "religious legislation" (*haqiqah datit*). This meant urging the Knesset to incorporate halakha into state law in a piecemeal fashion through laws that, for example, restricted the operation of businesses and public transport on the Sabbath and that gave the state rabbinate exclusive control over kosher certification.[1] On the whole, however, religious Zionists adopted a pragmatic attitude toward politics, tending to prioritize the flourishing of the state over their hopes for halakhic control.[2] Their accommodation to the secular state, though, was only superficial. It masked a powerful internal resolve to protest the secular state. Law played a central role in this protest. Religious Zionists used law not only as a tool for achieving political goals but also as a way of organizing their own community and strengthening their long-term commitment to the idea of the halakhic state, even as the prospects of its immediate success were very slim. From the 1950s, arguing about Israel's law helped religious Zionists to signal their support for the Zionist project and, simultaneously, their opposition to what they saw as the secular betrayal of religion.

The Setback

Very soon after the establishment of the state, it became clear to religious Zionist leaders that their constitutional plans would come to naught. The Zionist establishment was dominated by Jews whose attitude toward religion ranged from indifference to active opposition. Ben-Gurion had reached a "status quo" agreement with the Ultra-Orthodox Agudat Yisrael party in 1947, an agreement that

The Invention of Jewish Theocracy. Alexander Kaye, Oxford University Press (2020). © Oxford University Press.
DOI: 10.1093/oso/9780190922740.001.0001

guaranteed, among other things, public funding for religious education, and the rabbinical courts' exclusive jurisdiction over marriage and divorce. But this agreement was a matter of expediency only. Ben-Gurion wanted to be sure that the Orthodox would join the forthcoming Zionist delegation to the UN Special Committee on Palestine that visited Palestine later that year.[3] Ben-Gurion himself did not really think of the agreement as a compromise; he believed that the future of Orthodox Judaism was tentative at best and that commitments to that community had little political cost. He showed no interest in the constitutional discussions among religious Zionists. Herzog's work on a Jewish constitution, the books of halakhic civil legislation that were already being printed, and debates and discussions about the role of women and non-Jews in the Jewish state were ignored by the Zionist leadership. At no point in those early years was it a serious possibility that halakha would become the exclusive law of Israel.[4]

It is therefore justified to ask why religious Zionists themselves thought that their goal of a halakhic constitution had any chance of success. In a speech in the Great Synagogue in Jerusalem in July 1948, Herzog declared his continued commitment to the idea of a halakhic state. "We will not give up on the law of the Torah," he proclaimed. "I am ready to sacrifice my life for it."[5] The extreme nature of this declaration seems to indicate Herzog's continued belief in the possibility of a Torah constitution. Similarly, the rabbis who were composing halakhic civil law books under the leadership of Herzog and Rabinowitz-Te'omim continued their initiative into the early 1950s and presumably hoped that their labors would have immediate practical application.

This apparent optimism might have been sustained by a common tendency among religious Zionists to view divine impulses behind ostensibly secular processes.[6] Perhaps their ideological investment in the faith that the Zionist movement would produce a religious state obscured the evidence that their dreams were far from realization. It is also possible that the hopes of religious Zionists were fueled by a resurgence of interest in Mishpat Ivri just before the establishment of the state. Although the Mishpat Ivri movement had a secular orientation, and had therefore previously aroused Herzog's disdain, it ostensibly pursued the compatible goal of using Jewish law as a resource for Israeli law. In 1946, for example, Haim Cohn, who would later become Israel's Minister of Justice, spoke in favor of constructing a civil law "that would continue our ancient traditions" and that would reflect "the character and the destiny" of the Jewish people.[7] Sentiments like Cohn's, however, would never have resulted in the formal adoption of halakha as the law of the state. Even had the interest in Mishpat Ivri continued, the state would still have been a secular state whose laws, even as they drew from traditional sources, would have been given authority by the Knesset, not by God.

By the second half of 1948, though, Herzog had begun to doubt his chance of success. About two weeks before he declared his readiness to sacrifice his life for the sake of a Torah state, he wrote to Simhah Assaf, a rabbinical scholar, professor of Jewish law, and one of Israel's first Supreme Court Justices, admitting that he was "very doubtful whether they will agree" to his proposed constitutional clause that the laws of the state should be based on the laws of the Torah.[8] It seems, then, that Herzog's speech about self-sacrifice was a rhetorical call to arms at a time of impending failure rather than a sign of optimism. In later years, Moshe Una, a leader of the religious kibbutz movement and a member of Knesset for twenty years, also recorded his skepticism that the goal of a halakhic constitution could ever have succeeded. "It is unclear to me," he later wrote, "on what basis they hoped that it would be possible."[9] As early as mid-1948, therefore, it seems that the commitment to the idea of the halakhic state had become an identity marker of the religious Zionist community rather than a pragmatic template for political action.

The deliberations of the Zionist establishment over the constitutional and legislative structure of the state actually had an outcome that few could have predicted. Although Israel's Declaration of Independence called for the adoption of a constitution, the Knesset ended up postponing the adoption of a constitution indefinitely. Indeed, independence had little impact on most of its laws, which initially remained almost identical to those under the British mandate. (Decades later, Israel still has not completed its constitution, although many jurists argue that some of Israel's laws—those designated as "Basic Laws"—have constitutional standing.[10])

It is commonly believed that Israel's failure to adopt a constitution was the result of the opposition of religious parties, who considered the adoption of a written constitution to be a negation of the Torah. This is only partly true. Although the Ultra-Orthodox Agudat Yisrael party did oppose the constitution on these grounds, the other religious parties did not, at least at first.[11] In fact, it was Ben-Gurion himself who impeded the adoption of a constitution for fear that it would place limits on his executive powers. He took every opportunity to oppose the ratification of a constitution, believing that strong executive leadership, unencumbered by a written constitution, was necessary to place the young state, beset by war, on a firm footing.[12]

Primarily as a result of Ben-Gurion's opposition, plans for an immediate constitution were aborted. Indeed, initiatives for most new legislation were postponed in 1948, as war absorbed Israel's energies. The first law passed by the Provisional State Council (the forerunner of the Knesset) was the Law and Administration Ordinance, which established that the law in force on the last day of the British Mandate would continue to be in force in the new state, subject to legislation by the new government.[13] As under the British, and the Ottomans before them, personal status laws in Israel (marriage, divorce, etc.) remained under the jurisdiction of the religious courts, but the religious courts enjoyed no jurisdiction over civil or criminal law.[14]

This continuity marked the failure of the attempt by Herzog and his colleagues to implement a Torah constitution and halakhic rule. However much they doubted the success of their aspirations, they were no less distraught when they finally failed. In March 1948, the two chief rabbis, Herzog and Benzion Ousiel, wrote to the Jewish Agency to express their dismay over the decision to establish secular courts in the embryonic state:

> We were troubled to hear of your preparations to establish a secular court for all civil matters. This, the establishment of a permanent secular court on foundations foreign to the laws of Israel, means the uprooting of one of the basic and sacred principles of generations of Judaism. We Jewish leaders must protest against it with all our might and oppose it with every means at our disposal. We request of you and admonish you, in every possible way, that you remove this plan from your agenda and allow the law of the Torah to have its way.[15]

Ousiel, like Herzog, was a proponent of halakhic rule. On another occasion, he expressed his desire to have a halakhic legal system in Israel. "Now that God has blessed us with political deliverance, and a sovereign, independent Israeli government has emerged," he wrote, "it is incumbent upon us to establish beside it a national court that will judge according to the Torah."[16] The establishment of secular courts thwarted this dream.

Herzog's disappointment was palpable in his speech to the Eighteenth Council of World Mizrahi on August 16, 1949. The hope of the religious Zionists, he said, had been for the political elite to come to the rabbis to ask for advice about the law of the state. This move would have ensured that the democracy of the Jewish state would not just be a "pastiche, an aping of, and subordination to, the spirit of the democracy of other nations," but rather a democracy that drew from the Torah "the spring of our life, the source of Israel."[17] These hopes had been shattered. Instead, he lamented, "a mix of Turkish Ottoman and British law has taken the place of the law of the Torah of Israel in the State of Israel."[18] Given Herzog's beliefs in the superiority of Jewish civilization over both the Ottoman and the British, he felt this disappointment particularly acutely. "These peoples," he told the assembled members of Mizrahi, "did not reach the level of civilized peoples until thousands of years after we stood at Mount Sinai. The wisdom of their laws . . . is like a monkey before a human being when compared to the wisdom of our [Jewish] laws ... and I am talking to you as someone who is well versed in the laws of Rome and England."[19]

The fact that personal law remained under the jurisdiction of the rabbinical courts was small consolation. From the point of view of the state, the rabbinical courts now derived all of their legal authority from the secular state. This was not purely a theoretical matter; the state interfered in the workings of the religious courts. The most significant early intervention of the state in the practice of the rabbinical courts came in 1951, when the newly enacted Women's Equal Rights Law specified that "a man and a woman shall have equal status with regard to any legal proceedings."[20] The law explicitly imposed gender equality upon all courts in the state, including the rabbinical courts, except when they were dealing with cases of marriage and divorce.[21] Without such an exception, the application of Jewish law in the rabbinical courts would have ceased to have any meaning, given the fundamental place of gender difference in traditional Jewish marriage law. In other areas, however, the rabbinical courts were bound to observe total gender equality. This obligation affected in particular the administration of marital assets, regarding which halakha distinguishes between husband and wife.[22] Even when the law was still in its draft stages, Herzog expressed alarm at the threat that it posed to the operation of the rabbinical courts and the future of religious law in the state. He also expressed his fear that if the rabbinical courts did not have free rein in this area, a situation would develop in which Orthodox Jews in Israel would not trust the state to execute marriages and divorces properly. The result, he believed, would be a situation in which Orthodox Jews would avoid marrying other Jews, out of a fear that they were not eligible to marry under halakha.

> We are under threat of a bill regarding full equality between man and woman in all areas of the law. With this law, the arm of the sovereign will not only uproot the laws of Torah in the field of civil law but will also badly harm family law in Israel—marriage itself. This is likely to split, God forbid, the people of Israel in its land, to divide them in matters of marriage.[23]

The state did not heed the opposition of religious parties, however. Ben-Gurion himself told the Knesset that it would be "inconceivable" for the rabbinical courts to operate without state oversight.[24] Religious Zionists felt besieged. Their fight for a centralized halakhic regime had failed. Ultimately, they did find themselves under a legally centralized state, but the all-powerful law was secular legislation, not halakha.

Pragmatic Pluralism, Principled Centralism

By the early 1950s any hope of the realization of a Torah state, the cornerstone of religious Zionist thinking, had been dashed. The secular state ruled supreme. What was the response to this setback?

Religious Zionist leaders continued to subscribe in principle to a centralist philosophy of law. They did not stop believing that the State of Israel should have a single unified halakhic law. Some idealists continued openly to fight for this goal. Most, however, particularly religious Zionist politicians, recognized that it was no longer useful publicly to proclaim their commitment to this principle; the fight for the control of Israel's centralist legal infrastructure had already been decisively lost. But while not totally satisfied with the secular legal regime in Israel, they were willing to cooperate with the state in the political arena in the hope of preserving religious control over marriage and a separate religious educational stream.

As a result, from the early 1950s there developed an internal tension among religious Zionists between principle and pragmatism, resulting in a dual rhetoric. Externally, religious Zionists advocated a pluralist approach to law, an approach that allows for different legal systems with different sources of authority to coexist within the same political territory. This posture helped them to argue that rabbinical courts should be granted greater autonomy and that they should operate alongside, rather be subordinate to, secular courts. This pluralist rhetoric, however, was a strategic move only. Among themselves, religious Zionists continued to adhere to the doctrine of legal centralism that had guided them up to that point. They remained committed in principle to the ideal that the entire state and its law should be governed by halakha.[25]

This jurisprudential doublethink is clearly displayed in a speech that Herzog delivered to the Mizrahi council on August 6, 1949. Calling it a "programmatic proposal," Herzog began by noting the dissatisfaction of religious Zionists with the failure of the state to implement traditional Jewish law in its entirety:

> [Our duty is] . . . [t]o solemnly declare that we are not in principle ([though] in practice we have no power over this) in any way at peace with the current situation, which is the abolition of the vast majority of the law of the Torah, and that our most fervent desire is to return the law of the Torah to its place . . . under the leadership of the Chief Rabbinate of the Land of Israel.[26]

Conceding that this goal had become impractical in the short term, Herzog went on to describe a constitutional structure that, though less desirable than his ideal of a halakhic state, was still better than the current situation. According to this arrangement, rabbinical courts would constitute a parallel and entirely independent legal system to which any citizen of the state could have recourse. Like the civil courts, they would have jurisdiction in civil matters as well as in personal law. In this vision, cases heard in rabbinical courts could be appealed only to the Great Rabbinical Court; the Supreme Court of Israel would have no jurisdiction whatsoever in the rabbinical system. This structure would mean that the rabbinical courts would not be subsumed under the hierarchy of the state's secular legal system.

> Regarding civil cases, [even] outside the framework of personal status, there should be a law that every Jew who is taken to a state court has the choice to declare: "I am going to the Torah court." In such a case the Torah courts should have the full authority of law and their rulings appealed only before the Great Rabbinical Court of the Chief Rabbinate of the Land of Israel in Jerusalem. . . .

Herzog ended by conceding that if even this contingency could not be realized then at the very least the rabbinical courts must have independent and exclusive authority over the personal status laws that were traditionally within its jurisdiction. This authority was something over which no compromise could be tolerated.

> Whatever happens, we must insist with all force and power on the request for exclusive authority in the field of personal status. And ultimately I caution and warn from the bottom of my heart and soul that we must be ready to fight with absolutely all our power, even to the point that our ministers will leave the coalition and our representatives will leave the Knesset, against any law that is likely to impinge on the prohibitions of the personal laws of our holy Torah.[27]

Now that a centralized system of law meant the subordination of the rabbinical courts to a secular state, Herzog reluctantly encouraged his followers to make the case to the secular state for legal pluralism. His concession was a classic example of legal pluralism, exactly the kind of legal system that Gorontchik had suggested and Herzog had vigorously opposed only two years earlier. However, crucially, this pluralism was only part of a strategic argument toward the world outside religious Zionist circles. When talking to those inside his own camp, he made it clear that he still held fast to centralist principles. Herzog explicitly distinguished between the pluralistic rhetoric "facing outward, i.e. to the government authorities in the State of Israel" and the "internal requests" reserved for fellow religious

Zionists. Internally, his goal of centralization continued unabated and he persisted in his attempt to introduce "efficient procedures" into the rabbinical courts so that they would be more readily acceptable to the Israeli public. Everything rested on the success of these courts, "upon whose perfection, honor and glory the honor of our holy Torah and its influence to no small degree depend."[28]

The aspiration for centralization reached its apogee at the end of Herzog's speech, as he launched the idea of establishing a "world union of rabbis of Israel," which, he said, would be "like the Council of the Four Lands, based on its precedent and structure." He imagined a council "composed of Torah authorities from the Diaspora and Israel. It will be convened regularly by the Chief Rabbinate of the land of Israel, in Jerusalem our holy city, for the purpose of clarifying contemporary and future halakhic problems. It will be accepted as a supreme halakhic authority."[29]

As Herzog most likely knew, however, the Council of the Four Lands was nothing like the kind of institution that he wanted to establish. The Council of the Four Lands was an early modern institution made up of representatives of most of the Jewish communities in Eastern Europe. From the sixteenth to the eighteenth centuries, it was responsible primarily for assessing the tax responsibilities of its member communities. It also passed legislation on a wide variety of topics regarding the economic and religious lives of about a million Jews and served as a representative of Jewish communities before the Polish authorities. Crucially, though, the members of the Council of the Four Lands were not rabbis at all, but Jewish lay leaders. Rabbis were occasionally invited by the Council to compose legislation, but there was no doubt that they were subordinate to the lay leadership in the organization. Rather than being a precedent for a centralized system under a "world union of rabbis," the Council was, if anything, a paradigm of legal pluralism. It demonstrated the parallel existence of several sources of legal authority: the legislation of Jewish lay leaders, halakha as interpreted by rabbis, and non-Jewish political authority.[30] Herzog's reinterpretation of history underlines how committed he was to the principle of legal centralism even as he was encouraging his followers to argue for pluralism to the secular State of Israel. It illustrates the point that the pluralist position adopted by religious Zionists after 1949 was purely strategic. Internally, the philosophy of legal centralism continued to be a centerpiece of religious Zionist belief and rhetoric.

Resistance and Legal Rhetoric

After religious Zionist leaders failed to achieve their ideal goals, law took on an even more intense function as a focus of their identity. Legal rhetoric became a mode of resistance against the secular state that, many religious Zionists felt, had abandoned and oppressed them.

Law is not just a way of getting things done. It is also a way of understanding reality, shaping the categories through which we define ourselves.[31] Law is a discourse through which identity, power, and social roles are negotiated. For groups who feel marginalized or threatened by a state's hegemonic authority, the law can become a battlefield on which struggles for identity are fought and power imbalances addressed. Law can produce a "counter-hegemony" that challenges dominant power structures and prevailing cultural assumptions.[32] Thinking about law in this way allows us to see legal rhetoric from a different perspective. Legal rhetoric that appears ineffectual in practice may still be useful as a way of mounting resistance or shoring up identity.[33]

This analytical framework adds texture to the religious Zionist interest in religious legislation. Their interest reflected a desire to achieve specific political outcomes. But, perhaps even more importantly, it represented the urge to mount resistance against what they perceived to be the secular hegemony of the state. They imagined the law as the arena in which they would fight for their own identity and the creation of social meaning.

Zerah Warhaftig is the perfect character through which to illustrate the role of legal discourse as a tool of resistance. Warhaftig was born in Russia, received a law degree at the University of Warsaw, and later received a doctorate in law from the Hebrew University. During and after World War II he was extremely active in helping Jewish refugees from Poland and Lithuania, facilitating many of them in their escape to Japan. He came to Palestine in 1947 and represented Ha-Po'el Ha-Mizrahi in the Va'ad Le'umi, founding its department of law and justice. Warhaftig was a signatory to the Declaration of Independence and served in the Knesset until 1981 on the religious Zionist slate, first for Ha-Po'el Ha-Mizrahi and then for the National Religious Party.[34]

Warhaftig was a valuable asset for the religious Zionist community because he was a key participant in discussions over the drafting of legislation. He served on the Knesset's subcommittee that was charged with writing the state's constitution, serving as its chairman in 1948. Warhaftig's value was recognized by religious Zionist rabbinical leaders. Meir Bar-Ilan wrote to Warhaftig in March 1948, telling him, "It seems to me that the main key for bringing about the desires of the Mizrahi now rests in your hands more than any of our other representatives."[35] When Herzog was drafting his own halakhic constitution, Warhaftig composed three separate memoranda containing notes on the draft and offering advice about the legislative process.[36]

While fulfilling his obligations to the state, Warhaftig devoted himself to the goals of the religious Zionist community in legislation and politics. Both his public speeches and his private correspondence reveal that he understood arguments over law to be about identity as much as policy. He often explicitly portrayed his legislative activity in terms of the resistance of an oppressed minority against the state.[37] Warhaftig shared the principled legal centralism of Herzog and other religious Zionist leaders. His decision to participate with the secular legislature did not imply that he had come to terms with the failure to establish halakha as law. It was, rather, a strategic move in what Warhaftig believed would be a long-term battle with the state. The "war over Hebrew law," he wrote, "... will last for many years."[38]

Like Herzog, Warhaftig wanted the constitution to be based on Jewish sources. Before the Knesset decided to postpone the adoption of a constitution, Warhaftig made a speech in the Knesset, arguing as such. "We must search for material for our constitution in our own sources," he insisted. "The constitution of Israel [*yisra'el*] will be a Jewish [*yisre'eli*] constitution, only if it reflects the spirit of Israel. . . ."[39] He never gave up on this principle. As late as 1988, he compared the successful revival of the Hebrew language in Israel with what should have been the revival of Jewish law:

> [Hebrew] law is the language of the state and the spirit of the people.
> When we returned to the Land of Israel, we accepted the Hebrew language. We redeemed it from pages of books and brought it out to the city street. We did not go to seek other languages, despite the many difficulties in reviving an ancient language.[40] Similarly, the State of Israel should have announced its acceptance of Hebrew Law in its first constitution.[41]

Warhaftig marshaled the memories of Zionist resistance against British colonial rule to argue for the use of halakha in state legislation. He suggested that the failure to choose halakha over the law of imperial Britain in 1948 kept Israel as a colonial subject of the British Empire. Until Jewish law would be adopted, he declared in 1952, "we are still the slaves of Queen Elizabeth."[42] Warhaftig made this comment in Aramaic, rather than Hebrew, in order to paraphrase the talmudic phrase, "we are still the slaves of King Ahasuerus." Its original context is a talmudic discussion about the Purim story in the Book of Esther. The rabbis of the Talmud were pointing out that even after the apparently supremely successful Jewish victory at the end of that book, the Jews remained a people subservient to the Persian king.[43] So too, Warhaftig was intimating, despite its independence, and despite its military victory in 1948, Israel would remain a colony of Britain until it adopted a truly independent legal system that, in his mind, could only be halakha. In 1958, he was still arguing that, because Israeli legislation was interpreted by Israeli courts by reference to English law, "from this perspective we remain an English colony in every respect."[44]

Warhaftig felt so strongly about promoting the role of halakha in Israel that he surreptitiously enlisted the aid of religious Zionists outside of Israel to support that goal. In January 1948, for example, he wrote to Raphael Gold, the president of Ha-Po'el Ha-Mizrahi in New York, urging him to push the religious Zionist community there to put pressure on Israel to adopt Jewish law. "The battle for the religious character of the Jewish State will have to be waged and won here on the spot," he wrote, "but nonetheless the pressure of Jewish public opinion outside Palestine will surely be of value."[45] Warhaftig knew, however, that if it was discovered that he had been recruiting foreign pressure to achieve his own political ends, his own position might be compromised. He therefore implored Gold "to see to it that there is no needless publicity on my contacts with you in this matter which I intend to further in a private capacity."[46] The political risk that Warhaftig was willing to take to promote the idea of the halakhic state signifies the importance that it held for him.

Ultimately, though, despite all his political maneuvering, Warhaftig, like Herzog and others, recognized that the implementation of halakha in the state courts was a utopian dream. As a concession, Warhaftig pursued another strategy, which was to urge the Knesset to adopt a law stating that if a judge found a lacuna in Israeli law, he or she would be required to have recourse to halakha.[47] Warhaftig modeled his law on the procedure in force during the British Mandate that legal lacunae had to be filled by recourse to English Common Law.[48] His attempt failed, however, forcing him to follow Herzog's strategic retreat into pragmatic pluralism.[49] Herzog had told his followers that if the whole state could not be governed by halakha then they should at least fight for the rabbinical courts to be treated as an independent judicial system. Warhaftig adopted this strategy exactly, as he stated in a Knesset speech of 1954:

> We have in Israel two court systems. Most matters are under the legal authority of the general courts which judge not necessarily by original Hebrew law but according to the laws of the Knesset. . . . And there is a second system, of rabbinical courts. . . . The rabbinical courts rule according to the laws of the Torah. . . . The secular law does not get involved, and it cannot get involved, in the internal affairs of these rabbinical courts or in the cases that they hear. Secular law only defines the jurisdiction [of the rabbinical courts] . . . But it does not involve itself in their judicial activity because they are founded on the law of the Torah and not on human law.[50]

Warhaftig's assertion that Israel has "two court systems" was a direct attack on the jurisprudence prevalent among Israel's secular jurists. In the very same year of Warhaftig's speech, the Supreme Court ruled in Skornik v. Skornik that "every religious law, in its application in this country, flows from an act of the secular legislature."[51] In this view, the rabbinical courts were part of the state hierarchy and they had authority only to the extent that the secular legislature granted it to them. By contrast, Warhaftig insisted that the relationship between religious and state law is not the relationship between a higher and lower tier of a single hierarchy but rather the relationship between two independent legal systems, each with its own source of authority. Once the original hope of rabbinical law governing the entire state had failed, Warhaftig pushed for this pluralist position as a pragmatic strategy to enhance the authority of the rabbinical courts.

Perhaps Warhaftig's most striking statement about the independence of the rabbinical courts came in the context of a discussion about the oaths that were taken by rabbinical judges. Judges in the civil courts, Warhaftig noted, swear to "be faithful to the State of Israel and to its laws." Rabbinical judges swear only to "be faithful to the State of Israel," omitting the phrase "and to its laws." Warhaftig's explanation was that

> [t]he rabbinical judge … judges according to the laws of the Torah. … [The civil] law does not interfere with internal matters of the rabbinical court and so the rabbinical judge has no more obligation than any other citizen of Israel. He therefore has no reason to insert the phrase "and to its laws [into the oath.]"[52]

Warhaftig claimed that rabbinical judges, even though they were employed as judges by the state in state institutions, and empowered by state law, had no reason to swear loyalty to the laws of Israel. From the perspective of the state, this claim was utterly wrong. The judges in rabbinical courts were subordinate to the laws of the state. Their legal authority was derived from those laws and their verdicts were open to review by Israel's secular Supreme Court. But, as far as Warhaftig was concerned, the authority of the rabbinical courts was entirely independent of the state. The rabbinical courts drew their authority from halakha, not from the Knesset.

The practical outcome of Warhaftig's legal battles was not his only concern. To be sure, like other religious Zionists, Warhaftig continued to push for religious legislation to be enacted in the Knesset. He celebrated the fact that "through a difficult and ongoing struggle we have succeeded more than once to incorporate here and there aspects of our original Jewish law" into the law of the state.[53] Warhaftig's arguments over the law, however, also served as a tool of resistance and a way of strengthening the identity of a community that felt beleaguered and oppressed. In fact, sometimes the identity-forming function of legal discourse took precedence over its strategic efficacy.

One example of the primacy of the identity-forming function of law was the debate in the Knesset over the Capacity and Guardianship Bill in 1961. The proposed bill concerned the legal guardianship of minors and contained a clause requiring all children to "honor thy father and thy mother," a quotation from the Book of Exodus. One might expect the religious parties to have been in favor of this incorporation of religious law, one of the Ten Commandments no less, into an official statute. And yet, Warhaftig, then Minister for Religious Affairs, opposed the move: "There are things for which no law is needed," he told the Knesset. "Why repeat the Ten Commandments and thus, if I may say so, reduce the level of this eternal precept to a matter of transient law?"[54] Warhaftig worried that including one of the Ten Commandments in secular Israeli law would cheapen a divine command, presumably by implying that God's word is not sufficient authority without the endorsement of the Knesset. But from the perspective of the religious Zionist interest in "halakhic legislation," in which Warhaftig himself was deeply involved, this position is very curious. The incorporation of "eternal precepts" into Israeli law was one of Warhaftig's principle objectives. The counterintuitive nature of Warhaftig's argument was immediately recognized. Yitzhak Klinghoffer, a member of the Liberal Party, pointed out in response that the Law and Administration Ordinance (1948), Israel's first law, establishes Saturday as Israel's day of rest. He sarcastically asked whether that law also "reduce[s] the injunction 'and on the seventh day you shall not do any work' from its height to the level of a mere legality?"[55] Others also failed to make sense of Warhaftig's position, considering his strong support of incorporating halakha into legislation in general. Menachem Elon, an Orthodox jurist who became a Justice of Israel's Supreme Court, called Warhaftig's speech "exceptional and odd" and Moshe Una, another religious Zionist member of Knesset, supported the bill, against Warhaftig's objections.[56]

How, then, can we understand Warhaftig's speech? By way of explanation for his rejection of the clause, Warhaftig told a joke on the floor of the Knesset:

Forgive me for telling a famous joke. It is said that in a certain Jewish community they once put the Ten Commandments into the by-laws [pinqas] of the community. They asked, "Why are you putting the Ten Commandments into the community's by-laws?" They answered, "They don't observe what is written in the Torah but perhaps they will observe what is written in the by-laws of the community."[57]

With the joke, Warhaftig was trying to point out the absurdity of treating human law as more important than divine law. For Warhaftig, preservation of the independence and primacy of Jewish law was paramount. "Even if the legislator succeeded in incorporating the [halakhic] laws of personal status in their entirety into secular law (though here we are very far from that) even then I would oppose the tendency to make these things into the law of the state. Because then the court would be detached from its source; we would be detaching it from the well of living water."[58]

Warhaftig wanted halakha to be the law of Israel, but only if it retained its independent identity as halakha per se. He was concerned that if halakha was absorbed into the monolith of the state it would lose that identity. At that time, because of the legacy of British rule, the Israeli legislature was still interpreting Israeli law by reference to British precedent. Warhaftig was particularly fearful that halakha might be cut off from its own history of interpretation and made subject to the interpretation of the secular court. To address this concern, he insisted that if halakha was incorporated into secular law, it should be accompanied by a clause specifying that the interpretation of the law must be according to the halakhic tradition. Otherwise, he told the Knesset, the result would be the untenable outcome that "the court will interpret a law that is based on principles of Hebrew law according to English law. Then it will be a situation of a kind among a different kind [*min be-she-eno mino*], a kind of mixed threads [*sha'atnez*] or crossbreeding [*kila'im*] which are likely to destroy the law."[59] Warhaftig illustrated his position that it would be better to give up the chance of incorporating halakha into the law of the state rather that threaten its independence, with metaphors taken from halakhic literature. "A kind among a different kind" (*min be-she-eno mino*) is a term drawn from the laws of kashrut and priestly food laws; mixed threads (*sha'atnez*) is the biblical prohibition of wearing clothes that contain a mixture of wool and linen; and crossbreeding (*kila'im*) is a prohibition against mixing seeds or animals of different species. By using these halakhic metaphors one after the other, Warhaftig was, consciously or not, rhetorically emphasizing the centrality of halakha to his own identity.

The preceding examples of Warhaftig's legal rhetoric are mostly drawn from his debates in the Knesset. In that context, he kept to Herzog's policy of strategically appealing to legal pluralism when communicating with those outside religious Zionist circles. He also followed Herzog's lead of leaving that pragmatism aside, and making a more principled stand, when talking to fellow religious Zionists. In these internal conversations, he was more idealistic and less compromising, calling for the strengthening of halakhic legal centralism. Warhaftig urged religious Zionist leaders not only to resist the state's legal order but also to try to seize full legal control for themselves.

In 1953, Warhaftig delivered a speech to Israel's rabbinical judges. He summarized for them the various legal matters on which he was working and noted the practical benefits of having a state to enforce rabbinical rulings in matters of personal status law. Fundamentally, however, the speech was a call to arms, an invitation to mobilize in preparation for an extended war with the government. "We are," he said, "in a hard struggle with the Knesset and with the government over authority . . . fighting a war to save the oppressed from their oppression."[60]

Warhaftig told the rabbis that the secular state had overrun the entire legal landscape in Israel, laying exclusive claim to legal authority. He suggested that the only way to overcome this situation was to reverse it, to meet the expansive claims of the state with equally expansive claims of the rabbinate. He quoted with approval one of the rulings of the Great Rabbinical Court in Jerusalem: "In principle everything belongs to us, just that the law removes certain things from us."[61] The appropriate response to the state, he insisted, was to reject the state's claim to legal superiority. "The rabbinical courts need to be as imperialistic [imperialistiim] as possible," he said, "and not to give up on their authority."[62]

The strategy of counteracting the legal reach of the state had become both harder and more necessary, Warhaftig believed, with the global expansion of state power during the twentieth century. Elsewhere, in an unpublished essay, Warhaftig reflected on the changes in the ambitions of the state:

> What was perhaps possible at the end of the nineteenth century and the first years of the twentieth century, when the state was merely a political framework which did not penetrate into mens' souls, is impossible today, when the state is becoming more and more totalitarian. . . . The time has passed when the state filled the role of a "dog," guarding the borders, whereas social matters [and] problems of spirit and culture were left to the free initiative of society. The state today has returned to the age of absolutism.[63]

Whereas Warhaftig's references to totalitarianism and absolutism might conjure the image of fascist or communist states, it seems that Warhaftig was in fact referring to the growth of the power of Western democracies and the expanding reach of their administrative apparatus. In Warhaftig's understanding, the state had evolved from a kind of laissez-faire guard dog into a polity with an interest in the total control of its citizens' lives. One aspect of this development, he felt, was the encroachment of the state onto the territory of religious life, and religious law in particular. He now saw the state and religion as competing for the same ground, "both aspiring to encompass all of man and society."[64] His plan was to mount a religious defense against the state's absolutism, ideally reversing its tide. The battle for legal control, Warhaftig warned the rabbinical judges, was a zero-sum game in which either the government or the rabbinical courts, but not both, could win. Whatever his strategic rhetoric in the Knesset, Warhaftig's legal philosophy remained absolutely centralist in principle.

Religious Zionists were both idealists and pragmatists. They were not, on the whole, unrealistic about what they could achieve. Although crushed by the failure to achieve a halakhic state, they recognized that there was little they could do to change this state of affairs. As a result, most of them began to pursue a political strategy that deferred the dream of a halakhic legal system. Instead, they fought to bolster the independent footing of the rabbinical courts in their own realm and to champion "halakhic legislation" when possible. This pragmatism, however, should not be confused with an abandonment of principle. On the contrary: religious Zionists remained committed to the principle of centralized halakhic rule for the whole state, even as they accepted that it was an unattainable goal for the foreseeable future.

The dissonance between the ideals of the religious Zionist community and the reality in which they found themselves gave rise to a new element in their legal rhetoric. They saw debates over law not only as a tool to bring about practical change, but also as a way to protect and promote the identity and ideology of the religious Zionist community. Warhaftig acknowledged that in practical terms "we have stumbled far more than we have succeeded." But, as he himself recognized, "the essence of the struggle is important."[65] Even, or perhaps especially, in failure, the struggle over law performed an existential function. Religious Zionists held onto the principle of the halakhic state, even as they knew it could never succeed in practice, because it had become a core aspect of their identity, one that they were not willing to relinquish.

6   "GENTILE COURTS" IN A JEWISH STATE

Israel's Supreme Court was inaugurated in Jerusalem on September 15, 1948. Moshe Zmoira, the Chief Justice, opened his remarks with a statement taken from the High Holiday prayer service: "Behold, I stand here impoverished in good deeds, perturbed and frightened in fear of Him." He went on to portray the court as a fulfillment of an ancient Jewish prayer. "For almost two millennia," he said, "the Jewish people were praying three times a day, 'Restore our judges as at first, and our counselors as at the beginning.' We approach today the fulfillment of this vision."[1]

The justice's use of religious language belied the fact that, in the eyes of the state, the court was in fact a secular institution.[2] Its authority did not derive from God but from the will of the people. Indeed, for many religious Zionists the court was the ultimate symbol of the state's abandonment of halakha because it supplanted the rabbinical courts with a secular institution ruling by "foreign" laws. Although some rabbis did attend the inaugural ceremony, the Chief Rabbis of Israel, Isaac Herzog and Benzion Ousiel, both pointedly boycotted the ceremony and the reception that followed. Herzog explained his absence in a letter to Meir Bar-Ilan, the elderly head of the World Mizrahi Organization. This was not an occasion for celebration, he wrote, but for mourning. He lamented the fact that other religious leaders had chosen to attend. Had circumstances permitted, Herzog claimed, "it would have been fitting to declare a fast on that very day." The opening of the secular court, he believed, was nothing less than "the climax of the abolition of the Holy Torah from Israel."[3]

Herzog's acerbic rejection of the institution of the court was a natural outcome of his thinking about Israel's constitution. Herzog had long campaigned for a halakhic state with a centralized halakhic legal regime. The state indeed ended up as a centralized legal regime, but the law that governed it was not halakha but the secular law legislated by the Knesset. Herzog considered this outcome to be a catastrophic betrayal of the Jewish tradition. It was the state's civil courts that drew

The Invention of Jewish Theocracy. Alexander Kaye, Oxford University Press (2020). © Oxford University Press.
DOI: 10.1093/oso/9780190922740.001.0001

his particular ire. As he saw it, the only legitimate courts were those that ruled according to halakha. The civil courts represented an illegitimate revolt against the only true law. Herzog made this position clear in a speech delivered a few weeks after the establishment of the state:

> They have already set up courts [*batei dinim*], or courts [*batei mishpat*], and established a Ministry of Justice and the High Court [*bet din*], or High Court [*bet mishpat*]. And the Torah of Israel was not consulted, mentioned or appointed. They did not treat it "even like this lupine"[4] (see Betzah 33b) [*sic*]. It should have been the first responsibility of the government to announce and to publicize that its intention and goal was, at least after this period of transition, to return the law of the Torah, to renew its days as of old. The government of Israel [should have announced that it] was going to seek advice, guidance, and teaching from the mouths of Torah sages with regard to decrees and complementary [legislation] required in certain areas of Torah law, that would be given the force of the state.[5]

Herzog's perspective on Israel's courts was apparent in his choice of words as much as the substance of his comments. Twice, he referred to the court as a *bet din*, the traditional term for a rabbinic court, only to immediately correct himself, using instead the term *bet mishpat*, which was the name given to the secular courts by the government itself. With this pointed self-correction, Herzog emphasized the gap between his ideal, in which halakha would become the operative law in the state courts, and the reality, in which halakha had been abandoned. He expressed his outrage toward this abandonment by his use of the rather oblique term "like this lupine." According to the Talmud, the lupine is an extremely bitter plant that becomes sweet and edible after being boiled seven times. The Talmud portrays God bemoaning that the people of Israel have not even behaved like a lupine because they have not become "sweet" (i.e., they continue to bitterly reject God) even after they have been "boiled" (i.e., punished) seven times. By making this reference, Herzog indicated that he considered the state's forsaking halakha to be an idolatrous act of rebellion against divine law and God's will.

Some religious Zionists ostensibly became more accommodating to the secular courts than Herzog. Though they shared his disappointment, they worried that undermining the state's courts would threaten the state itself. As Zionists, they held the existence of a Jewish state, even a flawed one, to be a primary value. Ousiel, for example, boycotted the opening of the Supreme Court along with Herzog, but nonetheless warned that rejecting the authority of the Knesset would lead to anarchy. He wrote as much in a responsum of 1949:

We are now faced with a serious question that descends and penetrates to the depths.... How can the State of Israel survive if [the principle of] "the law of the land is the law" does not obligate every man and woman of Israel in the laws of the state for taxation and criminal law? It cannot be that [obedience to] the State of Israel will be a matter of personal discretion rather than a duty, such that each person will act however they wish.[6]

To avoid this outcome, Ousiel and other Zionist rabbis searched assiduously for halakhic precedent that would legitimize the state and its institutions, including the courts.

The efforts to find a halakhic basis for the authority of Israel's secular courts should not, however, be mistaken for outright approval. Religious Zionist rabbis in the 1950s trod a difficult path. As Zionists they wanted to uphold the legitimacy of the state, but as Orthodox Jews they balked at the state's rejection of halakha. As a result, they carved out various nuanced positions on the relationship between halakha and the law of the state, with a view to legitimizing the state while simultaneously challenging the extent of its authority. They articulated this relationship in different ways. For some, the institutions of state had relatively free rein as long as they did not directly contravene halakha. Others, though, were more restrictive. Many religious Zionist rabbis, including some who held official positions and were paid a salary by the state itself, explicitly ruled that the state's civil courts were illegitimate and that Jews were forbidden to use them. As a general rule, even religious Zionist rabbis who were more willing to recognize the importance of the state's judicial institutions continued to maintain that the exclusive legitimate source of law was halakha, to which the state was ultimately always subordinate. The writings of religious Zionism about the status of the state's courts were almost entirely internal and had no immediate influence on the actual policies of the state. In time, however, they had a profound practical significance by shaping the attitude of the religious Zionist community. The assertion of the supremacy of halakha over the state's institutions would become a significant trope in Israeli politics from the late 1970s.

In Israel's first decade, many discussions about the status of the state's courts and legislation were found in the pages of *Ha-torah veha-medinah* (*The Torah and the State*). The journal, which published thirteen volumes between 1949 and 1962, was produced by the Rabbinic Board of Ha-Po'el Ha-Mizrahi.[7] It called itself "a platform for the investigation of the halakha in matters pertaining to the state of Israel" and focused on the contemporary applications of halakha in many areas of Israeli politics and society.[8] Although many of its articles were too scholarly to be understood fully by the entire religious Zionist community, they nevertheless contributed to a widened consensus among the reading public about the desired direction of the Jewish state.

The editor of *Ha-torah veha-medinah* was Rabbi Shaul Yisraeli. Yisraeli was born in Belarus. His father was exiled to Siberia, never to see his son again, and his mother was killed by the Nazis. To escape the Russian Empire, Yisraeli crossed a frozen river from Russia into Poland. Caught by the Polish authorities, he narrowly avoided being transferred back to Russia and managed to immigrate to Palestine in 1934. Four years later he became the rabbi of Kefar Ha-ro'eh, a religious Zionist village in the north of Palestine. In 1953, he became a member of the Chief Rabbinical Council, a kind of executive committee of the Chief Rabbinate, in which he served as the head of the committee on halakha. In 1965 he was appointed to the rabbinical court of Jerusalem.[9]

In his introduction to the very first issue of *Ha-torah veha-medinah*, Yisraeli presented the tension between what he and his contributors considered to be the great religious potential of the State of Israel and their disappointment at the failure of the state to choose halakha as its law. On the one hand, Yisraeli made clear his excitement at the redemptive potential of the Jewish state.

> It is incumbent upon us to acknowledge clearly the greatness of the time in which we are living. For behold, the hope for redemption of the generations has arrived and is being realized. For we have merited to throw off the yoke of strangers from our necks. We are no longer beholden to crumbs from the table of foreign rulers. For all the institutions of government are ours. The ministers and the deputies, the officers and the military officers—they are from among our brothers.

The vicissitudes of his personal history lend a particular emotional moment to Yisraeli's words. As someone who had personally experienced the vulnerability of Jews under non-Jewish rule, his optimism was well earned. "For behold the dark and lengthy era of the concealment of [God's] face is ending and the era of the glory and splendor of the kingdom is beginning—the kingdom of Israel!"[10]

On the other hand, Yisraeli was explicit about his preference for a halakhic state, and his disappointment at its absence:

> If we had had foresight then we would have already designated a group of distinguished Torah scholars ten years ago, to devote themselves to the preparation of a constitution for the state of Israel and a comprehensive book of laws fit for immediate application by the [state's] courts.[11]

Yisraeli's regret over the failure of religious Zionists to create halakhic law for the modern state implies that he was not aware that Herzog and his followers had tried to do exactly that. Clearly, though, Yisraeli was aligned with Herzog's ideal of a halakhic state. Even as he embraced Israel's existence and explored avenues of practical accommodation with its secular legal regime, he never relinquished a principled commitment to the supremacy of halakha.

Contributions to *Ha-torah veha-medinah* drew on the legal pluralism that had characterized religious Zionist thinking earlier in the century. There was no other way to accept both the authority of secular legislation and the authority of halakha in the state. The resurrection of legal pluralism, however, did not mean that the religious Zionist turn to legal centralism in the late 1940s and early 1950s was forgotten. By contrast to their pre-state counterparts, religious Zionists thinkers in the 1950s no longer considered legal pluralism to be an ideal, but rather a concession to the catastrophic failure of the state to accept halakha as its law. They also granted far less power to non-halakhic law than earlier religious Zionist legal pluralists. Even as they looked for ways to legitimize the authority of the non-halakhic legislation of the Knesset, they also limited the scope of that authority.

From Monarchy to Democracy

The most common strategy for affirming the halakhic legitimacy of the State of Israel was to find precedent for it in the rabbinic corpus. This strategy had to contend with the fact that the democratic state is a modern phenomenon, meaning that analogies to earlier political structures inevitably fell short. Finding precedent therefore required creative reinterpretation of earlier sources, or extrapolations from them. It was often the assumptions of contemporary democratic thought that made these interpretations appear to be more convincing. In other words, although the novelty of the state posed a challenge to religious thinkers, it also provided them with the intellectual tools with which to solve that challenge.

Contributors to *Ha-torah veha-medinah* found precedents for the State of Israel in a wide variety of premodern Jewish political institutions. They found precursors to a democratic Jewish state in biblical kingdoms, in the medieval Kahal with its power to enforce communal regulations, in the principle of *dina de-malkhuta dina* (the law of the land is law), and in the mechanism of *qabalah* (acceptance) through which parties to a dispute are permitted to appoint judges to arbitrate between them.[12] Contributors to *Ha-torah veha-medinah* rarely insisted upon the use of one precedent over others. They generally searched for usable precedent wherever it could be found, sometimes switching between precedents in the course of a single article.[13]

The precedent put forward by Yisraeli himself, as well as many other religious Zionist writers, was the biblical king. In some ways, this king was a logical precedent for the modern government. Canonical sources from the Bible to the Middle Ages portray kings as engaging in activities that roughly correlate with the prerogatives of the modern state, such as engaging in foreign diplomacy, waging war, and maintaining social order. Yisraeli still had to contend, however, with the fundamental question of how a monarchy can serve as a model for a democracy. Yisraeli's answers to this question are particularly far fetched. He was willing to make any necessary intellectual move for the sake of legitimizing the state to which he was devoted.[14] His creativity is particularly interesting because his every significant interpretative leap takes for granted the principles of democratic thought. In other words, in order to legitimize the democratic state, Yisraeli first had to accept the principle of democracy.

Yisraeli was not the first person to suggest a parallel between monarchy and democratic government. During World War I, long before these constitutional questions were routinely discussed in Zionist circles, Abraham Isaac Kook had written a single pithy comment on the subject. He wrote, "It seems to me that when there is no king, since the king's laws relate to the general state of the nation, the rights of these laws return to the hands of the nation in its entirety."[15]

In other words, Kook had said, in the absence of a king, political authority resides in the entire people. Kook's statement was an elaboration on a theme common in premodern Jewish political thought, which is that the king's authority depended on the fact that the people desired his rule. This idea fits well with the biblical text, according to which the first Israelite king, Saul, was appointed over the Israelites only when they demanded a king.[16]

Yisraeli picked up on Kook's brief statement, but to make it useful he had to significantly widen its scope. After all, it was far from clear whether Kook's brief statement would grant full legitimacy to a modern democracy. The case of the king provides precedent only for the people consenting to the rule of a single individual, not to the rule of a rotating government made up of many individuals. Furthermore, the procedure for appointing a king, according to Maimonides, required the involvement of both a prophet and the Great Sanhedrin, neither of which was available in modern Israel.[17] And there was certainly no evidence that Kook would have considered a secular government, which disregarded the authority of halakha, as a corollary of the biblical monarchy.[18]

Yisraeli extended Kook's idea in an article entitled "The Authority of the President and Elected Institutions of Government in Israel."[19] He felt that Kook's argument ultimately depended, at least in part, on his intuition, so he set out to establish textual authority for Kook's position. "Today," he wrote, "when the question is not merely theoretical, it has become difficult to rely on what is apparent from logic and there is a need to find a basis for it in the sources of our forebears."[20] Ironically, in his eagerness to legitimize the State of Israel, Yisraeli himself came to conclusions that have a very weak basis in textual sources.[21]

Yisraeli insisted that the authority granted by the tradition to kings could equally be given to a democratic government. He wrote that "[s]ince the entire essence of the privileges [of the king] is from the consent of the people, they can be given also to the government and president." In other words, since political authority inheres in the people, the people are free to bestow it upon whomsoever it may wish. The monarchy described in the Bible, Yisraeli implied, was not the only form of government that the people could have chosen; a democracy would also have been legitimate.

Notwithstanding Yisraeli's argument that the Bible's endorsement of a monarchy would apply equally to a democracy, however, there remained obstacles to the straightforward application of biblical precedent to the modern state. For one thing, traditional authorities like Maimonides required that a king be appointed by a Sanhedrin and a prophet. This requirement posed a problem for applying the category of "king" to the State of Israel, for neither prophet nor Sanhedrin was available in the twentieth century. Even if the analogy between monarchy and democracy held up, how was the democratic government to be appointed in the absence of these institutions? Here, Yisraeli made a tenuous move. He noted that the biblical king of Israel, Omri, was regarded by the Bible as "more evil than all who had come before him." Given this point, Yisraeli conjectured that the Sanhedrin would surely not have agreed to appoint Omri as king.[22] (In fact, the Sanhedrin appears nowhere in the biblical narrative.) Yisraeli then asserted that the reason that Omri's appointment was legitimate even without the approval of the Sanhedrin was that, according to the biblical text, half the people followed him.[23] In other words, Yisraeli's interpretation presumes the democratic principle that the will of the majority is sufficient grounds to grant legitimacy to a political leader. He thereby concluded that Maimonides's requirement for the Sanhedrin to approve the appointment of a king applies only in cases in which the people do not consent. Where there is no popular consent, he wrote, the Sanhedrin and a prophet can override the people's disapproval and appoint the king. In the case in which the people do consent to the rule of a particular king, however, the approval of the Sanhedrin and prophet are not necessary to appoint him, for, as he put it, "since the people agree to this authority, what more is needed?"[24] But this point raised a question: If the consent of the people is the root of political authority, by what right could the Sanhedrin appoint a king even against the people's wishes? Here too Yisraeli mobilized a democratic principle. He stated, with only tenuous textual support, that the members of the Sanhedrin are themselves delegated by the people to represent their will. He wrote that "it must be that the Sanhedrin has the authority to appoint [a king] only because they are the faithful representatives of the people."[25] Yisraeli made this inference from the fact that the Talmud occasionally homiletically interprets biblical phrases such as "all the congregation" to refer to the Sanhedrin.[26] But beside the fact that this a homiletical reading, not intended to be taken literally, there is no indication that the Talmud regarded the Sanhedrin to be delegated representatives of the people. Yisraeli's entire analysis of the representative authority of the Sanhedrin is implicitly dependent on the assumption that people in authority must necessarily be delegated representatives of the people.

Yisraeli's entire discussion, then, was a defense of the idea that governmental authority, whether monarchic or democratic, is based on the democratic idea of popular consent. He went on to explore the question of how it can be properly established that the government has the consent of the people. He argued that it is fair elections that indicate popular consent, and which therefore grant halakhic legitimacy to the government's authority:

> Now it follows that all state [*mamlakhti*] appointments that are made in Israel, through elections by which the majority of the people decide, have validity and authority.... It consequently appears that a government chosen by way of fair elections will have authority to govern the nation, like the authority that the king had in Israel.[27]

This passage is striking, and not only because of Yisraeli's anachronistic implication that the Torah itself requires universal suffrage for the proper appointment of a governmental authority. His use of the adjective *mamlakhti* (state) is also very significant. This is one of the first times that the word appears in halakhic literature. There are many other words that Yisraeli could have used: *medini*, or *memshalti*, for example. The adjective *mamlakhti*, and its associated noun *mamlakhtiut*, refer to a particular ideology. It is the ideology, closely associated with Ben-Gurion, of supporting national sovereignty with strong and centralized institutions of state.[28] It is a modern notion, absent in traditional texts, which is derived directly from secular Israeli political theory. Yisraeli maintained, then, that the authority of the ancient king of Israel had the same nature as that of the contemporary Israeli parliament.

In short, every step of Yisraeli's analysis rested on interpretative leaps and depended on democratic principles. His contention that monarchic authority flowed from majority vote, his assertion that the people may bestow its authority upon any form of government, his claim that popular will has the power to override the disapproval of the Sanhedrin, his portrayal of the Sanhedrin as delegates of the people, and his reliance on elections to know the will of the people are all innovative interpretations with little textual support. They are convincing only once the principles of democracy have already been assumed. In other words, democracy is not only Yisraeli's conclusion but also his premise.

The reliance on democratic principles in drawing an analogy between the biblical king and modern democracy was not unique to Yisraeli; it occurred frequently in articles in *Ha-torah veha-medinah*. For example, in the first issue of the journal, from 1949, one author referred to "the king, or the body chosen in his place," apparently finding no need to justify the idea that an elected government could take the place of a monarch.[29] Another author made the same idea more explicit. Whenever the medieval sources mention a monarchy, he said, "they are referring to the laws and regulations of the state's government in accordance with the rules of democracy (*huqei ha-demoqratiah*), according to the spirit of the people and its will."[30] It is certainly true that traditional sources place certain limits on governmental authority. All of this, however, is worlds away from the democratic principle that the people are the very source of the king's authority. Indeed, there is no word in rabbinic sources for "democracy"; these authors had to resort to the Hebrew loan word *demoqratiah*.

Further testimony to the absorption of democratic ideas in religious Zionist writing is found in the work of Ovadiah Hadaya, a Jerusalem-born rabbi, a member of the Jerusalem rabbinical court, and, like Yisraeli, a member of the Chief Rabbinical Council. In one of his responsa, Hadaya considered the stipulation in some halakhic sources that communal regulations require the endorsement of a "distinguished person" (*adam hashuv*), which is normally interpreted as a rabbinic authority.[31] Given that the Knesset did not require any rabbinical approval to pass legislation, Hadaya investigated whether Israeli law was therefore automatically invalid according to halakha.[32] Although he was not a rabbi who tended to support halakhic innovation in the interests of modernization, when it came to the question of the requirement for rabbinical approval to legitimize state legislation Hadaya was quite creative.[33] Like Yisraeli's, Hadaya's halakhic reasoning depended on democratic principles: "It seems that since the town sage is one of the voters, it is *as if* he had initially given his consent to them, as long as it is for the good of the town and does not contravene the law of the Torah [Emphasis added]."[34] Hadaya's "as if" in the previous quotation deserves special attention. Democracy in general requires the acceptance of two fictions; two "as ifs." The first fiction is that the people endorse the state's actions. Whereas it is impossible in a modern state for all citizens to be physically present for every political decision, decisions made by elected representatives are regarded, through the mechanism of representation, "as if" they had been made by the people as a whole. The second fiction is that political actions even have the consent of people who voted against them. Because of their commitment to the constitution in general, all people live their lives "as if" they had consented to legislation that they voted against.[35]

Hadaya's "as if" can be taken in both of these senses. Because a rabbinical expert has, presumably, voted for elected officials, it is "as if" he had given his consent to the decisions of the representative assembly, even though he is never consulted on legislation. Second, the fact that the rabbi has voted makes it "as if" he had consented to legislation even if he might personally oppose it. Thus, Hadaya circumvented the halakhic requirement for explicit rabbinical approval of public legislation by employing democratic constitutional theory. It is significant that Hadaya could have used other halakhic methods to arrive at the same conclusion, which was effectively to annul the requirement for explicit rabbinical approval of Knesset legislation. There was ample precedent on which he might have relied. Some traditional halakhic authorities ruled that the approval of a "distinguished person" was required only for the regulations of trade associations and not for enactments of an entire community. Still others ruled that approval was not required at all according to the strict law, and was just a matter of custom. Indeed, historically there had been many communal enactments for which the approval of a "distinguished person" was neither sought nor provided.[36] Hadaya did not, however, appeal to any of these precedents. In fact, he quoted no textual authority of any kind to support his position. He relied solely on the proposition that elected officials are presumed to have the approval of the electorate. For Hadaya as for Yisraeli and others, a thoroughly modern democratic principle lay at the heart of the halakhic defense of the legal and political authority of the State of Israel.

The Limits of Law

As the writings of Yisraeli and others demonstrate, the belief that a secular legal regime was an abandonment of God and the Torah did not stop religious Zionists doing all they could to justify the legitimacy of the state's authority from religious sources. Their desire for a halakhic state was tempered by their commitment to the success of the State of Israel. Their decision to recognize both the authority of the Knesset and halakha meant that their approach was fundamentally legally pluralistic in that it had room for more than one system of law within the polity. In this respect, the legal and political theory of religious Zionists from the 1950s has something in common with that of religious Zionism in the 1930s and early 1940s. However, the later version of religious Zionist legal pluralism insisted on a far more prominent role for halakha in the state. It also limited, drastically in some cases, the scope of the authority of the Knesset and its laws. Even as their writings legitimized the state and its law, religious Zionist rabbis in the 1950s and 1960s refused to relinquish their belief in the supremacy of halakha.

This orientation of religious Zionists had two important consequences. On a theoretical plane, it emphasized the resistance among religious Zionists to the state's self-understanding as the exclusive source of all legal and political authority. This quiet resistance preserved the theoretical grounds for a more active opposition to the state in later years, when religious Zionists were less accommodating to the state's policies and laws. More immediately, affirming the primacy of halakha over state law made it possible for religious Zionists to formulate a distinction between legitimate and illegitimate state legislation and between legitimate and illegitimate state courts. Historically, halakhic authorities issued stern prohibitions against the use of "Gentile courts" (*arkha'ot shel goyim*).[37] Religious Zionist rabbis often concluded that the civil courts of the Jewish state were in fact illegitimate "Gentile courts," and prohibited their followers from using them. It is an astonishing fact that, from the 1950s until the present, rabbinic leaders of the religious Zionist community have commonly publicly prohibited Jewish use of Israel's civil courts.

In order to walk this tightrope, to legitimize the state while maintaining the supremacy of halakha, religious Zionists tended to adopt two strategies, which might be called distinction and limitation. The first strategy, distinction, placed Knesset legislation in a different category from halakha. Effectively, this strategy preserved the category of "law" exclusively for halakha. In this view, the state had no authority to legislate "law" but it could legitimately enact other kinds of norms, lower in the hierarchy of normativity than law itself. This strategy allowed rabbis to have their cake and eat it, too. They could continue to maintain that only halakha was actually law while also recognizing the binding authority of legislation produced by the Knesset.

There were a number of attempts by religious Zionist leaders to distinguish between the "law" of halakha and the lesser status of Knesset legislation. Shaul Yisraeli's was the most explicit attempt and deserves some attention.[38] The crux of Yisraeli's argument is his distinction between norms that non-halakhic institutions have the authority to enact and those that are exclusively within the purview of halakha:

> There are matters and legal problems which fundamentally require an intellectual [*sikhli*] determination. In this regard, the goal of the law is to discern the true and just outcome and to fix the law according to it. These matters may not be dealt with [merely] by issuing a regulation; an intellectual determination is required. Therefore, these matters are given to the determination of the legal sages [i.e., rabbinical judges and courts] who

are knowledgeable in the matter. The law is fixed by their mouths. There are also laws which are fundamentally only the drafting of regulations. Here, intellectual determination is not required, but rather the setting of a custom or rule, in accordance with the general foundations of justice.

Here, Yisraeli distinguished between two types of rules, one that might be called "laws" and one that might be called "regulations."[39] This distinction is reminiscent of the historical distinction in Continental European legal systems between "law" and "policy." As the administrative state began to grow in the Early Modern period, it enacted regulations for the sake of good governance, social order, and, increasingly, security. These regulations were issued directly by the state rather than the legislature. They aspired not to justice but to practical government. They were, then, distinct from "law" even as they had binding authority on the state's subjects.[40]

In a similar vein, Yisraeli distinguished between halakhic norms ("law") and non-halakhic norms ("regulations"). For Yisraeli, laws legislate the right way to act. To formulate such laws requires a kind of wisdom that can determine what truth and justice require.[41] Rabbinic experts have such wisdom. By contrast, regulations are rules that are intended to bring about social order and not to achieve the ends of truth and justice per se. They require only practical, not theoretical, reasoning: a knowledge of how society works rather than the essential nature of truth and justice.[42] The authority to make these two kinds of rules lies with two kinds of norm-making bodies. Non-halakhic institutions may legitimately create regulations. Therefore, if a king promulgates a regulation for the sake of social order, it is binding. But only halakhic institutions may legitimately create laws. So if a king legislates a law, wrongly purporting to have access to the powers of "intellectual" determination, such a law is invalid.

Yisraeli's distinction between the legitimate and illegitimate legislation of the state allowed him to define the scope of the prohibition of "Gentile courts." He considered non-halakhic courts that enforce regulations for the sake of social order to be legitimate. But he defined as "Gentile courts" non-halakhic courts that implement laws that purport to operate on the basis of theoretical reason. These are the courts that Jews are forbidden to use. Yisraeli put it as follows:

This distinction between matters that are fundamentally an intellectual determination and matters that are fundamentally about making a [practical] improvement in the world, is what creates the distinction between the "Gentile courts" [which are forbidden] and kingship [which is permitted]. Anything that depends on an intellectual determination is covered by the law [that prohibits the use of] "Gentile courts." This is synonymous with Gentile legal scholars, whose law is not legitimate at all. Because when it comes to intellectual determination, we [rabbis] have the wisdom of the Torah and its decisions, and the decisions of the rabbinic sages of blessed memory, from which we will never diverge. By contrast, matters that are fundamentally about regulations for social order pertain to kingship, which must work for the benefit of its citizens. Regarding [these regulations], the law of the kingdom is the law [*dina de-malkhuta dina*].[43]

Yisraeli believed, then, that the biblical king's authority to legislate was limited to "regulations," norms issued to protect social order, but not to "law" proper, norms intended to achieve truth and justice. Given that Yisraeli's entire analysis was based on the analogy between a king and the government of Israel, it followed that the legislation of the State of Israel was legitimate only insofar as it limited itself to the promulgation of regulations for social order. Yisraeli was subtly subverting the conventional understanding of the state's power to legislate. From the perspective of its secular founders, the state had legislative, judicial, and executive functions. According to that model, the Knesset was the legislative branch, whose purpose was to make laws. Yisraeli, however, was claiming that the entire apparatus of the state, including the Knesset, had the function of the biblical king. Thus, the entire state was reduced to the executive arm of government, whose role was to maintain social order. For Yisraeli, the Knesset did not make laws. It simply helped to keep social order by creating regulations. The real law of the state was halakha, which existed by the authority of God, not of the people or its representatives.

Yisraeli's distinction between laws and regulations was not rigorous enough to determine unambiguously what kind of rule would belong in which category. He assigned criminal law to the category of regulations, which the state is permitted to legislate. Civil law, however, he seemed to believe fell under the auspices of halakha alone. This belief meant that state legislation in civil law would be illegitimate.[44] So whereas Yisraeli resisted explicitly placing Israel's courts in the category of "Gentile courts," he did seem to rule that Jews should not use the state's courts in matters of civil law. Therefore, although Yisraeli worked hard to find precedent for the state's authority in the traditional canon, he also placed severe limitations on the authority of the Knesset to legislate and on the legitimacy of the state's courts.

If Yisraeli sought to defend the primacy of halakha through a strategy of distinction, by which he established a hierarchy of regulatory activity, others used a strategy of limitation. Rather than distinguishing between norms on the basis of the kind of intellectual capacity needed to enact them, this strategy distinguished between norms on the basis of the different spheres of life to which they pertained. This approach, which is found frequently in the pages of *Ha-torah veha-medinah*, entailed limiting the authority of the Knesset and the secular courts to certain legal realms, placing other legal realms under the exclusive auspices of halakha.

For those rabbis who wanted to limit the state's legal authority in this way, the question became which spheres of life fell under the legislative authority of the state and which did not. Some religious Zionists ceded quite a large sphere of authority to the state, following the position of the nineteenth-century Turkish rabbi Haim Palache, that the government has the authority to enact laws "in any matter that pertains a little to the government of the state."[45] The vagueness of this formulation generated a great deal of discussion among religious Zionists about which areas of law fell inside this category, and which outside. One author interpreted these words to allow the Knesset to make laws "for the sake of protecting the people, as well as taxes and municipal taxes which are imposed on the people for the sake of strengthening the system of government and similar things."[46] Some laws, however, presumably, fell outside these categories.

All agreed that the state was not permitted to enact legislation that directly challenged the authority of halakha. Even Ousiel, who strongly endorsed the authority of the state to legislate, wrote that Knesset legislation is "limited by the laws of the Torah" because even a Jewish legislature "is not permitted to uproot anything in the Torah."[47] A similar tone was struck by Ovadiah Hadaya. He also defended the authority of the state "to legislate according to their discretion for the good of the state," while simultaneously insisting that the state "may not impose [a law] that is against the Torah."[48] This position is echoed in many other writings of the period.

Other contributors to *Ha-torah veha-medinah* went further still, moving from a negative limitation on the Knesset's authority, accepting all Knesset legislation unless it contravened halakha, to a positive requirement that Knesset legislation is legitimate only if it is for the sake of God. One author insisted that if Knesset legislation is not "for the sake of heaven," then it has no force.[49] Another developed this position even further. Yisrael Be'eri agreed with Yisraeli that the state had legislative authority based on the precedent of the ancient monarchy, but he added the significant caveat that "if the main reason for the legislation is because they are not satisfied with the law of the Torah, and they choose the law of [other] nations and their decrees, then their laws have no authority."[50] Be'eri went on to make clear that he believed that the State of Israel was creating new legislation simply for the purpose of abandoning halakha. Its courts, therefore, are illegitimate. "In our case where they are rebelling against God's Torah and erring, and seeking out 'broken wells'[51] who are not fit to judge, any individual may ignore [the state's civil courts]."[52] Moreover, he declared, even if the Knesset is not actively rebelling against halakha but merely believes that other laws will serve the nation better, the state's courts still have the status of "Gentile courts." Disagreeing with Yisraeli, Be'eri wrote that if the people agree to accept the law of other nations, as Israel did in 1948 when it accepted the law of the British Mandate as its own law, then the state's courts are "absolutely Gentile courts" (*arkha'ot mamash*) and are therefore illegitimate.[53]

This reasoning was taken to an even further extreme by other writers. One contributor, Yehudah Segal, insisted that it was totally forbidden for Jews to use the state's courts under any circumstances:

> I was asked to explain the prohibition on using the secular courts in our holy land, which to our pain and embarrassment are not in accordance with our holy Torah. Even if they sometimes have a certain similarity to the laws of our holy Torah, nevertheless the legal basis is different and the entire legal procedure is far from the spirit of our eternal Torah.[54]

Segal believed that despite the fact that many Orthodox Jews in Israel used the state's courts, they were wrong to do so. Even courts run mostly by Jews in the Jewish state, he wrote, are in fact no different from the courts established by Gentile rulers during the long centuries of exile. Any Jew attending the courts of the State of Israel, he proclaimed, "scorns the Torah and its judges and prefers judges according to Gentile law."[55] In fact, even if the Knesset happened to legislate laws that were the same as halakha, this act would not diminish the offense, because the laws would not be divine commands but laws that "arose out of their own [human] intelligence."[56] State courts are, therefore, irredeemably illegitimate: "Anyone who is judged before idolaters [*aku"m*]—and the same goes for Jews who judge according to the laws of idolaters—is absolutely evil [*rasha gamur*], scorns the laws of our holy Torah and honors the laws of idolaters and is obligated to repay damages to the other party as a result of this [court case]."[57] This passage is uncompromising. Segal uses the condemnatory term "idolater" (*aku"m*) to refer to Gentiles, rather than a less pejorative term like *goy* or *nokhri*. He not only considers the state's courts illegitimate but also states that any Jew who uses them is considered a *rasha* (literally, "evil"), a gravely sinful status. Because Segal considered the state's civil courts to be illegitimate, he also considered anyone who accepted a payment awarded by the courts to be a thief until the money had been repaid.

The legal writings of religious Zionists rabbis in the 1950s displayed a deep tension. On the one hand, they wanted to embrace the State of Israel and they endeavored to find precedents for it in the Jewish canon. On the other hand, they could not forget what they perceived as the state's betrayal of halakha. Even while endorsing the authority of the state within certain parameters, they continued to insist upon the supremacy of halakha. They therefore placed the state's legislature and judiciary beneath halakha in the normative hierarchy. The state, they believed, was legitimate, but only to the degree that it remained in that subordinate position.

Religious Zionists in the 1950s were relatively weak politically and had no realistic chance of achieving their goal of establishing halakha as the state law. Despite this limitation, however, they did not give up on their ideals. Although, in practice, religious Zionists accommodated themselves to the state as it then operated, their legal and political theory remained, in principle, fundamentally at odds with that of the state itself. The state's leaders understood the Knesset, as the parliamentary body of a sovereign democracy, to be the exclusive source of all law. From this perspective, halakhic courts had authority only to the extent that the state granted it to them. From the perspective of religious Zionists, however, these roles were reversed. The Knesset and the civil courts had authority, but only to the extent permitted by the Torah. Sovereignty belonged not to the people, but to God.

7 THE PERSISTENCE OF JEWISH THEOCRACY

According to Amnon Rubinstein, a liberal Israeli politician and professor of law, religious Zionists in Israel's first two decades "bore the message of humanism and universalism bequeathed by enlightened Zionism."[1] Although they did not see eye to eye with the secular majority on every issue, he wrote, they were willing to compromise with the establishment for the greater good. But then, in the aftermath of the 1967 war, a "new religious militancy" arose, which transformed the religious Zionist community into a more assertive, less cooperative, and sometimes more violent group.[2] This narrative, in which the euphoric victory of 1967, and the controversial "land for peace" diplomacy that followed it, changed religious Zionism from a marginal element in Israeli politics to an active social force with theocratic tendencies, is widely believed.[3] The historical evidence, however, complicates the picture and calls upon us to question whether 1967 really marked such an abrupt break in the history of religious Zionism.

It is true that religious Zionists in the state's first decades were committed to the success of its institutions and sympathetic to democratic culture.[4] But many religious Zionists, especially rabbinical leaders, had other commitments, too. They were faithful in their desire for Israel, in principle, to become a halakhic state. "Facing outward," the spiritual leaders of religious Zionism continued to endorse compromise and they did what they could to legitimize the state that they believed to be messianic, despite its fundamental shortcomings.[5] Internally, however, the ideal of the halakhic state remained a guiding light. It was subdued, suppressed, and rarely expressed outside of the religious Zionist leadership. But it persevered.

The legal and political philosophy of religious Zionists before 1967 continues to have an impact today. Indeed, secular-religious tensions in twenty-first-century Israel cannot be understood without a careful consideration of its legacy. Herzog, Warhaftig, Yisraeli, Ousiel, and others discussed in this book would have opposed the political extremism exhibited by many religious Zionists today. Their

The Invention of Jewish Theocracy. Alexander Kaye, Oxford University Press (2020). © Oxford University Press.
DOI: 10.1093/oso/9780190922740.001.0001

theocratic principles were balanced by a sense of duty to national unity in the service of the state, even if that state did not fulfill their deepest religious aspirations. In recent years, however, the religious Zionist enchantment with the secular state has diminished. The ideology of the halakhic state is no longer tempered by an affiliation with liberal democratic culture, at least to the degree that it was for religious Zionists of previous generations. Unfettered by a countervailing liberalism, that ideology, laid down in the early years of the state, is finding expression in a new, more forceful way. In some religious Zionist circles, this development has given rise to a kind of religious fanaticism that would have been unheard of in the 1950s, and would certainly have been repudiated by Herzog and his followers. This new phenomenon, however, has old roots. Its origins lie in the ideology of the founding generation, which created a theocratic orientation that lay dormant for many years until it re-emerged in an unforeseen way and drastically altered the Israeli political landscape.

Such a claim may seem far-fetched. After all, religious society in Israel has changed substantially since its founding. Israel's Ultra-Orthodox population has grown in both real and relative terms and its rabbinical leaders have a far more significant role in the country's Jewish religious institutions than they once did. The Chief Rabbinate, once primarily the preserve of religious Zionist rabbis, is now dominated by Ultra-Orthodox rabbis.[6] In the religious Zionist community itself, there has been a gradual erosion of rabbinic authority, partly as a result of the increased interest in individualistic, rather than communal, religious expression.[7] Since the rise of Gush Emunim in the 1970s, religious Zionism has also redirected much of its ideological energy away from the cause of the public enforcement of halakha and toward the Jewish settlement of the Occupied Territories. Despite these developments, however, it remains the case that the early development of the idea of the halakhic state is a major cause of social tensions in Israel today. Although the intellectual output of elites is only one significant historical factor among many, ideas do matter. The ideology created by religious elites in the 1940s and 1950s continues to resonate in contemporary Israeli society and to exacerbate tensions in the twenty-first century.

The belief that the law of the State of Israel should be halakha is a pervasive and persistent element of religious Zionist thought. Even today, the majority of religious Zionist rabbis, many of whom are state functionaries themselves, only provisionally recognize Israel's democratically legislated laws. Many rabbis consider Israel's laws legitimate only if they do not contradict halakha, and it is often a matter of debate whether this condition has been satisfied. For example, Avraham Shapira, who succeeded Zvi Yehudah Kook as the head of the Merkaz Ha-rav Yeshiva and served as the Ashkenazic Chief Rabbi of Israel from 1983 to 1993, devised a religious test for secular legislation. During his tenure as Chief

Rabbi, he wrote that legislation was legitimate only if it had not been opposed by religious representatives in the Knesset:

> If a law passed without opposition from the religious representatives in the Knesset, there is an assumption that it is "kosher." And if [the religious representatives] opposed it, there is the assumption that it contradicts halakha and is not binding because the religious representatives are aware of the laws on the one hand, and they consult with rabbis on the other hand. So they would not agree to a law that contradicts halakha.[8]

Because Shapira assumed that religious politicians would take direction from rabbis, he deemed their support for legislation as a condition of its legitimacy. Whether or not Shapira was correct in implying that religious parties in the Knesset always vote according to their understanding of halakha rather than political considerations, his position seems to make all of Israel's laws provisional on religious approval. In his view, if religious representatives vote against a bill in the Knesset (which, of course, happens regularly), then it is not legitimate, even if it is passed as law by the majority.

Other rabbis impose even more stringent conditions before recognizing state law. Mordekhai Eliyahu, for example, who was the Sephardic Chief Rabbi from 1983 to 1993, believed that most of Israel's criminal law is automatically illegitimate because its procedure is different from that of halakhic criminal law.[9] Yaakov Ariel, the chief rabbi of the city of Ramat Gan and an influential religious Zionist leader, accepts only state law that does not address an area of law already addressed by halakha. By this standard, much of Israel's civil law is illegitimate. Even those religious Zionist rabbis who do accept the state's laws often do so only grudgingly. Shlomo Aviner, for example, the rabbi of the Bet El settlement and head of the Ateret Kohanim yeshiva in Jerusalem's Muslim Quarter, endorses Israeli democracy (as long as it is what he calls an "ethnocentric democracy") but still believes that "in principle, the law should be according to the Torah."[10]

The ambivalence of many religious Zionist rabbis toward secular legislation is expressed most emphatically in their antipathy to Israel's civil courts. Since 1948, when both chief rabbis boycotted the opening of Israel's Supreme Court, many religious Zionist rabbis have continued to see Israel's civil courts as a symbol of the state's abandonment of halakha and have consistently questioned their legitimacy.[11] This approach is not universal. Some contributors to the journal *Ha-torah veha-medinah*, for example, found precedent for Israel's civil courts in talmudic accounts of Jewish judges ruling according to non-halakhic law. Many, however, defined Israel's civil courts as "Gentile courts." This definition automatically amounts to a halakhic ruling that the civil courts are illegitimate and that Jews are prohibited from making use of them. Ovadiah Yosef, Sephardic Chief Rabbi from 1973 to 1983, whose teachings are still extremely authoritative (and whose son Yitzhak Yosef, the current Sephardic Chief Rabbi of Israel, adheres closely to his father's rulings) was uncompromising on this point: "It is strictly prohibited to deal in any of these laws [inheritance law, or civil law more generally] in courts that judge according to the laws of Gentiles . . . whether the judges are Gentiles or Jews who judge according to the laws of Gentiles, which are not like the law of the Torah."[12]

Similarly, Haim Druckman, the head of the Bnei Akiva youth movement popular among religious Zionist youth, and the leader of the prominent Ohr Etsion Yeshiva in the West Bank, believes that Israel's courts are fundamentally flawed and that they should in principle be replaced with halakhic civil and criminal courts.[13] Yaakov Ariel also wrote harshly in support of this position:

> A religious Jew who knows that there is Torah law and that there are Torah scholars who know [rabbinical] law, but nonetheless prefers to be judged by these [civil judges], who are sinful heretics, is considered a blasphemer and reviler and a rebel against the Torah of Moses. Their transgression is considered by Torah law to be a desecration of the name of God.[14]

Jewish judges in the civil courts, writes Ariel, are heretics. Jews who make use of those courts, knowing that they could instead take their case to rabbinical judges, are desecrating God's name. While particularly vehement in its formulation, Ariel's basic position is quite common. Well into the twenty-first century, it appears that a large majority of Israel's rabbis consider the state's civil courts to be illegitimate "Gentile courts."[15]

While most religious Zionist rabbis believe that halakha should control civil law, most secular Israeli jurists hold the inverse belief that civil law should control the rabbinical courts. This approach to law is quite common in the modern state. Proponents of modern legal regimes generally claim that state law has the monopoly on legal authority within the territory of its jurisdiction.[16] Thus, both religious Zionist and secular jurists share the belief that, in principle, they alone should have control of the legal apparatus of the state. Given these conflicting claims to legal supremacy, religious-secular tensions in Israel are almost inevitable. According to Israeli legal scholar Yedidia Stern, proponents of halakha and civil law in Israel see themselves in a "zero-sum game" in which the supremacy of one kind of law requires the subordination of the other.[17]

The most public recent manifestation of this conflict has been a debate in the Knesset and the Supreme Court with regard to the authority of the state rabbinical courts to hear civil cases. Although the state grants jurisdiction to rabbinical courts only in the realm of personal status law, rabbinical courts have historically heard cases in the realm of civil law also. Indeed, because many rabbis think that it is forbidden for Jews to use the state's civil courts, they believe that the rabbinical courts are the only legitimate forum in which civil cases can be adjudicated between Jews. The rabbinical courts claim that their authority to hear civil cases derives from the Torah. But they also support this claim with a legal argument that appeals to secular legal institutions. They demand that even the state should recognize their authority in civil law because, even if they are not recognized as official civil courts in the state system, they should still be recognized as binding courts of arbitration, with the agreement of the parties. In 2006, however, the Supreme Court decided in *Amir v. the Great Rabbinical Court in Jerusalem* that the rabbinical courts do not have the authority to hear cases outside their jurisdiction, even as courts of arbitration.[18] According to the majority opinion, written by Supreme Court Justice Ayala Procaccia, the authority of the state's rabbinical courts to hear cases is limited to the jurisdiction determined by the state. Because the rabbinical courts "derive their power and authorities from the state statute," she ruled, "they have no authority other than what is vested in them by the statute."[19] The Supreme Court therefore decided that state rabbinical courts are not permitted to hear civil cases, even as courts of arbitration.

For their part, the rabbinical courts have always rejected the claim that their authority derives from state legislation. In the early 1980s, for example, Shlomo Daikhovsky, a judge in the rabbinical courts for over thirty years, wrote that "[a]ccording to the Torah, the authority of the rabbinical courts is unlimited because it derives from the divine legislator not from the human legislator." For this reason, Daikhovsky rejected any authority on the part of the state to limit the jurisdiction of rabbinical courts. He even rejected the possibility of discussing the question of jurisdiction with the civil courts because such a deliberation would itself "constitute a kind of admission of limits delineated by the human legislator, against the law of the Torah."[20]

In keeping with this position, the rabbis reacted sharply to the Amir decision of 2006, which prohibited them from hearing civil cases, even as courts of arbitration. A month after the verdict of the High Court was issued, rabbinical judges issued a statement calling the ruling "a severe blow to the status quo and to the relations of the rabbinical court with the civil courts." They continued,

> The rabbinical courts were not born with the establishment of the state. These courts have existed since the revelation on Mount Sinai . . . There have been rabbinical courts in the Land of Israel for thousands of years . . . [Although the state] granted them formal authority in a narrow

segment of family law, the status of the courts remains intact in all other areas, with the consent of the parties.[21]

As often before, the rabbis insisted that the authority of the rabbinical courts preexisted the establishment of the state and that the state has no authority to undermine the capacity of rabbinical courts to arbitrate in civil cases. Moreover, the rabbinical judges noted, the use of the rabbinical courts in all areas of law is a requirement of halakha: "Note that citizens observant of the Jewish law are commanded by the halakha to litigate in rabbinical court, and they do so by agreement of both parties."[22] This remark amounted to a counterclaim against the High Court. Just as the state's civil justices rejected the authority of the state's rabbinical courts to hear civil cases between Jews, the rabbis rejected the authority of the state's civil courts to do the same.

This dispute about the limits of the authority of the rabbinical courts is far from over. In early 2017, a bill was proposed in the Knesset to reverse the effects of the Amir decision by explicitly allowing state religious courts to arbitrate in civil cases. The bill was proposed by members of a Jewish religious party, United Torah Judaism, and passed its first reading in the Knesset in February 2017. If it passes into law, it will once again expand the authority of the rabbinical courts and override the limits placed upon it by the state's civil judicial institutions.

In recent years, numerous new institutions have promoted a rabbinical judiciary and challenged the state's claim to being the exclusive source of legal authority. Since 1988, several private rabbinical courts have been founded, which attempt to attract Israel's Jewish citizens to use them instead of the state's civil courts. They now exist in towns in Israel and the Occupied Territories, such as Qiryat Arba, Qiryat Ono, Neve Nof, Har Nof, and Alon Shevut.[23] A network of private rabbinical courts, called Gazit, is associated with Eretz Hemdah, a yeshiva founded under the auspices of Shaul Yisraeli. In keeping with Yisraeli's ideology of support for the state while also promoting the superiority of halakha, the Gazit courts offer to arbitrate cases in keeping with both halakha and Israeli civil law. They encourage Israeli Jews to use their courts in place of the state's courts, claiming that they process cases more quickly and cheaply. They also appeal to religious and nationalist sensibilities. "Sizeable portions of Israeli society are alienated" from Israel's courts, the Gazit website proclaims, "feeling that they are not based on the foundations of Jewish law." Indeed, using Israel's civil courts is a "severe halachic problem" and also a "cultural-social problem" because the "Zionist vision" requires that "the judicial system reflect the Jewish judiciary tradition and Jewish values of justice." The website also professes that halakha can deal with "even the most complex, sophisticated problems of the modern economy" and that the Gazit courts "will apply the principles of the Torah and halachah in all aspects of public and commercial life and in the ever-changing modern world."[24]

Alongside the private rabbinical courts, a number of rabbinical training institutes have also been established, in order to train rabbinical judges to serve on them. Halakhic scholars associated with these institutes frequently publish research in Jewish law that is designed to demonstrate how it can be applied in the circumstances of the modern state. One such institute is Mishpetei Eretz, situated in the West Bank settlement of Ofrah. According to its head, Rabbi Abraham Geisser, its aim is to undo the "strategic decision" by the State of Israel to bring about the "abandonment of the Torah legal system." Jewish law, according to Geisser, should "take first place" in Israel and "displace foreign expressions and laws which have found a place of honor in the halls of Israeli justice."[25]

Other supporters of the rabbinical courts have openly called for the replacement of civil law in Israel with halakha. An example is a 2008 lecture by Reuven Heller, a rabbi of the city of Hod Ha-sharon entitled "The Transition from the Laws of the Gentiles to the Laws of the Torah: How?" Heller lamented the fact that most people did not know about "the wonderful treasure of Torah laws," including "the moral level of rabbinical judges and of the speed of judgment in the Torah courts." Heller believed that if private rabbinical courts operated for long enough in areas permitted by the state, then this "treasure" would become better known. This would "create a pressure from below, which will eventually bring about a reversal, making Hebrew law into the official law book of the State of Israel."[26] Promises of lower cost and greater efficiency were meant to attract people to the court but the long-term goal was a revolution in which halakha would officially govern the entire state.

This opinion is by no means marginal. It plays a role in politics at the national level. In June 2019, Bezalel Smotrich, the head of the right-wing nationalist religious party Tequmah, made a bid for the position of Minister of Justice. Speaking to a gathering at the religious Zionist yeshiva Merkaz Harav, Smotrich said that he wanted this particular portfolio, in order to "restore the system of Torah justice." In other words, a politician on the national stage publicly sought responsibility for the state's judiciary in order to implement halakhic law in Israel. In an interview the day after the speech, Smotrich confirmed that he believed that halakhic civil law was better than the state's civil law, and that the rabbinical courts should be granted "a higher status." When asked by his interviewer whether he was calling for a halakhic state, Smotrich seized the opportunity to criticize the Supreme Court. Right-wing politicians in Israel frequently lament what they see as the liberal activism of the Supreme Court, particularly under its influential president Aharon Barak, who retired from the court in 2006, and they often stand on a platform of reining in future activism of the judiciary. (Needless to say, this characterization of the judiciary is disputed by many politicians on the left.) With clear irony, Smotrich said that the return of Torah law would be superior to the "halakhic state founded by Aharon Barak." The implication was that he considered the liberal judiciary, not the rabbinical courts, to be coercive, and that he would prefer to see the state subordinate to halakhic rule than to secular law.[27]

The antagonism toward the state's laws and its courts by many rabbis today and the proliferation of institutions in support of the halakhic state are, at least in part, a consequence of the ideological positions established by religious Zionist leaders in the late 1940s and early 1950s. They are reminiscent of the call to religious Zionists issued in 1949 by Meir Bar-Ilan "to prepare immediately for war . . . for a state law that is based on the laws of our holy Torah . . . This law and no other."[28] Despite the failure of Bar-Ilan and his allies to achieve their goal in the short term, the principle of the halakhic state has remained an ideal for many religious Zionist rabbis since that time.

The role of the theocratic ideology formulated in the late 1940s in secular-religious tensions in Israel today complicates the standard historiography. According to the more common understanding, relations between religious Zionist Jews and Israel's political and judicial institutions deteriorated as a consequence of events that have transpired only since the 1970s.[29] By this account, in Israel's first thirty years religious Zionists were political pragmatists who supported the political establishment. Yosef Burg, a long-serving religious Zionist politician, was a typical representative of this friendly face of religious Zionism. In a famous, though undocumented, anecdote, Burg said that the most important element in "religious-Zionism" was the hyphen between the two terms. As the anecdote implies, religious Zionism in the early years of the state understood itself as a force able to bridge the secular-religious divisions in Israeli society.

According to this narrative, things began to change only in the late 1970s when Israel evacuated territories conquered in the war of 1967 as part of a peace agreement with Egypt and, for the first time, the press carried pictures of Israeli soldiers physically removing Israeli children with knitted skullcaps from their homes. Religious Zionist disillusionment with the government intensified after the signing of the Oslo Agreements in 1993 and the evacuation of Jewish settlements in the Gaza Strip in 2005. These events caused many in the religious Zionist community to come to the conclusion that the state was forcing them to abandon their sacred mission of settling the Land of Israel. It could no longer even be said, in the spirit of Abraham Isaac Kook, that the secular state was fulfilling the plan of God. On the contrary, the state appeared to some to be actively rebelling against God's plan. As a result, religious Zionists moved away from compromise and toward new kinds of engagement with the state. Rather than supporting the state's institutions, religious Zionists began to try to control them. They became far more prominent in the Israel Defense Forces, particularly among elite combat units and officer ranks. They also became increasingly hostile to the state's secular leaders. The nadir of this hostility was the assassination of Yitzhak Rabin by a religious Zionist student. A brief period of soul-searching after the assassination was followed by a further intensification of antagonism toward the state in the wake of the evacuation of Jewish settlements from Gaza in 2005.[30] It is against this background, the argument goes, that religious Zionists began to challenge the state's institutions, and to attack the courts, which many of them saw as a tool of the liberal secular elite.

This account is largely correct. There is no question that events from the late 1970s and onward precipitated a transformation of religious Zionism and its relationship to the state. Placing too much emphasis on that period, however, risks obscuring an earlier, and possibly more fundamental, source of religious-secular tension in Israel. It was in the first decade of the state, long before the religious settlement movement, that religious Zionists developed the ideology of the halakhic state. Already by the 1950s, secular and religious Zionists were committed to mutually exclusive visions of Israel's constitution and legal regime. The stage was set for a simmering confrontation between those who believe that the ultimate authority of law derives from God and those who believe that it derives from the will of the people. The principled pursuit of the halakhic state persisted beneath the pragmatic accommodations of religious Zionists in the state's early years. In this sense, Isaac Herzog's 1949 speech set the tone for religious Zionists for decades to come. Even as he cooperated with and supported the state, he urged his supporters to remember that "we are not in principle . . . at peace with the current situation. . . . [O]ur most fervent desire is to return the law of the Torah to its place."[31] Even as religious Zionists supported the State of Israel and its secular legal regime, they never gave up on this dream.

The developments among religious Zionists since the 1970s are not the result of the emergence of a new ideology but rather the erosion of the value of compromise that had previously kept the halakhic-state ideology in check. Many religious Zionists began to question whether the success of the Jewish state really depended on their compromise with the secular regime and wondered instead if they could be successful only if they refused to compromise. Some of those who have adopted this new position have been called Ultra-Orthodox Zionists (*haredim le'umi'im*, or *hardalim* for short) because they combine the religious Zionist belief in the redemptive nature of modern Zionism with a fundamentalist rejection of secular culture that has a lot in common with Ultra-Orthodoxy.

An example of the changing attitude to compromise is the writings of Elyakim Levanon, rabbi of the Elon Moreh settlement in the West Bank. In the aftermath of Israel's disengagement from Gaza in 2005, Levanon called for a change. For most of the twentieth century, he said, religious Zionists followed a "pathway of partnership and cooperation" with secular Zionism and the State of Israel.[32] This was a pragmatic choice, he claimed. Because secular politics was balanced between the left and right wing, "the religious bloc could always tip the scales." In other words, the participation of religious Zionists in secular institutions was a strategy to exert political influence despite having relatively little power. When the state began to evacuate Jewish settlements in the name of peace, however, Levanon believed that God was sending a message that things had changed. The state was no longer balanced; it had fallen to the "liberal-labor" camp. As a result, religious Zionists had to adopt a different policy; they had to take total control: "No more integration—only leadership."[33] Levanon called on his community to "establish systems that will slowly but surely replace those of the state."[34] In particular, he called for the religious takeover of the education system and the judicial system. The judicial system "has already reached the heights of absurdity," he claimed. "This system simply constitutes an attack on all the sanctity of Israel, an attack on the Land of Israel."[35] In response, he called for religious Zionists "to establish, slowly but surely, a parallel system of rabbinical courts that judge fairly and justly."[36] He believed that this rabbinical judicial system, parallel to that of the state, would attract the general public and pave the way for the establishment of a halakhic state.

Levanon adhered to the principle of the halakhic state developed by religious Zionist rabbis of the state's first decades, but renounced their attitude of compromise that held it in check. The more a willingness to compromise is abandoned, the more fanatical and intransigent the idea of the halakhic state becomes. This effect can be seen in the writing of Shmuel Tal. Tal was the head of a yeshiva situated in the Gaza Strip, which was relocated after the Israeli disengagement from Gaza in 2005.[37] In response to the disengagement, Tal said, religious Zionists should "disengage from the state."[38] In a controversial interview, he declared that religious Zionists should no longer pray for the welfare of the state, or celebrate Israel's Independence Day.

> . . . [I]t has become evident to us, in the clearest possible way, that the leadership, both as a whole and in all its parts—the government, the press, the judiciary, academia, and culture—is a kingdom that defies God's kingship. These two kingdoms [the kingdom of God and the State of Israel] are entirely incompatible. We must decide: is God the ruler, or, heaven forfend, the kingdom that is alienated from Him and that fights against everything that is sacred and dear to Him?[39]

For Tal, Israel's territorial disengagement meant that the age of compromise was over. The state was at war with God's rule. Although Tal's suggestion to abandon the celebration of Independence Day was not widely followed, his basic despair in the direction of the state was perhaps more representative.

A yet more extreme version of this position is held by Yitzchak Ginsburgh. A rabbi affiliated with the Hasidic Chabad movement, Ginsburgh is influential among many fundamentalist religious Zionists. Ginsburgh founded an organization, "The Way of Life Movement" (*Tenu'at derekh hayim*), whose purpose is to replace Israel with "a Jewish state according to the Torah."[40] Unlike Bar-Ilan, Herzog, Yisraeli, and others before him, however, Ginsburgh lacks a moderating impulse. For him, Zionism has run its course and the State of Israel needs to be wiped away and replaced by a halakhic state. In 2005, at the height of the religious resistance to the Gaza disengagement, Ginsburgh delivered a Sabbath lecture in which he said that "we must uproot the Zionist spirit." He continued: "We must destroy the [Supreme] Court. . . . We must eliminate the Government, whether it is left-wing or right-wing. We must overthrow the Government, and when a new Government arises, we must overthrow it too, and so on and so forth, until the rule of Torah is established in the Land."[41] Ginsburgh's battle cry is like a distorted version of religious Zionist ideology of earlier years. In his call for a "state according to the Torah," it is easy to recognize the echo of Herzog and other religious Zionists of his generation but the spirit of compromise that softened the ideology of the previous generations has given way to fundamentalist intransigence.

In searching for the causes of religious-secular conflict in Israel, then, political developments since the late 1970s and the ascendency of the settlement movement should not be given exclusive attention. The conflict has been exacerbated by these developments but its genesis was much earlier. The ambivalence of religious Zionist rabbinical leaders to Israel's civil court system, their support for a centralized system of rabbinical courts, and the recent proliferation of organizations whose goal is to make halakha into the civil law of the state, all flow directly from the legal philosophy that religious Zionists began to promote in the late 1940s.

If this diagnosis is correct, can anything be done? Is it reasonable or realistic to expect anything other than conflict and confrontation between two mutually exclusive legal outlooks, one rooted in the will of the people, the other in the will of God? It is almost a contradiction in terms to expect the state to renounce its claim to legal supremacy. In the words of the anthropologist of religion Talal Asad, "the modern state describes itself as the law state. Law is central to how it sees its structures and processes."[42] At the same time, halakha is also perceived by many as a total law, given by God, which governs every aspect of Jewish life. By this definition, it seems no more reasonable to expect Orthodox jurists to relinquish the claim of halakha to legal supremacy than to expect secular jurists to relinquish the claim of the state to legal supremacy. So, is the conflict between mutually exclusive claims to legal supremacy inevitable, or do strategies exist that might ease the tension between them?

Some argue that halakha should abdicate any role in Israel's political and legal life and recede into the private sphere. To be sure, religious coercion and any discriminatory elements of halakha should have no place in Israel's public life, but the view that any reference to halakha must be banished comprehensively from the public square is problematic for several reasons. First, it is unrealistic. It is a secularist fantasy to imagine that the large number of Israeli Jews for whom halakha is of paramount importance will accept the elimination of their central beliefs from public discourse. Second, notwithstanding the position of orthodox liberal political philosophy that "comprehensive doctrines" like the metaphysical axioms of religious groups should be kept out of political discourse, critics have persuasively argued that it is both unfair and unrealistic to ask people to keep their most deeply held convictions out of public debate altogether.[43] Third, attempts to separate between "religion" and "state" tend to be incoherent, or even paradoxical, on a theoretical level. Such attempts necessarily require the state to make its own inevitably controversial assessments of what counts as "religious" and what does not, thereby interfering in religious life and undermining the "separation" that is their very objective.[44]

More than these problems, though, the view that halakha should be entirely banished from Israel's public life ignores the potential of religious traditions at their best to enhance the public good and to provide a source of legitimate and necessary critique of modern states. Modern states are imperfect and the State of Israel is certainly no exception. Religion can, of course, intensify violence and injustice. The prophetic mode of politics can be extremely dangerous. But it also has the capacity to act as a corrective to ethical limitations of state power.[45] Religious voices have, at key moments of history, brought a voice of "moral grandeur and spiritual audacity" to the realm of power and politics.[46] Religious rhetoric can divide society and incite hatred but it can also offer resistance against the total claims of the state, inspire the pursuit of justice, and encourage social unity.[47] The problem with much religious Zionist legal ideology is not the fact that it resists the state, but the nature of that resistance and the actions through which it is sometimes expressed. Rather than shining a critical light on the state's tools of power and coercion, religious Zionist thinkers too often simply aspire to co-opt them for their own ends.

Other religious Zionist voices exist, however. Religious Zionism is no monolith and, since the beginning of the state period, there have been thinkers within that community who offer a constructive critique of the State of Israel without attempting to appropriate its authority. These thinkers, typically outliers, insist that Jewish theology can act as a moral check on the instrumental rationality of liberal capitalism and on the coercive violence that inescapably accompanies modern statehood. Yeshayahu Leibowitz, for example, an Orthodox Jewish scientist who was one of Israel's most outspoken intellectuals, condemned the attribution of any religious value to the state. He endorsed the state as a political tool, but rejected the position of Abraham Isaac Kook that the Jewish state is the "foundation of God's seat in the world."[48] For Leibowitz, the role of religion in the state should always be one of opposition. He put it as follows:

> It is very important that in the framework of any well-ordered state...there is an opposition within it, a power that acts as a brake against the government. And I think that if religion has any political function ... then perhaps this is its function: To be the fundamental opposition to the government *qua* government. [To tell the government:] you are not the highest authority.[49]

Leibowitz did not want religious authority to take the place of the state apparatus. Nor did he think religious tradition should be used to formulate specific laws or policies. He wanted religion to have a symbolic function in politics. It would represent a moral authority beyond and above the state. Taking this authority seriously, he believed, would generate a humility in governmental politics that might counteract the state's propensity to expand its power.

A similar position was laid out more recently by the Israeli political philosopher Menachem Lorberbaum. Lorberbaum also thinks that theology can play the role of an external critic of the state:

> It is the task of a theological critique of the political to constantly call our attention to the tendency of states to elide the saeculum and to render metaphorical reifications absolute and sacral. . . . By attenuating the grounding of human structures of rule it makes the excluded, "the sojourner, the widow, and the orphan," visible, thus contributing to the circumstances of justice and charity.[50]

Here, Lorberbaum points out that states have a dangerous tendency to bolster their authority by appealing to religious metaphors. This tendency, he suggests, can be checked by refusing to allow the state to commandeer concepts like the sacred, thereby preserving the power of these concepts to protect the vulnerable and to spread justice.[51] In this understanding, God's sovereignty essentially undermines the claim of the state to supremacy and rejects its use of religious symbols and myths in the service of its own apotheosis.[52]

The reconstruction of the genealogy of the halakhic state supports the work of those who question halakhic supremacy on the basis of sources from within the Jewish tradition. The key to this effort is the recovery of the legacy of Jewish legal pluralism. Religious Zionist thinkers interested in this approach have already recognized the appeal of legal pluralism (though generally without using that terminology) as the basis for a legal philosophy that resists the hubris of the idea of the halakhic state but remains open to the possibility that traditional Jewish thought might be applied to contemporary politics in other ways.

An early example of this use of legal pluralism was Eliezer Goldman, a committed religious Zionist who was a leading intellectual of the religious kibbutz movement.[53] One arena in which Goldman explored the idea was in his review of *Jewish Theocracy*, a book by Gershon Weiler, who was one of the Israeli thinkers most critical of the encroachment of the idea of the halakhic state on Israeli politics and law.[54] Goldman recognized that the problem for Weiler was the belief that "halakha and the law of the state are two systems of norms, each of which claims supremacy."[55] But Goldman rejected Weiler's premise. He argued that halakha does not need to be a "totalitarian" system that is necessarily opposed to the state.[56] Goldman showed how halakha had historically recognized the legitimacy of non-halakhic legal orders, including the legislation of the king, of rabbis, of Jewish lay leaders, and of Gentile governments. His position is reminiscent of the legal pluralism of early religious Zionists, and of the interpretative strategies of people like Shaul Yisraeli. Goldman was unusual among religious Zionists in his continued endorsement of Jewish legal pluralism as an ideal even after the foundation of Israel. He demonstrated that the pluralistic strand in the history of halakha undercuts the claim that halakha demands supreme authority in a modern Jewish state.[57]

The Jewish historian and philosopher Aviezer Ravitzky has also argued compellingly that a Jewish theocracy, a state in which halakha alone can rule, is something that the religious sources of Judaism neither require nor condone.[58] Drawing on sources like the Eleventh Sermon of the Ran, he noted that halakhic thinkers have always assumed that even an ideal Jewish state "is intended to encompass a [human] governmental and legal system that deviates from 'the law of the Torah.'"[59] Elsewhere, Ravitzky proposed four models of the relationship between religion and politics that are attested in the Jewish tradition.[60] One of them, which he called, "mutual completion," is a model of legal pluralism in traditional Jewish jurisprudence.

Menachem Lorberbaum himself has also made a significant contribution to the resurrection of the tradition of legal pluralism in Jewish jurisprudence in his analysis of the "limits of law" in the halakhic tradition.[61] Lorberbaum's work goes further than Ravitzky's in some respects. Although Ravitzky held up the Ran as an example of a Jewish legal pluralist, he presented Maimonides, the greatest of medieval Jewish thinkers, as an advocate for a "unifying model" of religion and state.[62] By contrast, Lorberbaum argued that even Maimonides did not imagine halakha as an exclusive legal system. Lorberbaum's reading helps to explain why Maimonides acknowledged the extra-halakhic authority of the king:

> The breadth of extralegal authority [that Maimonides] accords the king is so wide it is more than merely an auxiliary mechanism intended to support the halakhic hegemony. The king's power to command on pain of death, to tax, to conscript, and to regulate political life by his decrees makes the king's law a system that fully encompasses the political life of society.[63]

Lorberbaum's interpretation of Maimonides shows that even those committed to a Maimonidean position need not pursue the ideal of the halakhic state. Maimonides himself recognized an entire realm of legal and political authority that is independent of halakha.

Yedidia Stern, an Israeli legal scholar and fellow of the Israel Democracy Institute, has brought this line of inquiry to bear more directly on contemporary Israeli society. Stern thinks that a fundamental source of the antagonism in Israeli society is the competition for supremacy between religious and secular legal systems. He writes that, in the eyes of their adherents, these two systems "entertain the idea of the totality of their scope in the regulation of reality, and both—at least on the rhetorical level—hold themselves to be exclusive in this regard." He calls this a position of "normative duality," in which the two systems are understood to be "mutually hostile." This outlook "brings into sharp focus the confrontation over Israel's cultural profile and over the identity of Jewish society in Israel."[64] Stern goes on to show that this perception of the mutual exclusivity of halakha and the secular state can be challenged by the history of Jewish legal pluralism. An understanding of this history, he believes, may help to ameliorate some of these tensions by showing that the Jewish tradition itself contains alternative views of the relationship between halakha and other kinds of law.

It is hard to predict how successful thinkers like Ravitzky, Lorberbaum, and Stern are likely to be in their attempts to reintroduce legal pluralism into religious Zionist discourse. But, given the entrenched place of the halakhic state in religious Zionist ideology, and given the fact that religious Zionists have more political power today than at any time in the past, it is difficult to imagine that the prevailing ideology will be easily abandoned. What is more, legal pluralism is not a panacea. Even some scholars who accept the descriptive power of legal pluralism as a theory consider it too vague and unstructured to be of practical utility or to manage social conflict effectively.[65] Furthermore, some liberal thinkers are wary of the possible unintended consequences of applying a strong version of legal pluralism in the modern state. They are concerned that promoting the independent legal authority of some non-state groups, especially those that do not recognize liberal rights, may threaten the well-being of individuals within those groups. Some women, for example, may find themselves vulnerable if the state is not willing to intervene in the autonomous governance of religious communities when the rights of individuals are compromised under religious law.[66]

The possible shortcomings of legal pluralism as an applied system, however, do not diminish its value as a critique of ideologies of legal supremacy, whether those of the state or those of religious Zionists. In this sense, the renewed interest in legal pluralism by some contemporary religious Zionist thinkers is a welcome development. A dramatic shift in religious Zionist legal thinking is unlikely in the short term but, given the extent to which ideologies of legal centralism underlie many of the social tensions in Israel today, voices critical of those ideologies should be promoted. If the historical revelations presented in this book can contribute to that effort, so much the better.

The history of the halakhic state also has consequences far beyond the specific case of modern Israel. One of the greatest political questions today is how states should navigate the relationship between religion and law. It is often thought that this question comes down to the simple choice of "separation of church and state" on the one hand or "religious establishment" on the other. In the popular imagination, this choice sets up a dichotomy between theocratic states on the one hand, in which the constitution is based on religious principles, and liberal states on the other, in which religion is confined to the private sphere. Some claim that only theocratic politics can save us from the social crises and moral perversions of the modern world. Others insist that theocracies are incompatible with democracy, that they inevitably oppress dissenters, and that only a secular state can provide a neutral and rational politics that will protect the rights of individuals.

In recent years, the neatness of this dichotomy has been deconstructed by scholars of religion and of political thought. They have pointed out that the model of separation emerged from, and remains intertwined with, the history of Protestant Christianity. John Locke's contrast between religion as a matter of "faith" and civil government as a matter of "laws" is underpinned by Martin Luther's doctrine that man is saved "by faith alone."[67] Similarly, Thomas Jefferson's call for a "wall of eternal separation between Church & State" rested on a long history of Puritan theology. Already in 1644, the Puritan minister Roger Williams had warned against making any "gap in the hedge, or wall of separation, between the garden of the Church and the wilderness of the world."[68] This Protestant conception of religion, though, is alien to traditions in which sacrament, ritual, and other communal means of belonging are no less significant than dogma. It is doubtful whether a clean separation between church and state is possible even in places with a Protestant history. In places like Israel (and countless other countries), where the Protestant legacy of religion as faith alone is quite foreign, separation is unlikely to be successful.

By the same token, it is impossible to attain a pure religious constitution. Those who want to escape the corrupting effects of modernity by establishing pure theocracies are chasing a phantasm. There is no such thing as an authentic core of a religious tradition that can be distinguished from external influences. Religious societies, like all societies, have porous boundaries. They are always in flux, endlessly negotiating their engagement with other people and ideas. Religion today cannot be immune from adulterations of modernity. It is therefore a fool's errand to try to impose either side of the separation/establishment dichotomy. Secular law and religion are always intertwined.[69]

Recent works have analyzed the complex relationships between the amorphous categories of religion, politics, and law in countries where Christianity, Buddhism, Islam, or other religions are dominant.[70] Jewish examples, though, are rarely discussed, perhaps in part because a halakhic state has never existed in fact. This book examines such a state, as it was imagined by religious Zionists. It shows how difficult it is to make an easy distinction between religious and secular, traditional and modern. Even the most uncompromising positions of religious Zionists, which unapologetically called for a Jewish theocracy, drew from the language and structures of modern European law. Conversely, many religious Zionists who endorsed the legal recognition of secular law did so not as a pragmatic concession to the modern state, but as a principled religious position drawing on a long history of Jewish legal pluralism.

These unexpected dynamics underline the fact that there is no simple, universal solution to the ordering of religion law and politics in Israel or anywhere else. There is no single formula that guarantees both the rights of individuals and the integrity of historical communities; that preserves the freedom of religion without regulating religion; that ensures an open and inclusive democratic society while defining where that society begins and ends. Balancing between these competing concerns requires constant and imperfect negotiation. To acknowledge these complexities, however, does not absolve us of responsibility. We persist in the collective goal of pushing our societies to deal with these issues ever more mindfully, toiling slowly, messily in the direction of equality, justice, and truth.[71]

NOTES

INTRODUCTION

The following abbreviations are used in the notes:

ISA   Israel State Archives
RZA-MRK Religious Zionist Archives, Mosad Ha-Rav Kook, Jerusalem
RZA-BI Religious Zionist Archives, Bar-Ilan University Library

1. Yair Ettinger, "Ne'eman: Yesh la-hafokh et ha-halakhah la-hoq ha-mehayev ba-medinah," *Haaretz*, December 7, 2009. All translations are my own, unless noted otherwise.
2. This criticism was made at the time by Haim Oron, the chairman of the Meretz party. Yair Ettinger, "Se'arah ba-ma'arekhet ha-politit be-ikvot devarav shel sar ha-mishpatim, ya'aqov ne'eman," *Haaretz*, December 8, 2009.
3. Yair Ettinger, "Justice Minister: Rabbinical Courts Should Support, Not Replace Civil Courts," *Haaretz*, August 12, 2009.
4. This event is reported in the memoirs of Isaac Herzog's son, Chaim, who served as President of the State of Israel from 1983 to 1993. Chaim Herzog, *Living History: A Memoir* (New York: Pantheon Books, 1996), 12. See also Dermot Keogh, *Jews in Twentieth Century Ireland: Refugees, Anti-Semitism and the Holocaust* (Cork, Ireland: Cork University Press, 1998), 77.
5. On the relationship between the two men, see Shulamit Eliash, *The Harp and the Shield of David: Ireland, Zionism and the State of Israel*, Israeli History, Politics and Society 48 (Abingdon, Oxon: Routledge, 2007), 50 ff.
6. For the broader relationship between Zionism and Irish nationalism, see Aidan Beatty, "Zionism and Irish Nationalism: Ideology and Identity on the Borders of Europe," *Journal of Imperial and Commonwealth History* 45, no. 2 (March 4, 2017): 315–38.
7. A terminological note: In this book, I use "Palestine" to refer to the British Mandate for Palestine before its termination in 1948 and "Israel" or "the State of

Israel" to refer to the state after its establishment. I occasionally use "Jewish state" to refer to the idea of a Jewish state in the abstract. This term is not intended as a synonym for "the State of Israel" per se. I generally employ it to describe the state that Zionists were planning to establish before its name had been decided. On the revolutionary nature of Zionism, see David Vital, "Zionism as Revolution? Zionism as Rebellion?" *Modern Judaism* 18, no. 3 (October 1, 1998): 205–15.

8. The political-theological aspect of secular Zionism does not negate this general point. See, for example, Shmuel Almog, Jehuda Reinharz, and Anita Shapira, eds., *Zionism and Religion*, Tauber Institute for the Study of European Jewry 30 (Hanover, NH, and London: University Press of New England, 1998), especially pp. 237 ff.; Yael Zerubavel, *Recovered Roots: Collective Memory and the Making of Israeli National Tradition* (Chicago: University of Chicago Press, 1995); David Ohana, *Nationalizing Judaism: Zionism as a Theological Ideology* (Lanham, MD: Lexington Books, 2017).

9. On Zionism as a "secular revolution" in the context of nationalist movements globally, see Michael Walzer, *The Paradox of Liberation: Secular Revolutions and Religious Counterrevolutions* (New Haven, CT: Yale University Press, 2015), xii.

10. Although they have been represented in every Knesset, religious Jewish parties combined have rarely received more than 15 percent of the vote.

11. Rachel Rafael Neis, "The Seduction of Law: Rethinking Legal Studies in Jewish Studies." *Jewish Quarterly Review* 109, no. 1 (Winter 2019): 119–38.

12. Before the establishment of the Chief Rabbinate in Mandate Palestine and the enforcement of new procedural rules, there are almost no examples of an appellate process in Jewish law. For very rare exceptions to this rule, see Simhah Assaf, *Batei ha-din ve-sidrehem aharei hatimat ha-Talmud* (Jerusalem: Defus Ha-po'alim, 1924).

13. The phrase comes from the writings of Herzog's colleague and senior religious Zionist rabbi, Meir Bar-Ilan. Meir Bar-Ilan, "Hoq u-mishpat be-medinatenu," in *Ha-mishpat ha-ivri u-medinat yisra'el*, ed. Yaakov Bazaq (Jerusalem: Mosad Ha-rav Kook, 1969), 22.

14. It has been well established that Jewish Orthodoxy should be seen as a modern expression of Judaism rather than a holdout of premodern society. In a sense, the transformation of Orthodox law in an independent Jewish state is another example of that phenomenon. Among many studies, see Jacob Katz, *A House Divided: Orthodoxy and Schism in Nineteenth-Century Central European Jewry* (Hanover, NH: Brandeis University Press, 1998); Haym Soloveitchik, "Rupture and Reconstruction: The Transformation of Contemporary Orthodoxy," *Tradition: A Journal of Orthodox Jewish Thought* 28, no. 4 (1994): 64–130; David Ellenson, *After Emancipation: Jewish Religious Responses to Modernity* (Cincinnati, OH: Hebrew Union College Press, 2004); Leora Batnitzky, *How Judaism Became a Religion: An Introduction to Modern Jewish Thought* (Princeton, NJ: Princeton University Press, 2011). For a contemporary case study, see David N. Myers and Nomi Stolzenberg,

"Rethinking Secularization Theory: The Case of the Hasidic Public Square," *AJS Perspectives*, Spring 2011: 37–8.

15. Eliezer Don-Yehiya, "Stability and Change in a Political Party: The NRP and the 'Young Guard' Revolution," *Medinah mimshal ve-yahasim ben-le'umi'im* 14 (1980): 26.

16. For an overview of the varieties of religious Zionism, see Dov Schwartz, *Religious-Zionism: History and Ideology* (Boston: Academic Studies Press, 2009). On religious Zionist theology, see Dov Schwartz, *Faith at the Crossroads: A Theological Profile of Religious Zionism* (Leiden; Boston: Brill, 2002).

17. Ehud Luz, *Parallels Meet: Religion and Nationalism in the Early Zionist Movement (1882–1904)* (Philadelphia: Jewish Publication Society, 1988).

18. Schwartz, *Religious-Zionism*, vii.

19. The phrase "sacred rebellion" (*ha-mered ha-qadosh*) was coined by Shmuel Haim Landau, a religious Zionist leader of Hasidic descent. See Haya Frumer, ed., *Shahal: Holem ve-lohem* (Jerusalem: Erez, 2008). Key texts by Landau were collected in Shmuel Hayim Landau, *Kitve Sh. H. Landau* (Jerusalem: Ha-tenu'ah ha-olamit shel ha-mizrahi-ha-po'el ha-mizrahi, "yad shapira," mif'al hantsahah le-zikhro shel H M Shapira, 1984).

20. Aviezer Ravitzky, *Messianism, Zionism, and Jewish Religious Radicalism* (Chicago: University of Chicago Press, 1996); Menachem Friedman, "The State of Israel as a Theological Dilemma," in *The Israeli State and Society: Boundaries and Frontiers*, ed. Baruch Kimmerling (Albany: SUNY Press, 1989), 165–215.

21. Despite the claim by some that Shai Agnon wrote the prayer, it has been demonstrated that the true author was Herzog. Yoel Rafel, "Zehuto shel mehaber ha-tefilah li-shlom ha-medinah," in *Masu'ah le-yitshaq*, ed. Shulamit Eliash, Itamar Warhaftig, and Uri Desberg, 2 vols. (Jerusalem: Yad Ha-rav Herzog; Mekhon Ha-entsiklopediah Ha-talmudit; Mekhon Ha-talmud Ha-yisre'eli Ha-shalem, 2008), 1:594–620.

22. Whether Reines genuinely saw Zionism as a political solution rather than a movement of messianic import is a matter for debate. In *Messianism, Zionism, and Jewish Religious Radicalism*, 32 ff. Ravitzky argues that Reines was interested principally in the physical safety of persecuted Jews, whereas Schwartz claims that Reines esoterically encoded his apocalyptic beliefs in his political writing. Schwartz, *Religious-Zionism*, 13–15.

23. Quoted in Dov Schwartz, *Faith at the Crossroads*, 165.

24. Ibid., 175.

25. Quoted in Ravitzky, *Messianism, Zionism, and Jewish Religious Radicalism*, 113.

26. Not all secular Zionists appreciated this position. See ibid., 115. Amos Oz, a secular Zionist writer, put it this way: "Zionism began among people who rebelled against the dominion of religious law, refused to live in accordance with it. . . . You can adopt a patronizing, insulting interpretation in which the early pioneers thought

they were acting from an idealistic world view but were really no more than an instrument of God and that the holy sparks flew out of their secular, socialist 'shell' without their intending it. This is trampling the spiritual autonomy of others, and it has always made me feel insulted and bitter." Amos Oz, *In the Land of Israel* (Orlando, FL: Houghton Mifflin Harcourt, 1993), 149.

27. Shlomo Zalman Shragai, "Hazon mizrahi u-matarato," in *Mizrahi: Qovets yovel le-melot k"h shanah le-qiyumah shel histadrut ha-mizrahi be-ameriqah (5671–5796)*, ed. Pinchas Churgin and Aryeh Leib Gelman (New York: s.n., 1936), 69.

28. For more on the Religious Kibbutz Movement, see Aryei Fishman, *Judaism and Modernization on the Religious Kibbutz* (Cambridge: Cambridge University Press, 1992).

29. On Kook's circle, see Dov Schwartz, *Etgar u-mashber be-hug ha-rav kook*, 224 (Tel Aviv: Am Oved, 2001).

30. Dov Schwartz, "Ideas vs. Reality: Multiculturalism and Religious-Zionism," in *The Multicultural Challenge in Israel*, ed. Avi Sagi and Ohad Nachtomy, Israel (Boston: Academic Studies Press, 2009), 200–225; Shlomo Fischer, "Fundamentalist or Romantic Nationalist: Israeli Modern Orthodoxy," in *Dynamic Jewish Belonging*, ed. Harvey Goldberg, Steven Cohen, and Ezra Kopelowitz (New York; Oxford: Berghahn Books, 2012), 91–111. A recent survey of the beliefs and practices of religious Zionists carried out by Bet Hillel, an organization of Israeli Jewish religious leaders, demonstrates the diversity of the religious Zionist community. Accessed October 12, 2019, https://eng.beithillel.org.il/docs/beit-hillel-religious-zionism-survey-2014.pdf.

31. Tamar Hermann et al., "Dati'im? Le'umi'im!—Ha-mahaneh ha-dati le'umi" (Jerusalem: Israel Democracy Institute, 2014). The survey discussed those identifying as *dati le'umi*, which is a term roughly equivalent to, though not identical with, religious Zionism.

32. "This data expresses, in our opinion, the advancement of this camp into the center of the social stage in Israel and its transformation into a focus for an attitude of identity and values above and beyond the Orthodox halakhic way of life." Hermann et al., "Dati'im? Le'umi'im!," 2. This data needs further analysis, especially given the complexity attending the concept of "identity." Rawi Abdelal et al., "Identity as a Variable," *Perspectives on Politics* 4, no. 4 (2006): 695–711.

33. The term "wall of separation between church and state" was coined by Thomas Jefferson in his 1802 letter to the Danbury Baptist Association. It was first used by the Supreme Court in Reynolds v. United States (1878). It was not until the late 1940s, however, that it became a real touchstone of American jurisprudence. Philip Hamburger, *Separation of Church and State* (Cambridge, MA: Harvard University Press, 2009), especially Part IV.

34. Pinhas Kohn [=Leo Kohn], "The State of Israel: Draft Constitution," March 5708, G-542524 43.06/2941, ISA. The constitutional draft bears the Hebrew date

of Marheshvan 5708, the month on the Jewish calendar that fell between mid-October and mid-November 1947. Other drafts were presented to the Provisional State Council Constitution Committee but Kohn's was officially accepted as the basis for the committee's deliberations. Amihai Radzyner, "A Constitution for Israel: The Design of the Leo Kohn Proposal, 1948," *Israel Studies* 15, no. 1 (2010): 2.

35. Kohn, "The State of Israel: Draft Constitution," 1.

36. Kohn, "The State of Israel: Draft Constitution," 2, 1.2, 1.4.

37. Quoted in Radzyner, "A Constitution for Israel, 7. Warhaftig's observation is complicated by the fact that Kohn himself identified as a religious Zionist. Kohn's constitutional writing, however, was shaped more by his academic scholarship than by his religious convictions.

38. Quoted in Arthur Hertzberg, *The Zionist Idea: A Historical Analysis and Reader* (Philadelphia: Jewish Publication Society, 1997), 550.

39. John Locke, *A Letter Concerning Toleration and Other Writings*, ed. Mark Goldie (Indianapolis, IN: Liberty Fund, 2010), 12.

40. Quoted in Michael Stanislawski, *Zionism and the fin de siècle: Cosmopolitanism and Nationalism from Nordau to Jabotinsky* (Berkeley: University of California Press, 2001), 19–20.

41. Although he was a deist, Ben-Gurion was opposed to traditional Jewish law halakha. Zvi Tsameret, "Judaism in Israel: Ben-Gurion's Private Beliefs and Public Policy," *Israel Studies* 4, no. 2 (1999): 64–89; Anita Shapira, *Ben-Gurion: Father of Modern Israel* (New Haven, CT: Yale University Press, 2014), 192–93.

42. Charles S. Liebman and Eliezer Don-Yehiya, *Civil Religion in Israel: Traditional Judaism and Political Culture in the Jewish State* (Berkeley: University of California Press, 1983), 90.

43. On the belief that all Jews would return to halakhic practice, and on some resistance to it, see Asher Cohen, *Ha-talit veha-degel: Ha-tsiyonut ha-datit ve-hazon medinat ha-torah bi-yeme reshit ha-medinah* (Jerusalem: Yad Yitshak Ben-Tsvi, 1998), chap. 7.

44. Menachem Friedman, *Hevrah va-dat: Ha-ortodoksiyah ha-lo-tsionit be-erets yisra'el, 1918–1936*, Sifriyah le-toldot ha-yishuv ha-yehudi be-erets yisra'el (Jerusalem: Yad Yitshak Ben-Tvi, 1977), 146–84; Zvi Zohar, "Traditional Flexibility and Modern Strictness: Two Halakhic Positions on Women's Suffrage," in *Sephardi and Middle Eastern Jewries: History and Culture in the Modern Era*, ed. Harvey E. Goldberg (Bloomington: Indiana University Press, 1996), 119–33.

45. United Nations General Assembly Resolution 181 2.2.

46. This is a common understanding of sovereignty, following the tradition of Thomas Hobbes. The term has also been used in other ways. Jens Bartelson, *A Genealogy of Sovereignty* (Cambridge: Cambridge University Press, 1995); Quentin Skinner, "The Sovereign State: A Genealogy," in *Sovereignty in Fragments: The Past,*

Present and Future of a Contested Concept, ed. Hent Kalmo and Quentin Skinner (Cambridge: Cambridge University Press, 2010), 26–46.

47. J. Griffiths, "What Is Legal Pluralism?" *Journal of Legal Pluralism and Unofficial Law 18, no. 24* (1986): 1–55, 3.

48. This definition follows Sally Engle Merry, "Legal Pluralism," *Law and Society Review* 22, no. 5 (1988): 870.

49. Griffiths, "What Is Legal Pluralism?" 39.

50. This is the position of Griffiths, for example, who posits that "legal pluralism is the fact. Legal centralism is myth, an idea, a claim, an illusion." Ibid., 4.

51. For a description of this state of affairs, see Brian Z. Tamanaha, "Understanding Legal Pluralism: Past to Present, Local to Global," *Sydney Law Review* 30 (2007): 377.

52. Lauren Benton, "Historical Perspectives on Legal Pluralism," *Hague Journal of the Rule of Law* 3, no. 1 (March 2011): 57–69.

53. Assaf Likhovski, "The Ottoman Legacy of Israeli Law," *Annales de la Faculté de droit d'Istanbul* 39 (2007): 71–86; Iris Agmon, *Family and Court: Legal Culture and Modernity in Late Ottoman Palestine* (Syracuse, NY: Syracuse University Press, 2006).

54. Assaf Likhovski, *Law and Identity in Mandate Palestine* (Chapel Hill: University of North Carolina Press, 2006); Assaf Likhovski, "Between Mandate and State: On the Periodization of Israeli Legal History," *Journal of Israeli History* 19, no. 2 (1998): 39–68.

55. Kohn's draft constitution, for example, at 5.70(5), laid out that among the state's courts would be "[r]eligious courts of the Jewish community, the Muslim community and the Christian community, which will judge matters of personal status and religious endowments."

56. Herzog included this comment in a speech in the Great Synagogue in Jerusalem at the end of July 1948, later published in the religious newspaper *Ha-tsofeh*, 25 Tammuz 5708 and quoted in Itamar Warhaftig, "Mavo," in *Tehuqah le-yisra'el al pi ha-torah*, ed. Itamar Warhaftig (Jerusalem: Mosad Ha-rav Kook; Yad Ha-rav Herzog, 1989), 1:28 fn. 11.

57. Derek J. Penslar, "Zionism, Colonialism and Postcolonialism," *Journal of Israeli History* 20, nos. 2–3 (June 2001): 85. For an updated version of that article, and a discussion by other scholars, see Ethan B. Katz, Lisa Moses Leff, and Maud S. Mandel, eds., *Colonialism and the Jews* (Bloomfield: Indiana University Press, 2017).

58. See, for example, Amnon Rubinstein, *The Zionist Dream Revisited: From Herzl to Gush Emunim and Back* (New York: Schocken Books, 1984), 47. Others place less emphasis on universalism in religious Zionist politics, but still maintain that pragmatism outweighed ideology in religious Zionist politics between 1948 and the rise of Gush Emunim. See, for example, Cohen, *Ha-talit veha-degel*, chap. 6.

59. Before 1977, the Allon Plan, which proposed Jewish Israeli settlements in strategic locations, in particular along the Jordan Valley, implicitly guided government policy, even though it was never officially endorsed by the Labor-led government. Benny Morris, *Righteous Victims: A History of the Zionist-Arab Conflict, 1881–1998* (New York: Vintage, 2001), 328. After the accession of Prime Minister Begin in 1977, governmental support for the settlements continued.

60. Anita Shapira, *Israel: A History* (Hanover, NH: University Press of New England, 2012), chap. 14.

61. David K. Shipler, "Israelis Assess Role of Religion," *New York Times*, October 26, 1981; Shulamit Aloni, *Ha-hesder: Mi-medinat hoq le-medinat halakhah* (Tel Aviv, 1970), 37.

62. Other scholars have placed less emphasis on 1967 as a turning point and have pointed to a certain continuity in the development of religious Zionism. Gideon Aran has argued that the ideological position of the settler movement was formulated among young religious Zionists as early as the 1950s. Specifically, he discusses the importance of the Gahelet group of the 1950s in laying the groundwork for Gush Emunim. Gideon Aran, "From Religious Zionism to Zionist Religion: The Roots of Gush Emunim," in *The Challenge of Modernity and Jewish Orthodoxy*, ed. Peter Medding, Studies in Contemporary Jewry 2 (Bloomington: Indiana University Press, 1986), 116–43; Gideon Aran, "Bein halutsi'ut le-limud torah: Ha-reqa le-ge'ut ha-datit le-umit," in *Me'ah shenot tsiyonut datit*, ed. Avi Sagi and Dov Schwartz, 3 vols. (Ramat Gan, Israel: Bar-Ilan University, 2003), 3:31–72. This position is disputed in Avi Sagi and Dov Schwartz, "Bein halutsi'ut le-limud torah: Zavit aheret," in *Me'ah shenot tsiyonut datit*, ed. Sagi and Schwartz, 3:73–75. Aran also, though, identifies the significance of 1967 in the development of the movement's mythology. Gideon Aran, "A Mystic-Messianic Interpretation of Modern Israeli History: The Six Day War as a Key Event in the Development of the Original Religious Culture of Gush Emunim," in *The Jews and the European Crisis, 1914–1921*, ed. Jonathan Frankel, Peter Y. Medding, and Ezra Mendelsohn, Studies in Contemporary Jewry 4 (New York: Oxford University Press, 1988), 263–75. Aran's most recent and comprehensive treatment of the subject is Gideon Aran, *Quqism: Shorshei gush emunim, tarbut ha-mitnahalim, te'ologiah tsi'onit, meshihi'ut bi-zmanenu* (Jerusalem: Carmel Publishers, 2013). Others have identified elements of intellectual and spiritual continuity between Gush Emunim and strands in the thinking of Abraham Isaac Kook, whose more moderate aspects were jettisoned by some of his spiritual heirs. See Schwartz, *Etgar u-mashber*. For an extended study of the ideological development of Kook's students, see Yehudah Mirsky, *Rav Kook: Mystic in a Time of Revolution* (New Haven, CT: Yale University Press, 2014), especially the conclusion.

63. Moshe Hellinger and Itzhak Hershkovits, *Tsiut ve-i-tsiut be-tsionut ha-datit: Mi-gush emunim ve-ad tag mehir* (Jerusalem: Israel Democracy Institute, 2015).

64. This widely reported comment was allegedly made by Netanyahu to Yaakov Vider, an Ultra-Orthodox member of Netanyahu's Likud party, in connection with discussions over a proposed Basic Law regarding the Jewish identity of the State of Israel. Ari Yashar, "Report: Netanyahu Promises Talmud Will Be Israeli Law," *Arutz Sheva Israel National News*, September 5, 2014; Marissa Newman, "Netanyahu Reported to Say Legal System Based on Talmud," *Times of Israel*, August 5, 2014.

65. Works such as José Casanova, *Public Religions in the Modern World* (Chicago: University of Chicago Press, 1994) and Peter L. Berger, *The Desecularization of the World: Resurgent Religion and World Politics* (Grand Rapids, MI: W. E. Eerdmans, 1999) have criticized secularization theory on an empirical basis, by pointing to the continued centrality of religion in contemporary society. They advocate the decoupling of the concepts of modernity and secularization. Others have complicated the definition of "religion" and have thereby observed religious vitality in previously under-examined corners of society. Hubert Knoblauch, "Spirituality and Popular Religion in Europe," *Social Compass* 55, no. 2 (2008): 140–53. Still others have pointed to the centrality of religious ideas in the creation of modernity, arguing in different ways that religion underpins the modern age, or at least helped to lay its foundations. Talal Asad, *Formations of the Secular: Christianity, Islam, Modernity* (Stanford, CA: Stanford University Press, 2003); Charles Taylor, *A Secular Age* (Cambridge, MA.: Belknap Press of Harvard University Press, 2007).

66. Mark Lilla, *The Stillborn God: Religion, Politics, and the Modern West*, reprint edition (New York: Vintage, 2008), 55 ff.

67. José Casanova, "The Secular, Secularizations, Secularisms," in *Rethinking Secularism*, ed. Craig Calhoun, Mark Juergensmeyer, and Jonathan VanAntwerpen (New York: Oxford University Press, 2011), 54–74.

68. One of the most influential claims that Western Christianity is distinctive in this respect is Samuel P. Huntingdon, *The Clash of Civilizations and the Remaking of the World Order* (New York: Simon and Schuster, 1996). Huntingdon's articulation has been the focus of significant debate. For a critique, see, for example, Alfred C. Stepan, "Religion, Democracy, and the 'Twin Tolerations,'" *Journal of Democracy* 11, no. 4 (2000): 37–57.

69. Lilla, *Stillborn God*, 9.

70. The term "immanent frame" is from Taylor, *Secular Age*.

71. See, for example, Eric Nelson, *The Hebrew Republic* (Cambridge, MA: Harvard University Press, 2010); Michael Allen Gillespie, *The Theological Origins of Modernity* (Chicago: University of Chicago Press, 2009).

72. Carl Schmitt, *Political Theology: Four Chapters on the Concept of Sovereignty*, 1st ed., trans. George Schwab (Chicago: University of Chicago Press, 2006), 36.

73. This position is forcefully expressed by José Casanova, a leading sociologist of religion: "Rather than seeing the common structural contexts of modern state

formation, inter-state geopolitical conflicts, modern nationalism and the political mobilization of ethno-cultural and religious identities, processes central to modern European history that became globalized through the European colonial expansion, Europeans prefer seemingly to attribute those conflicts to "religion"—that is, to religious fundamentalism and to the fanaticism and intolerance that is supposedly intrinsic to "pre-modern" religion, an atavistic residue which modern secular enlightened Europeans have fortunately left behind." José Casanova, "Religion Challenging the Myth of Secular Democracy," in *Religion in the 21st Century: Challenges and Transformations*, ed. Margit Warburg et al. (Farnham, Surrey, England; Burlington, VT: Ashgate, 2010), 27.

74. José Casanova, "The Stillborn God: The Great Separation," *The Immanent Frame*, accessed April 13, 2017, http://blogs.ssrc.org/tif/2007/12/07/the-great-separation/. For similar reflections on the relationship between religion, secularism and violence, see Ted A. Smith, *Weird John Brown: Divine Violence and the Limits of Ethics* (Stanford, CA: Stanford University Press, 2014); William T. Cavanaugh, *The Myth of Religious Violence: Secular Ideology and the Roots of Modern Conflict* (New York: Oxford University Press, 2009).

75. Quentin Skinner, *Reason and Rhetoric in the Philosophy of Hobbes* (Cambridge: Cambridge University Press, 1996), 113.

76. J. G. A. Pocock, "The Concept of Language and the *métier d'historien*: Some Considerations on Practice," in *The Languages of Political Theory in Early-Modern Europe*, ed. Anthony Robin Pagden (Cambridge: Cambridge University Press, 1987), 21. Ultimately, if we follow Quentin Skinner, the goal is to understand the thinkers under consideration from within their own worldview in order "to grasp their concepts, to follow their distinctions, to appreciate their beliefs and, so far as possible, to see things their way." Quentin Skinner, *Visions of Politics* (Cambridge; New York: Cambridge University Press, 2002), 1:3.

77. Lawrence Rosen, *Law as Culture: An Invitation* (Princeton, NJ: Princeton University Press, 2006). Of course, the field of legal history is quite diverse. At least twelve distinct approaches to the relationship between law and culture have been identified by Menachem Mautner, "Three Approaches to Law and Culture," *Cornell Law Review* 96 (2010): 839.

78. For one articulation of this insight, see Austin D. Sarat, "Redirecting Legal Scholarship in Law Schools," *Yale Journal of Law & the Humanities* 12, no. 1 (2013): 129–150, 134.

79. Ashkenazim constituted the clear majority of the leadership of religious Zionism during the period that is the focus of this book. For the approach of Sephardic rabbis to Zionism, see, for example, Marc Angel, *Loving Truth and Peace: The Grand Religious Worldview of Rabbi Benzion Uziel* (Northvale, NJ: Jason Aronson, 1999); Zvi Zohar, "Sephardic Tradition on Galut and Political Zionism: The Halakhic Position of Rabbi Ya'akov Moshe Toledano," in *From Iberia to Diaspora: Studies*

in Sephardic History and Culture, ed. Yedida Kalfon Stillman and Norman A. Stillman (Leiden: Brill, 1999), 223–34; Marc Angel and Hayyim J. Angel, *Rabbi Haim David Halevy: Gentle Scholar and Courageous Thinker* (Jerusalem: Urim Publications, 2006); Zvi Zohar and Avi Sagi, eds., *Yahadut shel haim: Iyunim be-yetsirato ha-hagutit-hilkhatit shel ha-rav hayim david halevi* (Jerusalem: Mekhon Shalom Hartman; Keter, 2007); Zvi Zohar, *Rabbinic Creativity in the Modern Middle East* (New York: Bloomsbury Academic, 2013).

CHAPTER I

1. The slogan appeared in David Grossman's lyrics for the *Sticker Song* by the band *Hadag Nahash*. Its chiasmus exploits the fact that the letters *h-l-kh-h* in Hebrew can be read either as *halakhah* (Jewish law, literally "the way") or as *halkhah* ("it has gone").

2. Aloni, *Ha-hesder*, 37.

3. Gershon Weiler, *Te'oqratiah yehudit* (Tel Aviv: Am Oved, 1976). The quotation is from the book's English translation, Gershon Weiler, *Jewish Theocracy* (Leiden: Brill, 1988), 331.

4. Shipler, "Israelis Assess Role of Religion."

5. Isaac Herzog, *Tehuqah le-yisra'el al-pi ha-torah*, ed. Itamar Warhaftig (Jerusalem: Mosad Ha-rav Kook; Yad Ha-rav Herzog, 1989), 1:3. The passage from which this quotation was taken appears in translation in Isaac Herzog, "Rabbi Herzog on the Chief Rabbinate (ca. 1948)," in *The Origins of Israel, 1882–1948: A Documentary History*, ed. Eran Kaplan and Derek Penslar, trans. Alexander Kaye (Madison: University of Wisconsin Press, 2011).

6. Meir Bar-Ilan, "Hoq u-mishpat be-medinatenu," in *Ha-tsi'onut ha-datit veha-medinah: Qovets ma'amarim li-shloshim shenot ha-medinah*, ed. Yosef Tirosh and Avraham Tirosh (Jerusalem: Ha-histadrut ha-tsionut ha-olamit; Ha-mahlaqah le-hinukh ule-tarbut torani'im ba-golah, 1978), 327.

7. Ze'ev Falk, "Proposal for a Constitution of the State of Israel," RZA-BI PA/1616000171. Falk wrote a great deal over the years about the relationship between Jewish law, and about human values and the place of Jewish law in modern society. See, for example, Ze'ev W. Falk, *Law and Religion: The Jewish Experience* (Jerusalem: Mesharim, 1981).

8. The plan of the Peel Commission was not ultimately implemented, but ten years later the United Nations approved a similar resolution for the partition of Palestine.

9. For a biography of Grodzinski, see Shlomo Yosef Zevin, *Ishim ve-shitot: Shurat ma'amarim al ishei halakhah ve-shitotehem ba-torah* (Tel Aviv: A. Tsioni, 1966), 189–223. See also the biographical sketch at Benjamin Brown, "Grodzenski, Hayim Ozer," *The Yivo Encyclopedia of Jews in Eastern Europe*, accessed July 19, 2017, http://www.yivoencyclopedia.org/article.aspx/Grodzenski_Hayim_Ozer. For the relationship

between Mizrahi and Agudat Yisrael, see Daniel Mahla, "No Trinity: The Tripartite Relations between Agudat Yisrael, the Mizrahi Movement, and the Zionist Organization," *Journal of Israeli History* 34, no. 2 (July 3, 2015): 117–40. Although Agudat Yisrael never totally accommodated itself to Zionism, it collaborated with the Zionist organization and eventually lent its support to the establishment of Israel in 1948. Menachem Friedman, "The Structural Foundation for Religio-Political Accommodation in Israel: Fallacy and Reality," in *Israel: The First Decade of Independence*, ed. S. Ilan Troen and Noah Lucas (Albany: SUNY Press, 1995), 51–81.

10. Isaac Herzog, *Tehuqah le-yisrael*, 2:75.

11. Ibid., 2:75 fn. 10. The translation is based on that in Michael Walzer et al., eds., *The Jewish Political Tradition* (New Haven, CT: Yale University Press, 2000), 1:475 with some modifications. See also Warhaftig, "Mavo," 31 fn. 19.

12. Herzog, *Tehuqah le-yisrael*, 1989, 2:75.

13. Aviezer Ravitzky, *Religion and State in Jewish Philosophy: Models of Unity, Division, Collision and Subordination* (Jerusalem: Israel Democracy Institute, 2001), 13; Suzanne Last Stone, "Religion and State: Models of Separation from within Jewish Law," *International Journal of Constitutional Law* 6, nos. 3–4 (2008): 641. Stone's article summarizes this position well: "It does not require much guesswork to discern the motivations behind Grodzinski's response. Grodzinski was opposed to the state's creation altogether. For him, Zionism was blasphemy, the human forcing of a messianic ideal and, potentially, idolatry—the setting up of an alternative sovereign. He wished to protect the garden of religious halakha from any state but especially a Jewish state, by separating the two at the outset."

14. Tamanaha, "Understanding Legal Pluralism," 377.

15. Ido Shahar, "Legal Pluralism and the Study of Shari'a Courts," *Islamic Law and Society* 15, no. 1 (2008): 112–41.

16. The Talmud itself is replete with references to sources of law that operated in parallel with halakha. For example, rabbinic literature maintains that the Noahide Laws, a basic set of criminal, civil, moral, and theological norms, are binding on all of humanity. According to many rabbinic interpretations, the authority of these laws derives not from Sinaitic revelation but from a human intuition for moral norms. For a persuasive argument that the rabbinic tradition considers the Noahide Laws to apply to Jews even after the Sinaitic revelation, see Suzanne Last Stone, "Sinaitic and Noahide Law: Legal Pluralism in Jewish Law," *Cardozo Law Review* 12 (1990): 1157–1214. See also Steven Robert Wilf, *The Law before the Law* (Lanham, MD: Lexington Books, 2008).

17. For a study of the relationship between Jewish communities and kings, see Salo W. Baron, "'Plenitude of Apostolic Powers' and Medieval 'Jewish Serfdom.'" in *Ancient and Medieval Jewish History: Essays by Salo Wittemayer Baron*, ed. Leon Feldman (New Brunswick, NJ: Rutgers University Press, 1972), 308–22; Salo W. Baron, *A Social and Religious History of the Jews*, 18 vols. (New York: Jewish Publication

Society, 1952–1983), 4:36–43 and 9:135–92; Yosef Hayim Yerushalmi, "Servants of Kings and Not Servants of Servants: Some Aspects of the Political History of the Jews," in *The Faith of Fallen Jews: Yosef Hayim Yerushalmi and the Writing of Jewish History*, ed. David N. Myers and Alexander Kaye (Lebanon, NH: University Press of New England, 2013), 245–76; Yosef Hayim Yerushalmi, *The Lisbon Massacre of 1506 and the Royal Image in the Shebet Yehudah* (Cincinnati, OH: Hebrew Union College–Jewish Institute of Religion, 1976).

18. m. Avot 3:2.

19. The principle of *dina de-malkhuta dina* is attributed in several places in the Talmud to Samuel, a Jewish leader of the third century.

20. Robert Ignatius Burns, *Jews in the Notarial Culture: Latinate Wills in Mediterranean Spain, 1250–1350* (Berkeley, CA: University of California Press, 1996); Pinchas Roth, "Legal Strategy and Legal Culture in Medieval Jewish Courts of Southern France," *AJS Review* 38, no. 2 (November 2014): 375–93; Jessica M. Marglin, *Across Legal Lines: Jews and Muslims in Modern Morocco* (New Haven, CT: Yale University Press, 2016). Recent research on Early Modern Jewish communities has revealed that not only were Jewish courts familiar with the terminology and procedures of local Gentile civil law but Gentile civil courts were familiar with halakhic terminology also. See, for example, Edward Fram, *Ideals Face Reality: Jewish Law and Life in Poland, 1550–1655* (Cincinnati, OH: Hebrew Union College Press, 1997); Jay R. Berkovitz, *Protocols of Justice: The Pinkas of the Metz Rabbinic Court 1771–1789*, 2 vols. (Leiden: Brill, 2014).

21. See, for example, Simhah Assaf, *Ha-onshin aharei hatimat ha-talmud: Homer le-toldot ha-mishpat ha-ivri* (Jerusalem: Defus Ha-po'alim, 1924).

22. For a thorough examination of the principle in Jewish law and history, see Shmuel Shilo, *Dina de-malkhuta dina* (Jerusalem: Defus Akademi Bi-Yerushalayim, 1974). See also Samuel Atlas, "*Dina d'Malchuta* Delimited," *Hebrew Union College Annual*, 1975, 269–88.

23. 1 Samuel 8:11 ff.

24. See, for example, Maimonides, *Mishneh Torah*, "Laws of Kings and Wars," 4:1.

25. Menachem Elon, "On Power and Authority: The Halakhic Stance of the Traditional Community and Its Contemporary Implications," in *Kinship & Consent: The Jewish Political Tradition and Its Contemporary Uses*, 2nd edition, ed. Daniel Judah Elazar (New Brunswick, NJ: Transaction Publishers, 1997), 294. The historical origins of Jewish political authority are very old, stretching back earlier than talmudic times. Yitzhak Baer placed the origins of the kehilla in the talmudic period or earlier. Others have argued that the dual political-religious leadership of Jewish communities was structurally evident in the institutions of monarchy and priesthood in the Bible. See Yitzhak Baer, "Ha-yesodot veha-hathalot shel irgun ha-qehilah ha-yehudit be-yemei ha-benayim," *Zion* 15 (1950): 1–41. See also Stuart A. Cohen, "The Concept of the Three Ketarim: Their Place in Jewish Political

Thought and Implications for Studying Jewish Constitutional Theory," in *Kinship & Consent: The Jewish Political Tradition and Its Contemporary Uses*, 2nd edition, ed. Daniel Judah Elazar (New Brunswick, NJ: Transaction Publishers, 1997), 47–76; Daniel J. Elazar, "The Kehillah," in *Kinship & Consent: The Jewish Political Tradition and Its Contemporary Uses*, 2nd edition, ed. Daniel Judah Elazar (New Brunswick, NJ: Transaction Publishers, 1997), 233–36; Bernard Susser and Eliezer Don-Yehiya, "Prolegomena to Jewish Political Theory," in *Kinship & Consent: The Jewish Political Tradition and Its Contemporary Uses*, 2nd edition, ed. Daniel Judah Elazar (New Brunswick, NJ: Transaction Publishers, 1997), 117–38; Walzer et al., *Jewish Political Tradition*.

26. b. Bava Batra 8b.

27. For a historical overview of this communal legislation, see Louis Finkelstein, *Jewish Self-Government in the Middle Ages*, 2nd edition (New York: Jewish Theological Seminary of America, 1964). Avraham Grossman and Menachem Elon both effectively demonstrate that Jewish communities in the Middle Ages were governed by lay leaders rather than rabbis. Avraham Grossman, "Yahasam shel hakhmei Ashkenaz ha-rishonim el shilton ha-qahal," *Shenaton ha-mishpat ha-ivri* 2 (1975): 175–99; Menachem Elon, *Jewish Law: History, Sources, Principles*, (Philadelphia: Jewish Publication Society, 1994), 1:678–731. See also Gerald J. Blidstein, "On Lay Legislation in Halakhah: The King as Instance," in *Rabbinic and Lay Communal Authority*, ed. Suzanne Last Stone (New York: Michael Scharf Publication Trust of the Yeshiva University Press, 2006), 1–18.

28. Sometimes rabbis sat on these courts, but often the courts entirely comprised lay communal leaders. Grossman, "Yahasam shel hakhmei Ashkenaz ha-rishonim el shilton ha-qahal"; Assaf, *Batei ha-din*, 86–92 and passim.

29. Aharon Lichtenstein, "Religion and State," in *Contemporary Jewish Religious Thought: Original Essays on Critical Concepts, Movements, and Beliefs*, ed. Arthur Allen Cohen and Paul R. Mendes-Flohr (New York: Free Press, 1988), 774–75.

30. Aharon Lichtenstein, "Communal Governance, Lay and Rabbinic: An Overview," in *Rabbinic and Lay Communal Authority*, ed. Suzanne Last Stone (New York: Michael Scharf Publication Trust of the Yeshiva University Press, 2006), 42. On lay legislation, see Finkelstein, *Jewish Self-Government in the Middle Ages*; Elon, *Jewish Law*, 1:678–731.

31. Rashba, Responsa 3.393, translated in Walzer et al., *Jewish Political Tradition*. Rashba's talmudic quotation is from b. Bava Metzia 30b.

32. Nisim ben Reuben Gerondi, *Derashot ha-ran ha-shalem*, ed. Leon A. Feldman and Mordekhai Leyb Katzenelenbogen (Jerusalem: Mosad Ha-rav Kook, 2003). For a partial translation, see Walzer et al., *Jewish Political Tradition*, 1:156–61. The translations here are based upon that version.

33. Walzer et al., *Jewish Political Tradition*, 1:158.

34. Ibid., 1:157–58.

35. This is the most widespread modern interpretation of the Ran's sermon. See Stone, "Religion and State"; Suzanne Last Stone, "Law without Nation? The Ongoing Jewish Discussion," in *Law without Nations*, ed. Austin Sarat, Lawrence Douglas, and Martha Merrill Umphrey (Stanford, CA: Stanford University Press, 2011), 101–37. Another interpretation reads the Ran's sermon as a prototype of the doctrine of the separation of powers. See Warren Zev Harvey, "Liberal Democratic Themes in Nissim of Girona," in *Studies in Medieval Jewish History and Literature III*, ed. Isadore Twersky and Jay M. Harris (Cambridge, MA: Harvard University Press, 2000), 197–211. But see also Blidstein, "On Lay Legislation in Halakhah," 8. The debate over the original meaning of the Ran's sermon, while interesting, is tangential to our discussion because all of the religious Zionists discussed here understood the Ran according to the interpretation summarized previously.

36. Maimonides, for example, had a more restrictive understanding of the King's law than the Ran. However, it still performed an important function in his constitutional thinking: "Murderers and similar [criminals] who are not sentenced to death by a halakhic court [*bet din*]—if the king wishes to kill them under the king's law [*din malkhut*] and [his prerogative to] sustain society [*taqanat olam*], he is permitted to do so. Likewise, if a halakhic court [*bet din*] saw fit to kill them as an emergency measure, if the times require it, they are permitted to do as they see fit." *Mishneh Torah*, "Laws of Murder and the Preservation of Life," 2:4.

    Menachem Lorberbaum, a scholar of Maimonides's political thought, notes that, for Maimonides, the king's law is an "alternative system" to halakha. In Lorberbaum's strong formulation, "there is no 'halakhic polity,' and the term itself is an oxymoron.... There is therefore an inescapable conflict between the two sovereignties implicit in [Maimonides's] account—royal law and Torah law." Menachem Lorberbaum, *Politics and the Limits of Law: Secularizing the Political in Medieval Jewish Thought* (Stanford, CA: Stanford University Press, 2001), 75. According to Lorberbaum, "the breadth of extralegal authority Maimonides accords the king is so wide it is more than merely an auxiliary mechanism intended to support the halakhic hegemony. The king's power to command on pain of death, to tax, to conscript, and to regulate political life by his decrees makes the king's law a system that fully encompasses the political life of society." Ibid., 68.

37. The *Mishpat Ivri* movement was a notable example. See Assaf Likhovski, "The Invention of 'Hebrew Law' in Mandatory Palestine," *American Journal of Comparative Law* 46, no. 2 (1998): 339–73 and, more generally Likhovski, *Law and Identity in Mandate Palestine*.

38. Abraham Isaac Kook, *Mishpat kohen*, 2nd edition (Jerusalem: Mosad Ha-rav Kook, 1966), 144:14. The responsum was written on 19 Tevet, 5676, which corresponds to December 26, 1915.

39. Reuven Margulies, "Batei ha-mishpat be-erets yisra'el," in *Tal tehi'ah* (Lwow, Poland: Bet meshar sefarim hadashim ve-atiqim, 1922), 41–51.

40. Margulies, *Tal tehi'ah*, 3.
41. Margulies, "Batei ha-mishpat,"41.
42. Ibid., 41.
43. Ibid., 43.
44. This is a paraphrase of Numbers 23:9.
45. Margulies, "Batei ha-mishpat," 41. For Jews calling for minority rights, see James Loeffler, *Rooted Cosmopolitans: Jews and Human Rights in the Twentieth Century* (New Haven, CT: Yale University Press, 2018).
46. Margulies, "Batei ha-mishpat," 41.
47. Ibid., 42. cf. Proverbs 29:4.
48. Ibid., 45.
49. Ibid., 47.
50. Ibid., 51.
51. Ibid., 51.
52. Ibid., 51.
53. Shlomo [Goren] Gorontchik, "Huqah toranit ketsad?" in *Tehuqah le-yisra'el*, 1:146–56. The article was first published in three parts in 1948 in *Ha-tsofeh* on 19 Shevat (January 30) 3 Adar I (February 13) and 17 Adar I (February 27).
54. Gorontchik, "Huqah toranit ketsad?," 156.
55. Ibid., 146.
56. Ibid., 149.
57. Ibid., 147.
58. Ibid., 149.
59. In the Talmud, "Syria" generally refers to the area of the Roman Empire that was north and east of the Land of Israel.
60. "They taught [the teaching mentioned in the passage] with regard to Syrian courts and not with regard to experts." b. Sanhedrin 23a. To drive home the interpretation that the Talmud did not believe that "Syrian Courts" judged according to halakha, Gorontchik quoted also a lesser-known parallel passage in the Palestinian Talmud that makes the distinction between these courts and halakhic courts more explicit: "They said [the teaching] with regard to Syrian courts and not with regard to Torah law." p. Sanhedrin 3:2.
61. Gorontchik, "Huqah toranit ketsad?," 150.
62. Ibid., 151. This is the consensus of most traditional commentaries. Among modern scholars, Saul Lieberman, "Achievements and Aspirations of Modern Jewish Scholarship," *Proceedings of the American Academy for Jewish Research* 46–47 (1979): 369–80 suggests that the "Syrian Courts" were under the auspices of the Roman Empire, but were run by Jews and were expected to judge by Jewish law. It seems likely, however, that although their Jewish judges were sometimes familiar with Jewish law, or were willing to consult with rabbis, they were often ignorant of Jewish law and judged by precedent or common sense.

Gedalyahu Alon, *Mehqarim be-toldot yisra'el* (Tel Aviv: Ha-qibuts Ha-me'uhad, 1957), 2:30.

63. Gorontchik, "Huqah toranit ketsad?" 151. The phrases in quotation marks are taken from Meiri, quoted previously.

64. Gorontchik, "Huqah toranit ketsad?," 151.

65. Gorontchik discussed the status of non-Jews in the state in greater detail at ibid., 152–55. For more on this aspect of his constitutional thinking, see Alexander Kaye, "Democratic Themes in Religious Zionism," *Shofar: An Interdisciplinary Journal of Jewish Studies* 31, no. 2 (2013): 8–30.

66. Gorontchik, "Huqah toranit ketsad?" 156.

67. Ibid., 146.

68. Ibid., 156.

69. Shimon Federbusch, *Mishpat ha-melukhah be-yisra'el* (Jerusalem: Mosad Ha-rav Kook, 1952).

70. Ibid., 50.

71. Ibid., 48.

72. Ibid., 32. Federbusch slightly, though inconsequentially, misquotes de Tocqueville. The full quotation is "[t]he emigrants who came to settle the shores of New England all belonged to the comfortable classes of the mother country. Their gathering on American soil presented, from the beginning, the singular phenomenon of a society in which there were neither great lords, nor lower classes, neither poor, nor rich, so to speak." Alexis de Tocqueville, *Democracy in America: Historical-Critical Edition of "De la démocratie en Amérique,"* ed. Eduardo Nolla, trans. James T. Schleifer, bilingual French-English (Indianapolis, IN: Liberty Fund, 2010), 53. It is not clear which edition Federbusch used. His own footnote reads "Democratie en Amerique [*sic*], I, 48." In the 1848 edition, the quotation appears at vol. 1, p. 49. Alexis de Tocqueville, *De la démocratie en Amérique*, 4 vols. (Paris: Pagnerre, 1848).

73. De Tocqueville does mention in an aside in this passage that Europeans who migrated to America were "in general largely equal" and of course equality is a key theme in *De la démocratie en Amérique*. But it is not the import of the passage quoted by Federbusch.

74. Federbusch, *Mishpat ha-melukhah be-yisra'el*, 33.

75. Ibid., 35.

76. Reynolds v. U.S., 98 U.S. 145 (1878) referred to Jefferson's letter in the context of a ruling on Mormon polygamy but judicial references to the letter remained an exception until the mid-twentieth century, when the doctrine of separation began to be widely used American jurisprudence. For a historical overview, see Philip Hamburger, *Separation of Church and State*.

77. Everson v. Board of Education, 330 U.S. 1 (1947).

78. Jonathan D. Sarna, "Church-State Dilemmas of American Jews," in *Jews and the American Public Square: Debating Religion and Republic*, ed. Alan Mittleman,

Robert Licht, and Jonathan D. Sarna (Lanham, MD: Rowman & Littlefield, 2002), 57.

79. Federbusch, *Mishpat ha-melukhah be-yisra'el*, 27.

80. Ibid., 28–29.

81. In the rest of his book, Federbusch applied these theories to minority rights, criminal law, workers' rights, military law, and many other issues. There is sometimes a tension between his vision of a rather paternalistic state and his insistence on personal liberty, and between his doctrine of separation of church and state and his belief in religion as a moral presence in society. For an analysis, see Alan Mittleman, *The Scepter Shall Not Depart from Judah: Perspectives on the Persistence of the Political in Judaism* (Lanham, MD: Lexington Books, 2000), chap. 8.

82. Herzog, *Tehuqah le-yisra'el*, 1989, 2:75. This translation is taken from Walzer et al., *Jewish Political Tradition*, 1:475.

83. Isaac Herzog, "Be-qesher le-ma'amarav ha-hashuvim shel ha-rav r. shlomo gorontchik beha-tsofeh," in *Tehuqah le-yisra'el*, 1:174.

84. Herzog mentions Margulies' proposal in Herzog, *Tehuqah le-yisra'el*, 1989, 2:75.

85. Herzog, *Tehuqah le-yisra'el*, 2:76.

86. Ibid.

87. Ibid.

88. Herzog, "Be-qesher le-ma'amarav."

89. Gorontchik, "Huqah toranit ketsad?," 156.

90. Herzog is presumably referring to "United Nations General Assembly Resolution 181: Resolution Adopted on the Report of the Ad Hoc Committee on the Palestinian Question" (1947) Section I.C.2.2: "No discrimination of any kind shall be made between the inhabitants on the ground of race, religion, language or sex."

91. "The family law and personal status of the various minorities and their religious interests, including endowments, shall be respected." Ibid.

92. Herzog, "Be-qesher le-ma'amarav," 174.

93. Ibid., 175.

94. See Elon, *Jewish Law*, 1:132–37 and 2:707–12. For a classic example of this distinction, see the statement of the Ribash in fourteenth-century Spain, in his Responsa 305 quoted in ibid., 2:708: "If a community enacted that legal documents accepted in non-Jewish courts [but invalid in Jewish courts] are as fully valid for us as they are for non-Jews under their law . . . the community certainly may legislate on such matters, as these are conditions involving civil law and it is as if every single individual in the community so stipulated an undertook for himself. . . . Nevertheless, the community may not enact legislation that involves condoning usury, since usury is prohibited by the Torah even when the debtor pays it voluntarily."

95. Herzog referred to one proponent of this latter view, *Siftei Kohen* on Hoshen Mishpat 73:14, at Herzog, "Be-qesher le-ma'amarav," 175.

96. Herzog, "Be-qesher le-ma'amarav," 163.

97. Ibid., 163–64.

98. At the time of Herzog's writing, the authorship of the sermon was under question. It has since been demonstrated beyond doubt that the Ran was the author.

99. Herzog, "Be-qesher le-ma'amarav," 167.

100. Ibid., 166–77.

101. Ibid., 169.

102. Ibid., 169. See also Herzog, *Tehuqah le-yisra'el*, 1:53, 80–81.

103. Herzog, "Be-qesher le-ma'amarav," 169.

104. Menachem Lorberbaum has argued persuasively that Jewish political thought has always left room outside of halakha for an independent realm of politics. "The central question of Jewish political theory should not be whether to choose a secular or theocratic state but instead how to draw the line between the secular and the sacred." Lorberbaum, *Politics and the Limits of Law*, 156.

CHAPTER 2

1. Isaac Herzog, *Pesaqim u-khetavim*, vol. 9: *Teshuvot 'al hoshen mishpat* (Jerusalem: Mosad Ha-rav Kook, Yad Ha-rav Herzog, 1989), 405, quoted and translated in Amihai Radzyner, "Between Scholar and Jurist: The Controversy over the Research of Jewish Law Using Comparative Methods at the Early Time of the Field," *Journal of Law and Religion* 23, no. 1 (2007): 189–90. The dating of this excerpt follows Radzyner.

2. For somewhat hagiographic, but nonetheless useful, biographical material, see Shaul Mayzlish, *The Rabbinate in Stormy Days: The Life and Teachings of Rabbi Yitzhak Isaac Halevi Herzog, the First Chief Rabbi of Israel*, trans. Yoreh Tanhum (Springfield, NJ: Gefen, 2017) and Shaul Mayzlish, "Toldot ha-rav hertsog," in *Masu'ah le-yitshaq*, ed. Shulamit Eliash, Itamar Warhaftig, and Uri Desberg, 2 vols. (Jerusalem: Yad Ha-rav Herzog; Mekhon Ha-entsiklopediah Ha-talmudit; Mekhon Ha-talmud Ha-yisre'eli Ha-shalem, 2008), 1:13–53.

3. Herzog was ordained by Yaakov Dov Vilovski of Slotzk, Yosef Skuper of Slonim, and Meir Simha of Dvinsk. Ibid., 14. Some of Herzog's correspondence to Vilovski was appended to his father's book about the book of Genesis at Yoe'l Leib Halevi Herzog, *Imrei yo'el al sefer bereshit* (London: Express, 1921), 209 ff. Similar correspondence to Vilovski was appended to Herzog's commentary on Tractate Bekhorot, which was published alongside his father-in-law's commentary on the same tractate. Samuel Isaac Hillman, *Or ha-yashar al masekhet bekhorot* (London: Express, 1921), 140 ff. Herzog's father-in-law, Samuel Isaac Hillman, was a distinguished rabbi from Lithuania who eventually became a rabbinical judge in London before retiring to Jerusalem. In Jerusalem, he was the head of an advanced yeshiva for the training of rabbinical judges in Rehavia, Jerusalem, called *Ohel Torah*. When Herzog moved to Palestine, he taught a class there on Maimonides's laws of Sanhedrin, "to prepare [his students] to sit in the seats of

justice in the cities of Israel." Samuel Isaac Hillman, ed., *Mikhtevei ha-rabanim ha-gedolim de-ara de-yisra'el al ha-yeshivah gedolah "ohel torah" beit david bet midrash gavoah le-hishtalmut avrekhim rabanim* (Jerusalem: Ohel Torah, n.d.), 3. Many future rabbinical judges of the State of Israel studied in that institution, including Shlomo Zalman Auerbach, Yosef Shalom Elyashiv, and Shmuel Halevi Wozner.

4. Herzog's original dissertation was recently published along with other essays and scholarly apparatus in Isaac Herzog, *The Royal Purple and the Biblical Blue: Argaman and Tekhelet; The Study of Chief Rabbi Dr. Isaac Herzog on the Dye Industries in Ancient Israel and Recent Scientific Contributions* (Jerusalem: Keter, 1987).

5. Keogh, *Jews in Twentieth Century Ireland*, 107–8.

6. "Radio Programmes." *Irish Press*, November 27, 1934.

7. Shulamit Eliash, "Po'alo shel ha-rav hertzog be-inyanei hatzalah," in *Masu'ah le-yitshaq*, ed. Shulamit Eliash, Itamar Warhaftig, and Uri Desberg, 2 vols. (Jerusalem: Yad Ha-rav Herzog; Mekhon Ha-entsiklopediah Ha-talmudit; Mekhon Ha-talmud Ha-yisre'eli Ha-shalem, 2008), 1:54–83; Eliash, *Harp and Shield of David*, 49–70.

8. "Love of Zion," a Jewish nationalist movement established in Eastern Europe in the early 1880s. Its followers were called Hovevei Zion, "Lovers of Zion."

9. Meizlish, "Toldot," 13.

10. His most significant halakhic writings are his collections of responsa: Isaac Herzog, *Shu"t hekhal yitshaq* (Jerusalem: Agudah le-hotsa'at kitve rosh ha-rabanim ha-gria"h Hertsog zts"l, 1960-72); Herzog, *Pesaqim u-khetavim*. For a full bibliography, see Shmuel Katz, "Bibliografiah le-kitvei hgry"y hertsog zts"l," in *Masu'ah le-yitshaq*, ed. Shulamit Eliash, Itamar Warhaftig, and Uri Desberg, 2 vols. (Jerusalem: Yad Ha-rav Herzog; Mekhon Ha-entsiklopediah Ha-talmudit; Mekhon Ha-talmud Ha-yisre'eli Ha-shalem, 2008), 1:277–86.

11. Many of his English-language articles were collected into a volume overseen by his elder son, Chaim Herzog, later President of the State of Israel. Isaac Herzog, *Judaism: Law and Ethics* (London: Soncino Press, 1974). On the *Jewish Forum*, see Ira Robinson and Maxine Jacobson, "'When Orthodoxy Was Not as Chic as It Is Today': The Jewish Forum and American Modern Orthodoxy," *Modern Judaism* 31, no. 3 (2011): 285–313.

12. Isaac Herzog, vol. 1 of 2, *The Main Institutions of Jewish Law* (London: Soncino Press, 1936); Isaac Herzog, vol. 2 of 2, *The Main Institutions of Jewish Law* (London: Soncino Press, 1939).

13. For a classic account of this trend, see Richard Hofstadter, *Social Darwinism in American Thought* (Boston: Beacon Press, 1993), especially pp. 3–12. For a survey of the application of evolutionary theory to Anglo-American jurisprudence, see E. Donald. Elliott, "The Evolutionary Tradition in Jurisprudence," *Columbia Law Review* 85 (1985): 38–94. But see also the articles collected in Gralf-Peter Calliess and Peer Zumbansen, eds., "Law, the State and Evolutionary Theory," special issue, *German Law Journal* 9, no. 4 (2008): 389–548. For its impact on Victorian

social theory, see John W. Burrow, *Evolution and Society: A Study in Victorian Social Theory* (London: Cambridge University Press, 1966). (Chap. 5 deals with Henry Maine.) For Maine and the idea of social evolution and progress, see the articles in Alan Diamond, "The Victorian Achievement of Sir Henry Maine: A Centennial Appraisal" (Cambridge: Cambridge University Press, 1991), 55–69 and also Karuna Mantena, *Alibis of Empire: Henry Maine and the Ends of Liberal Imperialism* (Princeton, NJ: Princeton University Press, 2010), passim.

14. Robert R. Wilson, *Sociological Approaches to the Old Testament* (Minneapolis: Augsburg Fortress, 1984), 25.

15. It has been suggested that Maine intended to indicate his debt to Darwin by using the same publisher, but this notion is far from certain. Elliott, "Evolutionary Tradition in Jurisprudence," 43 fn. 22; Burrow, *Evolution and Society*, 139–40.

16. Henry Sumner Maine, *Ancient Law* (Boston: Beacon Press, 1963), especially pp. 8–14. Maine believed that a critical moment in the evolution of societies is the emergence of the capacity to create legal fictions. This ability allows individuals to enter into legal relationships independent of their blood ties. Families and tribes give way to voluntary associations. Maine famously described this effect as "a movement from Status to Contract." Ibid., 165.

17. Ibid., 18.

18. " . . . [T]here still exists a pervasive feeling that Jewish law is a 'religious' system (whatever that may mean), and therefore beyond the boundaries of legal history. The much misunderstood theories of Sir Henry Maine have implanted in the contemporary legal mind the view that early cultures are incapable of discriminating between religious and legal obligation. . . . Since Jewish law is a 'religious system,' it represents the law-religion 'stage,' and so falls outside the interest of the legal historian." Bernard S. Jackson, *Essays in Jewish and Comparative Legal History* (Leiden: Brill, 1975), 1.

19. Robert Cover, "The Supreme Court, 1982 Term: Foreword: Nomos and Narrative," *Harvard Law Review* 97, no. 4 (1983): 4–68. See also Suzanne Last Stone, "In Pursuit of the Counter-Text: The Turn to the Jewish Legal Model in Contemporary American Legal Theory," *Harvard Law Review* 106, no. 4 (February 1, 1993): 813–94.

20. Isaac Herzog, "Samkhut ha-torah be-medinat yisra'el," in *Tehuqah le-yisra'el*, 1:222.

21. Ibid., 1:226.

22. Republished in Isaac Herzog, "The Outlook of Greek Culture upon Judaism," in *Judaism: Law and Ethics* (London: Soncino Press, 1974), 211–23.

23. Matthew Arnold, *Arnold: "Culture and Anarchy" and Other Writings* (Cambridge: Cambridge University Press, 1993). Based on a series of articles, the book was originally published in 1869. The contrast between Greek and Hebrew was not new to Arnold. It has roots in antiquity and was a common literary trope in the nineteenth century. After Arnold's elaboration, however, the dichotomy

became a linchpin of Victorian cultural criticism, and was considered by many to be a key to the analysis of modernity. For more on how this dichotomy lay at the root of the "assertion of cultural and racial superiority on the part of its European exponents," see Tessa Rajak, "Jews and Greeks: The Invention and Exploitation of Polarities in the Nineteenth Century," in *The Jewish Dialogue with Greece and Rome: Studies in Cultural and Social Interaction* (Leiden: Brill, 2002), 554 and Jacob Shavit, *Athens in Jerusalem: Classical Antiquity and Hellenism in the Making of the Modern Secular Jew* (London; Portland, Or: Littman Library of Jewish Civilization, 1997), especially pp. 40 ff.

24. Arnold sometimes seemed to favor Hellenism as he associated Hebraism with the strict Puritanism that he believed was hampering social reforms. On other occasions, however, he advocated a balance between Hebraism and Hellenism. Donald D. Stone, "Matthew Arnold and the Pragmatics of Hebraism and Hellenism," *Poetics Today* 19, no. 2 (1998): 179–98. Many Christians, however, wanted to reject Judaism altogether, and attempted to distance Christianity from its Jewish roots. Shmuel Almog, "The Borrowed Identity: Neo-Pagan Reactions to the Jewish Roots of Christianity," in *Demonizing the Other: Antisemitism, Racism and Xenophobia*, ed. Robert S. Wistrich (Abingdon, Oxon: Routledge, 2013), 131–47.

25. For example, from Théodore Reinach, *Textes d'auteurs grecs et romains relatifs au judaïsme* (Paris: E. Leroux, 1895) and David Neumark and Samuel Solomon Cohon, *Toldot ha-pilosofiyah be-yisra'el* (New York: A. I. Shtibel, 1921). Reinach was a French Jewish scholar. Neumark was a German scholar who had recently moved to Hebrew Union College in Cincinnati.

26. Herzog, "Samkhut ha-torah be-medinat yisra'el," 226.

27. Herzog, "The Outlook of Greek Culture upon Judaism," 222.

28. Ibid., 214.

29. Ibid., 222.

30. Ibid., 222–3.

31. Isaac Herzog, "John Selden and Jewish Law," *Journal of Comparative Legislation and International Law* 13, no. 4 (1931): 236–45. The article was republished at Isaac Herzog, "John Selden and Jewish Law," in *Judaism: Law and Ethics* by Isaac Herzog (London: Soncino Press, 1974), 67–79. Page numbers refer to that edition.

32. See Amihai Radzyner, "Jewish Law in London: Between Two Societies," in *Jewish Law Annual 18*, ed. Berachyahu Lifshitz (London; New York: Routledge, 2009), 81–135.

33. On Selden's Jewish writings, see Jason P. Rosenblatt, *Renaissance England's Chief Rabbi: John Selden* (Oxford: Oxford University Press, 2006).

34. Herzog, "John Selden and Jewish Law," 68.

35. Ibid., 77, 79.

36. Ibid., 71.

37. Ibid., 79.

38. Ibid., 67.

39. Ibid., 78.

40. Isaac Herzog, *Main Institutions of Jewish Law*, 2 vols. (paperback) (London, New York: Soncino Press, 1980), 2:viii.

41. Isaac Herzog, "The Sources of Jewish Law," *Temple Law Quarterly* 5 (January 1930): 47–65; Isaac Herzog, "Possession in Jewish Law," *Temple Law Quarterly* 4 (1929–30): 329–38; Isaac Herzog, "Possession in Jewish Law Part II," *Temple Law Quarterly* 5 (January 1930): 260–71; Isaac Herzog, "Possession in Jewish Law Part III," *Temple Law Quarterly* 5 (January 1930): 598–612; Isaac Herzog, "Moral Rights and Duties in Jewish Law," *Juridical Review* 41 (1929): 60; Isaac Herzog, "The Assignment of Rights in Jewish Law," *Juridical Review* 43 (1931): 127; Isaac Herzog, "Legacies to Creditors and Satisfaction of Debt in Jewish Law," *Temple Law Quarterly* 6 (1931): 87.

42. Herzog, *Main Institutions*, 1936; Herzog, *Main Institutions*, 1939. A second edition of both volumes was published in 1965 and reissued in 1980. A Hebrew translation has just been issued as Isaac Herzog, *Ha-mosdot ha-ikari'im shel ha-mishpat ha-ivri*, trans. Moshe Hershkovits (Tel Aviv: Yediot Ahronot; Sifrei Hemed, 2016). Originally, five volumes were planned but the work was cut short by Herzog's work as Chief Rabbi along with, presumably, his efforts to aid refugees during and after World War II and his subsequent ill health. Herzog himself explained the gap between the publication dates of the first two volumes: "That a relatively long interval has elapsed between the appearance of Volume I and the present volume has been due to the fact that in the meantime I was suddenly transferred by the directing hand of Providence to an infinitely wider sphere of activity. My election to the Chief Rabbinate of the Land of Israel at a critical and momentous juncture in our history has had the inevitable effect of diverting my attention to other channels, while the severe trials and tribulations of Palestine Jewry, which, alas, have not yet ended, have not been conducive, to say the least, to that state of mind which is a necessary pre-requisite of literary work of this kind." Herzog, *Main Institutions*, 1939, vii.

43. Herzog, *Main Institution*, 1:xvii.

44. Ibid.

45. Ibid.

46. George Mousourakis, *Roman Law and the Origins of the Civil Law Tradition* (Cham, Switzerland: Springer, 2015); Peter Stein, *Roman Law in European History* (Cambridge: Cambridge University Press, 1999); Michael H. Hoeflich, *Roman and Civil Law and the Development of Anglo-American Jurisprudence in the Nineteenth Century* (Athens, GA: University of Georgia Press, 1997).

47. Herzog, *Main Institutions*, 1:xvi.

48. Likhovski, "Invention of 'Hebrew Law,'" 341 and passim.

49. Ibid., 342; Rudiger Schott, "Main Trends in German Ethnological Jurisprudence and Legal Ethnology," *Journal of Legal Pluralism* 20 (1982): 37–67.

50. Asher Gulak, *Yesodei ha-mishpat ha-ivri: Seder dine memonot be-yisra'el al-pi mekorot ha-talmud veha-poskim*, 4 vols. (Berlin: Devir, 1922). On Gulak, see David N. Myers, *Re-Inventing the Jewish Past: European Jewish Intellectuals and the Zionist Return to History* (New York: Oxford University Press, 1995), 88–89; Amihai Radzyner, "Mi-dogmatist le-historion: Asher gulak ve-heqer ha-mishpat ha-ivri be-universitah ha-ivrit 1925–1940," ed. Gershon Bacon et al., *Mada'ei yahadut* 43 (June 2005): 169–200.

51. For more on Gulak, and this work in particular, see Likhovski, *Law and Identity in Mandate Palestine*, 162–66; Radzyner, "Between Scholar and Jurist."

52. Radzyner, "Between Scholar and Jurist," 206; Radzyner, "Jewish Law in London."

53. A reasonable distinction between the methodologies of halakhah and Mishpat Ivri was made by Mishpat Ivri scholar Shmuel Shilo in "The Contrast between Mishpat Ivri and Halakah," *Tradition: A Journal of Orthodox Jewish Thought* 20, no. 2 (1982): 92–93. Writing in 1982, Shilo took pains to observe that the study of Mishpat Ivri does not per se imply a rejection of the sanctity of halakhah: "It should be noted that for either type of halakhist Jewish law is first and foremost a religious law, that is to say, a law commanded by God. For the secularist, however, Jewish law is of interest because of its cultural-national components, as a part of the Jewish heritage, independent of the autonomous authority of the halakhah. The great interest in Jewish law in our century was and is undoubtedly linked with the idea of a Jewish homeland in the land of Israel and a cultural renaissance; it is similar to the type of cultural aspiration best reflected in the rebirth of the Hebrew language as a spoken, modern means of communication. That the scholar engaged in Mishpat Ivri does not, in his work, emphasize its religious normative dimension, does not negate that dimension, just as the Hebrew language can be treated as a secular tongue without negating its sanctity, or even the land of Israel can be considered in terms of national-cultural import for the Jewish people without negating its religious importance. The orientation of Mishpat Ivri thus does not contradict that of halakhah, but, nonetheless, serves as a basis of differentiation." Herzog would likely have rejected Shilo's analysis of Mishpat Ivri, at least as it pertained to its practitioners before 1948.

54. This view was particularly, though not exclusively, true of the cultural Zionist program. Joseph E. David, "Beyond the Janus Face of Zionist Legalism: The Theo-Political Conditions of the Jewish Law Project," *Ratio Juris* 18, no. 2 (2005): 223.

55. Shmuel Eisenstadt, *Tsion be-mishpat* (Tel Aviv: Hamishpat, 1967). Quoted and translated in Radzyner, "Between Scholar and Jurist," 194–95.

56. For a discussion of Herzog's critique of comparative Jewish law in general, see Radzyner, "Between Scholar and Jurist," passim.

57. Herzog, "Possession in Jewish Law [Part I]," 329.

58. Herzog, *Main Institutions*, 1:xvi. See also Radzyner, "Between Scholar and Jurist."

59. Herzog, *Main Institutions of Jewish Law*, 1:xv.

60. Ibid., 1:xxi.

61. "The Palestinian *Talmud* is much older than Justinian, and although direct dependence is improbable, the idea of the all-embracing *praescriptio longissimi temporis* may have been partly suggested by some juridic practice in the eastern provinces." Ibid., 1:231–32.

62. Ibid., 1:xxi.

63. Ibid., 1:xxii.

64. Ibid., 1:xxiv–xxv.

65. John William Salmond, *Jurisprudence: Or the Theory of the Law* (London: Stevens and Haynes, 1907); William Reynell Anson, *Principles of the English Law of Contract* (Oxford: Clarendon Press, 1879). Salmond was in fact from New Zealand, which, as a Commonwealth country, had the same law as England at the time. Anson's work on contract is still in print today.

66. Buckland made the comment at a meeting of the Society of Public Teachers of Law in 1931. His comment was transcribed at H. G. Hanbury, "The Place of Roman Law in the Teaching of Law to-Day," *Journal of the Society of Public Teachers of Law* (1931): 25.

67. Herzog, *Main Institutions*, 1:xvii.

68. Ibid., 1:232.

69. Isaac Herzog, "The Administration of Justice in Ancient Israel," in *Judaism: Law and Ethics,* by Isaac Herzog (London: Soncino Press, 1974), 141.

70. Ibid.

71. Ibid.

72. Ibid.

73. Herzog, "Administration of Justice," 1974, 142.

74. Ibid., 141. Herzog was not the only modern scholar of halakha who addressed the question of the death penalty. For an overview of approaches, see Beth A. Berkowitz, *Execution and Invention: Death Penalty Discourse in Early Rabbinic and Christian Cultures* (New York: Oxford University Press, 2006), 44 ff.

75. Herzog, *Main Institutions*, 1:xxii–xxiv fn. 3.

76. Herzog, "Administration of Justice," 1974, 141.

77. Gulak, *Yesodei ha-mishpat ha-ivri*, 1:171.

78. Herzog, *Main Institutions*, 1:227.

79. Ibid., 1:228.

80. A. H. Manchester, *A Modern Legal History of England and Wales 1750–1950* (London: Butterworths, 1980), 126–29.

81. William Blackstone, *Commentaries on the Laws of England*, 5th edition (Oxford: Clarendon Press, printed for William Strahan, Thomas Cadell, and Daniel Prince, 1773), 3:382.

82. Jeremy Bentham, "An Introductory View of the Rationale of Evidence for the Use of Nonlawyers as Well as Lawyers," in *The Works of Jeremy Bentham with an Outline of His Opinions on the Principal Subjects Discussed in His Works*, ed. John Bowring, 11 vols. (Edinburgh: W. Tait, 1843), 6:43.

83. Manchester, *Modern Legal History of England and Wales 1750–1950*, 175 ff.

84. Walter Bagehot, *The English Constitution* (New York: Cambridge University Press, 2001), 194.

85. For an overview of the role of codification in European jurisprudence, see John Henry Merryman and Rogelio Pérez-Perdomo, *The Civil Law Tradition: An Introduction to the Legal Systems of Europe and Latin America* (Stanford, CA: Stanford University Press, 2007), 27–33; R. C. van Caenegem, *An Historical Introduction to Private Law* (Cambridge: Cambridge University Press, 1992).

86. The argument for a uniform German legal code was made by A. F. Thibaut, who believed that a unified legal system was an essential tool of unification. Initially, Thibaut was opposed by Von Savigny and his Historical School, who believed that laws should emerge from the societies that they govern and not be indiscriminately imposed by a small elite. Tellingly, though, Thibaut's position won out. The Historical School itself was instrumental in the gradual adoption of Roman law as the model for the German code. See Susan Gaylord Gale, "Very German Legal Science: Savigny and the Historical School," *Stanford Journal of International Law* 18 (1982): 123–46. The move to centralization continued during the course of the nineteenth century when jurists like Paul Laband continued to argue that law was nothing more than the will of the state and that therefore all laws and all institutions of state had, by definition, to be coordinated with one another. Peter Caldwell, *Popular Sovereignty and the Crisis of German Constitutional Law: The Theory & Practice of Weimar Constitutionalism* (Durham, NC: Duke University Press, 1997), 13–39.

87. "I believe that scholarly accounts of the early history of Jewish Law have been much affected by the dominant legal positivism of the modern age, leading to an unreflecting importation of models of the operation of law and justice which are simply inappropriate." Bernard S. Jackson, "Judaism as a Religious Legal System," in *Religion, Law and Tradition: Comparative Studies in Religious Law*, ed. Andrew Huxley (Abingdon, Oxon: Routledge, 2012), 36–37. Jackson's comment pertains primarily to jurists like Menachem Elon but apply equally well to some of Herzog's writings.

88. The articles were originally published as Isaac Herzog, "The Administration of Justice in Ancient Israel: 1. The Reconstruction of the Judiciary by Ezra," *Jewish Forum* 14, no. 3 (March 1931): 84–88; Isaac Herzog, "The Administration of Justice in Ancient Israel: 2. The Bet Din," *Jewish Forum* 14, no. 11 (November

1931): 404–8; Isaac Herzog, "The Administration of Justice in Ancient Israel: 3. The Appointment of Judges and Their Ordination," *Jewish Forum* 14, no. 12 (December 1931): 436–39; Isaac Herzog, "The Administration of Justice in Ancient Israel: 4. The Sanhedrin," *Jewish Forum* 15, no. 5 (May 1932): 165–70. They were republished as Herzog, "Administration of Justice." 1974. Page numbers here refer to that publication.

89. Maimonides, *Mishneh Torah, Hilkhot Sanhedrin*, chap. 1. See also b. Sanhedrin, especially chap. 1.

90. b. Sanhedrin 16b.

91. Herzog, "Administration of Justice," 1974, 137.

92. Ibid., 137–38. Gulak's discussion is at Gulak, *Yesodei ha-mishpat ha-ivri*, 4:9.

93. Herzog, "Administration of Justice," 1974, 136.

94. Ibid., 140.

95. Ibid., 120.

96. Ibid., 120–1.

97. Ibid., 122.

98. Ibid., 113. The reference is to Ezra 7:25 where Ezra is commanded to appoint *shaftin* and *daynin*, Aramaic for *shoftim* and *dayanim*.

99. Herzog, "Administration of Justice," 1974, 114.

100. Ibid.

101. Isaac Herzog, *Tehuqah le-yisra'el*, 3:289.

102. Herzog, "Administration of Justice" (1974), 135–36.

103. Herzog, *Tehuqah le-yisra'el*, 2:75. This translation is from Walzer et al., *Jewish Political Tradition*, 1:475.

CHAPTER 3

1. Herzog, *Tehuqah le-yisra'el*, 1:3.

2. See, for example, the constitutions of Iran (1979) and Iraq (2005).

3. Shulamit Eliash, "The 'Rescue' Policy of the Chief Rabbinate of Palestine before and during World War II," *Modern Judaism* 3, no. 3 (1983): 291–308; Eliash, "Toldot"; Mordecai Paldiel, *Saving One's Own: Jewish Rescuers during the Holocaust* (Lincoln: University of Nebraska Press, 2017), 69–70. Zerah Warhaftig was also instrumental in these rescue missions. Zerah Warhaftig, *Refugee and Survivor: Rescue Efforts during the Holocaust* (Jerusalem: Yad Vashem; Torah Education Dept. of the World Zionist Organization, 1988).

4. Herzog visited Maisky in London in 1940. Eliash, "Toldot," 68.

5. Ibid., 60–66.

6. Ibid., 66–76.

7. Ibid., 69.

8. Warhaftig, "Mavo," 26.

9. Ibid., 26 fn. 6. See also Warhaftig's own description of this period in Zerah Warhaftig, *Huqah le-yisra'el: Dat u-medinah* (Jerusalem: Mesilot, 1988) especially pp. 22–85.

10. Elyaqim Rubinstein, *Shoftei erets* (Jerusalem; Tel Aviv: Schocken, 1980), 46.

11. A proposed table of contents for the work was found in Herzog's archive and published in Herzog, *Tehuqah le-yisra'el*, 1:243.

12. The chapter about the king's law and its relationship to halakha was included in a pamphlet that Herzog wrote in an attempt to make Jewish inheritance law more egalitarian. It was published in an American Jewish journal as Isaac Herzog, "Din ha-melekh ve-din ha-torah," *Talpiyot* 7, no. 1 (Tishrei [5]718 [1947]): 4–32 and republished in Herzog, *Tehuqah le-yisra'el*, 1989, 2:65–89. For Herzog's writings on inheritance law, see *Tehuqah le-yisra'el*, 1989, 2:passim. See also the discussion at Ben Tzion Greenberger, "Rabbi Herzog's Proposals for Takkanot in Matters of Inheritance," in *The Halakhic Thought of R. Isaac Herzog*, ed. Bernard S. Jackson, Jewish Law Association Studies V (Atlanta: Scholars Press, 1991).

13. Isaac Herzog, *Tehuqah le-yisra'el al-pi ha-torah*, ed. Itamar Warhaftig, 3 vols. (Jerusalem: Mosad Ha-rav Kook; Yad Ha-rav Herzog, 1989). Herzog originally called the book *The Foundations of the Constitution, Law and Its Orders, and the State Government in the Jewish State in the Framework of the Torah*. He also referred to it by other titles, such as *The Constitution in Israel According to the Torah*. It was eventually published by Warhaftig under the title *A Constitution for Israel According to the Torah*. The title of the book is discussed at Warhaftig, "Mavo," 33.

14. Isaac Herzog, "Ha-tehiqah veha-mishpat be-medinah ha-yehudit," *Yavneh: Qovets akadema'i dati* 3 (1949): 9–13. The article was published in 1949 but an editorial comment indicates that it was received in Shevat 5708, which corresponds to January or early February 1948. It was republished as Herzog, "Ha-tehiqah veha-mishpat be-medinah ha-yehudit," in *Tehuqah le-yisra'el*, 1:205–9. Page numbers will refer to the latter publication.

15. On the contested election, see Friedman, *Hevrah va-dat*, 383–4. Friedman notes that Herzog's victory marked the end of the domination of the "Old Yishuv" of Ashkenazic Ultra-Orthodox rabbis in the Chief Rabbinate.

16. Herzog, "Ha-tehiqah," 205.

17. Ibid.

18. United Nations General Assembly Resolution 181.

19. Herzog, *Tehuqah le-yisra'el*, 1:3. See also his similar comments at ibid., 1:96.

20. Herzog, "Ha-tehiqah," 209.

21. Herzog, *Tehuqah le-yisra'el*, 1:1, 39.

22. Ibid., 1:26.

23. Ibid., 1:39.

24. Herzog, *Tehuqah le-yisra'el*, 1:43. The question of women's involvement in politics had a contentious history in the religious Zionist community. In 1919–20 Herzog's predecessor as Ashkenazic Chief Rabbi of Palestine, Rabbi Abraham Isaac

Kook, had ruled that women should not be allowed to vote. (Women's suffrage was, though, allowed by Rabbi Benzion Hai Ousiel, who was at the time the Chief Rabbi of Tel Aviv and, in 1939, became the Sephardic Chief Rabbi of Palestine.) See Friedman, *Hevrah va-dat*, 146–84; Zohar, "Traditional Flexibility and Modern Strictness."

25. Beverly B. Cook, "Women Judges: A Preface to Their History," *Golden Gate University Law Review* 14, no. 3 (1984): 576. In France, women were admitted to the bench only in 1946. Sara L. Kimble, "No Right to Judge: Feminism and the Judiciary in Third Republic France," *French Historical Studies* 31, no. 4 (2008): 609–41.

26. Herzog, *Tehuqah le-yisra'el*, 1:43.

27. Ibid., 1:2.

28. Ibid., 1:3.

29. Ibid., 1:18–19.

30. Ibid., 1:19.

31. Ibid., 1:19.

32. Ibid., 1:2.

33. Josephus, *Contra Apionem* II.17.

34. Baruch Spinoza, *Spinoza: The Complete Works*, ed. Michael L. Morgan, trans. Samuel Shirley (Indianapolis: Hackett Publishing, 2002), 544.

35. Thomas Erastus himself believed that the state and not the church should control the power of excommunication but he did not hold as extreme a position about the civilian control over ecclesiastical matters as devotees of "Erastianism," an idea that came to bear his name only in the 1640s and was popularized by English thinkers like Richard Hooker. See Weldon S. Crowley, "Erastianism in England to 1640." *Journal of Church and State* 32, no. 3 (1990): 549–66, 558; John Neville Figgis, *The Divine Right of Kings* (Cambridge: University Press, 1922), 293–342.

36. Nelson, *The Hebrew Republic*, 130–131. Julie E. Cooper points out that Spinoza's discussion of theocracy was also directed toward the Jewish community, as a way of talking about, and critiquing, the possibility of sustainable politics in the absence of a sovereign. Julie E. Cooper, "Reevaluating Spinoza's Legacy for Jewish Political Thought," *Journal of Politics* 79, no. 2 (January 18, 2017): 473–84.

37. Herzog, *Tehuqah le-yisra'el*, 1:2.

38. Other religious Zionists were also wary of this term. Making reference to Josephus, Shimon Federbusch wrote, somewhat apologetically, about how "theocracy" means simply a state under the law of God, in contradistinction to a "hierocracy," which is a state run by the priesthood (or, in the case of Israel, the rabbinate). Federbusch, *Mishpat ha-melukhah be-yisra'el*, 26 ff. See also Aviezer Ravitzky, "Is a Halakhic State Possible? The Paradox of Jewish Theocracy," *Israel Affairs* 11, no. 1 (2005): 137–64; Eliezer Goldman, "Hoq ha-medinah veha-halakhah—Ha-omnam

setirah?" in *Mahshavot al demoqratiah yehudit*, ed. Benny Porat and Aviezer Ravitzky (Jerusalem: Israel Democracy Institute, 2010), 165–75.

39. Isaac Herzog, "Ha-medinah ha-yisre'elit ap"i hashqafat ha-mesoret veha-demoqratiah," in *Tehuqah le-yisra'el*, 1:11.

40. Ibid., 1:8.

41. Henry Hart Milman, *The History of the Jews: From the Earliest Period down to Modern Times*, 5th edition (London: J. Murray, 1883), 1:215–16.

42. Oscar S. Straus, *The Origin of Republican Form of Government in the United States of America* (New York: G. P. Putnam's Sons, 1901), 108.

43. Herzog, *Tehuqah le-yisra'el*, 1:4.

44. Herzog, "Ha-medinah ha-yisre'elit," 1:8.

45. Herzog made this remark in the course of his comments on Leo Kohn's draft constitution. Herzog, *Tehuqah le-yisra'el*, 1989, 3:28.

46. Ibid., 3:289.

47. Herzog, *Tehuqah le-yisra'el*, 1:25.

48. Technically, Herzog wanted the jurisdiction of the rabbinical laws to be expanded so that they would have exclusive jurisdiction of all cases in their remit. Under the British Mandate, as under Ottoman rule, rabbinical courts had exclusive jurisdiction over certain kinds of law and concurrent jurisdiction over others. Rabbinical courts therefore had, in fact, a narrower jurisdiction than the Muslim religious courts. The fact that this difference between Muslim and Jewish courts was in fact preserved in the early years of the State of Israel was a source of great disappointment to many rabbis. See, for example, Herzog, *Tehuqah le-yisra'el*, 1:26, 239–42. On the jurisdiction of the different religious courts in the early years of the state, see Chigier, "Rabbinical Courts," 147–81.

49. Herzog, *Tehuqah le-yisra'el*, 1:26.

50. Ibid., 1:26.

51. Ibid., 1:25.

52. Ibid., 1:25.

53. Ibid., 1:28.

54. Ibid., 1:28.

55. Ibid., 1:20.

56. Ibid., 1:20. Herzog considered the possible difference between forging a partnership with Muslims and Christians, whom he did not categorize as idolaters, and others like "Indians, Chinese and Japanese." He concluded that a "partnership" would also be legitimate with these peoples and noted that he had not done sufficient research to establish whether those nations were, in fact, defined idolatrous according to his interpretation of halakha.

57. This is the description given in the official Prayer for the State of Israel produced by the Chief Rabbinate.

58. Deuteronomy 17:15.

59. Maimonides, *Mishneh Torah* "Hilkhot melakhim" 1:4.

60. Herzog, *Tehuqah le-yisra'el*, 1:23, 44–45.

61. Ibid., 1:41.

62. Ibid., 1:41.

63. Ibid., 1:28. cf. Leviticus 24:22.

64. Shulamit Eliash, "Ha-rav veha-medina'i, ha-rav ke-medina'i: Ha-yehasim bein ha-rav hertsog ve-emon de valera," in *Bein masoret le-hidush: Mehqarim be-yahadut tsionut u-medinat yisra'el*, ed. Eliezer Don-Yehia (Ramat Gan, Israel: Bar-Ilan University, 2005), 297–319.

65. Herzog, *Living History*, 12; Keogh, *Jews in Twentieth Century Ireland*, 77.

66. Herzog, *Living History*, 12.

67. Ibid.

68. Keogh, *Jews in Twentieth Century Ireland*, 77.

69. Herzog publicly criticized British policy in Palestine even when he was still a rabbi in Ireland. An example of this criticism is the following sermon. The sermon was presumably a response to the Passfield White Paper, published a few days earlier, which was anti-Zionist in tone, restricted Jewish immigration to Palestine, and was understood by many Zionists to be an abrogation of promises made under the 1917 Balfour Declaration. This is a rare extant example of Herzog's sermonizing in English. That, and the strength of his statements about Britain, make it worth quoting the sermon at some length, as it was reported in the Irish press:

"Rev. Dr. Isaac Herzog, M.A., D.Litt., Chief Rabbi of the Jewish community in the Free State, preaching at the Adelaide Rd., Dublin, Synagogue, on Saturday morning, referred to the Palestine question, and condemned the British Government's recent statement of policy. 'We stand amazed,' he said. 'How did it come about that the British Government has dared to turn into a sham, into a farce, most solemn obligations contracted towards an ancient, historic race of 17 millions; towards a race which has given to the world religion and morality; towards a race which has outlived all its tormentors and would-be destroyers, including the mightiest empires of antiquity; towards a race which is now in the forefront of every sphere of progress—humanitarian, industrial, scientific, literary and artistic? We refuse to believe that the British people are at one with the present Government in this singular breach of faith. When the latent conscience of the British public has been aroused to the true facts of the case, when it realises what a travesty, what a parody, the present Government has made of the Palestine Mandate, Englishmen throughout the Empire may yet proceed to echo the great cry of sorely-disappointed Israel. But come what may, we shall never lose heart. Palestine is the land of Israel, not by virtue of the Balfour Declaration, but by a Divine Declaration embodied in the Book of Books. No power on earth can tear us away from our prophetic cradle-land to which we are bound by ties innumerable, indissoluble.'" "Dublin Rabbi's Protest." *Irish Independent*, October 27, 1930.

70. Eliash, *Harp and the Shield of David*, 24–26.

71. Reuter, A. P. Agence France-Presse. "Palestine Tensions Grow: Fortified Camps Erected by the British," *Irish Press*, February 7, 1947. This comparison was not accepted by all readers. A letter to the editor in response to the article, from a London address, claimed that in fact the Jews in Palestine were more like Ulster Unionists and that "the quarrel between British and Jewish Imperialism is simply an example of thieves falling out." Reginald Reynolds, "Palestine and Ireland," *Irish Press*, February 11, 1947.

72. "Dr. Sokolow Received by Mr. de Valera," *Irish Press*, May 19, 1933.

73. Keogh, *Jews in Twentieth Century Ireland*, 91.

74. Isaac Cohen, "De Valera's Wartime Condolences." *Irish Times,* March 29, 2005.

75. Keogh, *Jews in Twentieth Century Ireland*, 110. Keogh notes that the official documents do not mention Herzog as a participant. On the basis of an oral interview, however, he maintains that Herzog was consulted about the constitutional clause relating to minorities in Ireland.

76. Samuel Moyn has called this "religious constitutionalism," defined as "a new form of constitutionalism navigating between the vehement rejection of the secular liberal state . . . and the widespread demand for an integrally religious social order." Samuel Moyn, *Christian Human Rights* (Philadelphia: University of Pennsylvania Press, 2015), 27.

77. "Constitution of Ireland," 1937. Preamble.

78. Moyn has shown that "human dignity" in the Irish constitution was "a religiously inspired root concept connected (as in the later West German case) to the subordination of the otherwise sovereign democratic polity to God—and, for many, to the moral constraints of His natural law." Moyn, *Christian Human Rights*, 31.

79. "Constitution of Ireland," Art. 44.1.

80. Ibid., Art. 44.1.

81. Ibid., Art. 44.3.

82. Under the fifteenth amendment, a court may grant a "dissolution of marriage" only if the spouses have lived apart for at least four years and there is no reasonable prospect of reconciliation between them.

83. Herzog, *Tehuqah le-yisra'el*, 1989, 3:29–30. For more on Herzog's references to the Irish example, see Amihai Radzyner, "The Irish Influence on the Israeli Constitution Proposal, 1948," in *The Constitution of Ireland: Perspectives and Prospects*, ed. Eoin Carolan (Haywards Heath: Bloomsbury Professional, 2012), 84 ff. The translation here is based on Radzyner's.

84. It is interesting to note that Leo Kohn, whose draft constitution formed the basis for the discussions of the constitutional committee of the Jewish Agency, also thought of Ireland as a model. Kohn's doctoral dissertation was a study of the constitution of the Irish Free State and he subsequently consulted in the drafting of the 1937 constitution of Ireland. Certainly, his study of Ireland played a role in his own

constitutional thinking for Israel, although he also studied many other constitutions as part of that process. On Kohn, see Radzyner, "Constitution for Israel," See also Radzyner, "The Irish Influence on the Israeli Constitution Proposal, 1948."

85. "Colonial states did not in an important sense exist as states in the early centuries of colonialism. They did not claim or produce a monopoly on legal authority or on the assignment of political and legal identity." Lauren Benton, *Law and Colonial Cultures: Legal Regimes in World History, 1400–1900* (Cambridge: Cambridge University Press, 2002), 229.

86. Ibid., passim and especially 28, 264.

87. Likhovski, *Law and Identity in Mandate Palestine*, 106. Arnulf Becker Lorca, "Universal International Law: Nineteenth-Century Histories of Imposition and Appropriation," *Harvard International Law Journal* 51 (2010): 475–552, 475, for example, discusses "the work of non-Western jurists who studied international law in Europe, internalized the categories of classical international law, and ultimately used them in order to change, in the direction of equality, the rules of international law applicable vis-à-vis their polities."

88. Writing of national liberation movements, Michael Walzer observed that "the militants go to school with the very people whose imperial rule they are fighting, and they have a view of their own nation that is remarkably close to what Edward Said called 'orientalism.'" Walzer, *Paradox of Liberation*, xiii.

89. For the hegemonic effects of imperial education, see Gauri Viswanathan, *Masks of Conquest: Literary Study and British Rule in India* (New York: Columbia University Press, 1989).

90. Filip Reyntjens, "The Development of the Dual Legal System in Former Belgian Central Africa (Zaire-Rwnda-Brundi)," in *European Expansion and Law: The Encounter of European and Indigenous Law in 19th- and 20th-Century Africa and Asia*, ed. W. J. Mommsen and J. A. de Moor (Oxford; New York: Berg, 1992), 126.

91. Esin Örücü, "The Impact of European Law on the Ottoman Empire and Turkey," in *European Expansion and Law: The Encounter of European and Indigenous Law in 19th- and 20th-Century Africa and Asia*, ed. W. J. Mommsen and J. A. de Moor (Oxford; New York: Berg, 1992), 49.

92. Ibid., passim.

93. Assaf Likhovski, "In Our Image: Colonial Discourse and the Anglicization of the Law of Mandatory Palestine," *Israel Law Review* 29, no. 3 (Summer 1995); Likhovski, *Law and Identity in Mandate Palestine*; Assaf Likhovski, "Two Horwitzian Journeys," in *Transformations in American Legal History: Essays in Honor of Professor Morton J. Horwtiz*, ed. Morton J. Horwitz, Daniel W. Hamilton, and Alfred L. Brophy (Cambridge, MA: Harvard Law School; distributed by Harvard University Press, 2009), 300–318.

94. Despite the high regard in which Maine was held by his contemporaries, his historicist theories did not have a serious impact on English jurisprudence. Legal

scholars and legislators in the United Kingdom, unlike those in the colonies, were suspicious of a theory that understood law to develop from the bottom up. They preferred a more analytical theory, positing that law was made up of pure categories, unaffected by context and history, in order to justify the imposition of legal reform by a political and academic elite. Raymond Cocks, *Sir Henry Maine: A Study in Victorian Jurisprudence* (Cambridge: Cambridge University Press, 2002), 141–95. In the colonies, however, even though his ideas were sometimes criticized, Maine was extremely influential. Elliott, "Evolutionary Tradition in Jurisprudence," 45–46.

95. Mantena, *Alibis of Empire*.

96. "The colonized are relegated to a timeless past without a dynamic, to a 'stage' of progression from which they are at best remotely redeemable and only if they are brought into History by the active principle embodied in the European. It was in the application of this principle that the European created the native and the native law and custom against which its own identity and law continued to be created." Peter Fitzpatrick, *The Mythology of Modern Law, Sociology of Law and Crime* (Abingdon, Oxon: Routledge, 1992), 110.

97. Likhovski, *Law and Identity in Mandate Palestine*, 52.

98. Judge Anthony Bertram in 1909, quoted in ibid., 54.

99. Ibid., 114 ff.

100. Ibid., 114–15.

101. Ibid., 116.

102. Norman Bentwich, "The Application of Jewish Law in Palestine," *Journal of Comparative Legislation and International Law* 9, no. 1 (1927): 65.

103. Ismar Schorsch, "The Myth of Sephardic Supremacy," *Leo Baeck Institute Yearbook* 34, no. 1 (1989): 47–66.

104. Likhovski, *Law and Identity in Mandate Palestine*, 144–50; Likhovski, "Invention of 'Hebrew Law' in Mandatory Palestine," 362–65.

105. Likhovski, "Between Mandate and State," 60–64; Rubinstein, *Shoftei erets*, 45–49.

106. Yehudit Karp, "Ha-mo'atsa ha-mishpatit: Reshit alilot haqiqa," in *Sefer Uri Yadin*, ed. Aharon Barak and Tara Shpanitz (Tel Aviv: Bursi, 1990), 2:209–56.

107. Moshe Silberg, *Talmudic Law and the Modern State* (New York: Burning Bush Press, 1973), 148–49.

108. Emanuel Rackman, *Israel's Emerging Constitution, 1948–51* (New York: Columbia University Press, 1955).

109. Shlomo Aronson, "David Ben-Gurion and the British Constitutional Model," *Israel Studies* 3, no. 2 (1998): 193–214.

110. Nir Kedar, "Law, Culture, and Civil Codification in a Mixed Legal System," *Canadian Journal of Law and Society* 22, no. 2 (2007): 177–95; Likhovski, "Between Mandate and State," 64–66.

111. Kedar, "Law, Culture, and Civil Codification in a Mixed Legal System."

112. Many secular Jewish jurists had been educated in Germany or in universities that sought to emulate German legal scholarship. This legal education took place in the period during which positivism, and particularly the theories of Hans Kelsen, an influential theorist of the centralized legal state, were dominant. Fania Oz-Salzberger and Eli Salzberger, "The Secret German Sources of the Israeli Supreme Court," *Israel Studies* 3, no. 2 (1998): 159–92. Kelsen's theories remained very popular in Israeli legal circles. Izhak Englard, a jurist who became a Supreme Court Justice, based his entire legal philosophy on Kelsen's theories. See, for example, Izhak Englard, *Religious Law in the Israel Legal System* (Jerusalem: Hebrew University of Jerusalem Faculty of Law, Harry Sacher Institute for Legislative Research and Comparative Law, 1975). Kelsen himself published the very first article of the first issue of the *Israel Law Review* in 1967. Hans Kelsen, "On the Pure Theory of Law," *Israel Law Review* 1, no. 1 (1966): 1–7. Other jurists were educated in Poland and cited the new postwar Polish constitution as precedent in Israeli constitutional law. Assaf Likhovski, "Peripheral Vision: Polish-Jewish Lawyers and Early Israeli Law," *Law and History Review* 36, no. 2 (2018): 235–66.

113. Guido (Gad) Tedeschi, "On the Choice between Religious and Secular Law in the Legal System of Israel," in *Studies in Israel Law*, ed. Guido (Gad) Tedeschi (Jerusalem, 1960), 274. Note that this article was first published in its Hebrew original in 1952. Although he was writing during the state period, the author is explicitly talking about the legal regime of the British Mandate.

114. Warhaftig, *Huqah le-yisra'el*, 130.

115. Quoted in Nir Kedar, *Ben-Gurion veha-huqah* (Or Yehudah: Devir; Bar-Ilan University Press, 2015), 101.

116. Skornik v. Skornik C.A. 191/51. *Piskei Din* 8:179–180. Quoted in Englard, *Religious Law*, 43.

117. Englard, *Religious Law*, passim.

118. For a long list of similar cases, see Asher Maoz, "Ha-rabanut u-vet ha-din: Ben patish ha-hoq le-sadan ha-halakhah," *Shenaton ha-mishpat ha-ivri* 16–17 (January 1990): 33 ff.

119. Balaban v. Balaban C.A. 313/59. *Piskei Din* 14:285.

120. Quoted in Menachem Elon, *Haqiqah datit* (Tel Aviv: Ha-kibuts ha-dati, 1968), 39.

121. Quoted in ibid., 39.

122. Billett C.A. 291/74. *Piskei Din* 29(1):102. Quoted in Yitzhak Kohen, "Shiput rabani ve-shiput hiloni," *Diné Israel* 7 (1976): 205.

123. Aharon Barak, "The Tradition and Culture of the Israel Legal System," in *European Legal Traditions and Israel*, ed. Alfredo Mordechai Rabello (Jerusalem: Harry and Michael Sacher Institute for Legislative Research and Comparative Law; Hebrew University of Jerusalem, 1994), 474.

CHAPTER 4

1. For a summary of the literature on the Sanhedrin, see James S. McLaren, *Power and Politics in Palestine: The Jews and the Governing of Their Land, 100 BC–AD 70* (Sheffield, UK: JSOT Press, 2015), 18–23.

2. For the history of attempts to restore the Sanhedrin, see Julius Newman, *Semikhah (Ordination): A Study of Its Origin, History, and Function in Rabbinic Literature* (Manchester, UK: Manchester University Press, 1950).

3. See, for example, Maimonides, *Perush ha-mishnayot*, Sanhedrin 1:3. Maimonides's opinion was based on Isaiah 1:26: "I will restore your judges as before and your counselors as at first. After that you shall be called city of justice, faithful city." Maimonides interprets the verse to mean that there will be a return of judges to Jerusalem ("city of justice") before the messianic restoration of Jerusalem as the "faithful city." For Maimonides, this indicates that the restoration of the Sanhedrin is a precondition for the Messiah's arrival. This belief posed a problem for Maimonides because he also believed that the restoration of the Sanhedrin required the restoration of the Mosaic chain of ordination. According to the rabbinic tradition, rabbinical authority was granted to Moses by God. Moses transmitted this authority to his student Joshua through a process called *semikhah* (literally, the "laying" of hands, but often translated as "ordination"). Joshua, in turn, transmitted this authority to his students, and so on through the generations in an unbroken line. However at a certain point, probably in the fourth century, the chain of rabbinic transmission was interrupted. From that point, rabbis were qualified to rule Jewish law but they did not have the authority of their predecessors. They could not, for example, impose corporal or capital punishment. Nor could they constitute a Sanhedrin.

   For many rabbinic thinkers, the Mosaic line of ordination would be restored by the Messiah himself but this was not an acceptable solution for Maimonides, because, in his interpretation, the messiah's arrival itself depended on the reinstitution of the Sanhedrin, which in turn depended on the restoration of Mosaic ordination. Maimonides resolved the problem by asserting, entirely without precedent, that Mosaic rabbinic authority could be resurrected: "It seems to me that if all the sages in the Land of Israel would agree to appoint judges and to ordain them, then they are ordained" (Maimonides, *Mishneh Torah* "Hilkhot Sanhedrin" 4:11).

   In 1538, the rabbis of Safed under the leadership of Jacob Berab attempted to use Maimonides's innovation to reinstitute Mosaic ordination. Berab himself became the first person formally to receive *semikhah* in over a thousand years, and others received it from him, including Joseph Karo, the most influential halakhic authority of the Early Modern period. Ultimately, though, the ordination initiative ended up making little impact and fizzled out within a few generations.

4. Zvi Makovsky, *Ve-ashiva shoftayikh* (Tel Aviv: Defus A. Moses, 1938), 7.

5. Ibid., 7. There is a mistake in the original source. *Emdo* should read *amenu*.

6. Ibid., 37. Kook's letter was first published in an article by Makovsky in the religious newspaper *Ha-hed*. Zvi Makovsky, "A"d yesod by"d ha-gadol bi-yerushalayim," *Ha-hed* 12 (1935).

7. Makovsky, *Ve-ashiva shoftayikh*, 37.

8. See, for example, Mirsky, *Rav Kook*, 202–4.

9. Fishman-Maimon was born Fishman. He and his sister Ada, a pioneering feminist leader in the Yishuv, changed their name to Fishman-Maimon in 1949 as a reference to their ancestor, Maimonides. A full biography of Fishman-Maimon was written by his daughter. Geulah Bat-Yehudah, *Rabbi Maimon in His Generations* (Jerusalem: Mossad Harav Kook, 1998).

10. Tsameret, "Judaism in Israel," 67; Zvi Tsameret, "Ben-Gurion, ha-'shulhan arukh' veha-'shulhan' ha-hadash: Le-shorshei ha-metah bein Ben-Gurion u-vein ha-yahadut ha-datit," in *Me'ah shenot tsi'onut datit*, ed. Avi Sagi and Dov Schwartz (Ramat Gan, Israel: Bar-Ilan University, 2003), 3:403–4.

11. The article, entitled "Justice in the State of Israel," was published in *Ha-tsofeh* on January 23, 1949. Quoted and translated in Bat-Yehudah, *Rabbi Maimon in His Generations*, 642.

12. Quoted in Bat-Yehudah, *Rabbi Maimon in His Generations*, 644.

13. The articles were collected shortly thereafter in Yehudah Leib and Hakohen Maimon Fishman, *Hidush ha-sanhedrin bi-medinatenu ha-mehudeshet*, 2nd edition, Kitvei ha-rav Y. L. Maimon 4 (Jerusalem: Mosad Ha-rav Kook, 1951).

14. Maimon's protest is quoted at Bat-Yehudah, *Rabbi Maimon in His Generations*, 646.

15. Quoted in Herzog, *Tehuqah le-yisra'el*, 1989, 3:261.

16. Quoted in ibid., 3:261.

17. Quoted in ibid., 3:261–2.

18. For more on the topic, including its other supporters and detractors, see Cohen, *Ha-talit veha-degel*, chap. 3.

19. Aryeh Morgenstern, *Ha-rabanut ha-rashit le-erets yisra'el: Yisodah ve-irgunah* (Jerusalem: Shorashim, 1973), 72.

20. For a full account of the establishment of the Chief Rabbinate and its early history, see ibid. See Itamar Warhaftig and Shmuel Katz, *Ha-rabanut ha-rashit le-yisra'el: Shivim shanah le-yisudah, 5681–5751; Samkhutah, pe'uloteha, toldoteha*, 3 vols. (Jerusalem: Hekhal Shlomo, 2001); Shulamit Eliash, "The Political Role of the Chief Rabbinate of Palestine during the Mandate: Its Character and Nature," *Jewish Social Studies* 47, no. 1 (1985): 33.

21. They were published, some years after their initial promulgation, as "Sidrei ha-mishpatim be-vatei ha-din be-erets yisra'el," *Ha-Mishpat* 2 (1921): 241–50, 290–98.

22. Amihai Radzyner, "Al reshitan shel taqanot ha-diyun be-vatei din ha-rabani'im: 'Sidrei ha-mishpatim,' [5]681," *Bar-Ilan Studies in Law* 25, no. 1 (2009): 37–76 passim, and especially 22–31.

23. The Talmud establishes that a rabbi may not overturn the ruling of a colleague: "What a sage has declared impure, his colleague may not declare pure. What he has forbidden, his colleague may not permit." (b. Hullin 44b, b. Niddah 20b.) Also, "[a]court does not scrutinize the decision of another court." (b. Baba Batra 138b.) Many premodern commentators allowed for a rabbi to overrule a colleague's ruling in the case of a clear mistake in the law or, according to some, in the case of a mistake in judgment. Some allow for a rabbi to overrule any ruling of a less eminent colleague. (See, for example, Rama on Yoreh De'ah 242:31 and Shakh on Yoreh De'ah 242:53.) Even these interpretations, though, imagine an ad hoc process resting on the eminence and learning of particular judges rather than a permanent institution, whose role is to inspect and potentially overrule the decisions of other courts. There are, though, some historical examples of rabbinical courts that functioned as appeal courts. The Council of the Four Lands, for example, an Early Modern interregional Jewish body, sometimes performed this function, although this was not its primary function. Simhah Assaf, a law professor in Mandate Palestine, noted other precedents for rabbinical courts of appeal. Assaf, *Batei ha-din*, 74–86. Herzog appreciated Assaf's work and quoted it in his book on the constitution. Zerah Warhaftig also referred to Assaf's work in defense of the idea of the rabbinical court of appeals. Warhaftig's apologetic tone hints at the rabbinic opposition to which he was implicitly responding: "The rabbinical court of appeals should not be considered a revolutionary innovation because rabbinical courts of appeal have existed for centuries in several places. And I do not want to return to that discussion. Only, for those who are interested, I mention the research of Rabbi Professor S. Assaf, "Rabbinical Courts and Their Procedures after the Talmudic Period." " *Divrei ha-keneset* 16 (1954) p. 2182. The protests of Herzog, Warhaftig, and others notwithstanding, the idea of a rabbinical appeals court remained largely foreign to the Jewish tradition, and many rabbis in Palestine, and later Israel, were unconvinced that the Chief Rabbinate had the authority to overturn their decisions. For more on the role of appeals and precedent in Jewish law, see J. David Bleich, "The Appeal Process in the Jewish Legal System," in *Contemporary Halakhic Problems*, vol. 4, (New York: KTAV Publishing House, Inc., 1995), 17–45.

24. *Shulhan Arukh Hoshen Mishpat*, 14:4.

25. Amihai Radzyner, "Reshitan shel taqanot ha-diyun be-vatei din ha-rabani'im: Taqanot [5]703," *Diné Israel* 25 (2008): 117.

26. See the contemporary report in Paltiel Dickstein, "Sidrei ha-din be-vatei dinenu ha-leumi'im," *Ha-mishpat ha-ivri* 3 (1928): 191–95. See also Radzyner, "Reshitan shel taqanot ha-diyun," 153 fn. 70.

27. Radzyner, "Reshitan shel taqanot ha-diyun," 117.

28. One scholar, who wrote an entire book about rabbinical procedure, later claimed that, in 1942, laws of legal procedure were drafted "for the first time in the history of the literature of halakha." Eliav Shochetman, *Seder ha-din le-or meqorot ha-mishpat*

ha-ivri: Taqanot ha-diyun u-fesiqat batei ha-din ha-rabani'im be-yisra'el, Library of Jewish Law (Jerusalem: Misrad ha-mishpatim: Moreshet ha-mishpat be-yisra'el: ha-qeren le-qidum ha-mishpat ha-ivri, 1988), 11.

29. Radzyner, "Reshitan shel taqanot ha-diyun," suggests that the success of the 1942 regulations is a result of the capitulation of the Chief Rabbinate in the face of external pressure from the Mandate authorities and the Va'ad Le'umi. This opinion is true, but a deeper reason is needed to explain the different response to the almost identical regulations in 1921.

30. ISA B/23517/83.

31. Radzyner, "Reshitan shel taqanot ha-diyun," 131.

32. For the approach of the Rabbinical Court of Appeals to the procedural irregularities of the courts of first instance, see Zerah Warhaftig, ed., *Osef pisqei din* (Jerusalem: Ha-midpas Ha-memshalti, 1950), 1:20–24, 48–52, 72–79, 91–92, 132–39.

33. Herzog, *Pesaqim u-khetavim*, vol. 9, Siman 9.

34. Since the Mandate period or earlier, the rabbinical courts had functioned as arbitration tribunals in areas outside of their legal jurisdiction. This role of the rabbinical courts was recognized in law under the British Mandate. In 2006, however, in HCJ 8638/03 Amir v. the Great Rabbinical Court in Jerusalem, the state ruled that Israel's state-funded rabbinical courts were prohibited from acting as arbitration tribunals, even where the private parties submitted themselves to their binding authority, and were allowed to adjudicate cases only that the state explicitly placed under their jurisdiction. Legislation currently passing through the Knesset might make the Amir ruling irrelevant. See Menachem Mautner, *Law and the Culture of Israel* (Oxford; New York: Oxford University Press, 2011), 189–90; Adam S. Hofri-Winogradow, "Plurality of Discontent: Legal Pluralism, Religious Adjudication and the State," *Journal of Law and Religion* 26, no. 1 (2010): 76–78 and passim.

35. Herzog, *Pesaqim u-khetavim*, vol. 9, Siman 11.

36. Warhaftig, *Osef pisqei din*, 1:71. For more about the way the official position of the Chief Rabbinate affected the perception of its courts in the halakhic mind, see Maoz, "Ha-rabanut u-vet ha-din."

37. Warhaftig, *Osef pisqei din*.

38. In family cases, the rabbinical reports, like secular law reports, generally conceal names in order to preserve the anonymity of the parties: for example, "The plaintiff A (the wife); The respondent B (the husband)."

39. ISA B/23527/15.

40. The fact that the published court records were summaries written by lawyers rather than by the rabbinical judges themselves is made clear in a note by Warhaftig in the forward to the first collection of edited decisions: "The selection of the rulings herein published was guided by the desire accurately to portray the workings of the Court. . . . The opinions of the judges, with a few exceptions, are not published as

written, but have been abstracted by the editors from the contents of the pamphlets appended to the case files. This volume thus does not constitute a formal record and the editors assume full responsibility for the adaption and wording of the judicial opinion." Warhaftig, *Osef pisqei din*, 1:3.

41. Zerah Warhaftig, "Precedent in Jewish Law," in *Authority, Process and Method: Studies in Jewish Law*, ed. Hanina Ben-Menahem and Neil S. Hecht Jewish Law in Context 2 (Amsterdam, The Netherlands: Harwood Academic Publishers, 1998), 13 fn. 73.

42. Ibid., 14.

43. Warhaftig originally spoke these words at a conference for a lawyers' organization under the auspices of the national religious party. They were later published as Zerah Warhaftig, "Ha-mishpat ha-ivri be-haqiqat medinat yisra'el ba-esor ha-rishon," *Ha-tsofeh*, September 14, 1958.

44. Ibid.

45. Warhaftig, "Precedent in Jewish Law," 14.

46. On the occasion of the establishment of the Chief Rabbinate in 1921, Abraham Isaac Kook spoke in his inaugural speech about the potential, in rare circumstances, for the Chief Rabbinate to introduce halakhic legislation: "In our national life in the Land of Israel, there will surely at times be a dire necessity to issue some significant legislation, which, if agreed upon by a majority of the rabbinate, the generally recognized sages of Israel, and accepted by society, will then gain the status and power of Torah law." Warhaftig and Katz, *Ha-rabanut ha-rashit le-yisra'el*, 1:23. Kook, however, never himself embarked on this vision of rabbinical legislation.

47. The full text of the statutes and associated contemporary material is at Herzog, *Tehuqah le-yisra'el*, 1989, vol. 3. See also Zorach Warhaftig, "Rabbi Herzog and Rabbinic Legislation," in *The Halakhic Thought of R. Isaac Herzog*. (Note that Zorach is an alternative transliteration of Zerah.)

48. Ashkenazim ceased the practice of polygamy long before it was formally outlawed in the tenth century under Rabenu Gershom. Finkelstein, *Jewish Self-Government in the Middle Ages*, 23 ff.

49. Aharon Gaimani, "Marriage and Divorce Customs in Yemen and Eretz Israel," *Nashim: A Journal of Jewish Women's Studies & Gender Issues*, no. 11 (2006): 43–83.

50. Attorney General v. Melnik Criminal Appeal no. 85 (1938), *Palestine Law Reports* 6 (1939): 34. See Emanuel Rackman, "The Religious Problems in the Making of the Israeli Constitution (1948–1951)," *Lawyers Guild Review* 13 (1953): 71.

51. For the criminalization of bigamy under the British Mandate, see Amihai Radzyner, "Milhamot he-yehudim: Itsuvo shel isur ha-bigamiah la-yehudim be-erets yisra'el ha-mandatorit," in *Huqah ahat u-mishpat ehad la-ish veha-ishah*, ed. Ruth Halperin-Kaddari, Margalit Shilo, and Ayal Katvan (Ramat Gan, Israel: Bar-Ilan University, 2010), 151–98.

52. For the ethnic dimensions of the policies over levirate marriage, see Elimelech Westreich, "Levirate Marriage in the State of Israel: Ethnic Encounter and the Challenge of a Jewish State," *Israel Law Review* 37, nos. 2–3 (July 2004): 426–99. This entire episode can perhaps be best understood in the highly politicized context of the relationship between Sephardic and Ashkenazic Israelis in Israel, particularly after the troubling policies of the state with the regard to the Yemenite immigration of 1949. See, for example, Tom Segev, *1949: The First Israelis*, trans. Arlen Neal Weinstein (New York: Free Press; Collier Macmillan, 1986), pt. II.

53. *Yabi'a Omer*, vol. 6, Even Ha-Ezer 14 (9).

54. For more on Yosef's resistance to "Ashkenazic imperialism," particularly in the context of polygamy, see Elimelech Westreich, "Haganat ma'amad ha-nisu'in shel ha-ishah ha-yehudi'ah be-yisra'el: Mifgash ben mesorot mishpati'ot shel edot shonot," *Pelilim* 7 (5759 [1999]): 273–347; Binyamin Lau, *Mi-maran ad maran: Mishnato ha-hilkhatit shel ha-rav Ovadiah Yosef* (Tel Aviv: Yedi'ot Aharonot; Sifrei Hemed, 2005), 192 ff.; Amihai Radzyner, "Halakhah, Law and Worldview: Chief Rabbis Goren and Yosef and the Permission to Marry a Second Wife in Israeli Law," *Diné Israel*, no. 32 (2018): 261–304, 281 ff. The imposition of Ashkenazic custom, and Yosef's resistance to it, can also be seen in the politics of the discussion about the pronunciation of Hebrew. Isaac B. Gottlieb, "The Politics of Pronunciation," *AJS Review* 32, no. 2 (2008): 335–68.

55. Hertzberg, *Zionist Idea*, 550.

56. Bar-Ilan, "Hoq u-mishpat be-medinatenu," 29–33 and 151. Republished as Bar-Ilan, "Hoq u-mishpat be-medinatenu," 1969 and later as Bar-Ilan, "Hoq u-mishpat be-medinatenu," 1978. Page numbers refer to the latter publication.

57. Bar-Ilan, "Hoq u-mishpat be-medinatenu," 1978, 324.

58. Ibid., 327.

59. Ibid., 325.

60. Ibid., 325.

61. Ibid., 326.

62. Ibid., 326.

63. Ibid., 326. Bar-Ilan is presumably here referring to the agreement, later called the "status-quo agreement," made between Ben-Gurion and the Agudat Israel party in June 1947. Part of that agreement granted the rabbinical courts continued control over personal status law, but reserved the right of the state to control all other realms of law. The full text of the agreement is at Itamar Rabinovich and Jehuda Reinharz, *Israel in the Middle East: Documents and Readings on Society, Politics, and Foreign Relations, Pre-1948 to the Present* (Waltham, MA: Brandeis University Press; Hanover: University Press of New England, 2008), 58–59. For a full discussion, see Friedman, "Structural Foundation for Religio-Political Accommodation in Israel."

64. Bar-Ilan, "Hoq u-mishpat be-medinatenu," 1978, 326–27.

65. Ibid., 327–28.

66. Ibid., 328.

67. This date, Sivan 5708, is reported in Zvi Kaplan, "Avodat va'adat ha-haqiqa she-al-yad ha-merkaz ha-olami shel ha-mizrahi" (Jerusalem, April 23, 5709), RZA-MRK 330/38/4/1949.

68. "*Batei mishpat*." This term refers specifically to state civil courts, as opposed to rabbinical courts, which are called *batei din*.

69. Zvi Kaplan, "Avodat va'adat ha-haqiqa she-al-yad ha-merkaz ha-olami shel ha-mizrahi".

70. Bar-Ilan, Correspondence of 12 Av 5708, RZA-MRK, 330/38/4/1948.

71. They were Avraham Shapira, Aharon Bialistotski, Yaakov Ginzburg, A. Z. Gerber [?], Sh. A. Yedelewitz, Dr Y. Z. Kahana, Binyamin Rabinowitz-Te'omim, Avraham Shadmi, and Mordekhai Elon. A further three rabbis also worked for a short time on the committee: D. Kreuzer, G. Arieli, Y. Salmon. (The list is taken from ibid.) Bar-Ilan, in a meeting of the same month, said there were sixteen workers on the project rather than twelve. It seems there were also other members of the committee not included on Kaplan's list: for example, Bezalel Zolti and M. D. Bakesht, who were both present at a meeting of 11 April 1949. "Du"ah hever ovdei avodat ha-haqiqah," 12 Nisan 5709, RZA-MRK, 330/38/4/1949.

72. Ibid.

73. Lit. "to greaten and ennoble the Torah" i.e., to study the Torah as an exercise of religious devotion, rather than for practical purposes.

74. Letter from Zvi Kaplan to Avraham Shadmi, 2 Elul 5708, RZA-MRK, 330/38/4/1948.

75. Mordekhai Elon to Bar-Ilan 17 Av 5708, RZA-MRK, 330/38/4/1948.

76. Avraham Shapira to Bar-Ilan 24 Av 5708, RZA-MRK, 330/38/4/1948.

77. Ibid.

78. "Du"ah hever ovdei avodat ha-haqiqah," 12 Nisan 5709, RZA-MRK, 330/38/4/1949.

79. Binyamin Rabinowitz-Teomim, *Ha-haqiqah al-pi mishpat ha-torah: Erkah, ba'ayotehah, u-derakhehah* (Jerusalem: Bet ha-midrash le-mishpat ha-torah, mahlakat ha-hakika, 1950).

80. In 1907 Switzerland had enacted its own civil code, similar to the German BGB. The Swiss code had been adopted by Turkey in the 1920s.

81. Yitzhak Ginzberg, *Mishpatim le-yisra'el: Ha-hoq ha-pelili ve-dinei ha-onshin bizman hazeh le-fi mishpat ha-torah, ha-talmud u-meforshim* (Jerusalem: Mechon Harry Fischel, 1956); Binyamin Rabinowitz-Teomim, *Hilkhot mekhira* (Jerusalem: Mechon Harry Fischel, 1957).

82. Ginzberg, *Mishpatim le-yisra'el*, 116 ff.

CHAPTER 5

1. Religious Zionists sometimes found secular partners for this kind of legislation. The desire of secular Zionists for cultural hegemony and the symbolic significance of pork products in Jewish tradition, for example, played a role in establishing legislation around kosher laws. Daphne Barak-Erez, *Outlawed Pigs: Law, Religion, and Culture in Israel* (Madison: University of Wisconsin Press, 2007).

2. An analysis of the idealistic and pragmatic streams within religious Zionism is found in Cohen, *Ha-talit veha-degel*, chap. 8. Cohen maintains that the pragmatic stream ultimately dominated. His analysis is sound but I believe that the role of principle even among the pragmatists is important to recognize, as I argue later.

3. Friedman, "The Structural Foundation for Religio-Political Accommodation in Israel."

4. The main constitutional proposal under consideration, by Leo Kohn, was amended over time to include additional symbolic references to the Jewish tradition but the substantive impact of Jewish law on the proposal was very minimal. Radzyner, "Constitution for Israel."

5. Isaac Herzog, "Tehei yerushalayim birat yisra'el ve-torato—huqatah," *Ha-tsofeh*, August 1, 1948.

6. Dov Schwartz, *Faith at the Crossroads*, 159.

7. Quoted in Likhovski, "Between Mandate and State," 62. Cohn's statement is particularly striking, given that he would become a clear opponent of the use of Jewish law in Israel, advocating instead a thoroughly modern legal system. For more on the temporary interest in Mishpat Ivri just before the establishment of the state, see ibid., 60–64 and especially fn. 101. For more on Cohn and the changes in his thinking about Jewish law, see Amihai Radzyner and Shuki Friedman, "Ha-mehoqeq ha-yisre'eli veha-mishpat ha-ivri: Hayim kohn ben mahar le-etmol," *Iyunei Mishpat* 29, no. 6 (2005): 167–244.

8. The letter is published in Herzog, *Tehuqah le-yisra'el*, 1:229.

9. Moshe Una, "Mashma'utah shel ha-hashpa'ah ha-hilkhatit 'al ha-haqiqah," in *Ha-mishpat ha-ivri u-medinat yisra'el*, ed. Yaakov Bazaq (Jerusalem: Mosad Ha-rav Kook, 1969), 101–9. Other religious Zionists were similarly skeptical. See Warhaftig, *Huqah le-yisra'el*, 351.

10. Technically, some have argued that Israel does indeed have a constitution, albeit one that is unwritten or incomplete. At the very least, Israel's Basic Laws are often treated by the judiciary to have the status of constitutional law and are used as a basis for finding individual rights and justifying judicial review. Gideon Sapir, Daphne Barak-Erez, and Aharon Barak, eds., *Israeli Constitutional Law in the Making* (Oxford: Hart Publishing, 2013). In the words of Aharon Barak, former president of Israel's Supreme Court, "Despite a common misconception, Israel does have a formal constitution as well as judicial review of constitutionality." Aharon Barak, "The Values of the State of Israel as a Jewish and Democratic State," in *Israel*

as a Jewish and Democratic State, ed. Asher Maoz, Jewish Law Association Studies XXI (Atlanta: Scholars Press, 1991), 6.

11. This fallacy was noted in an early study of the constitution-making process. The study observed that "notwithstanding popular opinion to the contrary there was opposition to a written constitution from political parties other than the religious ones." Rackman, *Israel's Emerging Constitution, 1948–51*, x. See also ibid., 27–32; Rackman, "Religious Problems in the Making of the Israeli Constitution (1948–1951)," 72.

12. According to an analysis of the papers in the Israel State Archive, "Ben-Gurion stood like a wall against those who wanted a constitution. In discussions with supporters and opponents, in the Knesset and outside it, he found countless reasons to belittle the importance that the supporters of the constitution adduced to the document. Moreover, by pushing off the need for a constitution here and now, he sought to set himself up as the supreme defender of the democracy." Eli She'altiel, *David Ben-Gurion: Rosh ha-memshalah ha-rishon; mivhar te'udot (1947–1963)* (Jerusalem: Medinat yisra'el, arkhi'on ha-medinah, 1997), 139. See also Amihai Radzyner and Shuki Friedman, *Huqah she-lo ketuvah ba-Torah* (Jerusalem: Israel Democracy Institute, 2006). For more historical background, and a more charitable view of Ben-Gurion's opposition to a written constitution, see Nir Kedar, *Ben-Gurion veha-huqah*.

13. Law and Administration Ordinance No.1, 1948, Section 11.

14. Religious courts would probably have maintained their jurisdiction over personal law even had a constitution been adopted. There was a clause along these lines in Leo Kohn's draft constitution, the most likely blueprint for a constitution in 1948. Radzyner, "Constitution for Israel."

15. The letter was written on March 11, 1948 and was published in Warhaftig and Katz, *Ha-rabanut ha-rashit le-yisra'el*, 295.

16. Ousiel, *Hegyonei uziel*, vol. 1, p. 177, quoted in Dov Schwartz, *Faith at the Crossroads*, 174.

17. Herzog, "Samkhut ha-torah be-medinat yisra'el," 222.

18. Ibid., 222.

19. Ibid., 226.

20. Women's Equal Rights Law, 1951, para. 1.

21. Ibid., para. 7.

22. For more on the administration and precise jurisdiction of the rabbinical courts, see Chigier, "Rabbinical Courts in the State of Israel"; Chigier, *Husband and Wife in Israeli Law*. For a helpful collection of Knesset regulations pertaining to religion and state, see Warhaftig, Hefetz, and Glas, *Dat u-medinah be-haqiqah*, 42–104. For the consequences of the Women's Equal Rights Law, see Elon, *Ma'amad ha-ishah*.

23. Herzog, "Samkhut ha-torah be-medinat yisra'el," 223.

24. Quoted in Shapira, *Ben-Gurion*, 191.

25. Dov Schwartz finds three levels of motivation in religious Zionism: An "overt" level, which affirms concrete political life; a "subconscious" level, which views events in terms of a naturalistic messianism; and an "unconscious" level, which expects an apocalyptic messianism. For Schwartz, "[a]lthough the daily routine of religious-Zionists conveys an accommodation with secularization, the subconscious layer, for instance, views this routine as a realization of the first stages of natural redemption." Schwartz, "Ideas vs. Reality," 205–6. The distinction between pragmatism and idealism that I describe in this chapter is not identical to Schwartz's taxonomy, but might roughly correspond to his first two levels. My distinction, however, does not describe a psychodynamic process. As I show later, Herzog is quite explicit about the need for internal and external rhetoric.

26. The speech was delivered on 21 Av 5709 at the Mizrahi Council. It is published in Herzog, *Tehuqah le-yisra'el*, 1:221–8.

27. Herzog, "Samkhut ha-torah be-medinat yisra'el," 1:226–27.

28. Ibid., 1:227.

29. Ibid., 1:228.

30. For more on the role of rabbis in the Council of the Four Lands and in Poland in general, see Adam Teller, "Rabbis without a Function? The Polish Rabbinate and the Council of Four Lands in the 16th–18th Centuries," in *Jewish Religious Leadership: Image and Reality*, ed. Jack Wertheimer (New York: Jewish Theological Seminary, 2004), 371–400; Fram, *Ideals Face Reality*.

31. "Law shapes society from the inside out by providing the principal categories in terms of which social life is made to seem largely natural, normal, cohesive, and coherent." Sarat, "Redirecting Legal Scholarship in Law Schools," 134.

32. "When they begin to find a voice, peoples who see themselves as disadvantaged often [resist] either by speaking back in the language of the law or by disrupting its means and ends." John L. Comaroff, "Foreword," in *Contested States: Law, Hegemony and Resistance*, ed. Mindie Lazarus-Black and Susan F. Hirsch (New York: Routledge, 2012), xii.

33. For the ways that the British used law as a tool of social construction, and the way that Zionists and Arabs used law as a site of resistance or collaboration, see also Likhovski, *Law and Identity in Mandate Palestine*; Ronen Shamir, *The Colonies of Law: Colonialism, Zionism and Law in Early Mandate Palestine* (Cambridge: Cambridge University Press, 1999).

34. For more on Warhaftig, see Itamar Warhaftig, *Alayikh zarah: Hayav u-po'alo shel ha-sar d"r zerah varhaftig zts"l* (Ma'alaeh Adumim, Israel: Itamar Warhaftig, 2018).

35. Letter from Bar Ilan to Warhaftig, 24 Adar I 5708. ISA G-472722/98/04.

36. Warhaftig, *Huqah le-yisra'el*, 441–53.

37. See, for examples, Zerah Warhaftig, *Al ha-shiput ha-rabani be-yisra'el: Neumim* (Tel Aviv: Moreshet, 1955), 12.

38. Zerah Warhaftig, "Ba'ayot ha-mishpat be-medinat yisra'el," *Ha-tsofeh*, September 2, 1949.

39. Bar-Ilan, "Hoq u-mishpat," 20.

40. This romantic view of the revival of Hebrew and the abandonment of other languages was not entirely true to reality. See Liora R. Halperin, *Babel in Zion: Jews, Nationalism, and Language Diversity in Palestine, 1920–1948* (New Haven, CT: Yale University Press, 2014); Anat Helman, *Becoming Israeli: National Ideals and Everyday Life in the 1950s* (Waltham, MA: Brandeis University Press, 2014), chap. 2.

41. Warhaftig, *Huqah le-yisra'el*, 45.

42. *Divrei ha-keneset* 11 (1952), 2107.

43. b. Megilla 14a.

44. *Divrei ha-keneset* 25 (1958), 232.

45. Letter from Zerah Warhaftig to Raphael H. Gold, 18 January, 1948. ISA G-472722/98/04.

46. Ibid.

47. Warhaftig, *Huqah le-yisra'el*, 45–46.

48. This procedure was legislated under Article 46 of the King's Order in Council, a kind of constitution for the British Mandate of Palestine.

49. Although Warhaftig failed, a version of this law was eventually legislated in Israel's *Foundations of Law Act (1980)*, which reads, "Where the court, faced with a legal question requiring decision, finds no answer to it in statute law or case-law or by analogy, it shall decide it in the light of the principles of freedom, justice, equity and peace of Israel's heritage." The act, however, makes no reference at all to halakha and its vague language allows for many possible interpretations.

50. Quoted at Warhaftig, *Huqah le-yisra'el*, 429.

51. C.A.191/51 Leib Skornik v. Miriam Skornik.

52. *Divrei ha-keneset* 16 (1954), 2184.

53. Warhaftig, "Ha-mishpat ha-ivri be-haqiqat medinat yisra'el ba-esor ha-rishon."

54. *Divrei ha-keneset* 32, no. 1 (1961), 54–57. For one treatment of Warhaftig's speech, see Izhak Englard, "The Problem of Jewish Law in a Jewish State," *Israel Law Review* 3 (1968): 260–2.

55. Quoted in Englard, "The Problem of Jewish Law in a Jewish State," 260 fn. 18. I could not locate this comment in *Divrei ha-keneset*.

56. Menachem Elon, "Ha-mishpat ha-ivri be-mishpat ha-medinah: Al ha-matsui ve-al ha-ratsui," *Ha-praklit* 25 (September 1968): 27–53. I am grateful to Amihai Radzyner for this reference.

57. *Divrei ha-keneset* 32, no. 1 (1961), 56.

58. Ibid., 57.

59. Ibid., 57.

60. Warhaftig, *Al ha-shiput ha-rabani*, 12.

61. Ibid., 17.

62. Ibid., 17.

63. RZA-BI PA/16001211. The nature of this source is unclear. It is certainly written by Warhaftig and seems to be a draft of an article or book that he did not publish.

64. Ibid.

65. Warhaftig, "Ha-mishpat ha-ivri be-haqiqat medinat yisra'el ba-esor ha-rishon."

CHAPTER 6

1. Moshe Zmoira, "Speech by Moshe Zmoira at the Inauguration of the Supreme Court," *Ha-Praklit* 5 (1948): 187, quoted in Pnina Lahav, "The Supreme Court of Israel: Formative Years, 1948–1955," *Studies in Zionism* 11, no. 1 (March 1990): 49. The translation here is Lahav's.

2. See ibid.

3. ISA 80-4253/10. I am grateful to Amihai Radzyner for bringing this document to my attention.

4. The reference should be b. Betzah 25b.

5. Isaac Herzog, "Al mishpat ha-torah be-yisra'el," in *Halakhah pesuqah: Mishpat ha-torah li-meqorotav be-talmud u-posqim al seder ha-shulkhan arukh* (Jerusalem: Mechon Harry Fischel, 1962), 1:11–15. These words were originally delivered by Herzog in a speech on July 23, 1948.

6. Ousiel originally wrote these words in a responsum sent on March 1, 1949 to the head of the rabbinical court of Tiberias, Refa'el Ha-Kohen Kook. The responsum was later published as Bentsion Meir Hai Ousiel, "Yesodot din ha-malkhut be-yisra'el uva-amim," *Ha-torah veha-medinah* 5–6 (1953–54): 16.

7. On the Rabbinic Council of *Ha-po'el ha-mizrahi*, see Asher Cohen and Aaron Kampinsky, "Religious Leadership in Israel's Religious Zionism: The Case of the Board of Rabbis," *Jewish Political Studies Review* 18, nos. 3–4 (October 1, 2006): 119–40.

8. For more on *Ha-torah veha-medinah*, see Mark Washofsky, "Halakhah and Political Theory: A Study in Jewish Legal Response to Modernity," *Modern Judaism* 9, no. 3 (October 1989): 289–310.

9. Many of these bibliographic details come from the account of his son-in-law. Yisrael Sarir, "Sha'ul yisra'eli, ha-rav," *Entsiklopedia yahadut le-nosa'im be-tarbut yisra'el li-tehumeha*, accessed June 11, 2019, http://www.daat.ac.il/encyclopedia/value.asp?id1=1070. See also Shmuel Katz, "Toldot hayav shel ha-rav sha'ul yisra'eli zts"l," accessed June 11, 2019, http://www.eretzhemdah.org//Data/UploadedFiles/SitePages/896-sFileRedir.pdf. For more about Yisraeli, and particularly his halakhic work, see Yitzchak Roness, "Mishnato ha-hilkhatit shel ha-rav sha'ul yisra'eli" (Ph.D. Dissertation, Bar–Ilan University, 2012).

10. Shaul Yisraeli, "Im ha-qovets," *Ha-torah veha-medinah* 1 (1949): 11.

11. Ibid.

12. For an overview of the application of these precedents in *Ha-torah veha-medinah*, see Washofsky, "Halakhah and Political Theory."

13. Appeals to these diverse precedents might in theory have yielded different conceptions of the State of Israel. Their ramifications are explored in Benny Porat, "Hamishah musagim yehudi'im shel demoqratiah yisre'elit: masat petihah," in *Mahshavot al demoqratiah yehudit*, ed. Aviezer Ravitzky (Jerusalem: Israel Democracy Institute, 2010), 17–27. In practice, however, the contributors to *Ha-torah veha-medinah* were often more interested in legitimizing the State of Israel than in the detailed consequences of choosing one kind of precedent over another. Their willingness to alternate between different precedents for non-halakhic law may reflect their intuition that extra-halakhic laws of any kind ultimately find their source in a Noahide law, a pre-Sinaitic natural law that applies to all peoples. Stone, "Sinaitic and Noahide Law," especially pp. 1202 ff. See also Avraham Hayim Burgansky, "Qehilah u-mamlakhah: Yehasim shel ha-rav y''a hertsog veha-rav sha'ul yisra'eli le-medinat yisra'el," in *Dat u-medinah ba-hagut ha-yehudit ba-me'ah ha-esrim*, ed. Aviezer Ravitzky (Jerusalem: Israel Democracy Institute, 2005), 267–94.

14. One scholar has noted that Yisraeli seemed willing to make whatever intellectual moves that were necessary to endorse the state's authority: "One might receive the impression that the overriding goal that guides his position, consciously or unconsciously, is nothing less than to grant a comprehensive approval to the state that had just been established, an approval both structural and functional." Gerald Blidstein, "Torat ha-medinah be-mishnat ha-rav sha'ul yisra'eli," in *Shenei ivrei ha-gesher*, ed. Mordechai Bar-On (Jerusalem: Ben Zvi Institute, 2002), 360.

15. Kook, *Mishpat kohen*, 144:14.

16. I Samuel 8. The principal biblical reference for the dependence of the appointment of a monarch on the people's consent is Deuteronomy 17:15 ("When you say 'I will set a king over me' . . . [y]ou shall surely set a king over yourself"), which was taken by many interpreters to imply that the consent of the people is necessary for the appointment of a king. This reading is born out by I Samuel 8. Neither source, however, implies that the king is subject to the consent of the people after his initial appointment, or provides for a legal method of removing a king should the people's consent be rescinded. In fact, I Samuel 8 strongly suggests that once appointed, he has very wide discretion in his prerogative.

17. Maimonides, *Mishneh torah*, "Laws of Kings and Wars," 1:3.

18. Blidstein, "Torat ha-medinah be-mishnat ha-rav sha'ul yisra'eli," 353 fn. 8; Yosef Ahituv, "Le-bituyav ha-hilkhati'im shel ha-rav ha-rashi yitshaq ha-levi hertsog be-esor ha-rishon li-tequmat yisra'el," in *Etgar ha-ribonut: Yetsirah ve-hagut be-esor ha-rishon la-medinah*, ed. Mordechai Bar-On (Jerusalem: Yad Yitshaq Ben-Tsvi, 1999), 205 fn. 14.

19. Many of Yisraeli's articles were collected and published in Shaul Yisraeli, *Amud ha-yemini* (Tel Aviv–Jaffa: Moreshet, 1966), which was reissued as Shaul Yisraeli, *Amud ha-yemini*, 2nd edition (Jerusalem: Hotza'at ha-torah veha-medinah al shem maran ha-rav sha'ul yisra'eli ztz'l, 2010). Unless stated otherwise, page references refer to the second edition. The article under discussion was first published as Shaul Yisraeli, "Samkhut ha-nasi u-mosdot memshal nivharim be-yisra'el," *Ha-torah veha-medinah* 1 (1949): 67–78. It was republished as Yisraeli, *Amud ha-yemini*, chap. 7.

20. Yisraeli, *Amud ha-yemini*, 35.

21. According to Gerald Blidstein, "[a]t least some of these conclusions seem fairly revolutionary; and if we pay attention to the halakhic argument of Rabbi [Yisraeli], we see that he enters into claims that are rather too forced to stand up." Blidstein, "Torat ha-medinah be-mishnat ha-rav sha'ul yisra'eli," 360.

22. Yisraeli, *Amud ha-yemini*, 39. The biblical quotation is from I Kings 16:25.

23. "Then the people of Israel were divided into two. Half of the people followed Tibni the son of Ginat, making him king; and half followed Omri" (I Kings 16:21). It is possible that Yisraeli picked a case in which only half the people supported the king in order to make the point that a majority is all that is needed to determine the will of the people.

24. Yisraeli, *Amud ha-yemini*, 39.

25. Ibid., 42.

26. See, for example, b. Yoma 73b, interpreting 2 Samuel 15:24.

27. Yisraeli, *Amud ha-yemini*, 40.

28. For more on *mamlakhtiyut*, see Nir Kedar, "Ben-Gurion's Mamlakhtiyut: Etymological and Theoretical Roots," *Israel Studies* 7, no. 3 (2002): 117–33; Nir Kedar, *Mamlakhti'ut: ha-tefisah ha-ezrahit shel david ben-gurion* (Beersheba, Israel: Mekhon Ben-Gurion le-heqer yisra'el, Ben-Gurion University in the Negev; Yad Yitzhak Ben Tsvi, 2009).

29. Shlomo Tenbitsky, "Dina de-malkhuta be-yisra'el uva-amim," *Ha-torah veha-medinah* 1 (1949): 41.

30. Natan Tsvi Friedman, "Samkhuyoteha shel memshelet medinat yisra'el," *Ha-torah veha-medinah* 1 (1949): 47.

31. For sources and discussion, see Elon, *Jewish Law*, 751–59.

32. Ovadiah Hadaya, *Yaskil avdi* (Jerusalem: n.p., 1931), 6:289 (Hoshen Mishpat 28:2:6). The context of this responsum is the question of the authority of the Knesset to levy taxes.

33. Hadaya opposed, for example, Herzog's attempt to make the halakha regarding inheritance the same for sons and daughters. Traditionally, halakhic inheritance laws favor male descendants. For Herzog's attempts at reform, see Herzog, *Tehuqah le-yisra'el*, 1989. See also Greenberger, "Rabbi Herzog's Proposals for Takkanot in Matters of Inheritance." For Hadaya's rebuttal, see Ovadiah Hadaya, *Yaskil avdi*, 6:278–9 (Hoshen Mishpat 22).

34. *Yaskil avdi*, 6:289 (Hoshen Mishpat 28:2:7).

35. Nadia Urbinati, *Representative Democracy: Principles and Genealogy* (Chicago: University of Chicago Press, 2008), 122.

36. Elon, *Jewish Law*, 753–58.

37. These prohibitions, however, were often observed in the breach. In many times and places, the use of non-Jewish courts by the Jewish community was widespread, and sometimes officially endorsed by rabbis and other communal leaders. See, for example, Berkovitz, *Protocols of Justice*; Marglin, *Across Legal Lines*.

38. Yisraeli, *Amud ha-yemini*, chap. 8.

39. Yisraeli is not always consistent with his terminology in the Hebrew original but he generally seems to use *hoq* as a generic term for legislation, *mishpat* to refer to law, and *taqanah* to mean regulation.

40. I am grateful to David Schorr for suggesting that the distinction between law and policy might help to describe Yisraeli's approach. On the Early Modern development of "policy," see Karl Härter, "Security and 'Gute Policey' in Early Modern Europe: Concepts, Laws, and Instruments," *Historical Social Research* 35, no. 4 (134) (2010): 41–65. On its place in the Anglo-American legal tradition, see Noga Morag-Levine, *Chasing the Wind: Regulating Air Pollution in the Common Law State* (Princeton, NJ: Princeton University Press, 2009), especially 67–70 and, for a linguistic analysis, see Arnold J. Heidenheimer, "Politics, Policy and Policey as Concepts in English and Continental Languages: An Attempt to Explain Divergences," *Review of Politics* 48, no. 1 (January 1986): 3–30. Some jurists and political theorists object to the massive growth of the administrative state during the course of the twentieth century. See, for example, Philip Hamburger, *Is Administrative Law Unlawful?* (Chicago: University of Chicago Press, 2014). For an alternative perspective, see, for example, Daniel R. Ernst, *Tocqueville's Nightmare: The Administrative State Emerges in America, 1900–1940* (Oxford: Oxford University Press, 2014).

41. Yisraeli calls this an "intellectual" [*sikhli*] determination. It is likely that Yisraeli here is alluding to Maimonides's notion of the intellect, which provides humans the potential for communion with God's own "intelligence" [*ha-sekhel ha-elohi*] through prophecy. See *Guide for the Perplexed* III 18. In his use of this terminology, Yisraeli is implicitly associating the ability to make halakhic determination with prophetic abilities.

42. Yisraeli's distinction between the kinds of expertise required to legislate these two kinds of rules roughly equates to Aristotle's distinction between *sophia* and *phronesis*. See *Nicomachean Ethics*, bk. 6.

43. Yisraeli, *Amud ha-yemini*, 46.

44. Ibid., 47.

45. Quoted in Shmuel Hayim Weingarten, "Huqei ha-medinah ve-toqfam le-fi ha-halakhah," *Ha-torah veha-medinah* 5–6 (1953–54): 311.

46. Ibid., 321.

47. Ousiel, "Yesodot din ha-malkhut be-yisra'el uva-amim," 21.
48. Hadaya, *Yaskil avdi*, 6:290 (Hoshen Mishpat 28:2:8).
49. Tenbitsky, "Dina de-malkhuta be-yisra'el uva-amim," 41.
50. Yisrael Be'eri, "Samkhut ha-malkhut be-medinat yisra'el," in *Be-tsomet ha-torah veha-medinah: Mivhar ma'amarim mi-tokh kovtsei "ha-torah veha-medinah" be-arikhah mehudeshet*, ed. Yehudah Shaviv 3 vols. (Alon Shevut, Gush Etsion, Israel: Mekhon Tsomet, 1991), 1:35. This collection is a selection of articles from *Ha-torah veha-medinah*.
51. The description of unfit leaders as "broken wells" comes from Jeremiah 2:13: "For My people have committed two evils: they have forsaken Me, a fountain of running water, and have hewn wells for themselves, broken wells, that cannot hold water."
52. Be'eri, "Samkhut ha-malkhut be-medinat yisra'el," 35.
53. Ibid.
54. Yehudah Segal, "Al ha-mishpat ha-hiloni ba-arets," *Ha-torah veha-medinah* 7–8 (1956–57): 74.
55. Ibid., 76.
56. Ibid., 77.
57. Ibid., 80.

CHAPTER 7

1. Rubinstein, *Zionist Dream Revisited*, 49.
2. Ibid., 99.
3. For example, see Avi Sagi and Dov Schwartz, *Religious Zionism and the Six Day War: From Realism to Messianism* (New York: Routledge, 2018).
4. There were exceptions to this rule. A group known as *Brit ha-qana'im* [Covenant of Zealots] attempted to use violent means to force traditional observance onto state institutions. This was a tiny radical fringe, however, that was quickly caught and imprisoned by the Israeli police. Ami Pedahzur and Arie Perliger, *Jewish Terrorism in Israel* (New York: Columbia University Press, 2009), 33–36.
5. Herzog, *Tehuqah le-yisra'el*, 1:227.
6. The trend to what has been called the "haredization" of the Chief Rabbinate was already recognized in the early 1990s. See, for example, Yehezqel Kohen, "Rabanut kevusha?" in *Ha-tsionut ha-datit be-re'iyah mehudeshet*, ed. Meir Roth (Ein Tsurim, Israel: Ne'emanei Torah Va-avodah, 1998), 215–19. Motti Inbari, *Messianic Religious Zionism Confronts Israeli Territorial Compromises* (New York: Cambridge University Press, 2014), also documents the increasing influence of Ultra-Orthodoxy on many religious Zionist leaders.
7. Indeed, the disparity between rabbinical ruling and the practices of the religious Zionist community has, if anything, become more pronounced over time. See, for

example, Schwartz, "Ideas vs. Reality," 214; Fischer, "Fundamentalist or Romantic Nationalist."

8. Avraham Shapira, "Mabat torani al huqei ha-medinah ve-hatqanat taqanot be-yamenu," *Tehumin* 3 (1982): 238.

9. Mordekhai Eliyahu, "Yahas ha-halakhah le-huqei ha-medinah," *Tehumin* 3 (1982): 243.

10. Yair Sheleg, *Aharei rabim le-hatot: emdot rabanim be-yisra'el klapei ha-demoqratiah*, Mehqar mediniut 67 (Jerusalem: Israel Democracy Institute, 2006), 22.

11. It must be noted that this is an area of halakha in which the religious Zionist public does not tend to follow the guidance of their rabbis. Although most religious Zionist rabbis prohibit the use of Israel's civil courts, the public uses them extensively. Maoz, "Ha-rabanut u-vet ha-din," 53; Yedidia Z. Stern and Yair Sheleg, eds., "Ma'amadam shel batei ha-mishpat be-yisra'el: halakhah, idi'ologiah u-metsi'ut," in *Halakhah tsionit* (Jerusalem: Israel Democracy Institute, 2017), 276–311. Indeed, sometimes the rabbis themselves have recourse to the civil courts. Yitzhak Nisim for example, used the state's civil courts during the time that he served as Chief Rabbi. See Maoz, "Ha-rabanut u-vet ha-din," 53 fn. 176.

12. Ovadiah Yosef, *She'elot u-teshuvot yehaveh da'at*, n.d., 4:65.

13. Sheleg, *Aharei rabim le-hatot*, 41.

14. Yaacov Ariel, "Ha-mishpat be-medinat yisra'el ve-isur arkha'ot," *Tehumin* 3 (1980): 327.

15. Yizhak Brand, *Arkhaot shel goyim be-medinat ha-yehudim* (Jerusalem: Israel Democracy Institute, 2010), 71. See also Maoz, "Ha-rabanut u-vet ha-din," 52 ff.

16. "[L]egal professionals and bureaucrats responsible for administering the law of a modern state typically claim that this state law prevails over every other law existing within its field of jurisdiction. . . . [T]he exponents of state law frequently seek to fortify their claims by asserting that no normative order other than state law can be properly given the title 'law.'" Gordon R. Woodman, "The Possibilities of Co-Existence of Religious Laws with Other Laws," in *Law and Religion in Multicultural Societies*, ed. Rubya Mehdi, 1st edition (Copenhagen: DJØF Pub, 2008), 24.

17. Yedidia Z. Stern, "Israeli Law and Jewish Law in Israel: A Zero Sum Game?" in *Institutionalizing Rights and Religion: Competing Supremacies*, ed. Leora Batnitzky and Hanoch Dagan (Cambridge: Cambridge University Press, 2017), 58.

18. Supreme Court acting as the High Court of Justice—HCJ 8638/03 Amir v. the Great Rabbinical Court in Jerusalem 8638/03 PD 61(1) 259. An English summary and translation of the case is at http://versa.cardozo.yu.edu/opinions/amir-v-great-rabbinical-court-jerusalem.

19. Amir, 287.

20. Shlomo Daikhovsky, "Samkhut batei ha-din ha-rabani'im be-re'i pesiqat batei ha-din," *Diné Israel* 10–11 (March 1981): 9.

21. Quoted in Amihai Radzyner, "The Impact of Supreme Court Rulings on the Halakhic Status of the Official Rabbinical Courts in Israel," in *Institutionalizing Rights and Religion: Competing Supremacies*, ed. Leora Batnitzky and Hanoch Dagan (Cambridge: Cambridge University Press, 2017), 225.

22. Quoted in ibid.

23. For further details and a more comprehensive list of private rabbinical courts, see Hofri-Winogradow, "Plurality of Discontent," 110 ff.

24. Accessed June 6, 2019, http://www.eretzhemdah.org/content.asp?PageId=36&lang=en and http://www.eretzhemdah.org/content.asp?pageid=194.

25. Ido Rechnitz, *Mishpat ha-torah be-medinat yisra'el* (Ofra, Israel: Makhon mishpetei eretz, 2007), 4, 5.

26. Reuven Heller, "Ma'avar mi-mishpetei ha-goyim le-mishpat ha-torah ketsad?," accessed July 17, 2017, http://www.yeshiva.org.il/midrash/6780.

27. "Smotrich Says He Wants to Be Justice Minister so Israel Can Follow Torah Law," *Times of Israel*, June 3, 2019, accessed June 6, 2019, https://www.timesofisrael.com/smotrich-says-he-wants-justice-ministry-so-israel-can-follow-torah-law/.

28. Bar-Ilan, "Hoq u-mishpat be-medinatenu," 1978, 327.

29. The account of contemporary Israeli scholar Yehonatan (Jonathan) Garb is typical: "In the period of the Yishuv and the first decades of the state, the basic decision of religious Zionism was to participate in the Zionist enterprise by, among other things, supporting the political establishment of the ruling Labor party. However, beginning in the 1970s, one can discern a decisive turn: religious Zionism gradually moves into a position of aspiring to lead and even to being made into the ruling establishment. This process led in the first years of the 1990s to a questioning of the very faith of wide circles of religious Zionists in the elected institutions of the state." Yehonatan Garb, "Tse'irei ha-mafda"l ve-shorshav ha-ra'ayoni'im shel gush emunim," in *Ha-tsionut ha-datit: Idan ha-temurot*, ed. Asher Cohen (Jerusalem: Bialik Institute, 2004), 171.

30. For the context of, and response to, the assassination of Rabin in the religious Zionist community, see Yoav Sorek, "Rega shel tsemarmoret: Ha-tsionut ha-datit le-nokhah retsah rabin," in *Ha-tsionut ha-datit: Idan ha-temurot*, ed. Asher Cohen (Jerusalem: Bialik Institute, 2004), 475–532.

31. Herzog, *Tehuqah le-yisra'el*, 1:226.

32. Yedidiah Meir and Sivan Rahav-Meir, eds., *Yamim ketomim: Ha-hitnatqut—Ha-heshbon veha-nefesh* (Tel Aviv: Yedi'ot Aharonot; Sifrei Hemed, 2006), 17.

33. Ibid., 24.

34. Ibid., 22.

35. Ibid., 22.

36. Ibid., 22–23.

37. In 2019, Tal was subject to further controversy after he was accused of sexual misconduct and abuse of power. Jacob Magid, "Top Rabbi Blows Lid off Rabbinic

Scandal, Rocking National Religious Public," *Times of Israel*, May 30, 2019, accessed June 12, 2019, https://www.timesofisrael.com/top-rabbi-blows-lid-off-rabbinic-scandal-rocking-national-religious-public/.

38. "Lo mitpalel li-shlomah—Ra'ayon im shmuel tal," *Mishpahah: Ha-shevu'on la-bayit ha-yehudi*, March 5, 2007, 18.

39. Ibid., 14. For Tal's response to his critics, see Shlomo Tal, "Mi-melekh evyon le-melekh elyon," *Ha-tsofeh*, January 6, 2007.

40. "Tenu'at derekh hayim," accessed July 17, 2017, http://www.derech-chaim.org/.

41. Yitzchak Ginsburgh, "Ha-zeman le-fatse'ah et ha-egoz," Yeshivat od yosef hai, accessed July 17, 2017, http://www.odyosefchai.org.il/TextHome/TextInfo/373.

42. David Scott and Talal Asad, "The Trouble of Thinking: An Interview with Talal Asad," in *Powers of the Secular Modern: Talal Asad and His Interlocutors*, ed. David Scott and Charles Hirschkind (Stanford, CA: Stanford University Press, 2006), 294.

43. The classical articulation of the liberal position was made by John Rawls in *A Theory of Justice* (Cambridge, MA: Harvard University Press, 2009). For one line of criticism, see Robert Audi and Nicholas Wolterstorff, *Religion in the Public Square: The Place of Religious Convictions in Political Debate* (Lanham, Maryland: Rowman & Littlefield, 1997).

44. Winnifred Fallers Sullivan, *The Impossibility of Religious Freedom* (Princeton, NJ: Princeton University Press, 2005).

45. This argument is made, for example, in Smith, *Weird John Brown*.

46. Abraham Joshua Heschel, *Moral Grandeur and Spiritual Audacity: Essays* (New York: Farrar, Straus and Giroux, 1997).

47. For one account of the uses of prophetic discourse, and a proposal about its limits, Cathleen Kaveny, *Prophecy without Contempt* (Cambridge, MA: Harvard University Press, 2016).

48. Abraham Isaac Kook, *Orot* (Jerusalem: Mosad Ha-rav Kook, 1961), 160.

49. Yeshayahu Leibowitz and Aviezer Ravitzky, *Vikuhim al emunah ve-filosofiyah*, Universitah Meshuderet (Tel Aviv: Ministry of Defence, 2006), 63.

50. Menachem Lorberbaum, "Questioning Territory: A Jewish Reflection on Holy Land," *The Immanent Frame*, June 29, 2017, accessed October 11, 2019, https://tif.ssrc.org/2017/06/29/questioning-territory-a-jewish-reflection-on-holy-land//.

51. For more on the use of the "sacred" in extremist religious Zionist politics, see, for example, the comments of Moshe Halbertal in Lawrence Susskind et al., "Religious and Ideological Dimensions of the Israeli Settlements Issue: Reframing the Narrative?" *Negotiation Journal* 21, no. 2 (2005): 177–91, 189–90.

52. These positions are reminiscent of Martin Buber, *Kingship of God* (New York: Harper & Row, 1967). For more on the critique of liberalism from the standpoint of Jewish political theology, see Randi Rashkover and Martin Kavka, eds., *Judaism, Liberalism, and Political Theology* (Bloomington: Indiana University Press, 2013).

53. For more on Goldman, see Avi Sagi, *Tradition vs. Traditionalism: Contemporary Perspectives in Jewish Thought* (Amsterdam; New York: Rodopi, 2008); Alexander Kaye, "Eliezer Goldman and the Origins of Meta-Halacha," *Modern Judaism* 34, no. 3 (January 10, 2014): 309–33; Alan Jotkowitz, "Eliezer Goldman and Judaism without Illusion," *Modern Judaism* 35, no. 2 (2015): 134–46. For the approach of the religious kibbutz movement to law, see Alexander Kaye, "The Legal Philosophies of Religious Zionism 1937–1967" (Ph.D. Dissertation, Columbia University, 2013), 12–61; Fishman, *Judaism and Modernization on the Religious Kibbutz.*

54. Goldman, "Hoq ha-medinah"; Weiler, *Te'oqratiah yehudit.*

55. Goldman, "Hoq ha-medinah," 165.

56. Ibid., 166.

57. For a different critique of Weiler's book from the same period, see Aharon Kirschenbaum, "Jewish Theocracy," *Diné Israel* 8 (1977): 223–34.

58. Ravitzky, "Is a Halakhic State Possible?"

59. Ibid., 152. This approach is mirrored by several articles of Gerald Blidstein, who has explored the ways in which religious Zionists have justified the legitimacy of Israeli democracy, even when it is in tension with halakha. See, for example, Gerald J. Blidstein, "Halakha and Democracy," *Tradition: A Journal of Orthodox Jewish Thought* 32, no. 1 (October 1, 1997): 6–39; Blidstein, "On Lay Legislation in Halakhah."

60. Ravitzky, *Religion and State in Jewish Philosophy.*

61. Lorberbaum, *Politics and the Limits of Law.*

62. Ravitzky, *Religion and State in Jewish Philosophy*, 30.

63. Lorberbaum, *Politics and the Limits of Law*, 68. As Lorberbaum pointed out, this position is different from the related position of Blidstein in Gerald J. Blidstein, "'Ideal' and 'Real' in Classical Jewish Political Theory," *Jewish Political Studies Review* 2, nos. 1–2 (Spring 1990): 43–66. There, Blidstein claimed that Maimonides's acceptance of a non-halakhic king's law pertains to the "real" world of unredeemed politics rather than an "ideal" halakhic regime. Lorberbaum, by contrast, maintained that Maimonides's acceptance of the need for a non-halakhic law is a permanent feature of politics and cannot be overcome even in an "ideal" Jewish polity.

64. Yedidia Z. Stern, "State, Law, and Halakhah—Part One: Civil Leadership as Halakhic Authority," Position Paper (Jerusalem: Israel Democracy Institute, 2001), 5–6.

65. William Twining, "Normative and Legal Pluralism: A Global Perspective," *Duke Journal of Comparative and International Law* 20 (2010): 485; Alexis Galán and Dennis Patterson, "The Limits of Normative Legal Pluralism: Review of Paul Schiff Berman, Global Legal Pluralism; A Jurisprudence of Law beyond Borders," *International Journal of Constitutional Law* 11, no. 3 (July 1, 2013): 785.

66. Even with the oversight of Israel's Supreme Court, the vulnerability of women in the rabbinical courts has been widely documented. See, for example, Ruth Halperin-Kaddari, *Women in Israel: A State of Their Own* (Philadelphia: University of Pennsylvania Press, 2004), chap. 11. Proponents of multiculturalism insist that it can be compatible, and even depends upon, liberal rights. Will Kymlicka, *Multicultural Citizenship: A Liberal Theory of Minority Rights* (Oxford: Clarendon Press, 1995). Some critics of multiculturalism, though, doubt the ability of states to recognize the rights of minority groups without endangering the rights of individuals within those groups. See, for example, Susan Moller Okin, *Is Multiculturalism Bad for Women?* (Princeton, NJ: Princeton University Press, 1999). Nonetheless, some secular jurists have begun to explore the application of theories of legal pluralism to Israeli law. Ruth Halperin-Kaddari, "Expressions of Legal Pluralism in Israel: The Interaction between the High Court of Justice and Rabbinical Courts in Family Matters and Beyond," in *Jewish Family Law in Israel*, ed. M.D.A. Freeman, Jewish Law Association Studies 13 (Binghamton, NY: Global Publications, State University of New York at Binghamton, 2002), 185–244. For a nuanced exploration of how to "strike a balance between the accommodation of minority group traditions, on the one hand, and the protection of individuals' citizenship rights, on the other," see Ayelet Shachar, *Multicultural Jurisdictions: Cultural Differences and Women's Rights* (Cambridge: Cambridge University Press, 2001), quotation: 1.

67. Locke, *A Letter Concerning Toleration and Other Writings*, 13–14.

68. Roger Williams, "Mr. Cottons Letter Lately Printed, Examined and Answered (1644)," in *The Complete Writings of Roger Williams* (New York: Russell & Russell, 1963), 1:392. For the theological history of the term, see Mark De Wolfe Howe, *The Garden and the Wilderness: Religion and Government in American Constitutional History* (Chicago: University of Chicago Press, 1967).

69. Winnifred Fallers Sullivan, Robert A. Yelle, and Mateo Taussig-Rubbo, "Introduction," in *After Secular Law*, ed. Winnifred Fallers Sullivan, Robert A. Yelle, and Mateo Taussig-Rubbo (Stanford, CA: Stanford University Press, 2011), 1–19. Not only do the categories of religion, law, and politics bleed into one another, but they also do so in different ways in different societies. There are diverse and "often unexpected ways in which the conjunction of religious, political, and legal texts and institutions inform, constrain and liberate human beings in various times and places." Lori G. Beaman and Winnifred Fallers Sullivan, eds., *Varieties of Religious Establishment* (Abingdon, Oxon: Routledge, 2016), 2. Even states that explicitly commit themselves to the separation model apply it in ways that vary, depending on their particular histories. Ahmet T. Kuru, *Secularism and State Policies toward Religion: The United States, France, and Turkey* (Cambridge: Cambridge University Press, 2009); Charles Taylor, "Modes of Secularism," in *Secularism and Its Critics*, ed. Rajeev Bhargava (Delhi; New York: Oxford University Press, 1998), 31–53.

70. Recent examples of such works include John Richard Bowen, *Islam, Law, and Equality in Indonesia: An Anthropology of Public Reasoning* (Cambridge: Cambridge University Press, 2003); Benjamin Schonthal, *Buddhism, Politics and the Limits of Law: The Pyrrhic Constitutionalism of Sri Lanka* (Cambridge: Cambridge University Press, 2016); Noah Salomon, *For Love of the Prophet: An Ethnography of Sudan's Islamic State*, reprint edition (Princeton, NJ: Princeton University Press, 2016).

71. Cf. Maimonides, *Mishneh torah*, "Laws of Kings and Wars," 4:10. For a philosophical articulation of what it means to move toward justice even without an a priori definition of what ideal justice is, see Amartya Sen, *The Idea of Justice* (Cambridge, MA: Harvard University Press, 2009); Iris Murdoch, *The Sovereignty of Good* (New York: Schocken Books, 1971).

BIBLIOGRAPHY

Abdelal, Rawi, Yoshiko M. Herrera, Alastair Iain Johnston, and Rose McDermott. "Identity as a Variable." *Perspectives on Politics* 4, no. 4 (2006): 695–711.

Agmon, Iris. *Family and Court: Legal Culture and Modernity in Late Ottoman Palestine*. Syracuse, NY: Syracuse University Press, 2006.

Ahituv, Yosef. "Le-bituyav ha-hilkhati'im shel ha-rav ha-rashi yitshaq ha-levi hertsog be-esor ha-rishon li-tequmat yisra'el." In *Etgar ha-ribonut: Yetsirah ve-hagut be-esor ha-rishon la-medinah*, edited by Mordechai Bar-On. Jerusalem: Yad Yitshaq Ben-Tsvi, 1999.

Almog, Shmuel. "The Borrowed Identity: Neo-Pagan Reactions to the Jewish Roots of Christianity." In *Demonizing the Other: Antisemitism, Racism and Xenophobia*, edited by Robert S. Wistrich, 131–47. Abingdon, Oxon: Routledge, 2013.

Almog, Shmuel, Jehuda Reinharz, and Anita Shapira, eds. *Zionism and Religion*. Tauber Institute for the Study of European Jewry 30. Hanover, NH, and London: University Press of New England, 1998.

Alon, Gedalyahu. *Mehqarim be-toldot yisra'el*. 2 vols. Tel Aviv: Ha-qibuts Ha-me'uhad, 1957.

Aloni, Shulamit. *Ha-hesder: Mi-medinat hoq le-medinat halakhah*. Tel Aviv: Otpaz, 1970.

Angel, Marc. *Loving Truth and Peace: The Grand Religious Worldview of Rabbi Benzion Uziel*. Northvale, NJ: Jason Aronson, 1999.

Angel, Marc, and Hayyim J. Angel. *Rabbi Haim David Halevy: Gentle Scholar and Courageous Thinker*. Jerusalem: Urim Publications, 2006.

Anson, William Reynell. *Principles of the English Law of Contract*. Oxford: Clarendon Press, 1879.

Aran, Gideon. "Bein halutsi'ut le-limud torah: Ha-reqa le-ge'ut ha-datit le-umit." In vol. 3 of 3, *Me'ah shenot tsiyonut datit*, edited by Avi Sagi and Dov Schwartz, 31–72. Ramat Gan, Israel: Bar-Ilan University, 2003.

Aran, Gideon. "From Religious Zionism to Zionist Religion: The Roots of Gush Emunim." In *The Challenge of Modernity and Jewish Orthodoxy*, edited by Peter Medding, 116–43. Studies in Contemporary Jewry 2. Bloomington: Indiana University Press, 1986.

Aran, Gideon. "A Mystic-Messianic Interpretation of Modern Israeli History: The Six Day War as a Key Event in the Development of the Original Religious Culture of Gush Emunim." In *The Jews and the European Crisis, 1914–1921*, edited by Jonathan Frankel, Peter Y. Medding, and Ezra Mendelsohn, 263–75. Studies in Contemporary Jewry 4. New York: Oxford University Press, 1988.

Aran, Gideon. *Quqism: Shorshei Gush Emunim, tarbut ha-mitnahalim, te'ologiah tsi'onit, meshihi'ut bi-zmanenu.* Jerusalem: Carmel Publishers, 2013.

Ariel, Yaacov. "Ha-mishpat be-medinat yisra'el ve-isur arkha'ot." *Tehumin* 3 (1980): 319–28.

Arnold, Matthew. *Arnold: "Culture and Anarchy: and Other Writings.* Cambridge: Cambridge University Press, 1993.

Aronson, Shlomo. "David Ben-Gurion and the British Constitutional Model." *Israel Studies* 3, no. 2 (1998): 193–214.

Asad, Talal. *Formations of the Secular: Christianity, Islam, Modernity.* Stanford, CA: Stanford University Press, 2003.

Assaf, Simhah. *Batei ha-din ve-sidrehem aharei hatimat ha-Talmud.* Jerusalem: Defus Ha-po'alim, 1924.

Assaf, Simhah. *Ha-onshin aharei hatimat ha-talmud: Homer le-toldot ha-mishpat ha-ivri.* Jerusalem: Defus Ha-po'alim, 1924.

Atlas, Samuel. "Dina d'Malchuta Delimited." *Hebrew Union College Annual*, 1975, 269–88.

Audi, Robert, and Nicholas Wolterstorff. *Religion in the Public Square: The Place of Religious Convictions in Political Debate.* Lanham, MD: Rowman & Littlefield, 1997.

Baer, Yitzhak. "Ha-yesodot veha-hathalot shel irgun ha-qehilah ha-yehudit be-yemei ha-benayim." *Zion* 15 (1950): 1–41.

Bagehot, Walter. *The English Constitution.* New York: Cambridge University Press, 2001.

Bar-Ilan, Meir. "Hoq u-mishpat be-medinatenu." *Yavneh: kovets akadema'i dati* 3 (1949): 29–33 and 151.

Bar-Ilan, Meir. "Hoq u-mishpat be-medinatenu." In *Ha-mishpat ha-ivri u-medinat yisra'el*, edited by Yaakov Bazaq, 20–24. Jerusalem: Mosad Ha-rav Kook, 1969.

Bar-Ilan, Meir. "Hoq u-mishpat be-medinatenu." In *Ha-tsi'onut ha-datit veha-medinah: Qovets ma'amarim li-shloshim shenot ha-medinah*, edited by Yosef Tirosh and Avraham Tirosh, 323–28. Jerusalem: Ha-histadrut ha-tsionut ha-olamit; Ha-mahlaqah le-hinukh ule-tarbut torani'im ba-golah, 1978.

Barak, Aharon. "The Tradition and Culture of the Israel Legal System." In *European Legal Traditions and Israel*, edited by Alfredo Mordechai Rabello, 473–92.

Jerusalem: Harry and Michael Sacher Institute for Legislative Research and Comparative Law; Hebrew University of Jerusalem, 1994.

Barak, Aharon. "The Values of the State of Israel as a Jewish and Democratic State." In *Israel as a Jewish and Democratic State*, edited by Asher Maoz, 6–18. Jewish Law Association Studies XXI. Atlanta: Scholars Press, 1991.

Barak-Erez, Daphne. *Outlawed Pigs: Law, Religion, and Culture in Israel*. Madison: University of Wisconsin Press, 2007.

Baron, Salo W. "'Plenitude of Apostolic Powers' and Medieval 'Jewish Serfdom.'" In *Ancient and Medieval Jewish History: Essays by Salo Wittemayer Baron*, edited by Leon Feldman, 308–22. New Brunswick, NJ: Rutgers University Press, 1972.

Baron, Salo W. *A Social and Religious History of the Jews*. 18 vols. New York: Jewish Publication Society, 1952–1983.

Bartelson, Jens. *A Genealogy of Sovereignty*. Cambridge: Cambridge University Press, 1995.

Bat-Yehudah, Geulah. *Rabbi Maimon in His Generations*. Jerusalem: Mossad Harav Kook, 1998.

Batnitzky, Leora. *How Judaism Became a Religion: An Introduction to Modern Jewish Thought*. Princeton, NJ: Princeton University Press, 2011.

Beaman, Lori G., and Winnifred Fallers Sullivan, eds. *Varieties of Religious Establishment*. Abingdon, Oxon: Routledge, 2016.

Beatty, Aidan. "Zionism and Irish Nationalism: Ideology and Identity on the Borders of Europe." *Journal of Imperial and Commonwealth History* 45, no. 2 (March 4, 2017): 315–38.

Be'eri, Yisrael. "Samkhut ha-malkhut be-medinat yisra'el." In Vol. 1 of 3, *Be-tsomet ha-torah veha-medinah: Mivhar ma'amarim mi-tokh kovtsei "ha-torah veha-medinah" be-arikhah mehudeshet*, edited by Yehudah Shaviv, 33–36. Alon Shevut; Gush Etsion: Mekhon Tsomet, 1991.

Bentham, Jeremy. "An Introductory View of the Rationale of Evidence for the Use of Nonlawyers as Well as Lawyers." In Vol. 6. of 11, *The Works of Jeremy Bentham with an Outline of His Opinions on the Principal Subjects Discussed in His Works*, edited by John Bowring. Edinburgh: W. Tait, 1843.

Benton, Lauren. "Historical Perspectives on Legal Pluralism." *Hague Journal of the Rule of Law* 3, no. 1 (March 2011): 57–69.

Benton, Lauren. *Law and Colonial Cultures: Legal Regimes in World History, 1400–1900*. Cambridge: Cambridge University Press, 2002.

Bentwich, Norman. "The Application of Jewish Law in Palestine." *Journal of Comparative Legislation and International Law* 9, no. 1 (1927): 59–67.

Berger, Peter L. *The Desecularization of the World: Resurgent Religion and World Politics*. Grand Rapids, MI: W. E. Eerdmans, 1999.

Berkovitz, Jay R. *Protocols of Justice: The Pinkas of the Metz Rabbinic Court 1771–1789*. 2 vols. Leiden: Brill, 2014.

Berkowitz, Beth A. *Execution and Invention: Death Penalty Discourse in Early Rabbinic and Christian Cultures*. New York: Oxford University Press, 2006.

Blackstone, William. *Commentaries on the Laws of England*. 5th edition. 4 vols. Oxford: Clarendon Press, printed for William Strahan, Thomas Cadell, and Daniel Prince, 1773.

Bleich, J. David. "The Appeal Process in the Jewish Legal System." In *Contemporary Halakhic Problems* 4:17–45. New York: KTAV Publishing House, Inc., 1995.

Blidstein, Gerald J. "Halakha and Democracy." *Tradition: A Journal of Orthodox Jewish Thought* 32, no. 1 (October 1, 1997): 6–39.

Blidstein, Gerald J. "'Ideal' and 'Real' in Classical Jewish Political Theory." *Jewish Political Studies Review* 2, nos. 1–2 (Spring 1990): 43–66.

Blidstein, Gerald J. "On Lay Legislation in Halakhah: The King as Instance." In *Rabbinic and Lay Communal Authority*, edited by Suzanne Last Stone, 1–18. New York: Michael Scharf Publication Trust of the Yeshiva University Press, 2006.

Blidstein, Gerald. "Torat ha-medinah be-mishnat ha-rav sha'ul yisra'eli." In *Shenei ivrei ha-gesher*, edited by Mordechai Bar-On. Jerusalem: Ben Zvi Institute, 2002.

Bowen, John Richard. *Islam, Law, and Equality in Indonesia: An Anthropology of Public Reasoning*. Cambridge: Cambridge University Press, 2003.

Brand, Yizhak. *Arkhaot shel goyim be-medinat ha-yehudim*. Jerusalem: Israel Democracy Institute, 2010.

Buber, Martin. *Kingship of God*. 1st American ed. New York: Harper & Row, 1967.

Burgansky, Avraham Hayim. "Qehilah u-mamlakhah: Yehasim shel ha-rav y"a hertsog veha-rav sha'ul yisra'eli le-medinat yisra'el." In *Dat u-medinah ba-hagut ha-yehudit ba-me'ah ha-esrim*, edited by Aviezer Ravitzky, 267–94. Jerusalem: Israel Democracy Institute, 2005.

Burns, Robert Ignatius. *Jews in the Notarial Culture: Latinate Wills in Mediterranean Spain, 1250–1350*. Berkeley, CA: University of California Press, 1996.

Burrow, John W. *Evolution and Society: A Study in Victorian Social Theory*. London: Cambridge University Press, 1966.

Caldwell, Peter. *Popular Sovereignty and the Crisis of German Constitutional Law: The Theory & Practice of Weimar Constitutionalism*. Durham, NC: Duke University Press, 1997.

Calliess, Gralf-Peter, and Peer Zumbansen, eds. "Law, the State and Evolutionary Theory." Special issue, *German Law Journal* 9, no. 4 (2008): 389–548.

Casanova, José. *Public Religions in the Modern World*. Chicago: University of Chicago Press, 1994.

Casanova, José. "Religion Challenging the Myth of Secular Democracy." In *Religion in the 21st Century: Challenges and Transformations*, edited by Margit Warburg, Lisbet Christoffersen, Hanne Petersen, and Hans Raun Iversen, 19–36. Farnham, Surrey, England; Burlington, VT: Ashgate, 2010.

Casanova, José. "The Secular, Secularizations, Secularisms." In *Rethinking Secularism*, edited by Craig Calhoun, Mark Juergensmeyer, and Jonathan VanAntwerpen, 54–74. New York: Oxford University Press, 2011.

Casanova, José. "The Stillborn God: The Great Separation." *The Immanent Frame*. Accessed April 13, 2017. http://blogs.ssrc.org/tif/2007/12/07/the-great-separation/.

Cavanaugh, William T. *The Myth of Religious Violence: Secular Ideology and the Roots of Modern Conflict*. New York: Oxford University Press, 2009.

Chigier, Moshe. *Husband and Wife in Israeli Law*. Jerusalem: Mechon Harry Fischel, 1985.

Chigier, Moshe. "The Rabbinical Courts in the State of Israel." *Israel Law Review* 2, no. 2 (1967): 147–81.

Cocks, Raymond. *Sir Henry Maine: A Study in Victorian Jurisprudence*. Cambridge: Cambridge University Press, 2002.

Cohen, Asher. *Ha-talit veha-degel: Ha-tsiyonut ha-datit ve-hazon medinat ha-torah bi-yeme reshit ha-medinah*. Jerusalem: Yad Yitshak Ben-Tsvi, 1998.

Cohen, Asher, and Aaron Kampinsky. "Religious Leadership in Israel's Religious Zionism: The Case of the Board of Rabbis." *Jewish Political Studies Review* 18, nos. 3–4 (October 1, 2006): 119–40.

Cohen, Stuart A. "The Concept of the Three Ketarim: Their Place in Jewish Political Thought and Implications for Studying Jewish Constitutional Theory." In *Kinship & Consent: The Jewish Political Tradition and Its Contemporary Uses*, 2nd edition, edited by Daniel Judah Elazar, 47–76. New Brunswick, NJ: Transaction, 1997.

Comaroff, John L. "Foreword." In *Contested States: Law, Hegemony and Resistance*, edited by Mindie Lazarus-Black and Susan F. Hirsch. New York: Routledge, 2012.

Cook, Beverly B. "Women Judges: A Preface to Their History." *Golden Gate University Law Review* 14, no. 3 (1984): 573–610.

Cooper, Julie E. "Reevaluating Spinoza's Legacy for Jewish Political Thought." *Journal of Politics* 79, no. 2 (January 18, 2017): 473–84.

Cover, Robert. "The Supreme Court, 1982 Term: Foreword: Nomos and Narrative." *Harvard Law Review* 97, no. 4 (1983): 4–68.

Crowley, Weldon S. "Erastianism in England to 1640." *Journal of Church and State* 32, no. 3 (1990): 549–66.

Daikhovsky, Shlomo. "Samkhut batei ha-din ha-rabani'im be-re'i pesiqat batei ha-din." *Diné Israel* 10–11 (March 1981): 9–26.

David, Joseph E. "Beyond the Janus Face of Zionist Legalism: The Theo-Political Conditions of the Jewish Law Project." *Ratio Juris* 18, no. 2 (2005): 206–35.

Diamond, Alan. "The Victorian Achievement of Sir Henry Maine: A Centennial Appraisal," 55–69. Cambridge: Cambridge University Press, 1991.

Dickstein, Paltiel. "Sidrei ha-din be-vatei dinenu ha-leumi'im." *Ha-mishpat ha-ivri* 3 (1928): 191–95.

Don-Yehiya, Eliezer. "Stability and Change in a Political Party: The NRP and the 'Young Guard' Revolution." *Medinah mimshal ve-yahasim ben-le'umi'im* 14 (1980): 25–52.

Eisenstadt, Shmuel. *Tsion be-mishpat*. Tel Aviv: Hamishpat, 1967.

Elazar, Daniel J. "The Kehillah." In *Kinship & Consent: The Jewish Political Tradition and Its Contemporary Uses*, 2nd edition, edited by Daniel Judah Elazar, 233–36. New Brunswick, NJ: Transaction Publishers, 1997.

Eliash, Shulamit. "Ha-rav veha-medina'i, ha-rav ke-medina'i: Ha-yehasim bein ha-rav hertsog ve-emon de valera." In *Bein masoret le-hidush: Mehqarim be-yahadut tsionut u-medinat yisra'el*, edited by Eliezer Don-Yehia, 297–319. Ramat Gan, Israel: Bar-Ilan University, 2005.

Eliash, Shulamit. *The Harp and the Shield of David: Ireland, Zionism and the State of Israel*. Israeli History, Politics and Society 48. Abingdon, Oxon: Routledge, 2007.

Eliash, Shulamit. "Po'alo shel ha-rav hertsog be-inyanei hatzala." In vol. 1 of *Masu'ah le-yitshaq*, edited by Shulamit Eliash, Itamar Warhaftig, and Uri Desberg, 54–83. Jerusalem: Yad Ha-rav Herzog; Mekhon Ha-entsiklopediah Ha-talmudit; Mekhon Ha-talmud Ha-yisre'eli Ha-shalem, 2008.

Eliash, Shulamit. "The Political Role of the Chief Rabbinate of Palestine during the Mandate: Its Character and Nature." *Jewish Social Studies* 47, no. 1 (1985): 33–50.

Eliash, Shulamit. "The 'Rescue' Policy of the Chief Rabbinate of Palestine before and during World War II." *Modern Judaism* 3, no. 3 (1983): 291–308.

Eliyahu, Mordekhai. "Yahas ha-halakhah le-huqei ha-medinah." *Tehumin* 3 (1982): 242–46.

Ellenson, David. *After Emancipation: Jewish Religious Responses to Modernity*. Cincinnati, OH: Hebrew Union College Press, 2004.

Elliott, E. Donald. "The Evolutionary Tradition in Jurisprudence." *Columbia Law Review* 85 (1985): 38–94.

Elon, Menachem. "Ha-mishpat ha-ivri be-mishpat ha-medinah: Al ha-matsui ve-al ha-ratsui." *Ha-praklit* 25 (September 1968): 27–53.

Elon, Menachem. *Haqiqah datit*. Tel Aviv: Ha-kibuts ha-dati, 1968.

Elon, Menachem. *Jewish Law: History, Sources, Principles*. 4 vols. Philadelphia: Jewish Publication Society, 1994.

Elon, Menachem. *Ma'amad ha-ishah*. Tel-Aviv: Ha-qibuts Ha-meuhad, 2005.

Elon, Menachem. "On Power and Authority: The Halakhic Stance of the Traditional Community and Its Conternporary Implications." In *Kinship & Consent: The Jewish Political Tradition and Its Contemporary Uses*, 2nd edition, edited by Daniel Judah Elazar, 293–326. New Brunswick, NJ: Transaction Publishers, 1997.

Englard, Izhak. "The Problem of Jewish Law in a Jewish State." *Israel Law Review* 3 (1968): 254–78.

Englard, Izhak. *Religious Law in the Israel Legal System*. Jerusalem: Hebrew University of Jerusalem Faculty of Law, Harry Sacher Institute for Legislative Research and Comparative Law, 1975.

Ernst, Daniel R. *Tocqueville's Nightmare: The Administrative State Emerges in America, 1900–1940.* Oxford: Oxford University Press, 2014.

Falk, Ze'ev W. *Law and Religion: The Jewish Experience.* Jerusalem: Mesharim, 1981.

Federbusch, Shimon. *Mishpat ha-melukhah be-yisra'el.* Jerusalem: Mosad Ha-rav Kook, 1952.

Figgis, John Neville. *The Divine Right of Kings.* Cambridge: University Press, 1922.

Finkelstein, Louis. *Jewish Self-Government in the Middle Ages.* 2nd edition. New York: Jewish Theological Seminary of America, 1964.

Fischer, Shlomo. "Fundamentalist or Romantic Nationalist: Israeli Modern Orthodoxy." In *Dynamic Jewish Belonging,* edited by Harvey Goldberg, Steven Cohen, and Ezra Kopelowitz, 91–111. New York; Oxford: Berghahn Books, 2012.

Fishman, Aryei. *Judaism and Modernization on the Religious Kibbutz.* Cambridge: Cambridge University Press, 1992.

Fitzpatrick, Peter. *The Mythology of Modern Law.* Sociology of Law and Crime. Abingdon, Oxon: Routledge, 1992.

Fram, Edward. *Ideals Face Reality: Jewish Law and Life in Poland, 1550–1655.* Cincinnati, OH: Hebrew Union College Press, 1997.

Friedman, Menachem. *Hevrah va-dat: Ha-ortodoksiyah ha-lo-tsionit be-erets yisra'el, 1918–1936.* Sifriyah le-toldot ha-yishuv ha-yehudi be-erets yisra'el. Jerusalem: Yad Yitshak Ben-Tvi, 1977.

Friedman, Menachem. "The Structural Foundation for Religio-Political Accommodation in Israel: Fallacy and Reality." In *Israel: The First Decade of Independence,* edited by S. Ilan Troen and Noah Lucas, 51–81. Albany: SUNY Press, 1995.

Friedman, Menachem. "The State of Israel as a Theological Dilemma." In *The Israeli State and Society: Boundaries and Frontiers,* edited by Baruch Kimmerling, 165–215. Albany: SUNY Press, 1989.

Friedman, Natan Tsvi. "Samkhuyoteha shel memshelet medinat yisra'el." *Ha-torah veha-medinah* 1 (1949): 46–49.

Frumer, Haya, ed. *Shahal: Holem ve-lohem.* Jerusalem: Erez, 2008.

Gaimani, Aharon. "Marriage and Divorce Customs in Yemen and Eretz Israel." *Nashim: A Journal of Jewish Women's Studies & Gender Issues,* no. 11 (2006): 43–83.

Galán, Alexis, and Dennis Patterson. "The Limits of Normative Legal Pluralism: Review of Paul Schiff Berman, Global Legal Pluralism; A Jurisprudence of Law beyond Borders." *International Journal of Constitutional Law* 11, no. 3 (July 1, 2013): 783–800.

Gale, Susan Gaylord. "Very German Legal Science: Savigny and the Historical School." *Stanford Journal of International Law* 18 (1982): 123–46.

Garb, Yehonatan. "Tse'irei ha-mafda"l ve-shorshav ha-ra'ayoni'im shel gush emunim." In *Ha-tsionut ha-datit: Idan ha-temurot,* edited by Asher Cohen, 171–200. Jerusalem: Bialik Institute, 2004.

Gerondi, Nisim ben Reuben. *Derashot ha-ran ha-shalem.* Edited by Leon A. Feldman and Mordekhai Leyb Katzenelenbogen. Jerusalem: Mosad Ha-rav Kook, 2003.

Gillespie, Michael Allen. *The Theological Origins of Modernity.* Chicago: University of Chicago Press, 2009.

Ginzberg, Yitzhak. *Mishpatim le-yisra'el: Ha-hoq ha-pelili ve-dinei ha-onshin bizman hazeh le-fi mishpat ha-torah, ha-talmud u-meforshim.* Jerusalem: Mechon Harry Fischel, 1956.

Goldman, Eliezer. "Hoq ha-medinah veha-halakhah—Ha-omnam setirah?" In *Mahshavot al demoqratiah yehudit,* edited by Benny Porat and Aviezer Ravitzky, 165–75. Jerusalem: Israel Democracy Institute, 2010.

Gorontchik, Shlomo (Goren). "Huqah toranit ketsad?" In vol. 1 of *Tehuqah le-yisra'el al-pi ha-torah,* edited by Itamar Warhaftig, 146–56. Jerusalem: Mosad Ha-rav Kook; Yad Ha-rav Herzog, 1989.

Gottlieb, Isaac B. "The Politics of Pronunciation." *AJS Review* 32, no. 2 (2008): 335–68.

Greenberger, Ben Tzion. "Rabbi Herzog's Proposals for Takkanot in Matters of Inheritance." In *The Halakhic Thought of R. Isaac Herzog,* edited by Bernard S. Jackson. Jewish Law Association Studies V. Atlanta: Scholars Press, 1991.

Griffiths, J. "What Is Legal Pluralism?" *Journal of Legal Pluralism and Unofficial Law* 18, no. 24 (1986): 1–55.

Grossman, Avraham. "Yahasam shel hakhmei Ashkenaz ha-rishonim el shilton ha-qahal." *Shenaton ha-mishpat ha-ivri* 2 (1975): 175–99.

Gulak, Asher. *Yesodei ha-mishpat ha-ivri: Seder dine memonot be-yisra'el al-pi mekorot ha-talmud veha-poskim.* 4 vols. Berlin: Devir, 1922.

Hadaya, Ovadiah. *Yaskil avdi.* Jerusalem: n.p., 1931.

Halperin, Liora R. *Babel in Zion: Jews, Nationalism, and Language Diversity in Palestine, 1920–1948.* New Haven, CT: Yale University Press, 2014.

Halperin-Kaddari, Ruth. "Expressions of Legal Pluralism in Israel: The Interaction between the High Court of Justice and Rabbinical Courts in Family Matters and Beyond." In *Jewish Family Law in Israel,* edited by M.D.A. Freeman, 185–244. Jewish Law Association Studies 13. Binghamton, NY: Global Publications, State University of New York at Binghamton, 2002.

Halperin-Kaddari, Ruth. *Women in Israel: A State of Their Own.* Philadelphia: University of Pennsylvania Press, 2004.

Hamburger, Philip. *Is Administrative Law Unlawful?* Chicago: University of Chicago Press, 2014.

Hamburger, Philip. *Separation of Church and State.* Cambridge, MA: Harvard University Press, 2009.

Hanbury, H. G. "The Place of Roman Law in the Teaching of Law to-Day." *Journal of the Society of Public Teachers of Law* (1931): 14–25.

Harvey, Warren Zev. "Liberal Democratic Themes in Nissim of Girona." In *Studies in Medieval Jewish History and Literature III,* edited by Isadore Twerski and Jay M. Harris, 197–211. Cambridge, MA: Harvard University Press, 2000.

Härter, Karl. "Security and 'Gute Policey' in Early Modern Europe: Concepts, Laws, and Instruments." *Historical Social Research* 35, no. 4 (134) (2010): 41–65.

Heidenheimer, Arnold J. "Politics, Policy and Policey as Concepts in English and Continental Languages: An Attempt to Explain Divergences." *Review of Politics* 48, no. 1 (January 1986): 3–30.

Hellinger, Moshe, and Itzhak Hershkovits. *Tsiut ve-i-tsiut be-tsionut ha-datit: Mi-Gush Emunim ve-ad tag mehir.* Jerusalem: Israel Democracy Institute, 2015.

Helman, Anat. *Becoming Israeli: National Ideals and Everyday Life in the 1950s.* Waltham, MA: Brandeis University Press, 2014.

Hermann, Tamar, Gil'ad Be'eri, Ela Heler, Hanan Kohen, Yuval Lavel, Hanan Mozes, and Kalman Neuman. "Dati'im? Le'umi'im!—Ha-mahaneh ha-dati le'umi." Jerusalem: Israel Democracy Institute, 2014.

Hertzberg, Arthur. *The Zionist Idea: A Historical Analysis and Reader.* Philadelphia: Jewish Publication Society, 1997.

Herzog, Chaim. *Living History: A Memoir.* New York: Pantheon Books, 1996.

Herzog, Isaac. "The Administration of Justice in Ancient Israel: 1. The Reconstruction of the Judiciary by Ezra." *Jewish Forum* 14, no. 3 (March 1931): 84–88.

Herzog, Isaac. "The Administration of Justice in Ancient Israel: 2. The Bet Din." *Jewish Forum* 14, no. 11 (November 1931): 404–8.

Herzog, Isaac. "The Administration of Justice in Ancient Israel: 3. The Appointment of Judges and Their Ordination." *Jewish Forum* 14, no. 12 (December 1931): 436–39.

Herzog, Isaac. "The Administration of Justice in Ancient Israel: 4. The Sanhedrin." *Jewish Forum* 15, no. 5 (May 1932): 165–70.

Herzog, Isaac. "The Administration of Justice in Ancient Israel." In *Judaism: Law and Ethics,* by Isaac Herzog, 107–43. London: Soncino Press, 1974.

Herzog, Isaac. "The Assignment of Rights in Jewish Law." *Juridical Review* 43 (1931): 127.

Herzog, Isaac. "Al mishpat ha-torah be-yisra'el." In vol. 1 of *Halakhah pesuqah: Mishpat ha-torah li-meqorotav be-talmud u-posqim al seder ha-shulkhan arukh,* 11–15. Jerusalem: Mechon Harry Fischel, 1962.

Herzog, Isaac. "Be-qesher le-ma'amarav ha-hashuvim shel ha-rav r. shlomo goront-chik beha-tzofe." In vol. 1 of *Tehuqah le-yisra'el al-pi ha-torah,* edited by Itamar Warhaftig, 57–80. Jerusalem: Mosad Ha-rav Kook; Yad Ha-rav Herzog, 1989.

Herzog, Isaac. "Din ha-melekh ve-din ha-torah." *Talpiyot* 7, no. 1 (Tishrei [5]718 [1947]): 4–32.

Herzog, Isaac. "Ha-medinah ha-yisre'elit ap"i hashqafat ha-mesoret veha-demoqratiah." In vol. 1 of *Tehuqah le-yisra'el al-pi ha-torah,* edited by Itamar Warhaftig, 7–11. Jerusalem: Mosad Ha-rav Kook; Yad Ha-rav Herzog, 1989.

Herzog, Isaac. *Ha-mosdot ha-ikari'im shel ha-mishpat ha-ivri.* Translated by Moshe Hershkovits. Rishon le-Zion, Israel: Yedioth Ahronoth Books; Miskal, Israel: Chemed Books, 2016.

Herzog, Isaac. "Ha-tehiqah veha-mishpat be-medinah ha-yehudit." *Yavneh: Qovets akademai dati* 3 (1949): 9–13.

Herzog, Isaac. "Ha-tehiqah veha-mishpat be-medinah ha-yehudit." In vol. 1 of *Tehuqah le-yisrael al-pi ha-torah*, edited by Itamar Warhaftig, 205–9. Jerusalem: Mosad Ha-rav Kook; Yad Ha-rav Herzog, 1989.

Herzog, Isaac. "John Selden and Jewish Law." *Journal of Comparative Legislation and International Law* 13, no. 4 (1931): 236–45.

Herzog, Isaac. "John Selden and Jewish Law." In *Judaism: Law and Ethics*, 67–79. London: Soncino Press, 1974.

Herzog, Isaac. *Judaism: Law and Ethics* by Isaac Herzog. London: Soncino Press, 1974.

Herzog, Isaac. "Legacies to Creditors and Satisfaction of Debt in Jewish Law." *Temple Law Quarterly* 6 (1931): 87.

Herzog, Isaac. "Moral Rights and Duties in Jewish Law." *Juridical Review* 41 (1929): 60.

Herzog, Isaac. *Pesaqim u-khetavim.* Vol. 9 of 9: *Teshuvot al hoshen mishpat.* Jerusalem: Mosad Ha-rav Kook; Yad Ha-rav Herzog, 1989.

Herzog, Isaac. "Possession in Jewish Law." *Temple Law Quarterly* 4 (1929–30): 329–38.

Herzog, Isaac. "Possession in Jewish Law Part II." *Temple Law Quarterly* 5 (January 1930): 260–71.

Herzog, Isaac. "Possession in Jewish Law Part III." *Temple Law Quarterly* 5 (January 1930): 598–612.

Herzog, Isaac. "Rabbi Herzog on the Chief Rabbinate (ca. 1948)." In *The Origins of Israel, 1882–1948: A Documentary History*, edited by Eran Kaplan and Derek Penslar, translated by Alexander Kaye. Madison: University of Wisconsin Press, 2011.

Herzog, Isaac. "Samkhut ha-torah be-medinat yisrael." In vol. 1 of *Tehuqah le-yisrael al-pi ha-torah*, edited by Itamar Warhaftig, 221–28. Jerusalem: Mosad Ha-rav Kook; Yad Ha-rav Herzog, 1989.

Herzog, Isaac. *Shu"t hekhal yitshaq.* 3 vols. Jerusalem: Agudah le-hotsaat kitve rosh ha-rabanim ha-gria"h Hertsog zts"l, 1960, 1960–72.

Herzog, Isaac. "Tehei yerushalayim birat yisrael ve-torato—huqatah." *Ha-tsofeh*, August 1, 1948.

Herzog, Isaac. *Tehuqah le-yisrael al-pi ha-torah.* Edited by Itamar Warhaftig. 3 vols. Jerusalem: Mosad Ha-rav Kook; Yad Ha-rav Herzog, 1989.

Herzog, Isaac. *The Main Institutions of Jewish Law.* Paperback. 2 vols. London, New York: Soncino Press, 1980.

Herzog, Isaac. "The Outlook of Greek Culture upon Judaism." In *Judaism: Law and Ethics*, 211–23. London: Soncino Press, 1974.

Herzog, Isaac. *The Royal Purple and the Biblical Blue: Argaman and Tekhelet; The Study of Chief Rabbi Dr. Isaac Herzog on the Dye Industries in Ancient Israel and Recent Scientific Contributions.* Jerusalem: Keter, 1987.

Herzog, Isaac. "The Sources of Jewish Law." *Temple Law Quarterly* 5 (January 1930): 47–65.

Herzog, Yoel Leib Ha-levi. *Imrei yo'el al sefer bereshit*. London: Express, 1921.

Heschel, Abraham Joshua. *Moral Grandeur and Spiritual Audacity: Essays*. New York: Farrar, Straus and Giroux, 1997.

Hillman, Samuel Isaac, ed. *Mikhtevei ha-rabanim ha-gedolim de-ara de-yisra'el al ha-yeshivah gedolah "ohel torah" beit david bet midrash gavoah le-hishtalmut avrekhim rabanim*. Jerusalem: Ohel Torah, n.d.

Hillman, Samuel Isaac. *Or ha-yashar al masekhet bekhorot*. London: Express, 1921.

Hoeflich, Michael H. *Roman and Civil Law and the Development of Anglo-American Jurisprudence in the Nineteenth Century*. Athens, GA: University of Georgia Press, 1997.

Hofri-Winogradow, Adam S. "Plurality of Discontent: Legal Pluralism, Religious Adjudication and the State." *Journal of Law and Religion* 26, no. 1 (2010): 101–33.

Hofstadter, Richard. *Social Darwinism in American Thought*. Boston: Beacon Press, 1993.

Howe, Mark De Wolfe. *The Garden and the Wilderness: Religion and Government in American Constitutional History*. Chicago: University of Chicago Press, 1967.

Huntingdon, Samuel P. *The Clash of Civilizations and the Remaking of the World Order*. New York: Simon and Schuster, 1996.

Inbari, Motti. *Messianic Religious Zionism Confronts Israeli Territorial Compromises*. Reprint edition. New York: Cambridge University Press, 2014.

Jackson, Bernard S. *Essays in Jewish and Comparative Legal History*. Leiden: Brill, 1975.

Jackson, Bernard S. "Judaism as a Religious Legal System." In *Religion, Law and Tradition: Comparative Studies in Religious Law*, edited by Andrew Huxley, 34–48. Abingdon, Oxon: Routledge, 2012.

Jotkowitz, Alan. "Eliezer Goldman and Judaism without Illusion." *Modern Judaism* 35, no. 2 (2015): 134–46.

Karp, Yehudit. "Ha-mo'atsa ha-mishpatit: Reshit alilot haqiqa." In vol. 2 of *Sefer Uri Yadin*, edited by Aharon Barak and Tara Shpanitz, 209–56. Tel Aviv: Bursi, 1990.

Katz, Ethan B., Lisa Moses Leff, and Maud S. Mandel, eds. *Colonialism and the Jews*. Bloomfield, Indiana University Press, 2017.

Katz, Jacob. *A House Divided: Orthodoxy and Schism in Nineteenth-Century Central European Jewry*. Hanover, NH: Brandeis University Press, 1998.

Katz, Shmuel. "Bibliografiah le-kitvei hgry"y hertsog zts"l." In vol. 1 of *Masu'ah le-yitshaq*, edited by Shulamit Eliash, Itamar Warhaftig, and Uri Desberg, 277–86. Jerusalem: Yad Ha-rav Herzog; Mekhon Ha-entsiklopediah Ha-talmudit; Mekhon Ha-talmud Ha-yisre'eli Ha-shalem, 2008.

Katz, Shmuel. "Toldot hayav shel ha-rav sha'ul yisra'eli zts"l." Accessed June 11, 2019. http://www.eretzhemdah.org//Data/UploadedFiles/SitePages/896-sFileRedir. pdf.

Kaveny, Cathleen. *Prophecy without Contempt*. Cambridge, MA: Harvard University Press, 2016.

Kaye, Alexander. "Democratic Themes in Religious Zionism." *Shofar: An Interdisciplinary Journal of Jewish Studies* 31, no. 2 (2013): 8–30.

Kaye, Alexander. "Eliezer Goldman and the Origins of Meta-Halacha." *Modern Judaism* 34, no. 3 (January 10, 2014): 309–33.

Kaye, Alexander. "The Legal Philosophies of Religious Zionism 1937–1967." Ph.D. Dissertation, Columbia University, 2013.

Kedar, Nir. "Ben-Gurion's Mamlakhtiyut: Etymological and Theoretical Roots." *Israel Studies* 7, no. 3 (2002): 117–33.

Kedar, Nir. *Ben-Gurion veha-huqah*. Or Yehudah: Devir ; Bar-Ilan University Press, 2015.

Kedar, Nir. "Law, Culture, and Civil Codification in a Mixed Legal System." *Canadian Journal of Law and Society* 22, no. 2 (2007): 177–95.

Kedar, Nir. *Mamlakhti'ut: Ha-tefisah ha-ezrahit shel david ben-gurion*. Beersheba: Mekhon Ben-Gurion le-heqer yisra'el, Ben-Gurion University in the Negev; Yad Yitshak Ben Tsvi, 2009.

Kelsen, Hans. "On the Pure Theory of Law." *Israel Law Review* 1, no. 1 (1966): 1–7.

Keogh, Dermot. *Jews in Twentieth Century Ireland: Refugees, Anti-Semitism and the Holocaust*. Cork, Ireland: Cork University Press, 1998.

Kimble, Sara L. "No Right to Judge: Feminism and the Judiciary in Third Republic France." *French Historical Studies* 31, no. 4 (2008): 609–41.

Kirschenbaum, Aharon. "Jewish Theocracy." *Diné Israel* 8 (1977): 223–34.

Knoblauch, Hubert. "Spirituality and Popular Religion in Europe." *Social Compass* 55, no. 2 (2008): 140–53.

Kohen, Yehezqel. "Rabanut kevusha?" In *Ha-tsionut ha-datit be-re'iyah mehudeshet*, edited by Meir Roth, 215–19. Ein Tsurim, Israel: Ne'emanei Torah Va-avodah, 1998.

Kohen, Yitzhak. "Shiput rabani ve-shiput hiloni." *Diné Israel* 7 (1976): 205–13.

Kook, Abraham Isaac. *Mishpat kohen*. 2nd edition. Jerusalem: Mosad Ha-rav Kook, 1966.

Kook, Abraham Isaac. *Orot*. Jerusalem: Mosad Ha-rav Kook, 1961.

Kuru, Ahmet T. *Secularism and State Policies toward Religion: The United States, France, and Turkey*. Cambridge: Cambridge University Press, 2009.

Kymlicka, Will. *Multicultural Citizenship: A Liberal Theory of Minority Rights*. Oxford: Clarendon Press, 1995.

Lahav, Pnina. "The Supreme Court of Israel: Formative Years, 1948–1955." *Studies in Zionism* 11, no. 1 (March 1990): 45–66.

Landau, Shmuel Hayim. *Kitve Sh. H. Landau* (Jerusalem: Ha-tenu'ah ha-olamit shel ha-mizrahi-ha-po'el ha-mizrahi, "yad shapira," mifal hantsahah le-zikhro shel H M Shapira, 1984).

Lau, Binyamin. *Mi-maran ad maran: Mishnato ha-hilkhatit shel ha-rav Ovadiah Yosef*. Tel Aviv: Yedi'ot Aharonot; Sifrei Hemed, 2005.

Leibowitz, Yeshayahu, and Aviezer Ravitzky. *Vikuhim al emunah ve-filosofiyah*. Universitah Meshuderet. Tel Aviv: Ministry of Defence, 2006.

Lichtenstein, Aharon. "Communal Governance, Lay and Rabbinic: An Overview." In *Rabbinic and Lay Communal Authority*, edited by Suzanne Last Stone, 19–52. New York: Michael Scharf Publication Trust of the Yeshiva University Press, 2006.

Lichtenstein, Aharon. "Religion and State." In *Contemporary Jewish Religious Thought: Original Essays on Critical Concepts, Movements, and Beliefs*, edited by Arthur Allen Cohen and Paul R. Mendes-Flohr, 773–78. New York: Free Press, 1988.

Lieberman, Saul. "Achievements and Aspirations of Modern Jewish Scholarship." *Proceedings of the American Academy for Jewish Research* 46–47 (1979): 369–80.

Liebman, Charles S., and Eliezer Don-Yehiya. *Civil Religion in Israel: Traditional Judaism and Political Culture in the Jewish State*. Berkeley, CA: University of California Press, 1983.

Likhovski, Assaf. "Between Mandate and State: On the Periodization of Israeli Legal History." *Journal of Israeli History* 19, no. 2 (1998): 39–68.

Likhovski, Assaf. "In Our Image: Colonial Discourse and the Anglicization of the Law of Mandatory Palestine." *Israel Law Review* 29, no. 3 (Summer 1995).

Likhovski, Assaf. *Law and Identity in Mandate Palestine*. Chapel Hill: University of North Carolina Press, 2006.

Likhovski, Assaf. "Peripheral Vision: Polish-Jewish Lawyers and Early Israeli Law." *Law and History Review* 36, no. 2 (2018): 235–66.

Likhovski, Assaf. "The Invention of 'Hebrew Law' in Mandatory Palestine." *American Journal of Comparative Law* 46, no. 2 (1998): 339–73.

Likhovski, Assaf. "The Ottoman Legacy of Israeli Law." *Annales de la Faculté de droit d'Istanbul* 39 (2007): 71–86.

Likhovski, Assaf. "Two Horwitzian Journeys." In *Transformations in American Legal History: Essays in Honor of Professor Morton J. Horwitz*, edited by Morton J. Horwitz, Daniel W. Hamilton, and Alfred L. Brophy, 300–318. Cambridge, MA: Harvard Law School. Distributed by Harvard University Press, 2009.

Lilla, Mark. *The Stillborn God: Religion, Politics, and the Modern West*. Reprint edition. New York: Vintage, 2008.

Locke, John. *A Letter Concerning Toleration and Other Writings*. Edited by Mark Goldie. Indianapolis, IN: Liberty Fund, 2010.

Loeffler, James. *Rooted Cosmopolitans: Jews and Human Rights in the Twentieth Century*. New Haven, CT: Yale University Press, 2018.

Lorberbaum, Menachem. *Politics and the Limits of Law: Secularizing the Political in Medieval Jewish Thought*. Stanford, CA: Stanford University Press, 2001.

Lorberbaum, Menachem. "Questioning Territory: A Jewish Reflection on Holy Land." *The Immanent Frame*. Accessed October 11, 2019. https://tif.ssrc.org/2017/06/29/questioning-territory-a-jewish-reflection-on-holy-land/.

Lorca, Arnulf Becker. "Universal International Law: Nineteenth-Century Histories of Imposition and Appropriation." *Harvard Internationall Law Journal* 51 (2010): 475–552.

Luz, Ehud. *Parallels Meet: Religion and Nationalism in the Early Zionist Movement (1882–1904)*. Philadelphia: Jewish Publication Society, 1988.

Mahla, Daniel. "No Trinity: The Tripartite Relations between Agudat Yisrael, the Mizrahi Movement, and the Zionist Organization." *Journal of Israeli History* 34, no. 2 (July 3, 2015): 117–40.

Maimon Fishman, Yehudah Leib Hakohen. *Hidush ha-sanhedrin bi-medinatenu ha-mehudeshet*. 2nd edition. Kitvei ha-rav Y. L. Maimon 4. Jerusalem: Mosad Ha-rav Kook, 1951.

Maine, Henry Sumner. *Ancient Law*. Boston: Beacon Press, 1963.

Makovsky, Zvi. "A"d yesod by"d ha-gadol bi-yerushalayim." *Ha-hed* 12 (1935).

Makovsky, Zvi. *Ve-ashiva shoftayikh*. Tel Aviv: Defus A. Moses, 1938.

Manchester, A. H. *A Modern Legal History of England and Wales 1750–1950*. London: Butterworths, 1980.

Mantena, Karuna. *Alibis of Empire: Henry Maine and the Ends of Liberal Imperialism*. Princeton, NJ: Princeton University Press, 2010.

Maoz, Asher. "Ha-rabanut u-vet ha-din: Ben patish ha-hoq le-sadan ha-halakhah." *Shenaton ha-mishpat ha-ivri* 16–17 (January 1990): 289.

Marglin, Jessica M. *Across Legal Lines: Jews and Muslims in Modern Morocco*. New Haven, CT: Yale University Press, 2016.

Margulies, Reuven. "Batei ha-mishpat be-erets yisra'el." In *Tal tehi'ah*, 41–51. Lwow, Poland: Bet meshar sefarim hadashim ve-atiqim, 1922.

Margulies, Reuven. *Tal tehi'ah*. Lwow, Poland: Bet meshar sefarim hadashim ve-atiqim, 1922.

Mautner, Menachem. *Law and the Culture of Israel*. Oxford; New York: Oxford University Press, 2011.

Mautner, Menachem. "Three Approaches to Law and Culture." *Cornell Law Review* 96 (2010): 839.

McLaren, James S. *Power and Politics in Palestine: The Jews and the Governing of Their Land, 100 BC–AD 70*. Sheffield: JSOT Press, 2015.

Meir, Yedidiah, and Sivan Rahav-Meir, eds. *Yamim ketomim: Ha-hitnatqut—Ha-heshbon veha-nefesh*. Tel Aviv: Yedi'ot Aharonot; Sifrei Hemed, 2006.

Mayzlish, Shaul. *The Rabbinate in Stormy Days: The Life and Teachings of Rabbi Yitzhak Isaac Halevi Herzog, the First Chief Rabbi of Israel*. Translated by Yoreh Tanhum. Springfield, NJ: Gefen, 2017.

Mayzlish, Shaul. "Toldot ha-rav hertsog." In vol. 1 of 2, *Masu'ah le-yitshaq*, edited by Shulamit Eliash, Itamar Warhaftig, and Uri Desberg, 3–53. Jerusalem: Yad Ha-rav Herzog; Mekhon Ha-entsiklopediah Ha-talmudit; Mekhon Ha-talmud Ha-yisra'eli Ha-shalem, 2008.

Merry, Sally Engle. "Legal Pluralism." *Law and Society Review* 22, no. 5 (1988): 869–96.

Merryman, John Henry, and Rogelio Pérez-Perdomo. *The Civil Law Tradition: An Introduction to the Legal Systems of Europe and Latin America*. Stanford, CA: Stanford University Press, 2007.

Milman, Henry Hart. Vol. 1 of 3, *The History of the Jews: From the Earliest Period down to Modern Times*. 5th edition. London: J. Murray, 1883.

Mirsky, Yehudah. *Rav Kook: Mystic in a Time of Revolution*. New Haven, CT: Yale University Press, 2014.

Mittleman, Alan. *The Scepter Shall Not Depart from Judah: Perspectives on the Persistence of the Political in Judaism*. Lanham, MD: Lexington Books, 2000.

Morag-Levine, Noga. *Chasing the Wind: Regulating Air Pollution in the Common Law State*. Princeton, NJ: Princeton University Press, 2009.

Morgenstern, Aryeh. *Ha-rabanut ha-rashit le-erets yisra'el: Yisodah ve-irgunah*. Jerusalem: Shorashim, 1973.

Morris, Benny. *Righteous Victims: A History of the Zionist-Arab Conflict, 1881–1998*. New York: Vintage, 2001.

Mousourakis, George. *Roman Law and the Origins of the Civil Law Tradition*. Cham, Switzerland: Springer, 2015.

Moyn, Samuel. *Christian Human Rights*. Philadelphia: University of Pennsylvania Press, 2015.

Murdoch, Iris. *The Sovereignty of Good*. New York: Schocken Books, 1971.

Myers, David N. *Re-Inventing the Jewish Past: European Jewish Intellectuals and the Zionist Return to History*. New York: Oxford University Press, 1995.

Myers, David N., and Nomi Stolzenberg. "Rethinking Secularization Theory: The Case of the Hasidic Public Square." *AJS Perspectives*, Spring 2011: 37–8.

Nelson, Eric. *The Hebrew Republic*. Cambridge, MA: Harvard University Press, 2010.

Neumark, David, and Samuel Solomon Cohon. *Toldot ha-pilosofiyah be-yisra'el*. New York: A. I. Shtibel, 1921.

Neis, Rachel Rafael. "The Seduction of Law: Rethinking Legal Studies in Jewish Studies." *Jewish Quarterly Review* 109, no. 1 (Winter 2019): 119–38.

Newman, Julius. *Semikhah (Ordination): A Study of Its Origin, History, and Function in Rabbinic Literature*. Manchester, UK: Manchester University Press, 1950.

Ohana, David. *Nationalizing Judaism: Zionism as a Theological Ideology*. Lanham, MD: Lexington Books, 2017.

Okin, Susan Moller. *Is Multiculturalism Bad for Women?* Princeton, NJ: Princeton University Press, 1999.

Ousiel, Bentsion Meir Hai. "Yesodot din ha-malkhut be-yisra'el uva-amim." *Ha-torah veha-medinah* 5–6 (1953–54): 15–21.

Oz, Amos. *In the Land of Israel*. Orlando, FL: Houghton Mifflin Harcourt, 1993.

Oz-Salzberger, Fania, and Eli Salzberger. "The Secret German Sources of the Israeli Supreme Court." *Israel Studies* 3, no. 2 (1998): 159–92.

Örücü, Esin. "The Impact of European Law on the Ottoman Empire and Turkey." In *European Expansion and Law: The Encounter of European and Indigenous Law in 19th- and 20th-Century Africa and Asia*, edited by W. J. Mommsen and J. A. de Moor, 39–58. Oxford; New York: Berg, 1992.

Paldiel, Mordecai. *Saving One's Own: Jewish Rescuers during the Holocaust*. Lincoln, University of Nebraska Press, 2017.

Pedahzur, Ami, and Arie Perliger. *Jewish Terrorism in Israel*. New York: Columbia University Press, 2009.

Penslar, Derek J. "Zionism, Colonialism and Postcolonialism." *Journal of Israeli History* 20, nos. 2–3 (June 2001): 84–98.

Pocock, J. G. A. "The Concept of Language and the *métier d'historien*: Some Considerations on Practice." In *The Languages of Political Theory in Early-Modern Europe*, edited by Anthony Robin Pagden, 19–38. Cambridge: Cambridge University Press, 1987.

Porat, Benny. "Hamishah musagim yehudi'im shel demoqratiah yisre'elit: Masat peti-hah." In *Mahshavot al demoqratiah yehudit*, edited by Aviezer Ravitzky, 17–27. Jerusalem: Israel Democracy Institute, 2010.

Rabinovich, Itamar, and Jehuda Reinharz. *Israel in the Middle East: Documents and Readings on Society, Politics, and Foreign Relations, Pre-1948 to the Present*. Waltham, MA: Brandeis University Press; Hanover NH: University Press of New England, 2008.

Rabinowitz-Teomim, Binyamin. *Ha-haqiqah al-pi mishpat ha-torah: Erkah, ba'ayotehah, u-derakhehah*. Jerusalem: Bet ha-midrash le-mishpat ha-torah, mahlakat ha-hakika, 1950.

Rabinowitz-Teomim. *Hilkhot mekhira*. Jerusalem: Mechon Harry Fischel, 1957.

Rackman, Emanuel. *Israel's Emerging Constitution, 1948–51*. New York: Columbia University Press, 1955.

Rackman, Emanuel. "Religious Problems in the Making of the Israeli Constitution (1948–1951), The." *Lawyers Guild Review* 13 (1953): 69–78.

Radzyner, Amihai. "Al reshitan shel taqanot ha-diyun be-vatei din ha-rabani'im: 'Sidrei ha-mishpatim,' [5]681." *Bar-Ilan Studies in Law* 25, no. 1 (2009): 37–76.

Radzyner, Amihai. "Between Scholar and Jurist: The Controversy over the Research of Jewish Law Using Comparative Methods at the Early Time of the Field." *Journal of Law and Religion* 23, no. 1 (2007): 189–248.

Radzyner, Amihai. "A Constitution for Israel: The Design of the Leo Kohn Proposal, 1948." *Israel Studies* 15, no. 1 (2010): 1–24.

Radzyner, Amihai. "Halakhah, Law and Worldview: Chief Rabbis Goren and Yosef and the Permission to Marry a Second Wife in Israeli Law." *Diné Israel*, no. 32 (2018): 261–304.

Radzyner, Amihai. "The Impact of Supreme Court Rulings on the Halakhic Status of the Official Rabbinical Courts in Israel." In *Institutionalizing Rights and*

Religion: Competing Supremacies, edited by Leora Batnitzky and Hanoch Dagan, 224–40. Cambridge: Cambridge University Press, 2017.

Radzyner, Amihai. "The Irish Influence on the Israeli Constitution Proposal, 1948." In *The Constitution of Ireland: Perspectives and Prospects*, edited by Eoin Carolan. Haywards Heath: Bloomsbury Professional, 2012.

Radzyner, Amihai. "Jewish Law in London: Between Two Societies." In *Jewish Law Annual 18*, edited by Berachyahu Lifshitz, 81–135. London; New York: Routledge, 2009.

Radzyner, Amihai. "Mi-dogmatist le-historion: Asher gulak ve-heqer ha-mishpat ha-ivri be-universitah ha-ivrit 1925–1940." Edited by Gershon Bacon, Devorah Dimant, Ithamar Gruenwald, and Marc Hirshman. *Mada'ei yahadut* 43 (June 2005): 169–200.

Radzyner, Amihai. "Milhamot he-yehudim: Itsuvo shel isur ha-bigamiah la-yehudim be-erets yisra'el ha-mandatorit." In *Huqah ahat u-mishpat ehad la-ish veha-ishah*, edited by Ruth Halperin-Kaddari, Margalit Shilo, and Ayal Katvan, 151–98. Ramat Gan, Israel: Bar-Ilan University, 2010.

Radzyner, Amihai. "Reshitan shel taqanot ha-diyun be-vatei din ha-rabani'im: Taqanot [5]703." *Diné Israel* 25 (2008): 185–260.

Radzyner, Amihai, and Shuki Friedman. "Ha-mehoqeq ha-yisre'eli veha-mishpat ha-ivri: Hayim kohn ben mahar le-etmol." *Iyunei Mishpat* 29, no. 6 (2005): 167–244.

Radzyner, Amihai, and Shuki Friedman. *Huqah she-lo ketuvah ba-Torah.* Jerusalem: Israel Democracy Institute, 2006.

Rafel, Yoel. "Zehuto shel mehaber ha-tefilah li-shlom ha-medinah." In vol. 1 of *Masu'ah le-yitshaq*, edited by Shulamit Eliash, Itamar Warhaftig, and Uri Desberg, 594–620. Jerusalem: Yad Ha-rav Herzog; Mekhon Ha-entsiklopediah Ha-talmudit; Mekhon Ha-talmud Ha-yisre'eli Ha-shalem, 2008.

Rajak, Tessa. "Jews and Greeks: The Invention and Exploitation of Polarities in the Nineteenth Century." In *The Jewish Dialogue with Greece and Rome: Studies in Cultural and Social Interaction*, 535–58. Leiden: Brill, 2002.

Rashkover, Randi, and Martin Kavka, eds. *Judaism, Liberalism, and Political Theology*. Bloomington: Indiana University Press, 2013.

Ravitzky, Aviezer. "Is a Halakhic State Possible? The Paradox of Jewish Theocracy." *Israel Affairs* 11, no. 1 (2005): 137–64.

Ravitzky, Aviezer. *Messianism, Zionism, and Jewish Religious Radicalism*. Chicago: University of Chicago Press, 1996.

Ravitzky, Aviezer. *Religion and State in Jewish Philosophy: Models of Unity, Division, Collision and Subordination.* Jerusalem: Israel Democracy Institute, 2001.

Rawls, John. *A Theory of Justice.* Cambridge, MA: Harvard University Press, 2009.

Rechnitz, Ido. *Mishpat ha-torah be-medinat yisra'el.* Ofra, Israel: Makhon mishpetei eretz, 2007.

Reinach, Théodore. *Textes d'auteurs grecs et romains relatifs au judaïsme*. Paris: E. Leroux, 1895.

Reyntjens, Filip. "The Development of the Dual Legal System in Former Belgian Central Africa (Zaire-Rwnda-Brundi)." In *European Expansion and Law: The Encounter of European and Indigenous Law in 19th- and 20th-Century Africa and Asia*, edited by W. J. Mommsen and J. A. de Moor, 111–27. Oxford; New York: Berg, 1992.

Robinson, Ira, and Maxine Jacobson. "'When Orthodoxy Was Not as Chic as It Is Today': The Jewish Forum and American Modern Orthodoxy." *Modern Judaism* 31, no. 3 (2011): 285–313.

Roness, Yitzchak. "Mishnato ha-hilkhatit shel ha-rav sha'ul yisra'eli." Ph.D. Dissertation, Bar-Ilan University, 2012.

Rosen, Lawrence. *Law as Culture: An Invitation*. Princeton, NJ: Princeton University Press, 2006.

Rosenblatt, Jason P. *Renaissance England's Chief Rabbi: John Selden*. Oxford: Oxford University Press, 2006.

Roth, Pinchas. "Legal Strategy and Legal Culture in Medieval Jewish Courts of Southern France." *AJS Review* 38, no. 2 (November 2014): 375–93.

Rubinstein, Amnon. *The Zionist Dream Revisited: From Herzl to Gush Emunim and Back*. New York: Schocken Books, 1984.

Rubinstein, Elyaqim. *Shoftei erets*. Jerusalem; Tel Aviv: Schocken, 1980.

Sagi, Avi. *Tradition vs. Traditionalism: Contemporary Perspectives in Jewish Thought*. Amsterdam; New York: Rodopi, 2008.

Sagi, Avi, and Dov Schwartz. "Bein halutsi'ut le-limud torah: Zavit aheret." In vol. 3 of 3, *Me'ah shenot tsiyonut datit*, edited by Avi Sagi and Dov Schwartz, 73–75. Ramat Gan: Bar-Ilan University, 2003.

Sagi, Avi, and Dov Schwartz. *Religious Zionism and the Six Day War: From Realism to Messianism*. New York: Routledge, 2018.

Salmond, John William. *Jurisprudence: Or the Theory of the Law*. London: Stevens and Haynes, 1907.

Salomon, Noah. *For Love of the Prophet: An Ethnography of Sudan's Islamic State*. Reprint edition. Princeton, NJ: Princeton University Press, 2016.

Sapir, Gideon, Daphne Barak-Erez, and Aharon Barak, eds. *Israeli Constitutional Law in the Making*. Oxford: Hart Publishing, 2013.

Sarat, Austin D. "Redirecting Legal Scholarship in Law Schools." *Yale Journal of Law & the Humanities* 12, no. 1 (2013): 129–50.

Sarir, Yisrael. "Sha'ul yisra'eli, ha-rav." *Entsiklopedia yahadut le-nosa'im be-tarbut yisra'el li-tehumeha*. Accessed June 11, 2018. http://www.daat.ac.il/encyclopedia/value.asp?id1=1070.

Sarna, Jonathan D. "Church-State Dilemmas of American Jews." In *Jews and the American Public Square: Debating Religion and Republic*, edited by Alan

Mittleman, Robert Licht, and Jonathan D. Sarna, 47–68. Lanham, MD: Rowman & Littlefield, 2002.

Schmitt, Carl. *Political Theology: Four Chapters on the Concept of Sovereignty*. Translated by George Schwab. 1st edition. Chicago: University of Chicago Press, 2006.

Schonthal, Benjamin. *Buddhism, Politics and the Limits of Law: The Pyrrhic Constitutionalism of Sri Lanka*. Cambridge: Cambridge University Press, 2016.

Schorsch, Ismar. "The Myth of Sephardic Supremacy." *Leo Baeck Institute Yearbook* 34, no. 1 (1989): 47–66.

Schott, Rudiger. "Main Trends in German Ethnological Jurisprudence and Legal Ethnology." *Journal of Legal Pluralism* 20 (1982): 37–67.

Schwartz, Dov. *Etgar u-mashber be-hug ha-rav kook*. 224. Tel Aviv: Am Oved, 2001.

Schwartz, Dov. *Faith at the Crossroads: A Theological Profile of Religious Zionism*. Leiden; Boston: Brill, 2002.

Schwartz, Dov "Ideas vs. Reality: Multiculturalism and Religious-Zionism." In *The Multicultural Challenge in Israel*, edited by Avi Sagi and Ohad Nachtomy, 200–225. Boston: Academic Studies Press, 2009.

Schwartz, Dov. *Religious-Zionism: History and Ideology*. Boston: Academic Studies Press, 2009.

Scott, David, and Talal Asad. "The Trouble of Thinking: An Interview with Talal Asad." In *Powers of the Secular Modern: Talal Asad and His Interlocutors*, edited by David Scott and Charles Hirschkind, 255–303. Stanford, CA: Stanford University Press, 2006.

Segal, Yehudah. "Al ha-mishpat ha-hiloni ba-arets." *Ha-torah veha-medinah* 7–8 (1956–57): 74–95.

Segev, Tom. *1949: The First Israelis*. Translated by Arlen Neal Weinstein. New York: Free Press; Collier Macmillan, 1986.

Sen, Amartya. *The Idea of Justice*. Cambridge, MA: Harvard University Press, 2009.

Shachar, Ayelet. *Multicultural Jurisdictions: Cultural Differences and Women's Rights*. Cambridge: Cambridge University Press, 2001.

Shahar, Ido. "Legal Pluralism and the Study of Shariʿa Courts." *Islamic Law and Society* 15, no. 1 (2008): 112–41.

Shamir, Ronen. *The Colonies of Law: Colonialism, Zionism and Law in Early Mandate Palestine*. Cambridge: Cambridge University Press, 1999.

Shapira, Anita. *Ben-Gurion: Father of Modern Israel*. New Haven, CT: Yale University Press, 2014.

Shapira, Anita. *Israel: A History*. Hanover, NH: University Press of New England, 2012.

Shapira, Avraham. "Mabat torani al huqei ha-medinah ve-hatqanat taqanot be-yamenu." *Tehumin* 3 (1982): 238–41.

Shavit, Jacob. *Athens in Jerusalem: Classical Antiquity and Hellenism in the Making of the Modern Secular Jew*. London; Portland, Or: Littman Library of Jewish Civilization, 1997.

She'altiel, Eli. *David Ben-Gurion: Rosh ha-memshalah ha-rishon; mivhar te'udot (1947–1963).* Jerusalem: Medinat yisra'el, arkhi'on ha-medinah, 1997.

Sheleg, Yair. *Aharei rabim le-hatot: Emdot rabanim be-yisra'el klapei ha-demoqratiah.* Mehqar mediniut 67. Jerusalem: Israel Democracy Institute, 2006.

Shilo, Shmuel. "The Contrast between Mishpat Ivri and Halakah." *Tradition: A Journal of Orthodox Jewish Thought* 20, no. 2 (1982): 91–100.

Shilo, Shmuel. *Dina de-malkhuta dina.* Jerusalem: Defus Akademi Bi-Yerushalayim, 1974.

Shochetman, Eliav. *Seder ha-din le-or meqorot ha-mishpat ha-ivri: Taqanot ha-diyun u-fesiqat batei ha-din ha-rabani'im be-yisra'el.* Library of Jewish Law. Jerusalem: Misrad ha-mishpatim: Moreshet ha-mishpat be-yisra'el: ha-qeren le-qidum ha-mishpat ha-ivri, 1988.

Shragai, Shlomo Zalman. "Hazon mizrahi u-matarato." In *Mizrahi: Qovets yovel le-melot k"h shanah le-qiyumah shel histadrut ha-mizrahi be-ameriqah (5671–5796)*, edited by Pinchas Churgin and Aryeh Leib Gelman, 68–73. New York: s.n., 1936.

Silberg, Moshe. *Talmudic Law and the Modern State.* New York: Burning Bush Press, 1973.

Skinner, Quentin. *Reason and Rhetoric in the Philosophy of Hobbes.* Cambridge: Cambridge University Press, 1996.

Skinner, Quentin. "The Sovereign State: A Genealogy." In *Sovereignty in Fragments: The Past, Present and Future of a Contested Concept*, edited by Hent Kalmo and Quentin Skinner, 26–46. Cambridge: Cambridge University Press, 2010.

Skinner, Quentin. Vol. 1 of *Visions of Politics.* Cambridge; New York: Cambridge University Press, 2002.

Smith, Ted A. *Weird John Brown: Divine Violence and the Limits of Ethics.* Stanford, CA: Stanford University Press, 2014.

Soloveitchik, Haym. "Rupture and Reconstruction: The Transformation of Contemporary Orthodoxy." *Tradition: A Journal of Orthodox Jewish Thought* 28, no. 4 (1994): 64–130.

Sorek, Yoav. "Rega shel tsemarmoret: Ha-tsionut ha-datit le-nokhah retsah rabin." In *Ha-tsionut ha-datit: Idan ha-temurot*, edited by Asher Cohen, 475–532. Jerusalem: Bialik Institute, 2004.

Spinoza, Baruch. *Spinoza: The Complete Works.* Edited by Michael L. Morgan. Translated by Samuel Shirley. Indianapolis: Hackett Publishing, 2002.

Stanislawski, Michael. *Zionism and the fin de siècle: Cosmopolitanism and Nationalism from Nordau to Jabotinsky.* Berkely, CA: University of California Press, 2001.

Stein, Peter. *Roman Law in European History.* Cambridge: Cambridge University Press, 1999.

Stepan, Alfred C. "Religion, Democracy, and the 'Twin Tolerations.'" *Journal of Democracy* 11, no. 4 (2000): 37–57.

Stern, Yedidia Z. "Israeli Law and Jewish Law in Israel: A Zero Sum Game?" In *Institutionalizing Rights and Religion: Competing Supremacies*, edited by Leora

Batnitzky and Hanoch Dagan, 57–73. Cambridge: Cambridge University Press, 2017.

Stern, Yedidia Z. "State, Law, and Halakhah—Part One: Civil Leadership as Halakhic Authority." Position Paper. Jerusalem: Israel Democracy Institute, 2001.

Stern, Yedidia Z., and Yair Sheleg, eds. "Ma'amadam shel batei ha-mishpat be-yisra'el: Halakhah, id'iologiah u-metsiut." In *Halakhah tsionit*, 276–311. Jerusalem: Israel Democracy Institute, 2017.

Stone, Donald D. "Matthew Arnold and the Pragmatics of Hebraism and Hellenism." *Poetics Today* 19, no. 2 (1998): 179–98.

Stone, Suzanne Last. "In Pursuit of the Counter-Text: The Turn to the Jewish Legal Model in Contemporary American Legal Theory." *Harvard Law Review* 106, no. 4 (February 1, 1993): 813–94.

Stone, Suzanne Last. "Law without Nation? The Ongoing Jewish Discussion." In *Law without Nations*, edited by Austin Sarat, Lawrence Douglas, and Martha Merrill Umphrey, 101–37. Stanford, CA: Stanford University Press, 2011.

Stone, Suzanne Last. "Religion and State: Models of Separation from within Jewish Law." *International Journal of Constitutional Law* 6, nos. 3–4 (2008): 631–61.

Stone, Suzanne Last. "Sinaitic and Noahide Law: Legal Pluralism in Jewish Law." *Cardozo Law Review* 12 (1990): 1157–1214.

Straus, Oscar S. *The Origin of Republican Form of Government in the United States of America*. New York: G. P. Putnam's Sons, 1901.

Sullivan, Winnifred Fallers. *The Impossibility of Religious Freedom*. Princeton, NJ: Princeton University Press, 2005.

Sullivan, Winnifred Fallers, Robert A. Yelle, and Mateo Taussig-Rubbo. "Introduction." In *After Secular Law*, edited by Winnifred Fallers Sullivan, Robert A. Yelle, and Mateo Taussig-Rubbo, 1–19. Stanford, CA: Stanford University Press, 2011.

Susser, Bernard, and Eliezer Don-Yehiya. "Prolegomena to Jewish Political Theory." In *Kinship & Consent: The Jewish Political Tradition and Its Contemporary Uses*. 2nd edition. Edited by Daniel Judah Elazar, 117–38. New Brunswick, NJ: Transaction Publishers, 1997.

Susskind, Lawrence, Hillel Levine, Gideon Aran, Shlomo Kaniel, Yair Sheleg, and Moshe Halbertal. "Religious and Ideological Dimensions of the Israeli Settlements Issue: Reframing the Narrative?" *Negotiation Journal* 21, no. 2 (2005): 177–91.

Tamanaha, Brian Z. "Understanding Legal Pluralism: Past to Present, Local to Global." *Sydney Law Review* 30 (2007): 375–411.

Taylor, Charles. *A Secular Age*. Cambridge, MA: Belknap Press of Harvard University Press, 2007.

Taylor, Charles. "Modes of Secularism." In *Secularism and Its Critics*, edited by Rajeev Bhargava, 31–53. Delhi; New York: Oxford University Press, 1998.

Tedeschi, Guido (Gad). "On the Choice Between Religious and Secular Law in the Legal System of Israel." In *Studies in Israel Law*, edited by Guido (Gad) Tedeschi, 238–88. Jerusalem, 1960.

Teller, Adam. "Rabbis without a Function? The Polish Rabbinate and the Council of Four Lands in the 16th–18th Centuries." In *Jewish Religious Leadership: Image and Reality*, edited by Jack Wertheimer, 371–400. New York: Jewish Theological Seminary, 2004.

Tenbitsky, Shlomo. "Dina de-malkhuta be-yisra'el uva-amim." *Ha-torah veha-medinah* 1 (1949): 27–41.

Tocqueville, Alexis de. *De la démocratie en Amérique*. 4 vols. Paris: Pagnerre, 1848.

Tocqueville, Alexis de. *Democracy in America: Historical-Critical Edition of "De la démocratie en Amérique."* Edited by Eduardo Nolla. Translated by James T. Schleifer. Bilingual French-English. 4 vols. Indianapolis, IN: Liberty Fund, 2010.

Tsameret, Tsvi. "Ben-Gurion, ha-'shulhan arukh' veha-'shulhan' ha-hadash: Le-shorshei ha-metah bein Ben-Gurion u-vein ha-yahadut ha-datit." In vol. 3 of *Me'ah shenot tsi'onut datit*, edited by Avi Sagi and Dov Schwartz, 401–20. Ramat Gan, Israel: Bar-Ilan University, 2003.

Tsameret, Tsvi. "Judaism in Israel: Ben-Gurion's Private Beliefs and Public Policy." *Israel Studies* 4, no. 2 (1999): 64–89.

Twining, William. "Normative and Legal Pluralism: A Global Perspective." *Duke Journal of Comparative and International Law* 20 (2010): 473–517.

Una, Moshe. "Mashma'utah shel ha-hashpa'ah ha-hilkhatit 'al ha-haqiqah." In *Ha-mishpat ha-ivri u-medinat yisra'el*, edited by Yaakov Bazaq, 101–9. Jerusalem: Mosad ha-rav Kook, 1969.

United Nations General Assembly Resolution 181: Resolution Adopted on the Report of the Ad Hoc Committee on the Palestinian Question (1947).

Urbinati, Nadia. *Representative Democracy: Principles and Genealogy*. Chicago: University of Chicago Press, 2008.

van Caenegem, R. C. *An Historical Introduction to Private Law*. Cambridge: Cambridge University Press, 1992.

Viswanathan, Gauri. *Masks of Conquest: Literary Study and British Rule in India*. New York: Columbia University Press, 1989.

Vital, David. "Zionism as Revolution? Zionism as Rebellion?" *Modern Judaism* 18, no. 3 (October 1, 1998): 205–15.

Walzer, Michael. *The Paradox of Liberation: Secular Revolutions and Religious Counterrevolutions*. New Haven, CT: Yale University Press, 2015.

Walzer, Michael, Menachem Lorberbaum, Noam J. Zohar, and Yair Lorberbaum, eds. Vol. 1 of *The Jewish Political Tradition*. New Haven, CT: Yale University Press, 2000.

Warhaftig, Itamar. *Alayikh zarah: Hayav u-po'alo shel ha-sar d"r zerah varhaftig zts"l*. Ma'alaeh Adumim, Israel: Itamar Warhaftig, 2018.

Warhaftig, Itamar. "Mavo." In vol. 1 of *Tehuqah le-yisra'el al pi ha-torah*, edited by Itamar Warhaftig, 22–40 [Hebrew numbering]. Jerusalem: Mosad Ha-rav Kook; Yad Ha-rav Herzog, 1989.

Warhaftig, Itamar, and Shmuel Katz. *Ha-rabanut ha-rashit le-yisra'el: Shivim shanah le-yisudah, 5681–5751; Samkhutah, pe'uloteha, toldoteha*. 3 vols. Jerusalem: Hekhal Shlomo, 2001.

Warhaftig, Zerah (*see also* Warhaftig, Zorach). *Al ha-shiput ha-rabani be-yisra'el: Neumim*. Tel Aviv: Moreshet, 1955.

Warhaftig, Zerah. "Ba'ayot ha-mishpat be-medinat yisra'el." *Ha-tsofeh*, September 2, 1949.

Warhaftig, Zerah. "Ha-mishpat ha-ivri be-haqiqat medinat yisra'el ba-esor ha-rishon." *Ha-tsofeh*, September 14, 1958.

Warhaftig, Zerah. *Huqah le-yisra'el: Dat u-medinah*. Jerusalem: Mesilot, 1988.

Warhaftig, Zerah, ed. Vol. 1 of *Osef pisqei din*. Jerusalem: Ha-midpas Ha-memshalti, 1950.

Warhaftig, Zerah. "Precedent in Jewish Law." In *Authority, Process and Method: Studies in Jewish Law*, edited by Hanina Ben-Menahem and Neil S. Hecht, 1–32. Jewish Law in Context 2. Amsterdam, The Netherlands: Harwood Academic Publishers, 1998.

Warhaftig, Zerah. *Refugee and Survivor: Rescue Efforts during the Holocaust*. Yad Vashem, 1988.

Warhaftig, Zerah, Haim Hefetz, and David Glas. *Dat u-medinah be-haqiqah: Leket hiquqim u-pesiqah*. Jerusalem: Misrad Ha-Datot, 1973.

Warhaftig, Zorach. "Rabbi Herzog and Rabbinic Legislation." In *The Halakhic Thought of R. Isaac Herzog*, edited by Bernard S. Jackson. Jewish Law Association Studies V. Atlanta: Scholars Press, 1991.

Washofsky, Mark. "Halakhah and Political Theory: A Study in Jewish Legal Response to Modernity." *Modern Judaism* 9, no. 3 (October 1989): 289–310.

Weiler, Gershon. *Jewish Theocracy*. Leiden: Brill, 1988.

Weiler, Gershon. *Te'oqratiah yehudit*. Tel Aviv: Am Oved, 1976.

Weingarten, Shmuel Hayim. "Huqei ha-medinah ve-toqfam le-fi ha-halakhah." *Ha-torah veha-medinah* 5–6 (1953–54): 306–30.

Westreich, Elimelech. "Haganat ma'amad ha-nisu'in shel ha-ishah ha-yehudi'ah be-yisra'el: Mifgash ben mesorot mishpati'ot shel edot shonot." *Pelilim* 7 (5759 [1999]): 273–347.

Westreich, Elimelech. "Levirate Marriage in the State of Israel: Ethnic Encounter and the Challenge of a Jewish State." *Israel Law Review* 37, nos. 2–3 (July 2004): 426–99.

Wilf, Steven Robert. *The Law before the Law*. Lanham, MD: Lexington Books, 2008.

Williams, Roger. "Mr. Cottons Letter Lately Printed, Examined and Answered (1644)." In vol. 1 of *The Complete Writings of Roger Williams*, 313–96. New York: Russell & Russell, 1963.

Wilson, Robert R. *Sociological Approaches to the Old Testament*. Minneapolis: Augsburg Fortress, 1984.

Woodman, Gordon R. "The Possibilities of Co-Existence of Religious Laws with Other Laws." In *Law and Religion in Multicultural Societies*, 1st edition, edited by Rubya Mehdi, 23–42. Copenhagen: DJØF Pub, 2008.

Yerushalmi, Yosef Hayim. "Servants of Kings and Not Servants of Servants: Some Aspects of the Political History of the Jews." In *The Faith of Fallen Jews: Yosef Hayim Yerushalmi and the Writing of Jewish History*, edited by David N. Myers and Alexander Kaye, 245–76. Lebanon, NH: University Press of New England, 2013.

Yerushalmi, Yosef Hayim. *The Lisbon Massacre of 1506 and the Royal Image in the Shebet Yehudah*. Cincinnati, OH: Hebrew Union College–Jewish Institute of Religion, 1976.

Yisraeli, Shaul. *Amud ha-yemini*. Tel Aviv–Jaffa: Moreshet, 1966.

Yisraeli, Shaul. *Amud ha-yemini*. 2nd edition. Jerusalem: Hotza'at ha-torah veha-medinah al shem maran ha-rav sha'ul yisra'eli ztz'l, 2010.

Yisraeli, Shaul. "Im ha-qovets." *Ha-torah veha-medinah* 1 (1949): 11.

Yisraeli, Shaul. "Samkhut ha-nasi u-mosdot memshal nivharim be-yisra'el." *Ha-torah veha-medinah* 1 (1949): 67–78.

Yosef, Ovadiah. *She'elot u-teshuvot yehaveh da'at*, n.d.

Zerubavel, Yael. *Recovered Roots: Collective Memory and the Making of Israeli National Tradition*. Chicago: University of Chicago Press, 1995.

Zevin, Shlomo Yosef. *Ishim ve-shitot: Shurat ma'amarim al ishei halakhah ve-shitotehem ba-torah*. Tel Aviv: A. Tsioni, 1966.

Zmoira, Moshe. "Speech by Moshe Zmoira at the Inauguration of the Supreme Court." *Ha-Praklit* 5 (1948): 187.

Zohar, Zvi. *Rabbinic Creativity in the Modern Middle East*. New York: Bloomsbury Academic, 2013.

Zohar, Zvi. "Sephardic Tradition on Galut and Political Zionism: The Halakhic Position of Rabbi Ya'akov Moshe Toledano." In *From Iberia to Diaspora: Studies in Sephardic History and Culture*, edited by Yedida Kalfon Stillman and Norman A. Stillman, 223–34. Leiden: Brill, 1999.

Zohar, Zvi. "Traditional Flexibility and Modern Strictness: Two Halakhic Positions on Women's Suffrage." In *Sephardi and Middle Eastern Jewries: History and Culture in the Modern Era*, edited by Harvey E. Goldberg, 119–33. Bloomington: Indiana University Press, 1996.

Zohar, Zvi, and Avi Sagi, eds. *Yahadut shel haim: Iyunim be-yetsirato ha-hagutit-hilkhatit shel ha-rav hayim david halevi*. Jerusalem: Mekhon Shalom Hartman; Keter, 2007.

INDEX